In reflecting on the greatest war in human history, one cannot help but think about the terrible conflict as a whole, its leaders, its peoples, and the puzzles still open about its conduct. The leadership of both sides recognized that at stake from the very beginning was the complete restructuring of the world order. More than a conflict of imperial aggression, World War II was about who would live and command the globe's resources and which peoples would disappear entirely because they were believed to be inferior or undesirable by the aggressor.

This collection of special studies in twentieth-century German and world history illuminates the nature of the Nazi system and its impact on Germany and the world. Bringing together essays now widely scattered and several never previously published in English, this volume examines the Holocaust, the connections between the European and Pacific theaters of war, as well as the effects, leaders, and research problems of World War II. Emphasis is placed on illuminating key topics that have been badly misunderstood or misrepresented in the past, including the true impact of the Treaty of Versailles of 1919 and Germany's relations with England, the United States, and the Soviet Union.

GERMANY, HITLER, AND
WORLD WAR II

GERHARD L. WEINBERG

GERMANY, HITLER, AND WORLD WAR II

ESSAYS IN MODERN GERMAN AND WORLD HISTORY

CAMBRIDGE
UNIVERSITY PRESS

Published by the Press Syndicate of the University of Cambridge
The Pitt Building, Trumpington Street, Cambridge CB2 1RP
40 West 20th Street, New York, NY 10011-4211, USA
10 Stamford Road, Oakleigh, Melbourne 3166, Australia

© Cambridge University Press 1995

First published 1995

Printed in the United States of America

Library of Congress Cataloging-in-Publication Data
Weinberg, Gerhard L.
Germany, Hitler, and World War II / Gerhard L. Weinberg.
p.   cm.
Slightly rev. collection of conference lectures, periodical articles, etc.
Includes bibliographical references and index.
ISBN 0-521-47407-8
1. World War, 1939–1945 – Germany. 2. Hitler, Adolf, 1889–45. 3. Germany – History –
1918–1933. 4. Germany – History – 1933–1945. I. Title.
D757.W384   1995
940.53'43 – dc20   94-27076
CIP

A catalog record for this book is available from the British Library.

ISBN 0-521-47407-8 Hardback

CONTENTS

PREFACE

This collection presents in slightly revised form a selection of essays dealing with German history in the twentieth century and history's greatest war, which Germany initiated in 1939. One essay (Chapter 16) first appeared in German. It was scheduled to be included in a volume in honor of the eightieth birthday of Admiral Arleigh Burke, but I translated it when the Naval Institute declined to publish that book; the essay appears here on the basis of the original text. The appendix deals with fundamental problems in the writing of recent history. Originally given as a paper at the Ranke Conference in 1986, it was omitted from the conference volume at the insistence of Syracuse University Press. The issues it raises are, if anything, more pressing now than they were when I called attention to them a decade ago.

Designed to illuminate specific aspects of German and world history, the texts, some originally given as talks, others written for periodicals, have been slightly revised to call attention to some recent literature which deals with their subject. All are reprinted with the permission of the prior publishers. More details on the background of World War II may be found in my two volumes dealing with that subject: *The Foreign Policy of Hitler's Germany,* both now reprinted in paperback by Humanities Press with a new preface. The war itself is covered as a whole in my *A World at Arms: A Global History of World War II,* published by Cambridge University Press. I am very glad that the same publisher has now decided to issue this collection, which makes the scattered but related items available in one volume, and I am grateful to Frank Smith for his support, encouragement, and advice on the project.

INTRODUCTION

No event more precisely marks the transition from the nineteenth to the twentieth century than the First World War. Its length, cost, and impact anticipated by practically no one, this conflict, soon to be referred to as the "Great War," saw the Germans checked in the West in their rush to victory in 1914. Something of a stalemate developed there in the following years while Germany and its allies defeated in turn their enemies in the Southeast, South, and East. The Romanov dynasty in Russia, which had held onto the unoccupied parts of that country a century earlier when the forces of Napoleon had taken Moscow, lost its grip on the country in February 1917; the succeeding Provisional Government was unable to consolidate its rule and was overthrown by the Bolsheviks in October of the same year.

One reason that the Germans had assisted the Bolsheviks was the hope that they might take Russia out of the war, and this hope was realized as fighting stopped on the eastern front. The Germans could now resume major offensive operations in the West, but they were unable to inflict a decisive defeat on the Allies. Two factors were primarily responsible for this failure: the prior exertions of the war had weakened Germany considerably, and she had deliberately drawn the United States into the war against herself by an unrestricted submarine campaign which was supposed to knock out Great Britain but failed to do so.

Under these circumstances, as the Western Allies turned to a series of counteroffensives, the Germans were forced to fall back. Though their armies were still deep inside French and Belgian territory, Germany's military leaders decided in September 1918 to ask for an armistice lest their front be completely ruptured. This admission of defeat took the strained but still confident German home front, including most of the government, completely by surprise, and that shock of surprise produced a revolution and collapse at home – which the military in turn then blamed for their defeat. Here was the beginning of that stab-in-the-back legend – a reversal of defeat at the front and collapse at home – which poisoned German life and policy thereafter.

The peace treaty of Versailles, which was worked out in a series of compromises by the victors and which the Germans, after some significant adjustments had been made in it, were obliged to accept, would be the object of endless attacks then and in subsequent years. It is the subject of the first piece in this collection. Originally a paper at a session of the American Historical Association commemorating the fiftieth anniversary of the defeat of the Central Powers in 1918, it attempts to explicate the striking discrepancy between the widespread belief that Germany had been terribly weakened by the 1919 settlement and the reality of a Germany potentially relatively more, rather than less, powerful in the interwar years and hence in a position to strive for domination of Europe and even the globe once again.

Adolf Hitler will always – and quite correctly – be associated with that German effort to control the world. The second piece is an edition of a document which I found in the collection of captured German documents originally assembled by the prosecution in preparation for the trials of German war criminals after World War II. Not used at the trials, this piece, now with other items from the correspondence of Rudolf Hess in the National Archives, has the special interest and great advantage of providing a contemporary description of Hitler's party, person, and views written in 1927 by Hess, then Hitler's secretary and chief aide, in order to inform a close and sympathetic friend.

It is, therefore, one of many pieces of evidence from the period *before* Hitler became chancellor of Germany in January 1933 which was drawn on to present the views and conceptions this pivotal figure in twentieth-century history held and publicly espoused. "The World through Hitler's Eyes," first written as the introductory chapter to my study of the origins of World War II, is designed to provide a framework through which the worldview of this extraordinary individual can be understood, with every effort being made to exclude insights derived from his speeches and actions after 1933. Here one can, therefore, see the man who described himself as a Raumpolitiker, a politician of space, to distinguish himself from the Grenzpolitiker, the border politicians, a term he used to deride those on the German political scene who in his eyes demonstrated their own foolishness and stupidity by calling for undoing the peace of 1919 and returning to the borders of 1914 – a goal he always rejected as both insufficient for Germany's need for space and a ridiculous objective for the wars he believed Germany should wage.

The new system which the National Socialists installed in Germany beginning in 1933 with substantial initial and steadily growing support from the German public is described in the fourth and fifth pieces in this collection. While the former analyzes the internal structure of the state as established in 1933 and developed thereafter, the latter takes up the preparations for the series of wars Hitler intended but felt obliged to shield by dissembling in the first years of the regime.

No aspect of German foreign policy was subject to more distortion during the years of the Cold War than that of relations with Great Britain. Because of the realignments brought about after 1945, the fact that Hitler had by 1935 abandoned his temporary hope of an alignment with Britain but instead assumed that Germany would fight it as well as France, made it seem nicer for many to pretend that it all had been otherwise. The sixth essay, "Hitler and England," provides a corrective to these legends and shows how and why the German government came to steer toward a war with England in the face of all efforts by the latter to urge Germany to accept a peaceful settlement of what it claimed to be its grievances.

The seventh essay, on German policy toward Austria, originally given in Vienna on the fiftieth anniversary of the country's annexation by Germany, shows how the Nazi government first tried to annex Austria in 1933 and 1934 and then, after initial failures, succeeded in doing so in 1938. That annexation appeared to open the way for what Hitler had thought of as the first of his wars: the one against Czechoslovakia. Chapter 8 describes the circumstances under which the German dictator, to his lifelong regret, reversed his decision for war and, pushed by the British, abandoned by his prospective Italian ally, and worried by an unenthusiastic German public, settled in 1938 at Munich for what others considered a German triumph but he determined should never happen again.

The German "lesson" from Munich was that it was dangerous to advance plausible demands – in that case the annexation of land inhabited by a German majority – because one then risked having them accepted and thereupon being left without a war which could be presented to the home front as absolutely necessary, whatever the required sacrifices. The ninth piece, that on Danzig (now Gdansk), demonstrates this point in connection with one issue in German relations with Poland which Hitler believed important for whipping up resolution at home – and hence would under no circumstances allow to be settled. The tenth piece reveals the success of this strategy of his with a critical segment of the German people: the generals and admirals who were in charge of Germany's military forces and whose loyalty was essential to launching war. The eleventh then underlines the absolute insistence on war in 1939; Hitler would not wait even the one day his own timetable allowed.

A development which startled the world a few days before the German invasion of Poland was the signing of the Nazi–Soviet Pact of August 23, 1939. Having waved off all earlier approaches from Moscow, the Germans now reversed course and signed with the Soviet Union. This policy change and the way it fit into the broader aims and policies of the Third Reich – as well as the Soviet role and reaction – are covered by the twelfth and thirteenth essays.

The German and Soviet invasions of Poland were followed by the German attack in the West, originally scheduled for the late fall of 1939 but then postponed until May of 1940. Enabled by her pact with the Soviet Union to concentrate all her strength on one front for the only time in the war, Germany, not yet weakened as in 1917 and having not yet drawn the United States into the conflict, won a stunning victory. Unlike 1914, when the initial defeats suffered by France had been very much more costly in lives but the French government had rallied the unoccupied parts of the country and together with its allies had continued in the fight, this time the initial defeat produced a collapse of the French government and home front; a new regime established in the resort town of Vichy, and named after that community, imagined that it could find a place for a French state organized along new lines in a German-controlled Europe. A tiny number of Frenchmen, led and symbolized by Charles de Gaulle, fought on, but most accepted the German victory as irreversible. And both they and the Germans assumed that Great Britain would give in quickly, either out of good sense or after bombing and invasion by the seemingly invincible German armed forces.

The British government and people did not accept the German victory in the West as necessarily heralding their own total defeat; instead they resolved to continue. With the Royal Air Force successful in defeating the German air assault in the Battle of Britain, and the German navy without most of its major warships, which had either been sunk or damaged and hence temporarily out of service as a result of the Norwegian campaign, the Germans were, to put it simply, afraid to try an invasion which they were in the process of preparing. It would take the German leadership quite some time, however, to recognize this decisive setback for what it really was.

The Nazi regime had always expected and intended that victory in the West over Britain and France would clear the way for the seizure of vast territories from the USSR in the East. It was further assumed that the anticipated easy victory over the Soviet Union would, in turn, provide the needed expanded raw material base for war against the United States, a war which Hitler had considered essential since at least 1928[1] and for which major preparations in the air and naval field had been inaugurated in 1937.

The absence from German discussion and records of such debates as those in the Second Empire on whether a German invasion of the United States should begin with landings on the beaches of Cape Cod or those of Long Island has led some historians to the erroneous conclusion that this time no war with the United States was intended. The fourteenth and fifteenth essays in this volume eliminate this misunderstanding and show both why such a war was indeed a part of German planning early on and why the German government declared it in December 1941 when at last it believed that the great navy, considered necessary for that war, was available – though that of an ally, not its own.

In the interval between Germany's victory over France in 1940 and the declaration of war on the United States, the German invasion of the Soviet Union had been halted by the latter, and this to all intents and purposes doomed the Third Reich to defeat. The government of the Soviet Union succeeded in maintaining full control of the parts of the USSR not occupied by the Germans, and this made possible the mobilization of the country's human and material resources for a continuing fight against the German invader.

While Japan had joined the European war to its own prior war with China, drawing the United States into the conflict greatly altered its nature. This point, the interrelated character of a global conflict, is illustrated by several significant examples in Chapter 16. Too much of the existing literature appeared to me to ignore the interrelations and interdependencies of World War II. The Soviet breakthrough at Stalingrad, and the subsequent desperate German attempts to relieve and supply their forces surrounded there, on the one hand, and the race between the Western Allies and the Axis for control of Tunisia, on the other, are usually described not as simultaneous and interdependent events but as occurring not just on different continents but on different planets. It is obvious, once anyone mentions it, that the German could not send the same units to try to relieve Stalingrad and to seize Tunisia, and that the same transport planes could not be utilized to fly supplies to Stalingrad and to Tunisia simultaneously, but one would never know it from the vast majority of the existing accounts of either battle. I wrote the book *A World at Arms* in large part to counter such distorted and distorting perspectives; Chapter 16, "Global Conflict: The Interaction between

---

1 Gerhard L. Weinberg (ed.), *Hitlers zweites Buch: Ein Dokument aus dem Jahr 1928* (Stuttgart: Deutsche Verlags-Anstalt, 1961), p. 130.

the European and Pacific Theaters in World War II," provides numerous examples to illustrate this key point further.

An additional widespread but equally misleading image of World War II is the concentration on the purely military; the impression that the war was a rather more dangerous form of chess in which the participants engaged huge forces primarily because they did not know what else to do with them: they fought the others because they were there. In reality, the war was begun by Germany and fought through to the bitter end for very specific purposes, many of them already outlined in the second, third, and fourth essays of this collection.

It was not, however, the intent of the Germans to defer implementation of the demographic revolutionary transformation of the globe until they had won their wars. On the contrary, they began the process in the very first months of fighting by the initiation in the fall of 1939 of a massive program for the systematic collection and killing of those German fellow citizens defined as "not worthy of life" (*lebensunwertes Leben*). This meant that those defined as incurably ill or confined to mental institutions, babies with substantial birth defects, persons crippled by accidents, and others often defined in several vague categories – which came to include seriously wounded German World War I veterans – were taken to a new type of institution, the killing center, and murdered there.[2]

By the summer of 1941, this program of mass murder had brought two significant developments: first, the initial project of systematic, bureau-cratically organized killing had led to the evolution out of the necessary experimentation of techniques for the collection and the killing of vast numbers, the disposal of great numbers of corpses, the establishment of institutions for mass killing, and the recruitment of large numbers of men and women willing and accustomed to killing, not individuals, but masses as a regular "occupation" from morning until lunch break and thereafter for the rest of the "working day."

The second result of the program was a very obvious sense of unease among a large portion of the German population which, of course, had many familial ties with those murdered; there was the appearance of substantial open opposition in the form of written protests, occasional riots when buses appeared at old folks' homes and mental institutions to haul off inmates to the nearest killing center, and public sermons by clergymen, especially the outspoken Bishop Galen of Münster.[3] Under

2 A forthcoming book by Henry Friedlander covers both the so-called euthanasia program and its relationship to the Holocaust in detail.

3 There is now a collection of Galen's papers in Clemens August Graf von Galen, *Akten, Briefe und Predigten, 1933–1946*, ed. Peter L. Löffler, 2 vols. (Mainz: Matthias-Grünwald-Verlag, 1988).

these circumstances, the government decided in August 1941 to reduce the scope of this program and postpone portions of it to the postwar period – the first stages of the war in the East, begun with the invasion of the Soviet Union on June 22, 1941, was not the best time to have German soldiers contemplate the likelihood that if they were seriously injured in the fighting, their own government instead of helping and supporting them was likely to kill them as useless mouths.

There would, however, be plenty to do for those temporarily without many victims to kill as a result of the reduction in the so-called euthanasia program. With the invasion of the Soviet Union, the Germans initiated the systematic killing of a second group of people: the Jews, a people the Nazis believed was a race simultaneously inferior and dangerous. Not only those previously involved in the earlier killing program but tens of thousands of others would be needed for the huge task of killing the Jews first in the newly occupied USSR, then in the rest of Europe, and finally throughout the world as the Germans intended. A portion of this project, as well as its extension to the Sinti and Roma, the Gypsies, is reviewed in Chapter 17, which originally introduced the 1943–1993 commemoration volume published by the U.S. Holocaust Memorial Museum.

It took the victory of the Allies over Germany to end this terrible process and prevent the subjection of others to the demographic revolution the Germans wanted to carry out, but it must not be thought that all Germans agreed with the aims and methods of the National Socialist regime. The fifth essay briefly discusses internal German opposition to the Hitler government; Chapter 18, "July 20, 1944: The German Resistance to Hitler," does so in a more comprehensive manner. Originally given at Colorado State University on the twenty-fifth anniversary of the July 20, 1944, attempt on Hitler's life, this revised version of a description of those who dared defy the system surely deserves attention on the fiftieth anniversary as well, even if the massive support most of Germany's leaders and people still gave the Nazi regime prevented it from collapsing the way that of Erich Honecker fell in 1989.

For many observers of the war then and since, the invasion of northern France by the western Allies on June 6, 1944, marked the beginning of Nazi Germany's end. Its fiftieth anniversary attracted worldwide attention. If the invasion had failed – and a new attempt had then been made, most likely in the spring of 1945 – either all of Germany would have been occupied by the Red Army or the first atomic bombs would have been dropped on Germany. But the first attempt succeeded and enabled the Western Allies to project their power against Germany and into the center of Europe. Chapter 19, "D-Day after Fifty Years," was commissioned as the concluding piece for the anniversary commemorative volume of the Eisenhower Center in Abilene, Kansas. It reviews the major issues in the background, execution, and the aftermath of the D-Day invasion.

The success of the invasion and of the Soviet summer offensive of 1944, however, cannot be seen simply from the perspective of the Allies and their subsequent triumph. The Germans were fighting not for their defeat but for victory, and the broader perspectives behind the desperate struggles of 1944 and 1945 have to be seen from the German side as well. Chapter 20, entitled "German Plans for Victory, 1944–1945," was originally a talk at the German Historical Institute in Washington; it sets forth an aspect of the last portion of World War II which is generally ignored.

As one looks back on the greatest war in human history, one cannot help but think about the terrible conflict as a whole, its leaders, its peoples, and the puzzles still open about its conduct. Chapter 21, originally a special lecture at the State University at Albany, looks at the five most important leaders in the war: Adolf Hitler, Winston Churchill, Joseph Stalin, Franklin Roosevelt, and Tojo Hideki. The next essay raises some serious questions about the war as waged by its major participating nations and, in particular, suggests some significant questions which remain open and calls for the dropping of continuing restrictions on access for scholars to important records. There follows a short summation dealing with the new Germany which emerged into a very different and new world in the years after World War II; this essay was written especially for this volume and suggests how the war and its immediate aftermath affected Germany and its relationship with the rest of the world in a manner very different from the experience which followed World War I.

A problem of growing complexity for anyone wanting to understand not only World War II but also almost any other aspect of world history in the twentieth century is the interrelated issues of archives preservation and archives access. The appendix of this book is addressed to it. If records are not kept in a format which future generations can in fact access in a world of rapid technological change, if records are not made available until they have deteriorated physically beyond recall, human society will be cut off from its own past, from its own experiences. This danger, far greater than most realize, is with us today and threatens to darken our tomorrow. And for democratic societies, such an extinction of the past cannot but hamper the public discourse on which the effective functioning of democracy depends.

Part I

BACKGROUND

1

———— • ————

THE DEFEAT OF GERMANY IN 1918
AND THE EUROPEAN BALANCE
OF POWER

In 1919 Germany and her allies were crushed in war. The armistice and peace that followed were held to be ruinous for her by many. One might have expected Germany's removal as a major power in the European balance. Perhaps the time has come to examine how factors that operated to remove from the scene Germany's Austro-Hungarian ally had the opposite effect of maintaining and even strengthening Germany's position.

Twenty-five years after the end of World War I, Germany was in control of most of the European continent. Perhaps that ought to raise the question of how greatly her position in Europe had in fact been weakened at the end of World War I, if that position had provided a base from which she had gone further than she had managed to reach at the height of her strength in the prior conflict. Today, any German who suggests a return to the borders of Versailles is labeled an ultranationalist, a neo-Nazi, and a threat to the peace of Europe, if not of the world. Is it not strange that inside Germany the approval of boundaries that would once have been considered treasonous weakness in defense of what were alleged to be her national interest, should now be considered an outrageous demand, dangerous to her domestic institutions as well as her foreign relations? Does not this paradox suggest that we need to ponder some new general perspectives about the peace settlement?

By advocating new perspectives, I do not mean the application of hindsight. It is easy to say that now that the Sudeten Germans have been brought "Home into the Reich," some of them cannot wait to move out again; to suggest that in addition to building *Autobahnen*, Hitler ended the division of Upper Silesia, terminated the curious structure of the Free City of Danzig, and put an end to the supposedly intolerable separation of East Prussia from the rest of Germany. Such ironic comments

Revised from *Central European History* 2 (1969): 248–60.

on the imaginary accomplishments of the Third Reich are useful to an analysis of the peace treaties from only one aspect. They demonstrate that the fundamental assumption of German foreign policy in the inter-war years – that nothing could be worse for Germany than the peace settlement dictated to her and that any change would therefore neces-sarily be for the better – was in reality quite erroneous. It was the easiest thing in the world to devise arrangements much worse for her, and several ways to do so had been suggested in 1919. But although the German campaign against the Versailles settlement had included refer-ences to some of the more extravagant demands on Germany that had been refused, no inferences were ever drawn from this.

Instead of looking back from the present, it might be well to look back from 1918. Germany was a country less than fifty years old. Her war aims, which have become the subject of both research and dispute, had included one demand that survived the fluctuation in war aims since 1914: the end of Belgian independence. Though Belgium as a country was more than three decades older than Germany, it was assumed by most throughout the war aims debate in Berlin that Belgium's history as an independent country had ended in 1914. Once one examines this age discrepancy, we quickly find others even more startling. When the Prus-sian parliament discussed the annexation of the states of Hanover, Hesse-Kassel, Nassau, and Frankfurt after the war of 1866, no voice was raised for the continued existence of states some of which were ten times as old as what was to become the Germany of 1918. It was assumed that the disappearance of these states was only what they deserved for being on the wrong side in war, and that if their inhabitants did not appreciate the benefits of annexation to Prussia, that only showed how benighted they were. In any case, they would not be asked. The portion of the settlement of the same war in which there *was* a reference to the possi-bility of inhabitants being asked about their disposition – the section of the Treaty of Prague that provided for a plebiscite in North Schleswig – was subsequently deleted by a secret arrangement Bismarck made during the Eastern Crisis of 1878. In the major territorial settlement between those of 1866 and 1878, that of 1871, the territory of Alsace-Lorraine was transferred in a similarly cavalier fashion.

Such transfers were characteristic of the seventeenth and eighteenth as well as the early nineteenth centuries, but in the period immediately preceding 1864 had given way to new approaches. No one would assert that the plebiscites that accompanied the process of Italian unification would meet all the standards for fairness of the League of Women Voters, but the underlying assumption of those procedures deserves to be noted. They represented some recognition of a principle that had *not* been recognized before – for example, when the people of Lorraine found themselves transferred to France via the bedroom of Louis XV – the principle that areas ought not to be transferred from country to country in total disregard of the preferences, ascertained or assumed, of their inhabitants. The original promise to the people of North Schleswig had been made in recognition of that principle. The fact that the year in which that promise was withdrawn was also the year in which the Cypriots learned they were British subjects, certain people in the Balkans were informed that they were now "Eastern Rumelians," and the Bosnians were rewarded for their revolt against Ottoman rule by Austrian occupation is by no means a coincidence.

Surely the return of the national principle as a basic assumption among the peacemakers in Paris was a momentous event whose importance for Germany and for Europe cannot possibly be overestimated. The very fact that a peace treaty was signed with Germany, but not with Austria-Hungary, ought to focus attention on this point. It is not only the post–World War II experience that suggests that such a procedure was not preordained; the prior events just mentioned underline the importance of new, or revived, assumptions in setting the framework for the peace settlement. In 1878 the assumption had been that the troublesome problems of Southeast Europe should be settled to accommodate the power interests of Russia, Germany, Austria, and England; the question of what the Cypriots, Bosnians, or prospective "Eastern Rumelians" thought was never considered relevant. In the study of diplomatic history, our search for documentary evidence should not prevent recognition of the crucial importance of generally accepted assumptions so widely held that they are not much discussed.

It has been asserted by some that the acceptance of the principle of nationality as a basic element in the peace settlement was a result of the change in the war during 1917, with the two Russian revolutions and the entrance of the United States into the war.[1] This is only partly correct. The war assuredly did change in 1917, but in regard to the question of nationality, one ought not to ignore certain earlier predispositions in the same direction. The role of the demand for the restoration of Belgium and Serbia in conditioning people to the national principle should not be overlooked. To many contemporaries, the call for a return of Alsace-Lorraine to France appeared in the same light. The British government of the pre-1917 period was the government that had pushed Irish Home Rule through Parliament, enacted the Minto–Morley reforms for India,

---

1 Arno J. Mayer, *Wilson vs. Lenin: Political Origins of the New Diplomacy, 1917–1918* (New York: Meridian Books, 1964).

and attempted to reconcile the Boers after the South African war. No one would suggest that there were no contrary currents, or that there were no distortions or qualifications or even internal contradictions in the British view of nationality as a basic assumption of international territorial organization; but the assumption itself was clearly there.

The same thing was true of France. The very stubbornness of Georges Clemenceau grew out of his sharing the assumption that there was and would be a Germany. His bitter conflict with Foch and other French leaders revolved about this point. If he was assailed in France after the war for having lost the peace, it was precisely because he accepted the assumption of German statehood. Clemenceau had tried to erect defenses against the dangers that this statehood was thought to imply for France, and many of his critics thought the defenses inadequate; but very few argued that the best defense was to do away with the source of the danger. That, too, shows how widely the new assumptions were shared. Even the most extreme demands considered by Germany's enemies, which are often adduced as evidence of their desire to destroy Germany, in fact demonstrate the opposite. The secret Franco–Russian agreement of February 1917 assumes the continued existence of a united Germany; the relevant documents explicitly refer to the stationing of French troops in the new state that was contemplated for the left bank of the Rhine until Germany should have carried out her obligations under the peace treaty.[2] A continued Germany is taken for granted. Just as the elements in Germany that Bismarck had called the *Reichsfeinde*, the enemies of the state – the Socialists, the Catholics, and the non-Marxist Left – preserved Germany's unity from the *inside*, those who preserved Germany's unity from the *outside* were those who were presumed to be her external enemies – the powers of the Entente.

It may be argued that the application of the principle of nationality at Versailles was incomplete, and that it was used to deprive Germany of important, even vital territory. This issue is best considered in two phases: first, as regards the alleged inequities in the case of Germany herself, and then in regard to the rest of Europe. It is true that Germany was not allowed to annex additional territories such as Austria and parts of Bohemia. It hardly makes sense for a defeated power to complain that it has been denied immediate extensive expansion, but the point should be noted here – and will be reviewed in more detail subsequently – that even without those areas, Germany as defined by the treaty would have

2 The texts of the secret agreements were originally published by the Soviets in November 1917. They may be found in Friedrich Stieve (ed.), *Iswolski im Weltkriege: Der Diplomatische Schriftwechsel Iswolskis aus den Jahren 1914–1917* (Berlin: Deutsche Verlagsgesellschaft für Politik und Geschichte, 1926), pp. 212–15.

the largest population of any country in Europe other than Russia. That the powers at Paris could see little reason to sacrifice the independence of Czechoslovakia to Germany is hardly surprising; the important book of Johann W. Brügel should inaugurate a period of more rational discussion of that issue.[3] The real crux of the territorial issue for Germany was that of the eastern border.

Here 1917 was a turning point in that it attenuated the consideration that France and Britain were required to pay to Russia in any sponsorship of Polish independence. The problem itself was not new, of course, and the Germans themselves had helped revive it in 1916. The German handling of the Polish question together with the Treaty of Brest-Litovsk had set the stage for a reordering of that part of the continent. Where in the German–Polish borderland, areas were eventually divided between the two or allocated to Germany as a result of plebiscites, the situation showed that on Germany's eastern border the subjective willingness to consider oneself German went beyond the language border; just the opposite of the situation in the west, where the language border went beyond the subjective one.

The key question, however, was – and in discussion of the peace treaty remains – the Polish Corridor. Has not the time come for a new look at this topic, both in terms of time perspective and in terms of long-range German interests? In time perspective, the whole matter of territorial contiguity needs reappraisal. One of the signal developments of the previously mentioned annexations of 1866, regularly ignored by German historians in the interwar years, was that it ended the centuries when Prussian territory had been noncontiguous. Only in the brief period of Prussia's humiliation by Napoleon had all her territory been contiguous; in the years of her rise to greatness, Prussia had managed very well with all sorts of corridors between her provinces. Only in 1866 had that situation ended. In the following year, 1867, the United States purchased Alaska; since then there has been what could be called a "Canadian Corridor." Few in the United States lose much sleep over this problem, whatever the practical difficulties created by the situation. The key issue is not territorial contiguity, long atypical in the German area, but the perception of the onlooker.

In the Prussian–Polish borderlands, Frederick II arranged for a corridor across Poland to connect his Brandenburgian and Prussian territories, thereby separating the Danzig area, which remained with Poland, from the bulk of Polish territory. The corridor concept looked fine to Germans when arranged by one of their great heroes; what makes it so

3 Johann W. Brügel, *Tschechen und Deutsche, 1918–1938* (Munich: Nymphenburger, 1967).

preposterous when designed to assist a revived independent Poland? Surely the time has come to examine the possibility that of the various alternative solutions applied to or suggested for that area in the last two centuries, the 1919 arrangement was perhaps the least unjust? It is now gone beyond recall, but ought not historians to consider it – and its authors – in cooler perspectives?

When the same question is reviewed in terms of long-term German interests, one has to face the implications for a Germany, however defined, of an independent Poland. Any independent Poland was going to require territorial sacrifices on Germany's part. Were there any compensating benefits for Germany? Most Germans would have said "No!" – perhaps some still think so. Maybe that answer is incorrect. In the first place, an independent Poland would be a buffer between Germany and Russia. This would be useful quite aside from what the Germans might think of the Soviet system they had helped install in Moscow. Whatever the nature of the Russian government, a Europe organized on anything resembling the national principle would have only one unit larger than Germany – Russia – and it might indeed be helpful for Germany to be separated from that center of power by another state.

The other side of the coin was that this state in between was certain to be weaker in the long run than Germany herself. If confined to a Polish national core, Poland would be much smaller in population and resources than Germany; if greatly expanded eastward as before 1772, she would be weakened by internal dissensions and Russian enmity. If one may put it that way, the chains of Versailles that tied Germany down in the East also tied down her potentially most dangerous enemy. Germans' inability to grasp this point was as much a product of racist feeling toward allegedly inferior Poles as it was of dissatisfaction with the specific terms of the territorial settlement. Here too, new perspectives would appear to be in order.

This last consideration – the greater power of Germany compared to any new Poland – has an important bearing on Germany's relationship to the peace settlement of the rest of Southeast Europe. The defeat of Germany implied the defeat of her Austrian ally; but the real danger that such a defeat might have posed for Germany – the danger against which Bismarck had originally designed the Dual Alliance – was obviated by the circumstances of Austria's defeat. The prior defeat of Russia opened the way for the map of Southeast Europe to be redrawn not by Russia but by the forces of that area. The resulting appearance of such new countries as Czechoslovakia and the enlargement of old ones like Romania meant that on the south and east Germany would face a series of new and relatively weak states rather than a menacingly enlarged Russian empire.

The division of the Dobruja and Transylvania, the allocation of Tesin (Teschen), Fiume, or the Banat, were all questions of the utmost importance to the inhabitants of those territories and the countries disputing their ownership; but it all made no real difference to Germany. She would be infinitely stronger than any of the new or enlarged countries, regardless of how these disputes were resolved. Whether the decisions of the peace conference were wise or unwise – and usually they were a mixture of the two – it was really all the same to Germany's position on the continent. Just as any application of the national principle necessarily left Germany populous, large, and strong, regardless of how much hemmed in; so it would leave the countries of Eastern and Southeast Europe small and weak, regardless of how much the scales of justice might be tilted unfairly in the direction of one or the other of them.

If the national principle was bound to work in Germany's favor inside Europe, this was even more so outside the continent. At first glance, it would appear to have been the other way around, since Germany lost her colonies, bases, and investments abroad, while these were frequently appropriated by her enemies. This first impression is misleading in two ways. In the first place, the relative position of Germany did not depend on her worldwide holdings; and in the second place, some of her former enemies whose worldwide holdings *did* constitute a key element in their power position saw their international position weakened. Germany's colonial possessions were a great asset to her pride; but if the war had shown anything at all, it was that they contributed nothing to her position as a great power. It was impressive to talk about the heroism of Germany's garrison in East Africa or to extol the grandiosely suicidal mission of her Far East fleet, but what did it all add up to? It is instructive to note that Germany was most successful in rebuilding her commercial position in East Asia in the interwar years without the dubious benefit of bases or extraterritoriality; in fact there is evidence that the Chinese preferred to deal with Germans precisely for that reason. When Germany gave up her strong position in China in 1938, it was as a sacrifice to other policy objectives, not for lack of a foothold on the Shantung peninsula.

The power position of Germany's World War I enemies, however, was in many instances very much a product of their colonial empires and other foreign assets. Certainly in this category Britain had been weakened more in victory than Germany in defeat. The independence of the Dominions in international affairs had been sealed by the extent to which the military developments of the war had made England dependent upon them. If Italy had been made in the mud of the Crimea, Canada was forged in that of Flanders, while Australia and New Zealand had secured their independence at Gallipoli. The wartime promise of new changes leading to dominion status for India must be seen in the same context. When the allocation of separate votes to the Dominions in the League of Nations was used in the United States as an argument against ratification of the peace treaty for fear of excessive British influence, the object of the agitation was a symbol of the decline, not the rise, of British power. The impetus that the war and the peace gave to nationalistic stirrings throughout the world, even if their initial impact was limited, was certain to have a greater effect of undermining the power of countries *other* than Germany that bestrode the world like a colossus twice in this century without anything other than token extra-European interests on either occasion. It is true that the extra-European position of France was not affected as quickly and as dramatically as was England's, but France had suffered far more serious damage to the domestic base of her power position. This leads to the next major consideration: the impact of the fighting itself on the major European belligerents.

There was a school of thought in post–World War I Germany that argued that if they had only fought a little longer, they might have secured better terms. The fact of the matter, of course, was the reverse. The longer the Germans fought, the more the American pressure for unconditional surrender would have had behind it a larger role in the councils of the Allies. But that is not all. Just as all the brilliant schemes of Germany's post-1945 Monday-morning quarterbacks would at best have set up the Germans for the first atomic bombs, so the great strategists for the post–September 1918 fighting would have produced a total surrender following upon an allied invasion of German home territory with its attendant destruction inside Germany. The longer and slower that process, the greater the destruction would have been.

One of the signal implications of the First World War's ending as it did was that most of the destruction of war had taken place in the territory of Germany's enemies. The cost of the war to Germany should not be minimized, but her European enemies had not bought victory cheaply. The proportion of the population killed and wounded in the war was high in Germany, but it was higher in France and little lower in England; while Russia was still in the throes of civil war and intervention long after Germany had ceased to be exposed to death and damage from serious military operations. Her basic resources – population, industry, transportation system – had on the whole been weakened less than those of her enemies. Certainly the peace treaty imposed substantial burdens on Germany in this regard, but again one must look at the balance, at the fate of other countries and not only at Germany.

This leads to a consideration that in one way or another had played a major part in the German discussion of war aims: the position of Germany in a future war her leaders took almost for granted. Many of the proposed territorial acquisitions that loomed so large in that discussion were supposedly essential for her to have a sufficiently strong position in the next war. What was not taken into consideration was the possibility that the process of war itself might produce an equivalent. The disruption of Russia, the debility of Italy, the exhaustion of France, and the weakening of Britain were all products of the fighting that would have been enormously accentuated by a German victory, but could not be fully and permanently offset by Germany's defeat as long as her enemies allowed her to survive as a nation. She would then survive as a state potentially at least as strong relatively as before the war, if not stronger because of the creation of new states in Eastern Europe. The demilitarization of the Rhineland and the joint British–American guarantee of France were designed to guard against the dangers that were thought inherent in such a situation. The European powers were weakened by the war vis-à-vis the United States and Japan, but this was as true of the Entente as it was of Germany, if not more so.

All this is not to suggest that the peace settlement was somehow a great boon to Germany, but to show how any acceptance in even the most modified form of the national principle for the organization of Europe in the industrial age could not help but be favorable to Germany in very important respects:

1. She would be the second largest people in Europe.
2. She would face a large number of smaller and weaker rather than a few big powers on the south and east.
3. The growing extension of the national principle outside Europe was certain to undermine the strength of others rather than herself.
4. Her industrial facilities had been less damaged by war than those of either France or Russia and would, therefore, enable her to continue to capitalize on the skills, size, and energy of her population.
5. The recognition of the principle of nationality in Central and Eastern Europe did not preclude the maintenance of strong cultural and linguistic ties between Germany and the new countries. Only the later identification of German culture with treason shattered a sort of cultural hegemony that bound many – and not only those of German descent – to Germany.

Before the reasons for the German failure to recognize these realities are discussed, it may be well to consider briefly the way in which post–World War II developments reinforce this interpretation. The assumption of German unity that had not been challenged in World War I was very much in question during World War II. Was the unity of Germany compatible with the safety and survival of the rest of the world? The "dismemberment" of Germany, to use the contemporary term, was eventually dismissed in theory but enforced in practice, and upon a severely truncated Germany at that. But one should note the combined effect of two policies followed in Eastern Europe at the end of World War II. The Germans having developed the terrifying policy of adjusting population to boundaries, instead of boundaries to population, found this policy applied to themselves. The result in the short run was death and tragedy for millions; but in the long run, the expulsion of Germans from the countries of Southeast and Eastern Europe as well as the areas east of the Oder-Neisse line produced a West German state with a population only slightly less than that of post–World War I Germany as a whole.

The other policy was the territorial policy of Stalin. His scheme for Eastern Europe was exceedingly radical in the social, political, and economic spheres, converting all but Finland into small-scale replicas of Soviet Russia; but his territorial policy was very conservative. With certain modifications, the bulk of the East European territorial settlement followed the outlines of the Paris peace settlement. The Baltic states did not regain the independence they had lost in 1940, but none of the other countries created or enlarged in 1919 was taken into the Soviet Union itself. In the older terms of European power, only the annexation of the Carpatho-Ukraine, which put the Soviets across the Carpathian mountains, represented a significant change. But there is no reason to suppose that this will have any more long-term significance for Germany than the decision of 1818 to add a piece of Galicia to the German Confederation in order to implicate the latter in the defense of the Moravian Gap. What was left of the 1919 settlement as a result of Stalin's very traditionalist territorial perspectives continued to leave the German Federal Republic the largest and potentially most powerful country in Europe after Russia, with the possibility – realized in 1989 – of again having Russian power separated from herself by a buffer of weaker states.

This digression may serve to underscore the importance of the question why the Germans so uniformly failed to recognize their own true position after World War I. In the first place, the suddenness and the location of defeat obscured both the extent of that defeat and its possible repercussions. The notion that the independent existence of other countries might have to end had been a prominent part of the German war aims debate; so too had the idea of large-scale population transfers. It had, however, never seriously occurred to anyone in Germany that this sort of thing might happen to them; this was not because they were unwilling to attribute such evil designs to their enemies – they very readily did – but because a total German defeat did not appear within the realm of possibility. This illusion had been strengthened by the German triumphs over Russia and Romania that appeared to offset the impact of blockade and American intervention.

A second reason was the internal convulsions that gripped Germany in the period after October 1918, which imperiled German unity but seemed to make its maintenance a predominantly domestic concern. A third factor was a parochialism that persuaded the Germans that they were alone in suffering – and hence must be suffering because of the peace treaty – just as they were subsequently convinced that only they suffered really badly from the Great Depression. German revisionist propaganda tended to reinforce such misconceptions; who in Germany ever knew that more than half the value of the mark had vanished before the first pfennig was paid on reparations?

A fourth reason was that the very measures which the victors devised to contain the dangers they feared from the continued strength of Germany made the Germans most unhappy. The occupation and demilitarization of the Rhineland, the special status of the Saar, the restrictions on Germany's armed forces were all designed as protection against dangers which their imposition in a sense accentuated. Added to the territorial sacrifices Germany was called upon to make, these internal servitudes were resented so bitterly that the possibility of anyone else having some legitimate interest in them was not even considered.

Blinding many in Germany to a recognition of the long-term implications of the war and the settlement was a series of moral issues, of which by far the most dramatic was that of war guilt. There was no reference to war guilt in the peace treaties; but the German foreign minister, when receiving the text of the treaty at Versailles, decided to interpret in such a fashion the article John Foster Dulles had drafted in order to paper over a compromise between the British and French insistence on Germany's paying for the total cost of the war and the American position, eventually accepted by the others, that only the future, not the past, costs of the conflict should be imposed on Germany.[4] Once this issue had been raised by the Germans, it came to play a central role in the debate on the whole treaty; though, curiously enough, none of Germany's erstwhile allies interpreted the identical provision of their peace treaties in the same way. Having fastened on this issue, the Germans worked it over and over, persuading themselves even more than others that everyone but Germany had been responsible for the dreadful slaughter. The hysterical

---

4 The best treatment remains Philip M. Burnett, *Reparation at the Paris Peace Conference* (New York: Columbia University Press, 1940), esp. pp. 142–57. See also Fritz Dickman, "Die Kriegsschuldfrage auf der Friedenskonferenz von Paris 1919," *Historische Zeitschrift* 197 (1963): 1–101.

tone with which part of the German historical profession greeted the works of Fritz Fischer and Immanuel Geiss in the 1960s reflects the extent to which polemics over the war-guilt issue clouded German think-ing in the years after the First World War. Closely related to this actually inadvertent aspect of the peace treaty was what may have been one of the most serious mistakes of the peace conference: the refusal of League of Nations membership to Germany from the beginning. By the time this error had been rectified, the German attitude was beyond much hope of change.

None of the foregoing means that defeat followed by the Treaty of Versailles gave the Germans much cause for celebration. What it does indicate is that in spite of her defeat in a long and most bitter war, Germany was not dealt with as, for example, Prussia would have been had she lost the Seven Years' War – or as Germany intended to do with a number of countries if she won the war. Furthermore, it should be recognized that the greatest damage to Europe had been done by the fighting itself, not the settlement that ended it. It was the fighting that brought on the most dramatic changes, including the Russian revolutions and the entrance of the United States onto the stage where decisions affecting Europe were made. But the impact of these developments af-fected the power position of Germany's European enemies at least as much, if not more, than her own. They changed the world balance, but like the technological changes of the time, these alterations can hardly be charged to the defeat of the Central Powers or the peace treaties. With her industrial, technical, and population resources largely intact, Ger-many came out of defeat confirmed as still a major power on the conti-nent. It is known that she planned to exercise political and economic control over Austria-Hungary if the Central Powers won: with servitude in store for her main ally, can anyone suggest that her European enemies would have survived a German victory as major powers still?

2

———— • ————

NATIONAL SOCIALIST ORGANIZATION
AND FOREIGN POLICY AIMS IN 1927

The publication of Hitler's second book,[1] dictated in the summer of 1928, has helped to close the gap in our knowledge of National Socialism in the period between the reorganization of the party after Hitler's release from jail and the drive against the Young Plan in 1929. The letter from Rudolf Hess to Walter Hewel published in the following pages contributes substantial new insights to our picture of the National Socialist party in those years.[2]

Walter Hewel had been an early follower of Hitler. Having carried a flag in the attempted putsch of November 1923, he was sentenced to jail and served some time in Landsberg prison. After considerable travel, including a longer stay in England, Hewel spent several years on a plantation in Java before returning to Germany in the 1930s. Eventually he became the foreign minister's permanent representative in Hitler's headquarters; he was killed or committed suicide in early May of 1945. While in London in 1926–27, he sent several letters to his old friends Adolf Hitler and Rudolf Hess. The answer Hess wrote on March 30, 1927, gave Hewel a picture of the development of the party and of its views. Written frankly and clearly, the letter illustrates the complete triumph of Hitler's absolutist concept within the party. It also shows the wide-ranging foreign policy views discussed in the Nazi inner circle. In his remarks about the "world police" of the "racially best power" Hess reflects the kind of talk later reported by Hermann Rauschning[3] and the

Slightly revised from *Journal of Modern History* 36 (1964): 428–33. ©1964 by the University of Chicago. All rights reserved.
1 Gerhard L. Weinberg (ed.), *Hitlers zweites Buch: Ein Dokument aus dem Jahr 1928* (Stuttgart: Deutsche Verlags-Anstalt, 1961).
2 This is the carbon copy kept by Hess (Hess to Hewel, December 8, 1928, National Archives, Nuremberg document 3753-PS).
3 Hermann Rauschning, *The Voice of Destruction* (New York: G. P. Putnam's Sons, 1940). See on this: Theodor Schieder, *Hermann Rauschnings "Gespräche mit Hitler" als Geschichtsquelle* (Opladen: Westdeutscher Verlag, 1972).

various editions of Hitler's conversations. A defense of Benito Mussolini
against criticism by Hewel concludes the letter.

The original of this letter may not have reached Hewel, who moved to
the Netherlands East Indies in 1927, and Hess for a while considered
sending him a carbon copy.[4] When summarizing the struggles of the
party in 1928 in another letter, Hess again stressed the need for space
and the fight for it as the party's real aim:

> We are really all filled with the highest hopes. I firmly believe in our ultimate
> success. Certainly there will be a long, hard, and nerve-devouring [*nervenfres-
> senden*] struggle – especially for the highest leader – before the internal pre-
> requisites have finally been established for that space policy [*Raumpolitik*]
> which is essential for maintaining the life of the nation. This is the most
> important task of the movement – everything else is only preparation and a
> means to this end.
>
> Space! We at home suffocate for lack of space – you out there [in Java] suffer
> because you are in a kind of human vacuum. . . . Have you by any chance read
> the marvelous novel of German fate, "Volk ohne Raum" [People without
> Space] by Hans Grimm? Grimm is close to us; he visited H[itler] recently.[5]

Several studies of Hitler's ideas of world domination come to the
conclusion that Hitler did indeed hold such ideas and that they must
form a major part of any effort to understand him and his policies.[6] The
letter of Hess describing Hitler's concepts supports that interpretation
against those who still attempt to transmute the ruthless dictator with
worldwide ambitions into a statesman with limited aims.

Munich, March 30, 1927

To Mr. Walter Hewel
London – 112
23 Cleveland Square Hyde Park

Dear Mr. Hewel:

At last you are to hear something from us after two interesting letters of
yours have remained unanswered for so long.

I want to tell you above all that Hitler was most pleased by your letters.
There was much in them that was completely new to us. He wants me to thank
you very much. At the same time, however, I would like to recommend that you
send letters to the Chief (as Hitler is called in the inner circle) through me. I
mark the most interesting passages for the Chief, whose time is often very

4 Hess to Hewel, December 8, 1928, 3753-PS.
5 Ibid. In the same letter Hess also discussed his own planned and actual aeronautical
  exploits – he had planned to fly across the Atlantic!
6 Günter Moltmann, "Weltherrschaftsideen Hitlers," in *Europa und Übersee: Festschrift für Egmont Zechlin* (Hamburg: Hans Bredow-Institut, 1961), pp. 197–240; Jochen Thies, *Architekt
  der Weltherrschaft: Die "Endziele" Hitlers* (Düsseldorf: Droste, 1976).

short, and submit them to him. Furthermore, you will then get a somewhat faster reply than hitherto.

You want to hear news of the movement. Well, one can be more than satisfied. If you consider the forces that are employed against us, forces which have the whole organization of the state at their disposal, either in the form of the government itself and the physical power behind it, or in the form of the press, or in the form of the weight of the masses influenced by it, or all of these taken together, then the Chief can view what has been accomplished since his release from the fortress [of Landsberg] with satisfaction. All the prohibitions against speaking and other chicaneries have not been able to arrest the slow but therefore more healthy growth of the movement. There was doubtless an inflationary factor in the movement's development in 1923 also: those were not the most dependable people who came running suddenly in view of the events that seemed to lie in the air, and some of whom were driven by the fear induced in them by the monetary inflation. Those, on the other hand, who have stayed with us in recent years, the years of persecution in which the movement looked least likely to succeed, form a basis on which we can build and in which idealism greatly predominates. And because of disputes with other organizations such as the Freedom Party,[7] the paramilitary associations,[8] etc., it has become clear that there is now a homogeneous block standing underneath [*unter*] Hitler, in which there is not the slightest doubt as to who leads and gives the orders. Here, in our own ranks, there is the possibility of a dictatorship which is erected on the healthiest principle, the principle that all who receive orders are convinced that the person giving the orders will give the *right* orders and lead the *right* way. The Führer can employ, maneuver, and if necessary withdraw this block, thoroughly imbued with that conviction, with all the strength of unity inherent in it. When the prohibition against Hitler's speaking in Bavaria was recently lifted, the Bavarian People's Party wrote in a secret circular that ʰ NSDAP was doubtless the best-disciplined party and that it had to be taken correspondingly seriously and watched with the greatest care.

Naturally, the discipline, coherence, and strength of the party does not fail to have its effect on outsiders. It is an old experience that such structures exercise considerable powers of attraction. This has already become evident in areas where we have had the greatest successes. I am thinking first of all of the Ruhr area. There we had an excellent leader in Dr. Goebbels, who carried on fine preparatory work. After its initial establishment, which involved bloody struggles, the movement is now already so strong there that our people dominate the situation in many places. In a small factory town like Hattingen, for example, the situation is such that no other party can hold a meeting there any more against the will of the National Socialists. Even the radical Left, the Communists, has declined to relative insignificance: after careful and intensive

7 *Freiheitspartei*, the party officially known as the *Deutsch-völkische Freiheitspartei*, led by Albrecht von Graefe and Reinhold Wulle.
8 *Wehrverbände*, the paramilitary organizations active in the Weimar Republic. See James M. Diehl, *Paramilitary Politics in Weimar Germany* (Bloomington: Indiana University Press, 1977).

indoctrination work by us, a large proportion of them have come over to us. Here as in other cities these active elements of the Left often provide the best and most belligerent segment of our SA [Sturm-Abteilung, the brown-shirted Nazi paramilitary formation]. A short time ago Hitler, who in Prussia is allowed to speak only in closed membership meetings, held a membership meeting in the largest hall in Essen, the Stadthalle. Five thousand persons appeared for it, and the hall had to be closed by the police.

No matter to which German city he comes today, there is not a room in it that can hold the masses who wish to hear him. Fortunately, laborers, members of the radical Left, come in especially large numbers; at the end of the talk there is never the slightest opposition in the hall, Communists, etc., applaud enthusiastically. Hitler has also improved substantially as a speaker since 1920. You will probably be pleased by the fact that in large parts of his presentation he has become more factual and convincing without any loss in the effectiveness of his speech and its ability to stir enthusiasm. You will probably be most interested to learn that last year he spoke three times before invited [audiences of] industrialists from Rhineland-Westphalia, etc; twice in Essen and once in Königswinter. Each time it was as successful as that time in the Atlantic Hotel in Hamburg.[9] Because he could attune his speech to a fairly uniform audience, he was able to stick to a consistent line. As in Hamburg, so in this instance the attitude [of the audience] was at first rather cool and negative, and some sat smiling condescendingly at the people's tribune. It was a great pleasure for me to be able to observe how the men slowly changed their outlook, not without visible signs of their inner resistance. At the end they clapped in a way *these* men probably clap rarely.

The result was that at the second meeting of industrialists in Essen about five hundred gentlemen accepted the invitation. Hitler will probably speak to industrialists in Essen for the third time on April 27. It is planned to have the ladies invited this time also, because once they have been won, they are often more important than the men and exert an influence on their husbands that should not be underestimated. If you are interested in having one or the other of your acquaintances invited, I would ask you to send the addresses to me.

The Chief and I learned with the greatest interest of your connections with the English fascists. Please cultivate these connections as much as possible − assuming that you still have the opportunity and are not already growing coffee in Java. In any case, the Chief greatly welcomes reports from England or from Java, or about your trip, for the [*Völkische*] *Beobachter.* If you do not have the time, the reports do not have to be lengthy at all. Brief reports on impressions, a characterization of the manner of thinking of the people among whom you live, etc. − but he would be equally grateful to you for any description of the customs of the country, or in fact any scientifically interesting pieces that could be published in his newspaper. Please let us know with that whether your name may be given as author, but presumably you will prefer that that not be done.

It is very revealing that English fascism rejects the idea of a dictatorship and

9 On February 28, 1926. Text and commentary in Werner Jochmann (ed.), *Im Kampf um die Macht: Hitlers Rede vor dem Hamburger Nationalklub von 1919* (Frankfurt/M: Europäische Verlagsanstalt, 1960).

builds up more along democratic lines. It probably cannot be otherwise in England in view of the political tradition of the country which over the centuries has entered the very flesh and blood of the English. Nevertheless, I believe that in practice a sufficiently strong leadership personality will occupy a dictatorial position, without its being consciously recognized by the English and especially without his saying so and admitting it.

I believe that in the fortress [Landsberg] Hitler talked to you about the leadership principle [*Führerprinzip*] that he advocates; in short, absolute authority downward and responsibility upward. Inside the movement the structure is such that the Führer does consult with those he commands, [but] once he has made a decision, he carries it out in a dictatorial manner and is responsible only upward. He himself gives orders to the district leaders, the district leaders to the local leaders, the local leaders to the broad mass of members who are directly under them. Responsibility, as stated, always goes in the opposite direction. Once a year the Führer makes his report [*verantwortet sich*] to the general membership meeting, and thereby the circle to the mass of the people is closed. The whole system is called "Germanic democracy."

In the democracy of today, which might be called Western-Jewish, the relationship is the very opposite: authority upward and responsibility downward. Today's leader always keeps an eye on the dear people and conscientiously takes their feelings into consideration. The chosen leaders of the Reichstag have decided more than once against their own judgment in accordance with the will of the demonstrating masses and the will of those who make public opinion by writing for the newspapers.

The figure of 250,000 as the membership of the English fascists probably has to be taken very skeptically. Certainly the role played by English fascism in no way corresponds to this large number. It is probably based on superficial estimates and the optimistic reports of the lower leaders; there is probably no central card file in which every single member is registered and which precludes fraudulent reports by the lower leaders. Our central card file is perfect. Any day one can determine the current membership of the whole organization and each subsection with one motion. In addition to a name file, in which all members are filed by name regardless of residence and from which one can immediately determine whether any given person is a member or not, there is a second card file in which the members are filed according to district [*Gau*] and local group [*Ortsgruppe*]. A third card file, a file according to occupation, is in prospect; it will someday be of great value in the reconstruction of the state. The labor which has gone into the card file is naturally enormous, especially because there are constant additions and withdrawals. But it is worth it. Because the local leaders have to turn over to headquarters a fixed contribution for each member, it is obviously impossible to have excess members reported. Since the membership books are issued by headquarters, it is impossible on the other hand for any person to hold a membership card without being registered at headquarters. The card file is kept in four large theftproof and fireproof safes of the most modern design.

Nobody understands better than Hitler that you should think it unnatural and silly for Englishmen and Germans ever to shoot each other down again. At one point in his first volume he wrote how he really suffered in 1914 at seeing blond young Englishmen confront us and the best Aryan and Germanic blood destroy one another.[10] You may be certain that the Jews observed this fight between their natural enemies, this extermination of the higher race, with a triumphal smile. Let us hope that the world war is the last time that these two peoples fight each other. Upon the solution of the Jewish question we shall take a great step forward on the path of understanding among peoples, and especially among related peoples. World peace is certainly an ideal worth striving for; in Hitler's opinion it will be realizable only when one power, the racially best one, has attained complete and uncontested supremacy. That [power] can then provide a sort of world police, seeing to it at the same time that the most valuable race is guaranteed the necessary living space. And if no other way is open to them, the lower races will have to restrict themselves accordingly. Today's League of Nations is really only a farce which functions primarily as a basis for the Jews to reach their own aims. You need only note how many Jews sit in the League, or, if they do not appear directly, exert their influence there as the private secretaries of leading statesmen. Aside from this, in the League of Nations, as everywhere in the world, might decides in the final analysis; in today's power relationships the diplomatic aim is as decisive as ever; that is, in the final analysis it is only a question of which party can assemble the greatest power. It will then get its way and disregard the will of the League of Nations; might takes the place of right. But because the Jews still represent the greatest might, it is the will of the Jews that is carried out by the League, or [the will] of international Freemasonry, which is largely the same thing. It is indicative, as you wrote yourself, that the League of Nations rests on the Treaty of Versailles; but whom does the Treaty of Versailles in all its financial implications benefit?

Just one more word in answer to your remark about the "one-sidedness and silly smallness" of Mussolini in regard to foreign influence and foreign culture. You must not believe that as a thinking person Mussolini "thinks as small and restrictedly" as would appear from his speeches. Mussolini is a great psychologist and knows his people, and – this applies not only to the Italian people but in the final analysis to every [people] – the leader must be absolute in his propagandistic speeches. He may not weigh the pros and cons like a scientist; he cannot allow his listeners the freedom of thinking something else correct; nor, when referring to a people and its mission, to assert, say, that in addition to one's own people there are such and such other peoples who are just as good, just as able, just as destined to greatness as one's own. In this the great popular leader is like the great founder of a religion; an absolute belief must be conveyed to the listeners, because only then can the mass of followers be led wherever they are supposed to be led. Then they will even follow the leader if there are setbacks, but only if they are given an absolute belief in the absolute correctness of their own will, in the mission of the leader, and in our case in the mission of our own people. Mussolini, for example, wants to make his people great and strong, to provide [Italy] with the status in the world that it merits, and to give its increasing population a chance to live. For the sake of this goal he is obliged to use the means that may most likely lead to success, and a

10 Perhaps a reference to *Mein Kampf* (Munich: Eher, 1933), Vol. 1: p. 159.

German leader on the whole cannot act otherwise, allowing for the differences in the psychological makeup of the German people. Hitler sends you many greetings and thanks you very much for your letters. He hopes that they are not the last ones and you will be able to report to him often in such an interesting manner. I myself send you heartiest greetings.

Yours,
H[ess]

3

THE WORLD THROUGH HITLER'S EYES

When Adolf Hitler became chancellor of Germany at the age of forty-three in 1933, he had held no previous position of authority in government. He had neither read intensively nor traveled extensively. He knew no foreign language. Yet he had a clearly formulated set of ideas on major issues of foreign policy, and these ideas were intimately interwoven with his concepts of domestic affairs. It is essential for an understanding of world history since 1933 that these ideas be examined in some detail, for a great part of the impact of Hitler on Germany – and of Germany on the world – lies precisely in the fact that by exertion of his will and the response it elicited inside Germany, Hitler was able to impress his ideas on events rather than allow events and realities to reshape his ideas. It is true that the effort failed. Realities that did not conform to Hitler's visions proved stronger even than his fanatic will and the mighty energies and resources the German people harnessed to it. But the great burst of activity in Germany in the 1930s, which soon spilled over Europe and affected the whole globe, was no random excitement, no accidental explosion.

There have been those who argue that Hitler was a pure opportunist, a manipulator of power, without guideposts. The shifts in the pattern of his alliances – now with the center of world communism, now with one of the sources of the so-called yellow peril – have suggested to some that plan, pattern, and ideological considerations of continuing influence must have been absent from the National Socialist scene. Efforts to rehabilitate Hitler's diplomatic reputation have tended to base themselves on such a view. Alan J. P. Taylor, in *The Origins of the Second World War,* attempted to convert Hitler into an eighteenth-century diplomat, striving for revision of the most recent treaty in the same way Maria Theresa

Slightly revised from *The Foreign Policy of Hitler's Germany: Diplomatic Revolution in Europe, 1933–1936* (Chicago: University of Chicago Press, 1970; Atlantic Highlands, N.J.: Humanities Press, 1994), ch. 1.

attempted to recover Silesia for Austria from the Prussia of Frederick the Great. David Hoggan and Philip Fabry present Hitler in somewhat similar terms, only they show him victimized by unscrupulous opponents: Lord Halifax in one case, Josef Stalin in the other.[1] The available evidence, however, shows that Hitler had some very definite, fixed ideas on foreign policy before he came to power. This evidence comes primarily from his speeches and writings, a not unnatural source in the case of a man who devoted his full time to political agitation, and who did not hesitate to include in his published views ideas he knew to be unpopular alongside others likely to elicit frenetic applause.[2] The evidence also indicates that during the years from 1933 to 1939 Hitler kept these ideas very much in mind in the actual conduct of affairs, though he tended to reserve oral and written expression of them to the privacy of the conference room or the circle of his associates. The opportunism to which some have pointed as the essence of Hitler's policy was instead an integral element in his theory of political action, and many of the most extravagant and perplexing instances will be seen to fit most precisely into his general view.

The objection might be raised that those who see a plan in Hitler's steps will be tempted to read the evidence in a manner that supports their interpretation, but the unanswerable fact remains that new evidence, as it comes to light, not only fits into but in astonishing ways underlines the accuracy of that view. Thus the publication in 1961 of what can only be called an apologia for Field Marshal Keitel, who was executed at Nuremberg, includes an instance of a revelation of war plans by Hitler in a 1935 military gathering that moved the editor to comment on this new indication of Hitler's real policy at a time when peaceful liquidation of the Versailles Treaty was the officially proclaimed policy of the German government.[3] The proponents of other interpretations have based their positions, not on the discovery of new evidence, but on attempts to explain away or disregard the obvious meaning of documents long known.[4]

In 1933 Hitler's ideology consisted primarily of two related systems of

1 Alan J. P. Taylor, *The Origins of the Second World War* (London: Hamilton, 1961); David J. Hoggan, *Der Erzwungene Krieg* (Tübingen: Verlag der Deutschen Hochschullehrerzeitung, 1961); Philip W. Fabry, *Der Hitler-Stalin-Pakt, 1939–1941* (Darmstadt: Fundus, 1982).
2 See also the analysis in Eberhard Jäckel, *Hitlers Weltanschauung: Entwurf einer Herrschaft*, rev. ed. (Stuttgart: Deutsche Verlags-Anstalt, 1981).
3 Walter Görlitz (ed.), *Generalfeldmarschall Keitel: Verbrecher oder Offizier?* (Göttingen: Musterschmidt, 1961), p. 81, n. 89. The question posed in the title, "Criminal or Officer?" suggesting that Keitel could not have been both, indicates the general tenor of the book.
4 An excellent demolition of such attempts in Walter Hofer, *Die Entfesselung des Zweiten Weltkrieges: Eine Studie über die internationalen Beziehungen im Sommer 1939*, 3d ed. (Frankfurt/M: S. Fischer, 1964), pp. 419–75, 503f.

ideas, acquired and developed in chronological sequence. The doctrine of race took form first and is clearly delineated by 1923, the partly derivative doctrine of space came to be defined, in the formulation to which Hitler subsequently adhered, in the immediately following years.

Hitler's conception of foreign policy in his first years of political activity, that is, until November 1923, can be summarized as follows:[5] Germany was not defeated in World War I but stabbed in the back by Jews and those inspired by Jews. These same elements now controlled Germany internally and maintained themselves in part by their subservience to those foreign powers whom that stab in the back had made the victors. A preliminary to any successful foreign policy therefore must be an internal change, in fact a revolution. A nationally conscious group must assume power, ruthlessly displace whatever steps toward democratic government had been taken inside Germany, and rearm to provide the tools of an aggressive foreign policy. Such a policy must be directed primarily against France, Germany's eternal enemy. This might mean an alignment with Italy, since that power was also opposed to French hegemony in Europe. The inclusion of postwar Austria in a greater Germany was also required; and other territories, not very clearly defined, would be annexed. War was an unavoidable step on the road to national recovery, and would be victorious, as there would be no repetition of the home-front laxness responsible for Germany's recent defeat.

These views were based on Hitler's doctrine of race, a vulgarized version of Social Darwinism that found increasing acceptance in Germany, both in supposedly learned circles and, especially in the years between 1900 and 1914, among the masses.[6] According to this doctrine, the history of mankind can be understood in terms of racial analysis, that is, in terms of the supposed racial components of different societies. The rise or fall of Rome can thus be understood as the products of the racial purity of early and the racial mixture of later Roman society. The political division of France in the age of the French Revolution reflects the division between the Romanic, that is, racially "Westic" lower classes, and the Nordic descendants of the Franks who had unified and organized the country. The cultural accomplishments of civilizations are the product of their racial composition – the great artists of Renaissance times were all Nordics whose works reflect their own appearance, while the monstrosities of modern art only mirror the appearance of their creators. Botticelli must have been as slim as his famous Venus, Rubens must have

---

5 A survey of the subject in Günter Schubert, *Anfänge Nationalsozialistischer Aussenpolitik* (Cologne: Verlag Wissenschaft und Politik, 1961).

6 The sources for this period have been collected in Eberhard Jäckel (ed.), *Hitler: Sämtliche Aufzeichnungen, 1905–1924* (Stuttgart: Deutsche Verlags-Anstalt, 1980).

been as corpulent as the figures he painted, and Picasso presumably had three eyes.[7]

An especially significant facet of the racialist doctrine was its rejection of the biblical distinction between humans and other creatures. With the most drastic implications – assuming that one was prepared to follow them to their logical conclusion – the new paganism argued that racial purity and selective breeding are the necessary instruments of progress in the human as in the animal world, and insisted that social policy be oriented accordingly. The elimination of categories of people, like the elimination of categories of insects or plants, could be judged solely by standards of utility, not morality. It was within this framework that the allegedly alien racial stock represented by the Jews was particularly dangerous because of their wide distribution and imagined influence as well as the progress which their assimilation had made, especially in Germany.[8]

The racial element also provided a basis for Germany's hope. Her defeat in the war was due not to her inherent weakness; on the contrary, her ability to hold out for so long against a world of foes was in part a reflection of her inherent racial superiority. A full recognition of this superiority and the willingness to draw from it the necessary conclusions for domestic policy would combine to produce a different outcome next time. That this "next time" would come was beyond question. France was the great enemy. In Hitler's view, however, the enmity of Germany and France was based on more than the obvious reasons of recent war and contemporary (1920–23) French hegemony. There was a racial angle of special virulence that greatly affected Hitler's perception of France and his policies toward that country.

A key element in National Socialist hostility to France was the role of the latter as the European home of the concept of human equality, and especially the extension of *égalité* to the Negro. Because racialism in Germany focused most directly on the Jews and also the Sinti and Roma (Gypsies), it has generally been overlooked that the next great danger to European racial purity was supposed to be the Negro, introduced into

---

7 Anyone who considers this summary an unfair satire can examine Paul Schulze-Naumburg, *Kunst und Rasse* (Munich: Lehmann, 1928; 2d ed. 1935), since the illustrations convey its message to anyone who does not read German.

8 It is true that in his speeches Hitler particularly emphasized the least assimilated Jews, i.e., those who had recently immigrated into Germany, as a sure way to stir up his audiences. But he also left no doubt that his attacks were directed against *all* the Jews, as when he explained to a cheering crowd on April 6, 1920, his determination "to pull up the evil by its roots and exterminate it completely" (das Übel an der Wurzel zu packen und Stumpf und Stiel ausderzurotten). Jäckel, *Hitler*, p. 120. This reference to the extermination of all Jews, which is immediately followed by the assertion that all means for reaching this goal, including an alliance with the devil, would be appropriate, has not been given the attention it deserves.

Europe and sponsored by France. Unquestionably the experience of the world war had intensified, if it did not create, this concern. The large-scale deployment on European battlefields of soldiers recruited in Africa had made a major impact on German thinking. Partly because so many Negroes had been included in the French army, and partly because of the presence of African colonial units among the French forces stationed in the Rhineland during the postwar occupation, this whole process came to be associated with France in German eyes. National Socialist publications of the 1920s were filled with attacks on the supposed negroidization of France, and Hitler found ways to connect this directly with the "Jewish menace." Thus enmity for France was ordained by more than political or territorial factors.[9]

Hitler's views of other countries in these first years of his political activity were not yet as systematized as they were to become in the mid-1920s.[10] In his writings and speeches of those years his doctrine of space, built on that of race, was to provide a series of prescriptions for foreign policy in general and for policies toward certain countries in particular. This principle of space therefore requires scrutiny.[11]

Space, in Hitler's thinking, always referred to agriculturally usable land; the word is regularly employed in connection with the raising of food for the support of the population living on it. Hitler had no confidence in the possibility of increasing food production from available land. The struggle for existence in which the races of the world engaged, the basic element of life on earth, was fundamentally a struggle for space. In this struggle the stronger won, took the space, proliferated on that space, and then fought for additional space. Racial vitality and spatial expansion were directly related. A people always faced the question of bringing about a proper relationship between the space on which it lived and its population. In Hitler's view, a people could choose between adjusting the

9 Hitler speech of December 16, 1921, ibid., p. 531. See also Schubert, *Anfänge National-sozialistischer Aussenpolitik*, p. 29; Adolf Hitler, *Mein Kampf* (Munich: Eher, 1933), Vol. 1, p. 357, and Vol. 2, p. 730. Alfred Rosenberg, *Der Zukunftsweg einer deutschen Aussenpolitik* (Munich: Eher, 1927), pp. 36–39. This racial factor led Hitler to a low estimate of French military power and was a factor in his unwillingness to respond to French attempts at collaboration after the armistice of June 1940.

10 The contrast can be seen most clearly if Hitler's speeches in 1920–21 (to be found in Jäckel, *Hitler*), are contrasted with those after his release from jail (see n. 11).

11 The main sources for this period are *Mein Kampf*; Gerhard L. Weinberg (ed.), *Hitlers zweites Buch: Ein Dokument aus dem Jahr 1928* (Stuttgart: Deutsche Verlags-Anstalt, 1961); and the series being issued under the auspices of the Institut für Zeitgeschichte in Munich: *Hitler: Reden, Schriften, Anordnungen, Februar 1925 bis Januar 1933* (Munich: Saur, 1992–) (cited hereafter as *Hitler: Reden*). In a category by itself because written years later is Hermann Rauschning's *The Voice of Destruction* (New York: Putnam, 1940). On this source, see Theodor Schieder, *Rauschnings "Gespräche mit Hitler" als Geschichtsquelle* (Opladen: Westdeutscher Verlag, 1972).

population to a given space or adjusting space to population. The adjustment of population to a fixed space meant emigration, birth control, abortion, and suicide – all leading to eventual racial decay as each occurred with higher frequency among the racially superior elements of the population. Furthermore, this course generally involved dependence on others, because of the need to import food, even for the population that had been intentionally held down. Only a weak people would choose this course, and they would become weaker in the process.

The desirable alternative course, which Hitler consistently advocated in *Mein Kampf* and his political speeches from 1925 on, was the adjustment of space to population by the conquest of additional land areas whose native population would be expelled or exterminated, not assimilated. The availability of such land areas would in turn encourage the good, healthy Nordic couples settled on them to raise large families that would both make up for the casualties incurred in the conquest of the territory and assure adequate military manpower for subsequent wars *they* would need to wage.

Two facets of this last point need emphasis. Wars cost casualties – Hitler knew this as well as his audiences – but this did not mean that wars should be avoided. They were the only way to gain the land required for racial survival, and therefore necessary. But they should be fought for an adequate purpose: an amount of land believed worth the casualties in a calculation that applied to the prospective German dead the same extreme instrumentalization Hitler applied to all.[12] In Hitler's calculation, the German borders of 1914 were most certainly not such an adequate purpose and were not worth the sacrifices their recovery would require. Until 1933, therefore, he never ceased to attack as a ridiculously inadequate objective the idea of trying to regain the borders of 1914. In his second book, Hitler mentioned 500,000 square kilometers of additional space in Europe as his first goal.[13] Since Germany's European territorial losses in the war had slightly exceeded 70,000 square kilometers, it is no wonder that he wrote in *Mein Kampf*: "The borders of the year 1914 mean absolutely nothing for the future of the German nation."[14] The foreign policy Hitler advocated thus promised war for new land *beyond* Germany's prewar borders, and further specified that the land would be settled by German farmers.

12 For examples of this type of "casualty mathematics" before Hitler came to power, see *Mein Kampf*, Vol. 2, pp. 738–40; *Hitlers zweites Buch*, p. 48, where the editor has also noted an example from the World War II period.

13 *Hitlers zweites Buch*, p. 102. A few weeks earlier, Hitler was still prepared to settle for a mere 300,000 or 400,000 square kilometers; see his speech of May 2, 1928, in *Hitler: Reden*, Vol. 2/2, No. 268, p. 815.

14 *Mein Kampf*, Vol. 2, p. 738.

The second aspect of this expansionist program requiring attention is its potentially limitless character. The specific and immediate conclusions Hitler drew from his theories of race and space will be reviewed in detail, but first this inherent long-term trend toward world conquest must be noted. Clearly, if space is to be adjusted to an expanded population by conquest, and such conquest again enables the population to expand and facilitates further conquest, the only possible limitations are utter defeat on the one hand or total occupation of the globe on the other. A gifted German scholar, Günter Moltmann, called attention to the tendencies in this direction to be found in *Mein Kampf* and has suggested that the more explicit statements of 1932–1934, attributed to Hitler by Hermann Rauschning, may be accepted as consistent with them.[15] Evidence that has come to light since Moltmann wrote shows that in the years between the period reflected by *Mein Kampf* and by Rauschning's report Hitler himself recognized these implications.[16] Rudolf Hess in 1927 informed Walter Hewel, who had been in Landsberg prison together with Hess and Hitler, that Hitler was of the opinion that world peace could come only "when one power, the racially best one, has attained complete and uncontested supremacy." It would then establish a world police and assure itself "the necessary living space. . . . The lower races will have to restrict themselves accordingly."[17] The process was described aptly by Hitler himself in 1928: "We consider our (anticipated) sacrifices, weigh the size of the possible success, and will go on the attack, regardless of whether it will come to a stop 10 or 1,000 kilometers beyond the present lines. For wherever our success may end, that will always be only the starting point of a new fight."[18]

The combined doctrines of race and space had significant implications for the day-to-day conduct of foreign affairs. Hitler was publicly explicit about these before 1933; their influence will be apparent in his record after 1933, although he no longer discussed them quite so publicly. It has already been shown that war was to be a key instrument of policy; not the

---

15 "Weltherrschaftsideen Hitler," in *Europa und Übersee: Festschrift für Egmont Zechlin* (Hamburg: Hans-Bredow Institut, 1961), pp. 197–240.

16 See Jochen Thies, *Architekt der Weltherrschaft: Die "Endziele" Hitlers* (Düsseldorf: Droste, 1976).

17 Gerhard L. Weinberg (ed.), "National Socialist Organization and Foreign Policy Aims in 1927." *Journal of Modern History* 36 (1964): 432; the full text is to be found in the preceding chapter. Hitler expressed similar worldwide ambitions to Otto Strasser in May 1930; see Strasser's brochure, *Ministersessel oder Revolution* (Berlin: Kampf-Verlag, 1930), reprinted in his *Aufbau des deutschen Sozialismus* (2d ed., Prague: Heinrich Grunov, 1936), pp. 122–24, 132.

18 *Hitlers zweites Buch*, p. 77. Examples of references by Hitler to repeated wars leading to worldwide conquest from the World War II period are quite numerous; many are listed by Moltmann. The point here has been to document the conscious recognition of the idea in the years before 1933.

last resort, but in some instances the preferred approach. This role of war as a deliberate prior choice, not the *ultima ratio,* was to have a profound influence on German diplomacy. It meant, for example, that if you decided that your opponent must give in absolutely or you would go to war, the process of negotiations would be one in which your demands would be constantly raised as deadlock approached, not reduced as the parties moved toward a compromise.

A second way in which the doctrines affected the handling of international relations was their import for treaties. If treaties are to serve the struggle for space, their primary objective would be either the immediate gain of space by the partitioning of third countries or the postponement of troubles considered dangerous at the moment until they could be faced with safety. In either case, treaties were temporary instruments to be broken as soon as they were no longer useful in the struggle for space. Hitler assumed that there could be no alliance except on the basis of such gains for both parties. Once the prospect of gain was gone, or even obstructed by the treaty, it had to be dropped.[19]

With this view of treaties in mind, one can readily understand National Socialist opposition to all multilateral treaty commitments. It is easier to make and break a treaty with one partner than to join and subsequently disengage oneself from a complicated multilateral structure. For this reason, as well as opposition to the doctrine of the equality of states, the National Socialists did not approve Germany's adherence to the Locarno Treaty and the Kellogg–Briand Peace Pact and were strongly opposed to Germany's entrance into the League of Nations. Hitler's repeated public denunciations of the League were paralleled by the frequent introduction of resolutions calling on Germany to leave Geneva by the National Socialist members of the Reichstag.[20] After 1933 Hitler not only took Germany out of the League and tore up the Locarno Treaty at what seemed to him the earliest possible moments, but he was to avoid most carefully any new type of multilateral commitments.

Still another way in which the doctrines of race and space affected Hitler's view of international affairs was their relation to the traditional diplomatic service. Specific evidence of Hitler's attitude toward diplomats before 1933, as contrasted with the subsequent period, is slight. His denunciations of the elements of German society who controlled the

---

19 *Mein Kampf, Vol. 1, pp. 154–55; Hitlers zweites Buch,* pp. 94f.
20 Just as Hitler's views favoring new wars were publicly expressed, so the Nazi Party's opposition to the League of Nations and all measures for world peace were made the proud subject of Nazi propaganda. A compendium of the positions taken by the Nazi delegation in the Reichstag was issued by its chairman, Wilhelm Frick, in 1929 as No. 4 in the *Nationalsozialistische Bibliothek* and reissued in updated form as No. 37 in 1932 (*Die Nationalsozialisten im Reichstag,* Munich: Eher).

government in the prewar, wartime, and postwar periods, however, presumably included the diplomats. Certainly there was nothing to distinguish the German foreign service from what might be called the German
establishment, and all efforts to change that service during the Weimar
period were largely frustrated.[21] The prewar policy of alliance which
Hitler denounced was a product of their activities; they were implicated
in the allegedly weak and defeatist wartime government; and they implemented, willingly or unwillingly, the foreign policy of Weimar Germany
which Hitler considered treasonable in nature. Hitler's comments on
Count Johann Heinrich Bernstorff, former German ambassador to the
United States, who in 1928 represented Germany in the disarmament
negotiations, may serve as an indication of his assessment: "This man . . .
was a typical representative of Germany's prewar foreign policy, just as he
is a typical representative of the foreign policy of the [Weimar] Republic.
This character [*Subjekt*], who would have been hanged by order of a state
tribunal in every other country, is Germany's representative at the League
of Nations in Geneva. These men bear the guilt and responsibility for the
collapse of Germany."[22]

The diplomatic service Hitler inherited in 1933 consisted almost entirely of men whose background, education, and general orientation precluded full acceptance of Hitler's doctrines, although the vast majority
were in agreement with the policies Hitler used to implement his own
ideas in his first years in power. Here was a long-term personnel problem
for any National Socialist regime, but anticipations of it may be recognized when one considers the three men who in a way constituted the
foreign service of the party before 1933: Alfred Rosenberg, Kurt
Lüdecke, and Ernst (Putzi) Hanfstaengl.

Alfred Rosenberg was born in Riga, studied in Moscow, and had done
some other traveling before settling in postwar Munich as a professional
agitator for anti-Semitic causes. He became both one of the National
Socialist party's leading theoreticians and the foreign policy expert of its
Reichstag delegation. His interests in international affairs were concentrated on Eastern Europe and somewhat influenced Hitler's ideas; but
his efforts to play a key role in foreign affairs after January 1933 were
generally a failure. Rosenberg's unsuitability as a diplomat was at least
partially apparent to Hitler before 1933. Rosenberg was simply a dedicated theoretician with no organizational talent. It was for precisely this
reason that Hitler, while in jail, placed him temporarily in charge of the

---

21 See Paul Seabury, *The Wilhelmstrasse* (Berkeley: University of California Press, 1954), ch. 1;
    Hans-Jürgen Döscher, *Das Auswärtige Amt im Dritten Reich: Diplomatie im Schatten der
    Endlösung* (Berlin: Siedler, 1987), ch. 1.
22 *Hitlers zweites Buch*, p. 215.

party, certain that he could take over again once released from Landsberg. Even if Rosenberg could be given a diplomatic assignment for a short time, he was obviously no man to recruit or organize a foreign service or any other sort of diplomatic apparatus, a judgment that his later efforts in this direction proved correct.[23]

Kurt Lüdecke was an international adventurer and gambler who joined Hitler in 1922. Anti-Semitism was a key element in his original adherence to National Socialism, and he continued to preach the doctrines of racial purity between amorous adventures with women of rather varied origins of which he boasts in his memoirs.[24] Lüdecke's relevance to a study of Hitler's foreign policy lies in the fact that he was one of the very few early members of the party to have some experience of the world outside Germany and some knowledge of foreign languages.[25] He represented Hitler in his "diplomatic" contact with the Hungarian Gömbös and with Mussolini, and was delegated to raise funds for the party in the United States.[26] Lüdecke represented precisely the type of ideologically oriented adventurer Hitler could employ for diplomatic missions that would serve the new Germany; and the men who played this role in the 1930s – Joachim von Ribbentrop, Ferdinand Heye, Peter Kleist, Edmund Veesenmayer, Johannes Bernhardt, to name a few – bear a startling resemblance to Lüdecke. But Lüdecke's ideology was too doctrinaire for Hitler, who was more willing to be opportunistic in his means; and Lüdecke was not only frustrated in his hopes for a great diplomatic career after the National Socialists' assumption of power but found himself arrested for his pains. Though even his memoirs, published in 1937 after his escape to the United States, reveal his continued faith in National Socialism, and though he tried in 1939 to return to Hitler's fold,[27] the model diplomat had to observe the Third Reich from the sidelines.

The same fate overtook Ernst Hanfstaengl, whose personal quarrels and rivalry with Lüdecke must not be allowed to obscure the similarity in their outlook, careers, and relations to Hitler. The Harvard graduate and

---

23 For Rosenberg's pre-1933 role, see Schubert, *Anfänge Nationalsozialistischer Aussenpolitik*, pp. 99–138. A general account of his *Aussenpolitische Amt* is in Hans-Adolf Jacobsen, *Nationalsozialistische Ausssenpolitik, 1933–1938* (Frankfurt/M: Metzner, 1968), pp. 45–89.

24 Kurt G. W. Lüdecke, *I Knew Hitler* (New York: Scribner's, 1937). See also Roland V. Layton, Jr., "Kurt Lüdecke and *I Knew Hitler*: An Evaluation," *Central European History* 12 (1979): 372–86; Schubert, *Anfänge Nationalsozialistischer Aussenpolitik*, pp. 138–67.

25 Years later Hitler remembered Lüdecke as a man who spoke French, English, Spanish, and Italian like a native and by implication as a man who could be depended on to seduce the right women. Hugh R. Trevor-Roper (ed.), *Hitler's Table Talk* (London: Weidenfeld and Nicolson, 1953), October 30, 1941, p. 102.

26 Lüdecke, *I Knew Hitler*, pp. 128, 261–66; Alan Cassels, "Mussolini and German Nationalism, 1922–1925," *Journal of Modern History* 35 (1963): 137–57.

27 Interrogation of Fritz Wiedemann, November 10, 1945, National Archives, Nuremberg Trials materials.

member of a respected Munich family joined Hitler in 1922, to a large extent drawn by a common intensity of anti-Semitic feelings. In addition to introducing Hitler to members of Munich society, Hanfstaengl entertained Hitler by his jokes and piano playing, serving as a kind of court jester. Hanfstaengl's travels abroad made him an expert on international affairs among the beer hall politicians, and Hitler used him in his dealing with foreign journalists. Hanfstaengl became the foreign press chief of the party. Like Lüdecke, however, he was an independent-minded adventurer; he was rather too intent on chasing skirts; and his openly voiced criticisms of some of Hitler's associates and temporary departures from the true doctrine made it impossible for him to fit in. As Lüdecke had fled in 1934, so Hanfstaengl was to flee in 1937; and again like Lüdecke, he failed in his efforts to return to the Reich in 1939.[28]

Rosenberg, Lüdecke, and Hanfstaengl were all greatly concerned about getting the outside world to understand and appreciate Hitler's ideas. Rosenberg was prepared to accept whatever Hitler did and said; his experience was to prove that it would be impossible to arouse enthusiasm in the outside world; but since he never attempted to change anything, Hitler rewarded his loyalty by allowing him to continue in office. Lüdecke and Hanfstaengl, however, sought to have Hitler make minor modifications in his tactics in order to enhance his reputation abroad. For such men there was no room in National Socialist diplomacy, and soon they were succeeded by men who shared their interest in international intrigue and their lack of responsibility but were careful to keep to themselves their opinions of tactical details.

One other National Socialist figure who dabbled in foreign affairs before 1933 was Hermann Göring. He, too, had some international adventures behind him, and he was already representing Hitler in some external negotiations, in Danzig, for example.[29] He was to continue to play a role in the German-Danzig-Polish complex as well as some other aspects of foreign affairs after 1933; but his numerous offices in the

---

28 There is no scholarly study of Hanfstaengl's career. His memoirs, *Hitler: The Missing Years* (London: Eyre & Spottiswoode, 1957), show that just as Lüdecke's anti-Semitism survived his escape to America, so Hanfstaengl's survived World War II (see, e.g., pp. 31f., 80f.). See also the memorandum on Hanfstaengl in the unpublished memoirs of George S. Messersmith (then U.S. consul general in Berlin) in the University of Delaware Library. On his effort to return to Nazi Germany, the story in his memoirs (p. 290) is contradicted by the contemporary record, a memorandum of the British government accompanying a letter by Sir Ronald Campbell to John Franklin Carter of June 23, 1942, in the Henry Field papers, Franklin D. Roosevelt Library. I am indebted to Dr. Field for permission to use this document.

29 See Ernst Ziehm, *Aus meiner politischen Arbeit in Danzig, 1914–1939* (Marburg: Herder-Institut, 1960), pp. 143–45.

Third Reich were to direct most of his extensive energies to domestic affairs.

Upon Hitler's accession to power there was no ready-made apparatus to replace the established diplomatic service as the chosen implement of new policies. Hitler would have to utilize the old while experimenting with the new. The first was to prove much simpler and the second much more difficult than might have been anticipated.

The doctrines of race and space were not limited in their implications to general considerations of foreign policy aims and methods but had very specific import for the policies to be followed toward individual countries. The space Germany needed was to be found primarily in the East, in Russia. The major theme of the foreign policy sections of *Mein Kampf* and of most of Hitler's second book was this insistence on the conquest of territory toward the Urals. This theme, constantly reiterated in his speeches before 1933, was one in which Hitler's perception of Russia, primarily in terms of his doctrine of race, seemed to fit most precisely with the requirements of space policy. The land area the Germanic farmers would be settled on was inhabited by Slavs, an inherently inferior group according to Hitler. They were incapable of organizing a state or developing a culture. The only state organization ever successfully imposed on these inferior people had been established and maintained by individuals of Germanic racial stock whose Russification had been no more real in the racial sense than the supposed Germanization of Poles and Czechs had made real Germans of these groups. This stratum of good racial stock, however, had been weakened even in prewar Russia by political attacks from the developing Slavic bourgeoisie with its Pan-Slavic and anti-German ideology. The world war had drastically depleted the Germanic group: war always bears most heavily on the racially best elements who serve at the front while the racially inferior attempt to escape service. The enormous casualties Russia had suffered thus decimated the Germanic stock, especially in the officer corps, in which they were heavily represented. The final blow came during the Bolshevik Revolution, in which the last remnant was exterminated.

This process of elimination of the Germanic element in Russia had left behind an amorphous bloc of Slavs, ruled and exploited for the benefit of world capitalism by the Jews, Hitler claimed. Inherently, the Jews were even less capable of organizing and maintaining a state than the Slavs, and would in any case be destroyed on the triumph of Pan-Slavism among the Russian people. The remaining Slavic population, however, would constitute a permanently feeble and unstable society. The "Slavs have no organizational ability whatever," and a purely Slavic

Russia would have no power; in fact, it would fall into dissolution. That recent events – World War I and the Bolshevik Revolution – had so weakened Russia, therefore, constituted a piece of "good luck" for the future of a Germany that would know how to profit from it.[30] The vast number of Russians presented no problem in itself: Germany had defeated the great Russian armies in the war, and space and numbers alone were not important. Nobody, Hitler maintained, would ever arrive at the idea that there was any danger of Russian hegemony in the world because there was no inner value – meaning no racial value – in the Russian population, however numerous.[31] Since the reduction of the Russian population by slaughter and expulsion was implicit in his policies, it is not surprising that Hitler commonly referred to the rural areas of Eastern Europe, notoriously suffering from overpopulation, as being thinly settled.[32] Territorial conquest eastward was thus both necessary and simple, and the major areas to be conquered lay in Russia.

If Germany were to conquer Russian territory, a terminology he always used for the whole Soviet Union, she had to concern herself with the tier of new states that had gained their independence after World War I because all the great powers of Eastern Europe had been defeated in that conflict. Poland was the largest of these states. It should be noted that Hitler did not pay nearly so much attention to Poland as did many of his German contemporaries. To them, regardless of political orientation, Poland was an abomination, temporary, but most irritating. The Poles were, in German eyes, an East European species of cockroach, their state was generally referred to as a *Saisonstaat* – a country just for a season; and the expression *polnische Wirtschaft* – Polish economy – was a phrase commonly applied to any hopeless mess. The general orientation of German foreign policy with its goal of a return to the borders of 1914, at least in the East, hoped for a new partition of Poland, probably in cooperation with the Soviet Union. There is no evidence to suggest that anyone who occupied a leading position in Weimar Germany recognized that the existence of a strong and independent Poland might have great advantages for Germany. Until the Germans had broken what were commonly known as the "chains of Versailles," they did not notice that the same chains had bound Soviet Russia. Official German policy called for per-

---

30 The clearest presentation of Hitler's views, summarized here and from which the quotations are taken, is in *Hitlers zweites Buch*, pp. 155-59.

31 Ibid., p. 128. This would not preclude the convenient propaganda use of the Russian or Bolshevik menace as a tool, first of domestic and later of foreign propaganda by the National Socialists. Hitler explained to his associates that this was a device for the consumption of others; his own policy was based on the gross underestimation of Soviet power.

32 Ibid., p. 102.

manent hostility to Poland, manifested in a trade war as well as constant friction over questions of minorities and revisionist propaganda.[33]

In the Weimer period, German policy toward the Soviet Union was influenced to a great extent by the priority of revisionist hopes against Poland; in Hitler's view, policy toward Poland was incidental and subordinated to his aim of territorial aggrandizement at the expense of the Soviet Union. This certainly did not make him any friendlier toward the Poles than his predecessors, but he did not share their fixed objectives because he thought them inadequate. His desire for enormous territory rather than border revision automatically diminished the long-term importance of Poland and freed from rigid preconceptions Hitler's short-term tactics toward that country. He assumed Polish hostility toward Germany, understood Poland's close ties with France, and was aware of the possibility of a Polish preventive war against Germany; but in the conduct of relations with Poland, Hitler could proceed pragmatically, subordinating everything to the tactical requirements of other policies.

If the doctrine of space led Hitler to seek territorial expansion eastward, the presumptive increase in strength that would accrue to Germany from such expansion added yet another reason to the many existing ones making for enmity between Germany and France. Surely France would do anything to prevent such an enormous increase in German might. On this assumption, it seemed safe to defeat France first, that is, before moving east, so that Germany would not have a dangerous enemy at her back while engaged on the great enterprise. The first great war Germany would fight, therefore, would be against France; the second one would be against Russia. In fact, Hitler now asserted that in the long run the first war would prove useless unless it paved the way for the second.[34]

As the concept of space reinforced enmity for France, so it accentuated a hitherto only slightly apparent difference in Hitler's attitude toward England. Until about 1923, England was regularly included with France among Germany's present and future enemies, but with greater emphasis on the enmity of France. Perhaps British opposition to the French occupation of the Ruhr stimulated a more fundamental differentiation between the two powers. England now appears in Hitler's view of the world in a separate category. His new attitude toward Great Britain was a mixture of admiration and hate, never entirely untangled. He thought he recognized in the British upper classes the product of a process of selective breeding not entirely unlike what he hoped to accomplish in Ger-

33 For a comprehensive review, see Gaines Post, Jr., *The Civil-Military Fabric of Weimar Foreign Policy* (Princeton, N.J.: Princeton University Press, 1973).
34 *Mein Kampf,* Vol. 2, p. 741.

many. Similarly, he often referred to the ability of a small number of Englishmen to control the Indian subcontinent as a model for his own vast schemes of conquered areas and subdued peoples. On the other hand, Jews were allowed to play a part in British society, Britain had a democratic form of government, and the people of England were oriented more toward trade and industry than toward agriculture. The Jews were imagined to have all sorts of great influence; by definition democracy destroyed responsibility and leadership in a society; and trade and industry were not only less healthy occupations than agriculture but had a debilitating effect on the social structure. Nevertheless, the hegemony of France, apparently created by the Paris peace settlement, would strengthen France in world competition for trade and empire and was thus against the interests of Great Britain. Her opposition to the strongest power on the continent in defense of the European balance would logically place England alongside Germany in her conflict with France – even if that conflict eventually produced a Germany so strong that England would again turn against her, at a time when, presumably, it would be too late.[35]

In Hitler's eyes, the only thing required to persuade England of the wisdom of an alliance with Germany would be the abandonment of Germany's world trade and naval ambitions. These had threatened England before the war, and he believed them responsible for British entrance into an alliance against Germany with her former enemies, France and Russia. The new eastward-directed space policy that Hitler projected for Germany would entail finding food for Germany's people by competition for land in Europe instead of competition for trade in the world, and would thus remove any basis for hostility between Germany and England. Furthermore, if France was one great danger to England, Russia with her expansionist threats to the oil-rich Near East and toward India was a second danger, while the rising trade empire of the United States was a third.[36] With no cause for enmity against Germany, therefore, and with a shared hostility to France and Russia, there was no reason why England should not become an ally of Germany, at least temporarily. As already mentioned, there are explicit hints in Hitler's second book what such an alliance might subsequently give way to renewed enmity, but that was in a future in which Germany would have acquired the territory needed to take care of herself.

35 Schubert, *Anfänge Nationalsozialistischer Aussenpolitik*, pp. 74–75; A. V. N. van Woerden, "Hitler Faces England: Theories, Images, and Policies," *Acta Historiae Neerlandica* 3 (1968): 145–46; *Mein Kampf*, Vol. 1, p. 699; *Hitlers zweites Buch*, pp. 167, 173–74.
36 *Hitlers zweites Buch*, pp. 172–74.

The new emphasis on *Lebensraum* strengthened the apparent wisdom of a German alliance with Italy. Hitler had favored such an alliance on purely pragmatic grounds: Italy's ambitions in the Mediterranean clashed with those of France, and this common hostility to France could furnish the basis for joint action.[37] Hitler's plans for expansion eastward would upset France but not Italy. The divergent expansionisms of Italy and Germany constituted a potential tie between them; they would not bring the two powers in conflict with each other, but both could be achieved only over the opposition of France. The alliance between Germany and Italy that appeared to be the logical deduction from this set of facts was confronted by a negative factor in the form of a potential division between the two powers and a positive factor in the form of a potential additional tie. The potential tie was the ideological affinity of Italian fascism and national socialism; the potentially divisive factor was the question of South Tirol.

Hitler was an early and continuing admirer of Mussolini and his program. The Fascist Party's seizure of power in Italy seemed to him a harbinger of his own success. The attacks of the liberal newspapers in Germany and elsewhere on the Fascist leader confirmed Hitler's assessment of their spiritual kinship. Personal admiration for Mussolini played an undoubted part in this, and the curious type of friendship Hitler developed for his distant hero was to outlast shocks that would have sundered most personal relationships. In the period before 1933 the actual dictator of Italy and the prospective dictator of Germany dealt with each other by unofficial emissaries, Lüdecke performing this role for Hitler, while Major Giuseppe Renzetti acted in a similar capacity for Mussolini. Lüdecke merely made a few brief trips to Rome, but Renzetti as president of the Italian Chamber of Commerce in Berlin and later as Italian consul general provided a means of regular contact. While it is known from Lüdecke's memoirs that he made his first trip to Italy for Hitler in 1922, Renzetti first appears in the documents in 1931, already then referred to in a letter to Rosenberg as "our friend."[38] The earliest available reports of Renzetti to the Duce are those of October 15 and November 20, 1931.[39] The latter records that Renzetti brought Hitler some political advice from Mussolini and reports on Hitler's great desire

---

37 Walter Werner Pese, "Hitler und Italien, 1920–1928," *Vierteljahrshefte für Zeitgeschichte* 3 (1955): 113–26, first showed that Hitler favored common action with Italy before Mussolini's march on Rome.

38 Arno Schickedanz to Rosenberg, January 13, 1931, Nuremberg document 1148-PS, National Archives.

39 Renzetti to Mussolini, October 15 and November 20, 1931, National Archives Microcopy T-586, cont. 491, fr. 0505253–56.

to make a trip to Rome to see the Italian leader.[40] At that time, as during all of 1932, the ardent hopes of Hitler for a meeting with Mussolini came to naught, but the contact remained and would provide a continuing means of direct communication outside regular diplomatic channels even after Hitler came to power.[41]

The very first contact between the two leaders in 1922 was used by Mussolini to bring home to Hitler the danger to German–Italian relations in the question of South Tirol.[42] Germany's agitation for revision of the peace treaties constantly called attention to those people of German background who had been transferred from Austria to Italy by the Treaty of St. Germain and were being subjected to a process of Italianization. In the 1920s, the German minority in South Tirol was probably the one most subject to repression of their original nationality, and thus a plausible object for attention by those German parties that claimed to have a monopoly on national patriotism. Italy's insistence on the maintenance of the existing border on the Brenner made revision here incompatible with any German–Italian alliance. Although this was a most unpopular stand in Germany, where in any case public opinion was very anti-Italian because of Italy's alleged unfaithfulness to her alliance with the Central Powers, Hitler decided that the South Tirol must be sacrificed to the vastly greater interest in a German–Italian alliance and he publicly defended a renunciation of South Tirol.[43] The relevant portion of the second volume of *Mein Kampf* was published as a separate brochure in 1926, and the impetus for Hitler to prepare (though never to publish) a second book in the summer of 1928 was closely related to the problem that the unpopularity of his position on this issue created for him in German domestic politics.

The National Socialists constantly tried to deprecate the importance of the South Tirol issue and to point to the agitation over it in Germany and Austria as simply a convenient pretext for Jews, Marxists, Freemasons, and others to attack Mussolini. Within the party, Hitler defended his position on South Tirol as essential for Germany if she were to regain

---

40 See Renzetti's reports to Mussolini of January 12, June 9, June 30, 1932, ibid., fr. 050259–65.

41 The published Italian documents indicate that this channel remained in use for many years and was not unknown to the Italian diplomatic service. Attolico to Ciano, June 14, 1939, *I Documenti diplomatici Italiani*, 8th series, Vol. 12, No. 231; September 2, 1939, ibid., Vol. 13, No. 607.

42 The discussion of South Tirol, except where otherwise noted, is based on my introduction to *Hitlers zweites Buch*, pp. 21–25, 34ff., and Conrad F. Latour, *Südtirol und die Achse Berlin-Rom, 1938–1945* (Stuttgart: Deutsche Verlags-Anstalt, 1962).

43 The chronology of this reversal is traced in Schubert, *Anfänge Nationalsozialischer Aussenpolitik*, pp. 76–81; see also *I Documenti diplomatici Italiani*, 7th series, Vol. 1, No. 131.

her position of power and influence, a position she could secure only by alliance with Italy and England.[44] To Mussolini, Hitler reaffirmed his renunciation through Ettore Tolomei, the leading proponent of the policy of Italianization of South Tirol.[45] Of course, this should not be taken to mean that other circumstances might not lead to other perspectives. Hitler would refrain from a ruthless drive for colonies and world trade as a tactical sacrifice to secure the assistance of England, but that would not keep him from grandiose colonial plans when England refused to fulfill his expectations. He would ignore the South Tirol question as a tactical sacrifice to the needed alliance with Italy, but that would not prevent him from annexing that area, plus other large portions of northern Italy, once Italy had left the Axis. In few other areas is the relationship between Hitler's long-term aims and short-term opportunism more clearly revealed.

There was still one other potential source of difficulty between Germany and Italy, and on it Hitler was not prepared to make concessions so readily: the annexation of Austria.[46] Hitler always argued that Austria and Germany should be joined in one country, and he never ceased to make this opinion public. The very fact that tactical considerations led him to renounce claims to South Tirol probably made him all the more obdurate in regard to the *Anschluss*. It is clear from his writings – and later acts – that this desire was not due to any great love for the land of his birth. Rather, it was the desire to expand the racial base of the forthcoming German empire. He hoped that his renunciation of South Tirol would ease Italy's objections to the *Anschluss*, and that the time would come when Italy would see no reason to oppose a union of Austria with an anti-French Germany.[47] Subsequent developments were to prove this a miscalculation, but the policy which produced the abrupt confrontation of his illusions with the real world in 1934 can be understood only if the illusions and their place in his thinking are kept in mind.

If Austria was to be swallowed up completely, Hungary was another potential ally, even if not a very important one. A revisionist power,

---

44 See the report on the conference in the National Socialist Party headquarters in Munich on March 31, 1932, quoted in *Der deutsche Imperialismus und der Zweite Weltkrieg* (Berlin: Rüten und Loening, 1961), Vol. 2, p. 478.

45 The draft of Tolomei's report to Mussolini of September 30, 1928, on his meeting with Hitler on August 14, 1928, is published in Karl Heinz Ritschel, *Diplomatie um Südtirol: Politische Hintergründe eines europäischen Versagens* (Stuttgart: Seewald, 1966), pp. 133–37.

46 The questions of South Tirol and the *Anschluss* were closely related. Italy had little to fear as long as the agitation emanated from a small and weak Austria. If Austria ever joined Germany, Italy would face a neighbor both large and strong.

47 *Hitlers zweites Buch*, pp. 208ff. To Tolomei, Hitler described the *Anschluss* as certain but in the distant future (Ritschel, *Diplomatie um Südtirol*, p. 137).

opposed to Yugoslavia, which was backed by France and in turn opposed by Italy, Hungary might be fitted into the German alliance system.[48] The National Socialists and other extremist groups in Bavaria had been in contact with similarly oriented elements in Hungary in the years before 1923, and there had been talks about simultaneous revolutions in both places in November of that year.[49] Lüdecke had served in Hungary as Hitler's emissary, and a similar role had been played by another international adventurer, Max Erwin von Scheubner-Richter, whose career was ended by death in the putsch of November 9, 1923. It was to Scheubner-Richter as their intermediary of a decade before that the leader of the Hungarian rightists, Julius Gömbös, referred when, having become prime minister of Hungary, he sent greetings immediately after Hitler became chancellor of Germany.[50]

Another Central European country that figured in Hitler's perceptions and plans was Czechoslovakia. His analysis of prewar Austria dealt very extensively with the growing power of the Czechs in both Bohemia and Vienna itself, his attacks on the Habsburg dynasty were phrased to a great extent in terms of their failure to combat this trend, and his praise of the Pan-German movement was based heavily on the anti-Czech element in Georg von Schönerer's program. In Hitler's eyes, the nationality problem of Bohemia was the presence of Czechs in an area he believed appropriate solely for German settlement. He assumed that the Czech state would be hostile to Germany, and he kept in contact with sympathetically inclined elements among the German population of Czechoslovakia. When the time came, they were to be the tool of far-reaching schemes.[51]

Yugoslavia appeared in Hitler's mental world primarily in two ways. He thought of Yugoslavia, first, as an enemy of Italy and a friend of France and thus as a possible partner of France in a war against Mussolini's Italy, and second, as the country of the Serbs who had followed their national interest realistically and persistently by working for the destruction of Austria-Hungary. It should be noted that in Hitler's assessment of people in terms of their racial awareness and value, this point constituted something of a plus mark for the Serbs. Hitler was, of course, aware of the struggle over the border between Austria and Yugoslavia in Carinthia, but

---

48 *Hitlers zweites Buch*, p. 217. There are few references to Hungary and the Magyars in Hitler's written and oral comments.

49 See Schubert, *Anfänge Nationalsozialistischer Aussenpolitik*, pp. 168–80.

50 On Scheubner-Richter, see Walter Lacqueur, *Russia and Germany: A Century of Conflict* (London: Weidenfeld and Nicolson, 1965), pp. 58–68; Paul Leverkuehn, *Posten auf ewiger Wache* (Essen: Essener Verlagsanstalt, 193), pp. 191–94. The message of Gömbös given to Hitler on February 7, 1933, is in *Documents on German Foreign Policy, 1918–1945*, Series C, Vol. 1, No. 15.

51 *Hitlers zweites Buch*, pp. 78ff.; Rauschning, *Voice of Destruction*, pp. 37f.

there is nothing to suggest any special interest of his in that issue. Other European countries appear to have played little part in Hitler's thinking before 1933.

Outside the European continent and its colonial extensions, the major areas of importance for German foreign policy were East Asia and the United States. Hitler's vision was primarily continental, and he paid very little attention to either area, a habit that was to continue until 1945. He was not especially interested in the Far East, a fact that was to be reflected in a more than usual confusion in German policies toward that area after 1933. Three facets of Hitler's perspective on Far Eastern affairs deserve mention. In the first place, there can be no question that he shared in some way the aversion to the people of eastern Asia expressed in references to the "yellow peril," widespread in those early years of the twentieth century when so many of Hitler's ideas were formed.[52] His own racist orientation, of course, served only to intensify this attitude. Second, Hitler did not share the sinophilism current in the Germany of his day as a counterweight to the "yellow peril" fears. In the third place, he had somewhat kindlier feelings toward Japan. Though of "racially uncreative stock," the Japanese were at any rate very clever; and their aggressive moves in the Far East, which brought down upon them the attacks of the liberal press, were to their credit in Hitler's eyes.[53]

The United States originally drew very little attention from Hitler.[54] In his political speeches and writings Hitler echoed the denunciations of the United States in general and President Wilson in particular then current in Germany. He was sure that Jewish influence had been responsible for America's entrance into the First World War, but his references to the United States were few indeed. His interest was aroused, however, by American immigration legislation and by the very considerable importation of American automobiles into Germany. This latter fact drew Hitler's attention to the advantages of a large domestic living space, and thus market, for industrial as well as agricultural purposes. This evidence of American strength was related, in Hitler's eyes, to American immigration legislation. These laws seemed to Hitler, not without reason, to be basically racist in orientation. They reinforced a tendency he believed inherent in the process of migration from Europe to America: the best and most enterprising members of each community, that is, the Nordics, emigrated to America. The United States was, therefore, not the melting

---

52 See Heinz Gollwitzer, *Die Gelbe Gefahr: Geschichte eines Schlagwortes* (Göttingen: Vandenhoeck & Ruprecht, 1962).
53 *Hitlers zweites Buch*, p. 25; Hitler's speech of May 23, 1928, *Hitler: Reden*, Vol. 2/2, p. 851.
54 This is summarized from my essay "Hitler's Image of the United States," *American Historical Review* 69 (1964): 1006–11.

pot of the American imagination but the great meeting place of the
Nordics, who maintained their racial purity by strict immigration laws.
This gathering in of the finest Nordic racial stock from each European
country explained why the Americans had made such good use of their
living space. With a racial headstart over all others – especially the European countries drained of their best blood by the same process that had
made America strong – and with a vast space on which to proliferate, the
American people were exceedingly dangerous and a real threat to German domination of the world. Only a Eurasian empire under German
control could hope to cope with this menace successfully. A third big war
was added to the original two: after the wars against France and Russia
would come the war against the United States. One of the major tasks of
the National Socialists would be the preparation of Germany for this
conflict.

This assessment of the United States was to give way in the early
1930s to a far different one. Under the impact of the world Depression
and its effects on the United States – effects Hitler thought permanent –
Hitler concluded that the United States was really a very weak country.
Turning again to a racial explanation, he came to believe that America
was a racial mixture after all, a mixture that included Negroes and Jews.
Such a mongrel society, in which the scum naturally floated to the top,
could not construct a sound economy, create an indigenous culture, or
establish a successful political system. America was a weak country,
whose hope for strength had been destroyed in the past by the victory of
the wrong side in the Civil War and whose hope for the future, if there
were any, lay with the German-Americans. In any case, the United States
could not interfere with Hitler's plans, which in confidential discussions
were now said to include Mexico and much of Latin America. Thus
Hitler was to go forward in the 1930s, unconcerned about the United
States and generally uninterested in it. The basic hostility remained, but
the concern about America's racial strength had vanished. Since he was
subjectively entirely convinced that Germany had lost the world war
because of the stab-in-the-back, he could conclude without any doubt
whatever that it was the role of the United States in enabling the Allies to
defeat Germany which was the legend.

It should be noted that, with insignificant exceptions, the general nature of Hitler's views as summarized here was readily recognizable before
his assumption of power.[55] In fact, the rise of the National Socialist Party

---

55 I have been careful to avoid using evidence from a later period. Although almost none of
   Hitler's views on the subjects discussed here later ever changed, reliance on material of the
   pre-1933 period minimizes the danger of later events or documents influencing the interpretation.

was financed to a considerable extent by the thousands and thousands of Germans who paid admission to public meetings at which Hitler publicly proclaimed his belief in these ideas and policies. He tried to leave his audiences in no doubt about his meaning; on the contrary, he repeated the same ideas and even phrases over and over again. He assured them that if granted power, he would ruthlessly and brutally establish a dictatorship in Germany, build up Germany's military might after its republican institutions and ideas had been swept away, and then proceed to lead his country as its absolute dictator in a series of wars. In promising a ruthless dictatorship, he did not hesitate to say explicitly that it would be like that of Italy and of Soviet Russia.[56] In promising war, he was always personal and specific: "I believe that I have enough energy to lead our people whither it must shed its blood [*zum blutigen Einsatz*], not for an adjustment of its boundaries, but to save it into the most distant future by securing so much land and space that the future will receive back many times the blood shed," Hitler said on May 23, 1928.[57]

Why did millions of Germans respond so enthusiastically to these appeals? Certainly the terrible cost of the First World War had left many Germans disillusioned with war and fearful of its repetition. But it should be noted that the disillusionment in Germany was not quite like that in Western countries. There were books expressing such sentiments as characterized Erich Maria Remarque's *All Quiet on the Western Front* in other countries, but one would find it exceedingly difficult to match outside Germany the literature glorifying war that was typified by the works of Ernst Jünger and applied to the postwar period by the members of the Free Corps.[58]

More important, perhaps, than this survival of militaristic attitudes was the psychological disorganization produced by defeat. Unaware of the real situation, the German people had seen their hopes tumble from the vision of victory to the reality of collapse in a few months of 1918. After the glory of a powerful state, after the immense sacrifices of war, their world had crashed down around them. In the preceding decades, while the peoples of England and France were painfully learning to govern themselves, the German people had been trained to think that this was neither possible nor desirable for them. In the chaos and despair of a

56 An example of February 28, 1926, in Werner Jochmann (ed.), *Im Kampf um die Macht: Hitlers Rede vor dem Hamburger Nationalklub von 1919* (Frankfurt/M: Europäische Verlagsanstalt, 1960), p. 103.
57 *Hitler: Reden*, Vol. 2/2, p. 856.
58 There are important pointers on this subject in the first section of the first volume of the series on Germany in World War II prepared in the Military History Research Office of the Federal Republic of Germany, *Das Deutsche Reich und der Zweite Weltkrieg* (Stuttgart: Deutsche Verlags-Anstalt, 1979).

defeated country, it was easier for many to mock the brave few who tried hard to reconstruct a self-respecting society than to take a hand in the difficult task of rebuilding. It was simpler to put one's faith in one man who would take care of everything than to assume a share of the responsibility for the agonizing choices to be made in daily political life. Those who agreed that one man was to lead and decide, while they would obey and follow, could not thereby escape the responsibility for his decisions; they simply accepted that responsibility in advance.[59]

A further factor of great significance was the widespread acceptance of racial ideology, and especially anti-Semitism, among the people of Germany. Whether or not willing to agree to all its horrible implications, vast numbers were prepared to accept its premises, even more than in the nineteenth century. It is significant that in a country where academic persons were high in prestige, the pseudoscience of racism had made rapid and deep inroads in the academic community. Furthermore, it is clear from all accounts of National Socialist gatherings that anti-Semitism was the most popular part of Hitler's appeal to his audiences. If so many followed, it was in part that they were enthusiastic about the direction he wanted to take.[60]

Certainly one should not overlook the belief of many that the National Socialists did not necessarily mean precisely what they said; that Hitler's more extreme ideas should not be taken seriously; that once in power, the movement would find itself forced into a more reasonable course by the impact of responsibility and reality. Many of those who deluded themselves in this opinion were to argue after World War II that Hitler had deluded them. But he had not lied to them; they had misled themselves. In many instances this self-delusion was greatly facilitated by the hope that Hitler *did* mean what he said about destroying the Social Democratic Party and the trade unions, regardless of the methods used and the purposes for which this might be done.[61] There was also the hope of some of the older generation of German leaders that the dynamism of National Socialism could be harnessed to their own more limited goals. But above all there was the opposition of millions to the Weimar Republic, its ideals and its practice, and the whole tradition of liberalism and humanism to which they were related. The German people was to be the new all-powerful god and Hitler the all-powerful prophet; and already in

59 Because the jurisdictional disputes of the Third Reich have left behind such mountains of paper, scholars have tended to ignore the degree of consensus in the Third Reich; agreement produces fewer records than squabbles.

60 An excellent introduction is George L. Mosse's *The Crisis of German Ideology: The Intellectual Origins of the Third Reich* (New York: Grosset & Dunlap, 1964).

61 A fine local case study illustrating this process is William S. Allen's *The Nazi Seizure of Power: The Experience of a Single German Town*, rev. ed. (New York: Franklin Watts, 1984).

January 1933 there were many who identified the two.[62] He could lead Germany back to strength; he could overcome the psychological depression of past defeat and the economic depression of Germany's contemporary situation.

Many in Germany opposed Hitler's rise to power, some of them recognizing clearly the implications of his policies, especially in the field of foreign affairs.[63] Before 1933 the millions who pushed Hitler forward, and the small clique who installed him in office, by no means constituted the whole population. But there were vast reservoirs of support for the new leader to draw on, and for many years the support was to increase rather than lessen. The national acceptance of the leadership principle implied the unconditional surrender of the country to the will of a leader who had explained for years what he would do with power when he secured it. His people were not to be disappointed. They would get all the wars he had promised, and he would remain faithful to the ideas he had preached until the bitter end.

62 A thoughtful summary is that of Karl Dietrich Bracher, Wolfgang Sauer, and Gerhard Schulz, *Die Nationalsozialistische Machtergreifung* (Cologne: Westdeutscher Verlag, 1962), pp. 22–27.
63 A startlingly accurate pre-1933 analysis by the man who became the first president of the postwar Federal Republic may be found in Theodor Heuss, *Hitlers Weg: Eine historisch-politische Studie über den Nationalsozialismus* (Stuttgart: Union Deutsche Verlagsgesellschaft, 1932), pp. 96–105.

Part II

———— • ————

THE NAZI SYSTEM

4

———— • ————

THE NAZI REVOLUTION: A WAR
AGAINST HUMAN RIGHTS

The fourteenth of July has long been celebrated as the day on which the storming of the Bastille marked in the eyes of the French people and the world's public the opening of the French Revolution. Whatever the actual nature of that looming fortress, or the events of that stirring day, the Bastille symbolized the fetters imposed on mankind by the Old Regime. Its seizure in that attack was seen equally as a symbol of the breaking of those fetters, a liberation from royal bondage, and an affirmation of human rights. When Lafayette gave the key to the Bastille to George Washington (tourists can today view it at Mount Vernon), he did so to demonstrate in a concrete way the symbolic tie between the French and American revolutions, with both perceived as affording an opening for human rights not only in the two countries immediately affected by the two revolutions but in the whole world through the inspiration of example. There was hope that the example would find many imitators, and those who indeed saw in the American and French upheavals salutary lessons for the preferred structure of their own societies often considered July 14 their own special day. From the very beginning, the concept of human rights and equality was seen by both its supporters and its opponents as in some ways including the Jewish inhabitants of society.

In the Germany of 1933, July 14 was made the occasion for a very special set of actions by the government. The new National Socialist regime, which had come to power earlier that year, had been consolidating its hold on the country during the immediately preceding months. In what one leading scholar has called a "mammoth session of the cabinet,"[1] a whole series of major laws was enacted on July 14 under the new

This chapter was originally given at a symposium at Emory University in 1983; a slightly different text was published in Moses Rischin and Raphael Asher (eds.), *The Jewish Legacy and the German Conscience* (Berkeley, Calif.: Judah L. Magnes Museum, 1991), pp. 287–96.
1 Karl Dietrich Bracher (with Wolfgang Sauer and Gerhard Schulz), *Die Nationalsozialistische Machtergreifung*, 2d ed. (Cologne: Westdeutscher Verlag, 1962), p. 214.

procedures which had been instituted by the Enabling Act of March 23, 1933.[2] The Nazi Party was declared to be the only legal political party in the country, and all efforts to organize any other party were now made subject to severe penalties. In the future absence of genuine choice, the public could be periodically consulted in plebiscites by a government which would call upon the voters to acclaim its latest policy according to a format established that day. A new structure was to be provided for Germany's rural population, and a new name and constitution were decreed for the German Protestant Church. Those persons whom the regime did not like could, under the terms of another law of the same date, be stripped of their citizenship and their property, a procedure that would be applied to Willy Brandt and Albert Einstein to mention only two examples.[3] The centrality of racial doctrine in the system was affirmed by a law calling for the compulsory sterilization of those whom the regime defined as afflicted with hereditary ailments – characteristically the first of the Nazi regime's laws in the area of family and marriage.[4]

Implementing directives would subsequently tighten the restrictions and elaborate on the regulations; but the framework within which the new state would function until its defeat in war was set on July 14, 1933; and this choice of dates was deliberate. The regime perceived itself as the antithesis of the ideals of 1776 and 1789; its leaders had preached against them in the years before 1933; and they saw themselves as reversing the way in which those ideals had begun to affect the life of the world at large and of Germany in particular. The fact that those ideas were of limited influence in Germany only encouraged their opponents: there might still be an opportunity to reverse their impact, but allowed to continue unchecked, they might become established to an extent that would make them an integral and irremovable aspect of German society.

There has been a veritable flood of scholarly publications dealing with the topic of continuity in German history. Their authors have variously asserted in great detail that neither the revolution of 1918 nor that of 1933 was a revolution at all; that there were no really substantial upheavals in German society on either occasion; and that the persistence of old elites, structures, and policy impulses assured a continuum from the German empire of the late nineteenth century until the defeat of 1945

2 On the Enabling Act, see ibid., pp. 152ff. For a semiofficial presentation of the laws of July 14, 1933, see the first volume, entitled "Die Nationalsozialistische Revolution 1933," in Paul Meier-Benneckenstein (ed.), *Dokumente der Deutschen Politik* (Berlin: Juncker und Dünn-haupt, 1939), pp. 70, 179–80, 204–6, 244, 376–77.
3 See Hans-Georg Lehmann, *In Acht und Bann; Politische Emigration. NS–Ausbürgerung und Wiedergutmachung am Beispiel Willy Brandts* (Munich: C. H. Beck, 1976), esp. pp. 49–53.
4 This point is made in the useful survey by Dorothee Klinksiek, *Die Frau im NS-Staat* (Stuttgart: Deutsche Verlags-Anstalt, 1982), pp. 72–74.

and perhaps beyond. Whatever may be the elements of truth in these assertions, particularly as they relate to the persistence of elite groups, they entirely miss critical breaks in the history of Germany. The use of troops to reestablish the Prussian autocracy in 1849, the constitutional breaches with which Otto von Bismarck began his role as Ministerpresident of Prussia in 1862 and which he threatened at its end in 1890, the often successful efforts of the opponents of the Weimar Republic to murder its leading statesmen, and the tragically unsuccessful attempts of Hitler's German opponents to kill him, which in turn led to their deaths by the hundreds – all these involved neither fake issues nor minor differences or rivalries. Those tumultuous events revolved around an essentially correct recognition by those involved in them of fundamental differences about the proper ordering of Germany's public life and the individual rights to be enjoyed by its inhabitants.

If one may define the human rights issue in modern German history as one which placed in opposition to each other those who favored and those who opposed public control of government policy, institutionalized protection of individual rights, and equality for citizens in the eyes of the law, then the great struggles and the real breaks become clear to the observer. It was in opposition to these concepts that the Prussian autocracy triumphed over the revolutionary movement of 1848–49, that Bismarck won the constitutional conflict in Prussia and erected the German Empire of 1871 – and it was their supporters who won out in the upheaval of 1918–19.[5] Now for the first time in the history of the country the direction of policy was to be determined by freely elected representatives of the public. For the first time in the history of the country individual rights, including the right of opposition to the government of the moment, were to be protected against the arbitrary exercise of executive authority; and for the first time, there were to be no restrictions on the equal status of all citizens – including Jews – in all parts of the country.

Those who hated the Weimar Republic, vilified its policies, shouted down or even shot down its leaders, and publicly promised the German people an alternative structure with authority vested in one leader, the submission of all rights to central authority, and the imposition of legal distinctions in status between different segments of the population, understood a great deal more clearly than some contemporaries of theirs and many contemporaries of ours that there had indeed been a revolution in Germany in 1918 and that their own coming to power would mark a further dramatic break with the past.

5 A fine review of the whole issue in Dietrich Orlow, "1918/19: A German Revolution," *German Studies Review* 5 (1982): 187–203.

In this new break, that of the Nazi revolution, the race issue was of both symbolic and substantive significance. Its symbolic nature grew out of demographic and historic factors. The demographic factor was simply that the group immediately defined as racially distinct, dangerous, and to be degraded – namely the Jews – constituted less than 1 percent of the population and had for a century actually been declining as a proportion of the country's inhabitants. It was therefore electorally safe to attack this tiny group. It was also propagandistically simple to manipulate statistical slogans about them: if there were two Jews out of a hundred persons in some activity, that meant not that it was 98 percent non-Jewish but that there was a 220% overrepresentation of Jews!

The historic factor was that the process of emancipation of Germany's Jews was closely intertwined with the spread of human rights ideas in Central Europe from the impact of the French Revolution and Napoleon at the beginning of the nineteenth century to its completion in the Weimar Constitution of 1919. Already in the era of Prussian reform in the first decade of the nineteenth century, one of its leading opponents, Ludwig von der Marwitz, had attacked the reformers for trying to create what he called "ein neumodischer Judenstaat," a new-fangled Jew-state. Resentment against the France of the Napoleonic Wars and against the France of the First World War and its aftermath could be safely and effectively focused on the Jews as beneficiaries of the legal equality for all citizens which had really begun to be implemented in Napoleonic times and which the supporters of human rights had formally installed in a complete form by the constitution of Weimar Germany.

Legal discriminations against Jews were accordingly called for in the Nazi Party's program of 1920, then demanded with great fervor and applauded with equal fervor in the years from 1920 to 1933, implemented beginning immediately after the Nazi seizure of power, and always publicly boasted about as one of the regime's greatest accomplishments, up to and including the mass murders of World War II.[6] It was in this sense also that the opposition to parliamentary government and human rights was joined with anti-French and anti-Semitic agitation in the Germany of the 1920s as it is joined with anti-American and anti-Semitic agitation in the German Federal Republic. The symbolic and historical identification of human rights, parliamentary government, French and American ideas, and equality for Jews was maintained by the opponents of them all in both Germanies of the 1970s and 1980s and the unified country now as it was in the Germany of the 1920s. Only the self-

---

6 Hans-Heinrich Wilhelm, "Wie geheim war die 'Endlösung'?" in *Miscellanea: Festschrift für Helmut Krausnick*, Wolfgang Benz (ed.) (Stuttgart: Deutsche Verlags-Anstalt, 1980), pp. 131–48.

perception of those opponents has been altered: they see themselves now in many, though by no means all, instances as being on the left rather than the right of the political spectrum.

The race issue was of enormous substantive importance because it signified what might be called the new alternative vision of the society which was to be constructed in stages beginning in 1933. A perception of the past, present, and future in racial terms was opposed not only to the politically egalitarian society of Weimar but also to the allegedly racially blind and insufficiently alert society of pre-1918 Germany. The Second Empire was seen as hopelessly negligent in this regard, and it was asserted that it had been this negligence above all else which had been responsible for its defeat in war in 1918 by its domestic rather than its foreign enemies. The new government would certainly follow a different path and hence assure itself of a different fate.

The discriminations against Jews would be matched by new racial policies within the so-called "Aryan" community, ranging from the compulsory sterilization program already mentioned, through forgivable loans for early marriage and medals for numerous children, to a massive so-called euthanasia system to remove those considered unworthy of continued life and an unproductive drain on the nation's resources. The racially aware society to be developed and formed by these processes would conquer the lands it needed to feed itself, and, by expelling or exterminating those living on them, provide the basis for an ever-expanding agriculturally settled population. The numerous children raised on the newly conquered lands would more than make up for the casualties incurred in the wars required for the conquests, and would in turn provide both the need for additional conquests and the human resources to accomplish them. What would happen when the ever-expanding Germanic agricultural settlements eventually met on the other side of the globe was left as hazy as the world of Marxist theorists in which the state had withered away according to class rather than racial determinism; but that in the meantime, the one like the other required a dictatorship was always taken for granted, readily acknowledged, and boasted about as itself a sign of superior insight into the nature of the universe.

In one area of particular interest in recent years in this country and in many other parts of the world, that of women's rights, the new regime would also alter the direction of the evolution of German society. It can certainly be argued that the advances of women in Germany had been minimal before 1933, but then even these were perceived, entirely correctly in my judgment, as part and parcel of the movement for human equality that National Socialists believed should be reversed. The possibility – even if rarely realized – of women rising to positions of political, professional, academic, or economic power was too horrible to contemplate. There would be a blocking of all such avenues and a general redirection of women into a totally patriarchal society where women with healthy bodies brought vast numbers of healthy children into the service of the fatherland. Other pursuits would be closed as far as practicable – and even beyond. The already existing discrepancy in the sex ratio as a result of World War I, which would be greatly accentuated by World War II, was to be dealt with by the encouragement of illegitimacy during the new conflict.[7] For the postwar years there were projects for a new form of polygamy in what a British scholar has dubbed the National Socialist principle of crop rotation.[8] The fact that parental rights over the raising of children could be withdrawn if the parents were deemed politically unreliable certainly shows that all this had nothing to do with the maintenance of the family as an institution. The production of children for the all-powerful state was what counted.

The symbols, the rites, and the procedures of the new state all illustrated the deliberately different format of the new society. The supreme and constantly reiterated ritual of the new dispensation was the parade – thousands, millions, marching in cadence and in uniform. This was not a novel and energy-saving means of mass transportation; in fact of course the parades went from one nowhere to another nowhere and often imposed stupendous and energy-consuming burdens on the public transportation system. Their purpose lay in the march itself: in its ritualistic submerging of all individuality, in its insistence on a publicly visible community of preferably indistinguishable human beings ordered by a will exterior to themselves, and thus as effective a rite for those marching as for those summoned in analogously anonymous masses to cheer as onlookers.

The mass march in the form just described contrasts deliberately and dramatically with the symbolic act of the alternative kind of society, the one where each person goes individually into the secrecy of the voting

7 Himmler's notorious order of October 28, 1939, the so-called "Kinder-Erlass" or directive for children, has been reprinted in Klinksiek, *Die Frau im NS-Staat*, pp. 153–54. The official newspaper of the SS, *Das Schwarze Korps*, wrote on January 4, 1940: "A young woman who by one means or another evades her highest responsibility, that of giving birth inside or outside of marriage, is as much a deserter as a man who refuses to serve in the army." The German text and related materials can be found in Willi A. Boelke (ed.), *Kriegspropaganda 1939–1941: Geheime Ministerkonferenzen im Reichspropagandaministerium* (Stuttgart: Deutsche Verlags-Anstalt, 1966), p. 270.
8 Hugh R. Trevor-Roper (ed.), *The Bormann Letters* (London: Weidenfeld and Nicolson, 1954), p. xx. The subject itself comes up elsewhere in the records as well; see Oron J. Hale, ed., "Adolf Hitler and the Post-War German Birthrate," *Journal of Central European Affairs* 17 (1957): 166–73.

booth and quietly chooses the direction into which he or she prefers to be led. And if the elections for all sorts of levels of offices to which Americans and Frenchmen are called sometimes come with a frequency that seems as tiring as the endless marching in the Third Reich looks in the newsreels, it is because the founders of both types of systems understood the power of habit and the formation of social cohesion and basic assumptions somewhat better than a cynical world may be willing to admit.

The other side of cohesive uniformity can be seen in the treatment accorded to outcasts, whether from the supposedly superior or the supposedly inferior racial group. One example will illustrate each category. Many have heard of the case of Private Slovik, the one American soldier executed for desertion in World War II. The corresponding figure for the German army is in excess of 30,000 – an almost incredible statistic which cannot be given precisely because in the last months of the war soldiers were shot or hanged after summary proceedings of which no records were kept or if kept did not survive. If this was the treatment accorded to individual members of the superior "Aryan" group, it may be easier to comprehend why it has been so difficult to determine precise and accurate figures on the number of Jews murdered wholesale by the National Socialists. It was not considered important enough always to keep track of the numbers. The murderers thought it critical to record that twelve Paraguayan Peso notes valued at 60 pfennigs each had been taken from the victims, so that the Reichsbank could properly credit the account of the SS with RM 7.20;[9] but as for the number of dead, that was certainly not of equal significance.

If the individual, and the rights of the individual, were to play no role in the new society, and if the state as an entity, directed by the will of a dictator, was to command everything, then the permanent visible symbolism of such a political and social structure was, most appropriately, to be found in its buildings. Designed in the first place by Adolf Hitler himself for future construction during the 1920s, developed and begun not only for Berlin but for a long list of cities in the 1930s and 1940s, the buildings of the Third Reich were to be characterized by colossal size on the one hand and an absence of human amenities on the other.

Recent research has affirmed the great significance attached by Hitler and his associates to these mammoth construction projects which were to transform the appearance of Berlin and more than twenty other cities.

9 The example is taken from a long list included in the report on the "Reinhard" murder operation in Poland by Odilo Globocznik to Heinrich Himmler and can be found in *Trial of the Major War Criminals before the International Military Tribunal*, Vol. 34 (Nuremberg, 1949), p. 86. A very helpful effort on the question of statistics is Wolfgang Benz (ed.), *Dimensionen des Völkermords: Die Zahl der jüdischen Opfer des Nationalsozialismus* (Munich: Oldenbourg, 1991).

The largest single building in this vast program, on which the architectural firms were still working in the spring of 1945, was to be the world assembly hall in Berlin, reaching almost 1,000 feet into the sky, and topped by the eagle of the German Reich holding the globe in its claws. No vague notions here: the drawings and some of the models survive, as does one of the soil test forms from the beginning of construction. Designed to overawe both those inside and those outside, this structure would hold 150,000 to 200,000 persons – but they would all have to stand; and although the atmospheric conditions within this supersuperdome were likely to lead to the development of rain clouds inside the dome, there appear to be no provisions for umbrellas in the exceedingly detailed plans. When it came to the needs of the government, on the other hand, the frailties of mere mortals were given some consideration: the over 400,000 spectators who were expected to view the annual Nazi Party rally in the new monster stadium in Nuremberg would get to their lofty perches in elevators with a capacity of 32,000 and would be provided with special glasses so that they could actually see what was transpiring on the necessarily distant stadium floor.[10] And one should also note, rather more seriously, that all the plans for all construction for all cities, suburbs, and villages omit entirely one type of structure previously characteristic of German and other European communities: there would be no churches.[11]

Within the new museum structures and opera houses, concert halls and ministerial buildings, there would be only artistic works and performances which conformed to state rules, just as the libraries were to hold only books and newspapers approved by the state and party censors. People, not means of production, had to be nationalized; they would be exposed exclusively to such art forms and cultural artifacts as the state authorized. Only those artists and composers, authors and playwrights would be permitted to exercise their creativity who were prepared to subordinate their talents to the dictates of the authorities. No literary works out of harmony with the new standards would be published. Those musical forms which were perceived as alien to the "Aryan" race – jazz, to mention only one example – would disappear from the radio and the record shops, while most modern art could be seen only when included in an exhibition of "Degenerate Art" sent on tour to exemplify the alleged horrors of decadence.

The formation of human consciousness in a new mold was seen as requiring the greatest caution lest people be contaminated. The creations

10 Jost Dülffer, Jochen Thies, and Josef Henke (eds.), *Hitlers Städte: Eine Dokumentation* (Cologne: Böhlau, 1978), p. 212.
11 Ibid., p. 20.

of Walt Disney, for example, were banned because of his alleged Jewish ancestry. Observers may say to themselves: Donald Duck, Mickey Mouse, and Pluto don't look Jewish – but that is just the point. The less obvious the distinctiveness, the greater the danger of unrecognized and hence most insidious infiltration. The guardians of the system would accordingly exercise the greatest vigilance at precisely those points at which the ordinary and perhaps insufficiently alert German was most likely to become infected by undesirable cultural influences. It may all sound rather like a description of measures of the earlier government of South Africa or the utopia of the Moral Majority, but this actually summarized the construction and censorship policies of a regime that feared spontaneity and creativity, and which insisted that there could be no sphere outside state control for the unfettered flourishing of the human spirit.

If in referring to the plans and projects for the National Socialist version of urban, rural, and cultural renewal, this account in some instances goes beyond what was actually implemented and completed to refer to some of the plans and projects which were cut short by war and defeat, it is because a revolution halted in its tracks cannot be understood unless attention is paid to the direction of the tracks and the destination not reached. In one field of especial importance to the comprehension of National Socialism, however, a concluding episode of sorts was actually attained, and as early as April 1942 at that. Because of its revealing character, the episode deserves a brief retelling.

In the crisis on the Eastern Front before Moscow in the winter of 1941–42, as the German army met its first very serious defeat, one of the German commanders, General Erich Hoepner, saved a whole corps of tens of thousands of men subordinate to his Fourth Panzer Army by ordering it to pull back, a step he took without Hitler's prior approval. The dictator was livid and on January 8, 1942, ordered Hoepner not only removed from command but deprived of his pension and the right to wear his uniform as well. Hitler was thereupon told by some brave officers in headquarters that he could not order these last two measures by fiat: Hoepner could be deprived of his rights as an inactive four-star general only by a formal court martial proceeding. Hitler could relieve and replace him as Fourth Panzer Army commander; he could refrain from appointing Hoepner to any other command; but as an officer with thirty-five years of service, Hoepner had certain rights which could be taken away only by specified procedures. It will be easily understood that Hitler's mood was not improved by this piece of information, and the dictator decided to do something about it. No court martial proceedings were initiated against Hoepner; but long before the general had been hanged in August 1944 for his connection with the attempted coup of July 20, 1944, the rules governing such situations had been fundamentally altered.

Once the front situation in the East had been temporarily stabilized, Hitler summoned the Reichstag on April 26, 1942, for what would turn out to be its last session until October 1990. He gave a long speech, but the purpose of the meeting was not to cheer the speech but to approve a proposal formulated by Hitler and presented by Hermann Göring, the president of the Reichstag. It provided that the Führer could assign anyone of any rank to any position of his choice, could punish in any way he saw fit any person who did not carry out his orders, and that all this could be done without regard to legal procedures or earned rights.[12] There would be no procedures and no rights protecting any individual in the Third Reich which could not be forfeited at the whim of the dictator, and in this regard the Nazi system thus broke with the legal traditions of the old regime in Prussia as well as those struggling to assert themselves in the Weimar Republic. The end of all human rights had been formally confirmed in public with great publicity and to loud applause. The fact that this highly acclaimed action stripping all Germans of any procedural and substantive rights vis-à-vis their own government occurred in the same month as the beginning of mass killing by the use of gas in Auschwitz is a coincidence in timing but not in essence. No rights for Germans and no life for others.

Persons deprived of their peculiar and special qualities as human beings are converted into the equivalent of inanimate objects. The regime's reference to its own citizens as "Menschenmaterial," human matériel, illuminates the point linguistically. The state then disposes of its own people as it does of any other resource – German trees and rocks have no rights, so why should German persons? And if Germans have no rights, then anyone designated by those in charge as non-German is hardly worth counting. And where appropriate for the momentary benefit of the regime, even the allegedly scientific and unalterable racial distinctions can be amended: a prominent German airman who rose to the rank of field marshal had only to get his mother to certify in writing that she had committed adultery in order to clear up an otherwise embarrassing racial blemish in his ancestry. In the final analysis, all persons without rights become un-persons; they become things.

As is well known, the National Socialist revolution was cut short by defeat in war, though it would also be well to remember how extraordi-

---

12 Max Domarus (ed.), *Hitler: Reden und Proklamationen, 1932–1945*, Vol. 2 (Neustadt a.d. Aisch: Verlagsdruckerei Schmidt, 1963), p. 1877.

narily far that revolution had gone in twelve short years. The world had been turned upside down, tens of millions had died, and nothing anywhere could ever be the same again. One has only to think in comparison of the Soviet Union in 1929 or Italy in 1934 to see how much more dramatically the dozen years of National Socialist rule had altered not only the country in which the new regime had come to power but the rest of the world as well.

It had been the hope of the National Socialists that their empire would last at least a thousand years and that even its ruins might inspire subsequent millennia by an imposing and ubiquitous presence. With its rusting steel rods and crumbling cement, a reinforced concrete building is extremely unaesthetic in appearance once it is wrecked. Hitler therefore accepted the recommendation of his master builder Albert Speer that only stone would be used for the construction of the regime's monumental buildings. Like the picturesque Roman ruins which still testified all over Western and Central Europe and around the Mediterranean centuries later to the glory of the Roman Empire, so the Third Reich's structures would evoke admiration and perhaps imitation even in their ruined state into a far distant future.[13] In reality, the great projects were never completed, and the Germany of 1945 was instead a land of endless rubble piles. Appropriately enough, a vast quantity of this rubble was made into a real hill in the middle of Berlin; the highest monument of the Third Reich is not a metal eagle holding the globe above the winter clouds, but a new ski run in the old capital. And the American tourist who crosses the Potomac after looking at the key to the Bastille in Mount Vernon can see Hitler's last will in the National Archives.

13 Albert Speer, *Erinnerungen* (Frankfurt/M: Propyläen, 1969), p. 69.

5

———— • ————

PROPAGANDA FOR PEACE AND PREPARATION FOR WAR

Two explanations must precede any examination of National Socialist foreign policy in 1933 and thereafter. In the first place, the new regime did not come to power in Germany without previously developed views on the subject of an appropriate foreign policy for Germany. Quite to the contrary, although it was primarily internal disruption and the related reduction in the authority and prestige of the Weimar Republic which led to the appointment of Adolf Hitler to lead a new government, the newly installed masters had very much more detailed and far-reaching views about foreign policy than about internal and economic matters. These prior concepts must, therefore, be included in any review of developments.

Second, one should not attempt to make a clear distinction between domestic and foreign policy in studying National Socialism. There was no such separation in the reality of the time, and to speak of the priority of internal or foreign policy only obstructs any understanding of the evolution of the Third Reich. The concepts which can be recognized in the writings and speeches of Hitler and some of his followers during the time before their seizure of power, which then became historically significant in and after 1933, on the contrary called for a whole series of measures in both policy spheres. These measures were inextricably bound together, had to be fitted or adjusted to each other, and had mutual repercussions. This complex of interconnected concepts must be summarized first so that the attempt to implement them beginning in 1933 can be seen in the proper light.

A deterministic Social Darwinistic view of the world was the central focus around which all the thoughts of the new leaders had revolved for many years. They demanded additional *Lebensraum*, living space, for the

Translated and revised from Wolfgang Treue and Jürgen Schmädeke (eds.), *Deutschland 1933* (Berlin: Colloquium Verlag, 1984), pp. 119–35.

German people, and with *Lebensraum* they always meant land which could be utilized for agriculture. The Germans allegedly needed this land in order to feed themselves from its products, and in order to settle on it families whose numerous children would make up for the casualties incurred in conquering it. Furthermore, these large families would then both require and make possible the conquest of additional land. What the world would look like, and what would happen, when the Germanic settlers met on the other side of the globe was never explained by any of the Nazi politicians or advocates – presumably in analogy to the world in which according to Marxist views the state had withered away – but as to the way to reach the goal, there was certainty about several points.

Only a state organized according to racial principles could conduct such a policy, and it is no coincidence that the first law of the new government in the field of family policy was the "Law for the Prevention of Hereditarily Defective Progeny" with its provisions for compulsory sterilization. In addition, the Nazis since 1920 had been demanding that the equality of all citizens before the law provided for in the Weimar constitution be replaced by a racial classification of people. In this regard also the first important measures were enacted in 1933, measures which were directed primarily but not exclusively at the less than 1 percent of the German population which was Jewish. It was assumed that only a one-party dictatorship could effectively implement the measures required of a racially organized society, and Hitler had always explained this to his listeners. He had, for example, held up as examples worthy of imitation on this score fascist Italy and communist Russia (in his speech of February 26, 1926, to the Hamburg National Club of 1919).[1]

It had also always been made clear that the state reorganized on a racial basis would have to fight wars, but for other reasons and objectives than imperial Germany had fought them and than the wars those who wanted to recover the territories Germany had lost in 1919 anticipated. It had been precisely the lack of racialist foundations which had brought the loss of World War I by the stab-in-the-back. The belief in the truth of the stab-in-the-back legend had significant implications for domestic and foreign policies. On the one hand, the racial policies had as one objective the prevention of any stab-in-the-back in a future war, a danger which worried Hitler and many other Germans. On the other hand, belief in the stab-in-the-back turned the decisive influence of American participation in World War I into a legend. This makes it easier to understand why of

---

1 Werner Jochmann (ed.), *Im Kampf um die Macht: Hitlers Rede vor dem Hamburger Nationalklub von 1919* (Frankfurt/M: Europäische Verlagsanstalt, 1960), p. 103.

all the German declarations of war only the one against the United States was met by practically no cautions and warnings from the elites of the Third Reich.

Even more important, however, was the complete difference in *purpose* for which the wars were to be fought. Because even a recovery of the borders of 1914 would leave Germany incapable of feeding her population out of the products of its own agriculture, the Nazis believed it a terrible mistake to try to regain them. The hope of reclaiming the situation of 1914 was, in Hitler's eyes, characteristic of the stupidity of the German bourgeoisie. Although even today there are those who assert that Hitler strove for a revision of the peace treaty of 1919, he himself both publicly and in private invariably rejected such a policy as fatally flawed. Instead, he insisted, Germany must conquer enormous areas and expel or exterminate their non-German inhabitants. When one reads in his second book that he recommended that as a first installment Germany seize 500,000 square kilometers of land in Europe,[2] it is easier to understand why he rejected the recovery of the 70,000 square kilometers Germany had lost in 1919 as a goal. Obviously a territory larger than the whole of Poland, and almost the size of France, could be obtained only by one or several wars. In 1928 Hitler did not specify how large the next installment was to be; he only explained that the farmers settled on the first installment were to raise millions of soldiers for the conquest of additional lands.

The land to be acquired lay to the East, in the Soviet Union, where – due to what Hitler considered a stroke of good fortune for Germany – the incompetent Bolsheviks now ruled Slavs whose alleged hereditary racial inferiority incapacitated them for state building. In order to take advantage of the easy seizure of land in the East made possible by this development, and to do so without the risk of any attack on Germany's rear, Germany must first defeat its enemies in the West. Perhaps with the help of Italy and possibly with the help or at least abstention of Britain, France would have to be defeated in a new war. And as it became increasingly obvious that the two Western Powers could not be separated, Hitler was willing to fight them both. The main point for Hitler was the great war in the West as the prerequisite for the seizure of vast lands in the East; all other matters were secondary and had to be subordinated to this central aim.

The preparation of new wars therefore had to be the first priority of

2 Gerhard L. Weinberg (ed.), *Hitlers zweites Buch: Ein Dokument aus dem Jahr 1928* (Stuttgart: Deutsche Verlags-Anstalt, 1961), p. 102. A planned new edition of this work has been prohibited by the Bavarian government.

the new regime, and Hitler hastened to explain these views to Germany's military leaders on February 3, 1933, a few days after becoming chancellor.[3] On the assumption that the members of this audience had neither read *Mein Kampf* nor heard his speeches, he explained to them in some detail the domestic prerequisites for the building up of large armed forces and their subsequent employment for the conquest of *Lebensraum*. In the new cabinet he pressed for a transformation of Germany's internal structure, the formation of society on racial concepts, and enormous expenditures for the armament program. The dictatorship at home, which presupposed the absorption or dissolution of the labor unions and all other social, cultural, and other organizations within Germany which were not already dominated by the Nazis, the development of a society structured on a racial basis, and the immediately inaugurated preparations for war must be seen as the three sides of the triangle of Nazi policy at home and abroad. If in the following account the emphasis is on the third side of the triangle, it must again be emphasized that Nazi foreign and military policy can be understood only in its connection with the two others: the dictatorial system of government and the ordering of the state on a racial basis.

The policy of rearmament for a war to conquer living space was hardly without risks inside and outside the country, and the new government recognized these dangers. In the first place there was the fear of a new war. Both inside and outside Germany the experience of World War I had left behind great apprehension about any possibility of new hostilities. The enormous casualties were, in a sense, a cloud over the whole continent – in almost every family in Europe the war had either left behind a gapingly empty spot or a seriously wounded member. Most still recalled the privations war had imposed on those at home. Under these circumstances it was especially important for Hitler to calm those in the world who had been shocked by the Nazi seizure of power. As he explained at the time, the outside world had to be reassured as much as possible and as long as it took until a Germany restructured and rearmed according to his plans was ready to attack. During the early period of his regime, he hoped to avert the danger of a preventive strike by others by the tactic of launching a massive campaign of peace propaganda and, where necessary, by concessions in the diplomatic field.

The peace propaganda of the German government was to a large extent carried out by the chancellor himself. In his speeches, beginning

3 See Gerhard L. Weinberg, *The Foreign Policy of Hitler's Germany: Diplomatic Revolution in Europe, 1933–1936* (Chicago: University of Chicago Press, 1970; Atlantic Highlands, N.J.: Humanities Press, 1994), pp. 16–27.

with the one on the international situation of May 17, 1933, he spoke
of the desire of Germany to live at peace with its neighbors.[4] He insisted
in public ten days later that "war brings suffering and misfortune to
people," declared that "National Socialism knows no policy designed to
change borders at the expense of other peoples," and exclaimed that "We
shall never attempt to conquer foreigners who hate us by a process which
requires that we sacrifice millions who are dear to us, and whom we love,
on the field of battle."[5] There was lots more of this sort of thing in public,
but already on February 8 he had emphasized in the cabinet "that for the
next 4–5 years the highest principle must be: everything for the armed
forces."[6]

In a world filled with fear of war, pleasantly pacific themes emanating
from Berlin were always welcome, and in subsequent years – especially
when the government had just broken another treaty or planned to attack
a neighbor – such peaceful tones were sounded once again. After tearing
up the Locarno Treaty in March 1936 Hitler made a whole series of
pacifying offers; as soon as they had served their reassuring purpose all
were allowed to evaporate or were repudiated by the German government
itself. Right after giving the order for the attack on Poland in August
1939 Hitler sent a new message of peace and friendship to London, a
message which was supposed to arrive there at the same time as news of
Germany's beginning the war.[7]

A series of tactical concessions made by Germany in the foreign policy
arena must be seen in the context of the voluble propaganda which
promised peace and invariably insisted that the latest German breach of
treaties and raising of demands was the very last one. The renewal of the
Berlin Treaty of 1926 with the Soviet Union, the Concordat with the
Vatican, and the declaration of nonaggression with Poland – to enumer-
ate the three during Hitler's first year in power in chronological sequence
– must all be seen in this context. Precisely because the new policy
presupposed that all these agreements would be broken, Hitler could
make concessions in the negotiations for them which the prior governments of the Weimar Republic had refused to make or had postponed on
the contrary assumptions that Germany should and would abide by its
treaties. One more especially instructive example may be cited: in May
and June of 1935 – the very time when the Anglo–German Naval Agree-

4 Max Domarus (ed.), *Hitler: Reden und Proklamationen, 1932–1945* (Neustadt a.d. Aisch:
  Verlagsdruckerei Schmidt, 1962), Vol. 2, pp. 270–79.
5 Ibid., p. 279.
6 *Akten zur Deutschen auswärtigen Politik, 1918–1945*, Series C, Vol. 1, No. 16, p. 36.
7 Gerhard L. Weinberg, *The Foreign Policy of Hitler's Germany: Starting World War II, 1937–
  1939* (Chicago: University of Chicago Press, 1980; Atlantic Highlands, N.J.: Humanities
  Press, 1994) (cited hereafter as Weinberg, *1937–1939*), p. 632.

ment was being concluded – decisions were made to adopt measures violating that agreement, but in a manner calculated to remain concealed from the British for a long time.[8]

The new German government for years based its policy on the reluctance of other powers to go to war, and for some time it had a measure of success with this approach. The procedure of calming others and restraining their concern by peace propaganda and by fake concessions while Germany prepared itself for a series of wars, however, entailed some dangers of its own.

The first danger was that the German people itself might come to take the peace propaganda seriously. Especially because the new leaders actually believed in the stab-in-the-back legend themselves, they were most concerned about the internal cohesiveness of the German population, believing it an absolute prerequisite for any future war. Hitler dealt with the fear of the German public of war in the crisis of the fall of 1938, a fear which was too obviously manifest to overlook, in a speech before representatives of the German press on November 10, 1939. As he put it: "It is self-evident that such peace propaganda conducted for a decade has its risky aspect; because it can too easily induce people to come to the conclusion that the present government is identical with the decision and with the intention to keep the peace under all circumstances."[9] It was now necessary to take the opposite tack, and a new style of propaganda "had to present certain foreign policy events in such a fashion that the inner voice of the people itself slowly begins to shout out for the use of force."

The second dubious facet of this policy was that it would put the German government under time pressure after a few years. As Hitler himself recognized and repeatedly explained in closed meetings, the German headstart in rearmament was certain to drive other countries into an arms race. Because the other powers could then base their armament programs on later and hence possibly superior weapons systems, and because in addition they had a greater resource base at their disposal, Germany would have to strike before it was too late – otherwise its headstart would turn into a disadvantage. Since Hitler had always been of the opinion that imperial Germany had waited too long to start World War I and had missed what he considered the best moment for that, there can be no doubt that he himself was more likely to lead Germany too

8 Jost Dülffer, *Weimar, Hitler und die Marine: Reichspolitik und die Marine 1920 bis 1939* (Düsseldorf: Droste, 1973), pp. 379–80.
9 Wilhelm Treue (ed.), "Rede Hitlers vor der deutschen Presse (10. November 1938)," *Vierteljahrshefte für Zeitgeschichte* 6, no. 2 (1958): p. 182. Additional reports on this talk are listed in Weinberg, *1937–1939*, p. 515, n. 203.

soon rather than too late "whither it must shed its blood" (*zum blutigen Einsatz*), as he called it.[10]

These two problems which arose from the simultaneous and interrelated policy of propaganda for peace and preparation for war were in their general nature already understood by Germany's leaders during the 1930s. There was a third problem which they probably never grasped: that precisely those in other countries who had once believed or wanted to believe the promises of peace would, once disappointed in that belief, be practically impossible to get to the negotiating table again. There is a straight line connecting the British demand of the summer of 1939 for Germany to take a step backward before there could be new Anglo–German negotiations, via the demand of the winter 1939–40 that Germany restore the independence of Czechoslovakia and Poland before there could be peace negotiations, to the final demand for unconditional surrender by a country that for ten years had followed a regime that invariably broke its word.

These considerations, which already take us into the war years, raise the question, which is so often brought up, of how it could be that the German people accepted such a policy, could even cheer it on enthusiastically, and could support it with almost incredible exertions in a world war even more terrible than the preceding one, and for almost six years at that.

To begin with, once must point out that many Germans did not agree with this policy at all. From the beginning there were always contrary views among some elements of the population, but to the best of our knowledge, these tendencies appear to have diminished in the early years of the Nazi regime. But when they grew again, it was very late. Many of those who went along – perhaps it would be more accurate to say, who rode along – began to have doubts later on; but as the express train roared toward disaster, very few had the courage to jump off, to pull the emergency brake, or to try to seize the controls. Not everyone is ready to become a hero. The great catastrophe for Germany and for the world was that many were prepared so to conduct themselves in the struggle with the *outside* world but few could muster such courage for the struggle *inside* the country. But this makes it especially important that we remember those who did have the necessary insight and daring. It would be an unforgivable error if in astonishment at the vast crowds which hailed the government one forgot those who stood aside or warned or resisted because they cannot be seen in the newsreels showing the cheering

---

10 Hitler's speech of May 23, 1928, in Bärbel Dusik (ed.), *Hitler: Reden, Schriften, Anordnungen, Februar 1925 bis Januar 1933*, Vol. 2/2 (Munich: Saur, 1992), No. 280, p. 856.

crowds in the early years of the regime and because their later attempts to free Germany from Nazi rule failed.

The very fact that there were those who stood aside, who opposed, and those who warned, however, only serves to emphasize the extent to which the mass of the population simultaneously gave its support to the new government. As we know today, it was precisely this self-identification of so many with the Nazi regime which very much hindered the opponents in their planning and execution of attempts to overthrow it. If one searches for the sources of the massive cheering, one quickly comes upon self-deceptions and a whole series of mistakes and ideological preconceptions of which a few of special importance for foreign policy need to be emphasized here.

The most significant self-deception, which dealt with the lost war, was a double one. The stab-in-the-back legend has already been mentioned; some further implications of it have to be brought up. The belief that Germany had lost World War I at home rather than having been defeated at the front almost automatically led to speculation about a possible successful repetition. This speculating and planning, in turn, originated in part in another self-deception growing out of the same events. This was the widespread belief that the numerous difficulties and deprivations of the postwar era in Germany were due to the peace settlement and not the result of the war. Everything was the fault of others; all problems were blamed on the peace, not on the war. And this, naturally, meant the government of Weimar, not of the Empire. This distorted view of the past further blocked any clear look into the future because, like the stab-in-the-back legend, it suggested that a new war might have a different impact. If a man like Field Marshal Ritter von Leeb could carefully make entries into his diary after the *Second* World War on how best to defeat England in a *Third* World War,[11] it is perhaps not so surprising that many Germans were misled by self-deceptions about the outcome and effect of World War I into speculating about a second one.

These self-deceptions also closed the eyes of many Germans to the terrible effects which the war had had for the other nations of Europe, effects which had been all the more serious because almost all of the fighting of that war – and hence the destruction it had entailed – took place *outside* Germany. After a second world war, in which the German people could see that a modern war leads to the destruction not only of *other* peoples' cities and farms, it should be possible for German observers to look at this almost complete omission from their earlier view of

11 Diary entry of December 10, 1945 in Georg Meyer (ed.), *Generalfeldmarschall Ritter von Leeb: Tagebuchaufzeichnungen und Lagebeurteilungen aus zwei Weltkriegen* (Stuttgart: Deutsche Verlags-Anstalt, 1976), p. 80, n. 104.

World War I in a new light. It is in this context that one should also recall that the Great Depression was seen – and is still all too often regarded – as a German, not a worldwide, phenomenon, while the suffering else-where, which was frequently greater than in Germany, is simply ignored.

This incapacity for coming to terms with the experience of World War I may well be responsible for the fact that Germany was one of the very few countries in which there existed a segment of the literary world afterward which glorified war. There were pacifist themes in the litera-ture and art as well as the politics of every country, but it would be difficult to find in the literature of any other country something akin to such writings as those of Ernst Jünger. For this reason it is especially praiseworthy that the first portion of the first volume of the history of Germany in World War II being issued by the German Military History Research Office in Freiburg, *Das Deutsche Reich und der Zweite Weltkrieg,* is devoted to this particular topic.[12] Even though the psychological prep-arations pointing to another war were certainly not sucessful with every-one, the new leaders of Germany could build on a substantial basis in this regard which was already in place when they came to power.

A further substantial contribution to the willingness to accept the Nazi Party line was the widespread acceptance in pre-1933 Germany of racist fantasies. There is a most significant clue for today's readers in the reports on Hitler's public speeches during the 1920s. It was the attacks on the Jews which time and again were greeted by the audience with "applause" according to the police and newspaper reports. The belief in racism, moreover, had most important repercussions on foreign policy. In this regard, the longer I have worked with the relevant material, the more convinced I have become of the centrality of the question of relations with Slavic peoples; and for the Germans of that time this meant the Poles. Nothing illuminates this more clearly than the frequent use in the propaganda and by numerous writers of the time of such terms as "a state for a season" (*Saisonstaat*) and "a Polish economy" (*polnische Wirtschaft*), derogatory terms applied to what was assumed to be a temporary situa-tion and a complete mess.

The hatred for Poles and Poland fitted extremely well into the unend-ing campaign against the peace treaty of 1919. It is surely noteworthy that German propagandists against the Versailles Treaty were always eager to utilize the argument that the treaty had supposedly deviated from Wilson's Fourteen Points – but simultaneously denounced the effort to

---

12 *Das Deutsche Reich und der Zweite Weltkrieg,* Vol. 1: *Ursachen und Voraussetzungen der deutschen Kriegspolitik* (Stuttgart: Deutsche Verlags-Anstalt, 1979), pp. 25–106.

implement the thirteenth point, the restoration of an independent Poland with a free and secure access to the sea, as a particularly heinous misdeed of the peacemakers. It is at precisely this point that the learned professions, and especially the historians, failed their society completely. They were so busy attempting to prove that every country on the face of the earth except for Germany was responsible for the outbreak of World War I that they carefully kept quiet on this central issue in spite of their own knowledge of the facts. They assuredly knew that during the centuries of Prussia's rise to great power status its land had been on both sides of territory subject to the Polish crown, that territorial contiguity of states had been the exception, not the rule, in German history, and that the inventor of the concept of a corridor in the border area of Prussia and Poland had been none other than the much admired Prussian ruler Frederick the Great, who had separated Poland from its port by a corridor in 1772. They concealed these facts, which were shown in full color in their historical atlases, as if they were state secrets.

Hatred for Poles clouded people's vision, and no one had the courage to call attention to the truths hidden by the fog of propaganda. It is hardly a coincidence that it was precisely in regard to this issue that the tactical concessions Hitler was prepared to make in 1933–34 diverged from the more traditional views of the German Foreign Ministry, that it was at this point that war began in 1939, and that it was in this regard that there would be among those in the then critical positions of power – the leaders of Germany's armed forces – a renewed internal consensus (*Burgfrieden*) in support of the decision to initiate hostilities.

Still one more view of many Germans which was irreconcilable with the realities of the time would be of decisive importance for the Nazi seizure of power and the growing internal cohesion of the German public behind the foreign policy of the Nazis: allegedly a disarmed Germany stood in a world armed to the teeth. In reality, both Great Britain and the United States had voluntarily reduced their mass armies of 1918 to about the size which the peace treaty prescribed for Germany. France had steadily reduced its army also. Germany was protected against any repetition of the occupation of the Ruhr not only by the Treaty of Locarno but in addition could see how the steady reduction in the term of service required by France's conscription law – by 1928 to one year – had led to the decision in 1929 to build the Maginot Line and in 1930 to relinquish occupation of parts of the Rhineland five years ealrier than specified in the peace treaty. There was no danger in the West. In the East, Germany's neighbor Poland, in view of its lengthy border with the Soviet Union, had no plans whatever for any war with Germany; the Polish general staff only began to develop plans for such a contingency in March of 1939.[13]

Even the loudest advocates of German rearmament never claimed that Italy and Japan, which had fought on the Allied side in the World War, would take even the slightest steps directed against Germany. The Soviet Union – however one assessed its military strength at the time – was separated from Germany by states created by the supposedly bad peace treaties of 1919. In spite of all this, as early as the last years of the Weimar Republic, at a time when other countries were disarming further under the pressure of the Depression and pacifist sentiments among their population, Germany was beginning to head in the opposite direction.[14]

It should be easier to understand the delusions of masses of Germans at that time once one has noted that even now the German rearmament of the early years after the Nazi seizure of power (which was tolerated by foreign countries) is still frequently referred to by Germans as a success, and without quotation marks. Some years ago I asked the audience of a talk in Cologne to reconsider the alleged successes of the Nazi regime.[15] It seemed to me that the city which was the first one to be bombed by a thousand-plane air raid was the right place to raise the question of whether the building up of a German air force in a world practically without heavy bombers should really be regarded as a success. When one has the experience today of seeing people merely shake their heads when such a question is put to them, it is easier to understand the rejoicing of much of the population in the 1930s over the numerous new big war toys. That such a rearmament program would provoke others into rearming themselves was something Hitler had always anticipated, as has already been mentioned, and he saw this as an incentive to initiate hostilities early. Once the results of the arms race initiated by Germany started falling on Berlin, Cologne, and other German cities, it was too late to reverse the course of events.

It is into this context that one must fit the connection between rearmament, economic development, the reduction of unemployment, and the growing popularity of the Nazi regime. The economic crisis had passed its zenith by 1933, and into the slow economic recovery there poured enormous expenditures for rearmament much more quickly than many later wanted to recognize. Partly utilizing one of the swindles typical for

13 Friedrich Forstmeier and Hans-Erich Volkmann (eds.), *Wirtschaft und Rüstung am Vorabend des Zweiten Weltkriegs* (Düsseldorf: Droste, 1975), pp. 364–65.
14 Note Michael Geyer, *Aufrüstung oder Sicherheit: Die Reichswehr in der Krise der Machtpolitik, 1924–1936* (Wiesbaden: Steiner, 1980).
15 See Gerhard L. Weinberg, "National Style in Diplomacy: Germany," in Erich Angermann and Marie-Luise Frings (eds.), *Oceans Apart? Comparing Germany and the United States* (Stuttgart: Klett-Cotta, 1981), p. 152.

Hjalmar Schacht, the so-called Mefo-Bills of Exchange, the new regime quickly funneled great sums into the economy of the country and simultaneously withdrew large numbers of people from the labor market by conscription and labor service. The direct and indirect stimulation of the economy produced by this program led to an upswing which relatively rapidly eliminated unemployment.

It has been correctly pointed out that regulations by the regime kept the income of many at a low level and that the average wage of working people hardly rose. These findings, however, ignore a highly significant psychological factor. Just as large-scale unemployment had earlier had a demoralizing influence on those still holding jobs, inspiring them with fear of the future and doubts about the government, so the new image of steady work, whether well paid or not, contributed substantially to a positive attitude toward the new government, even if that inclination cannot be precisely measured. And hardly anyone asked questions about the wisdom and the possible outcome of the economic measures being taken.

Under these circumstances the foreign policy of the Nazi regime could be perceived as bringing the fulfillment of the hopes of many Germans. The peace propaganda not only calmed fears abroad but could also deflect a portion of the population at home from recognizing the dangers in the new policies. People were happy to believe in promises which corresponded to their own hopes. The building up of large armed forces was rejected by few, and the new authorities made certain that especially in this field no one criticized official policy. Numerous organizations inside Germany were "coordinated" (*gleichgeschaltet*) in 1933, from those for mathematicians to the ones for rabbit breeders, but all pacifist organizations were dissolved. The last German winner of the Nobel Peace Prize before 1939, Carl von Ossietsky, was awarded this honor while in a concentration camp. But many did not see, or did not want to see, what his death could tell them about the allegedly peaceful intentions of the government.

This is not the place to review the individual steps of National Socialist foreign policy. It is, however, important to comment on a few measures of the early years of the regime which pointed to future developments. This is not to assert that the whole process was planned in detail in advance. The new government was not operating with a precise schedule. For major state visits there was a so-called minute-by-minute plan (*Minutenprogramm*), but there was nothing like that for foreign policy. On the other hand, this does not mean that the regime moved purely opportunistically and without any clear goals. The main consideration was that of direction, of the major aims to be attained and the obstacles which it was believed needed to be removed along the way. An important hint on this last point has already been mentioned. As Hitler had always demanded in public and personally explained to the military leaders on February 3, 1933, all pacifist sentiments and organizations inside Germany were suppressed. This potential obstacle had to be removed right away, then as now an important indicator as to the direction the government did not under any circumstances wish to go. But what were the positive goals of the first steps of the regime and to what extent did they correspond to the concepts which have already been outlined as articulated before 1933?

Of all the steps taken publicly in 1933, Germany's exit from the League of Nations was surely the most characteristic and the one pointing most clearly to the future. For the postwar government of the Weimar Republic, entrance into the League of Nations accompanied by a permanent seat on the Council of the League had meant a normalization of Germany's position in the world and the return to recognition as a major power. It meant acceptance into a circle of nations which recognized one another as in principle equal as states, whatever their differences in size, population, and wealth. All the great powers – whether they really were such or not – were to have permanent seats on the Council, and all states were to be equal in the Assembly of the League. The National Socialists had always denounced the League; their members in the Reichstag, the German national legislature, had voted against Germany's entrance into it; and they had been proud of their opposition to the international organization. Some years would pass before the Third Reich began to show the public its own concepts of international structures such as the Anti-Comintern Pact and the Tripartite Pact, but they certainly wanted to clarify beyond any doubt and from the first year of their rule in 1933 that they would under no circumstances have anything to do with any system of equality of rights in the world.

While the Nazi government publicly demonstrated its direction, the implementing measures were carried out at least partially in secret, something which was entirely appropriate at a time when there was concern about any possible preventive measures by the outside world. In this connection I would like to call attention to a field of activity which is rarely discussed: that of naval rearmament. I do this not only because both public and scholarly interest in the Third Reich has paid insufficient attention to the question of how it came to be that this era in German history ended under the command of an admiral, but also because given the technology of the 1920s and 1930s the lead time, the time needed for the planning and construction of large warships, was longer than that for any other weapons system. And this special characteristic was well known both to Hitler and to the commander-in-chief of the German navy.

It is not necessary to enter into either the details or the various still open questions in this regard; that is neither needed nor relevant for our purposes. But in this field, where plans for a future more distant than in any other aspect of the rearmament program were needed, it is easier to obtain a general understanding of the hopes and aims which were entertained at that time.

The first installments of large infusions of money were allocated to the navy in February and March of 1933,[16] but the ships on which vast sums were spent in 1933 had, of course, long been on the drawing boards, even if they were not completed for several years. Thus the navy utilized the additional 80 million Marks allocated to it on May 1, 1933, to begin construction of the *Scharnhorst*. This ship, officially notified falsely as of 26,000 tons, was in reality a 31,300-ton battleship; launched on October 3, 1936, it was commissioned on January 7, 1939.[17] The fact that the navy's budget of 1932 was increased by two-thirds in 1933 and multiplied tenfold by 1938 only provides the external framework.[18] Of greater importance for our understanding are the huge warships jointly planned by Hitler and Admiral Raeder *after* the Nazis came to power. In 1935 the German government decided to build battleships of over 40,000 tons in violation of the Anglo–German Naval Agreement signed that year. The plans quickly went further; even during the 1930s these included battleships of over 56,000 tons, of which the keels for the first ones had been laid down before Germany attacked Poland in September 1939.

The question of the purpose and assumed enemy against whom these ships were being built will only be touched on briefly before we turn to the fate of one of the ships which was actually completed. Certainly nobody thought of floating the monster battleships down the Danube into the Black Sea or of running them on railway tracks to the Caspian Sea. The preparations for naval warfare, like those for land and air warfare, were directed toward the great war against the major powers in the West: Great Britain, France, and the United States.

This direction is exemplified by the first of the great ships planned and actually completed during the Third Reich. After prior detailed planning, the contract for the construction of the battleship *Bismarck* was issued on

---

16 Flottenintendant Thiele, "Die Entwicklung des Marinehaushalts von 1930 bis 1939," July 12, 1944, in *Trial of the Major War Criminals before the International Military Tribunal*, Vol. 35 (Nuremberg: Tribunal, 1949), pp. 590–91.

17 Weinberg, *1933–1936*, p. 32.

18 Dülffer, *Weimar, Hitler und die Marine*, p. 563.

November 16, 1935. The keel was laid on July 1, 1936; it was launched on February 14, 1939; and it was commissioned on August 24, 1940.[19] Needless to say, the Germans lied to the British government about the size of the ship; Berlin did not want to acknowledge the breaking of the naval agreement, planned even before that agreement was signed, and hoped to postpone discovery of the treaty breach as long as possible.[20] In this instance, the British did not discover that the treaty had been broken until after the ship was sunk in May of 1941; the London government had not awaited the completion of the two aircraft carriers ordered in 1935 on the same day as the *Bismarck*.

The sinking of the *Bismarck*, named after the founder of the unified Germany, is of both practical and symbolic significance for the history of the foreign policy of the Third Reich. Even before the attack on the Soviet Union, the great war in the West, which Hitler saw as the necessary prerequisite for the seizure of land in the East, had run into unanticipated difficulties. To get Japan to join in the war against England as soon as possible, Hitler had promised in April of 1941, that is, a month earlier, that Germany would fight alongside Japan against the United States if the Japanese saw such a conflict as an essential portion of any war with England. Germany at this time was willing to fight England and the United States – instead of England and France – at a time when preparations for the invasion of the Soviet Union were in their final stage. Although the Japanese waited longer than Hitler hoped, so that he went to war with the United States after rather than before attacking the Soviet Union, he was creating the great coalition against Germany in the spring of 1941.

The details of this development could not be foreseen in 1933. But the direction was proclaimed in public even before 1933, and after 1933 it was approached in secret and pursued with unbelievable consistency of purpose.

19 Ibid., p. 570.   20 Weinberg, *1937–1939*, pp. 29–30.

Part III

— • —

BACKGROUND FOR WAR

6

HITLER AND ENGLAND, 1933-1945:
PRETENSE AND REALITY

A subject of continuing interest in analyses of the origins and conduct of World War II is the policy of Germany toward England. It has been asserted time and again that Adolf Hitler and his government wanted good relations with Britain, preferred to avoid war with that nation, and, once war had started, were very interested in returning to peaceful relations. This picture is, in my judgment, largely mistaken, and ought to be subjected to a new examination.

The thesis of German desire for good relations with England is based on a number of events and arguments; a few of the most frequently mentioned will be examined here. It is obviously appropriate to exclude those published as Hitler's own views in a diary which turned out to be a forgery, but even some more substantial ones which are often cited by reputable scholars look rather dubious on closer inspection. The four which will be reviewed are the Anglo–German Naval Agreement of 1935, the mission of Joachim von Ribbentrop to London in 1936, the so-called alliance offer to England of August 25, 1939, and the scene in Berlin when Hitler learned of Britain's intention to declare war in 1939.

The Anglo–German Naval Agreement of 1935 is often mentioned as evidence that Hitler had indeed decided to forgo the challenge to British naval power which had poisoned Anglo–German relations before World War I. Whatever the British motives for this agreement, the German ones must be seen in the context of other German decisions in the same field and at that time. When one removes the blinders which confine vision to the purely diplomatic sphere and looks at what Hitler and Admiral Raeder, the commander-in-chief of the German navy, were doing in the way of naval planning in 1935, a very different picture emerges. As first

This is a slightly revised version of a piece which originally appeared in the *German Studies Review* 8 (1985): 299–309.

the works of Gemzell[1] and Zieb,[2] and subsequently the book of Dülffer[3] have shown, the critical decisions to build a "blue-water" navy of big battleships and aircraft carriers in violation of the 1935 treaty were made in the same year! The plans were developed before the treaty was signed, and the first contracts for construction were let on November 16, 1934.[4]

The Germans assumed, quite correctly, that these violations and those planned soon after would not become known to the British for years, and in the case of the battleship *Bismarck,* the British did not learn the true size of the ship until after it had been sunk. Moreover, many of the ships contracted were never completed; but to understand German intentions, the real as opposed to pretended policy, one must look at the ships actually ordered and not at the fairy tales told to the British and still accepted by some. The superbattleships ordered by Germany beginning in 1935 – the year of the Anglo–German Naval Agreement – were designed to surprise and outclass the British and the Americans;[5] and since Hitler and Raeder well knew that it took years to build such ships, it was anticipated that their surprising appearance on the naval scene would produce a dramatic shift in the world balance of sea power that others could not quickly redress. That in practice the program later had to be modified and only two of the planned ships were actually completed should not blind observers to the fact that the *direction* German naval policy in and after 1935 was the opposite of that then advertised.[6]

It is from this perspective perhaps easier to understand why Hitler's public renunciation of the Anglo–German Naval Agreement on April 28, 1939, no more led to a new program of naval building outside the bounds of the agreement than its earlier signature had imposed restraints. The reality of contracts and construction was governed by considerations quite different from those which affected the formulation of public gestures. This can be seen with equal ease in the fate of the Anglo–German declaration signed on September 30, 1938, the day after the Munich

1 Carl-Axel Gemzell, *Raeder, Hitler und Skandinavien: Der Kampf für einen maritimen Operationsplan* (Lund: Gleerup, 1965).
2 Paul W. Zieb, *Logistische Probleme der Kriegsmarine* (Neckargemünd: Vowinckel, 1961).
3 Jost Dülffer, *Weimar, Hitler und die Marine: Reichspolitik und Flottenbau 1920 bis 1939* (Düsseldorf: Droste, 1973).
4 Ibid., p. 570. Wilhelm Deist, *The Wehrmacht and German Rearmament* (Toronto: University of Toronto Press, 1981), pp. 74–79, penetrates the smokescreen only in part.
5 The implications of Hitler's own subsequent reference to his plan to build the world's strongest squadron of battleships are not discussed by those who imagine that he anticipated a long-term association with England. See Werner Jochmann (ed.), *Adolf Hitler: Monologe im Führer-Hauptquartier 1941–1944* (Hamburg: Albrecht Knaus, 1980), June 19, 1943, p. 402.
6 As I suggested earlier in this essay, the new monster battleships were presumably not to be sent down the Danube to the Black Sea or transported by railway to the Caspian Sea.

Conference, which provided for future consultations between the two powers on all other issues which might concern them.[7] It was at all times thereafter ignored by Germany; everyone knows that, and all have laughed at Neville Chamberlain's waving of this document on his return to England as a sign of "peace in our time." What most have overlooked is that the same document, which everyone ridicules without reading it, also contains the assertion that the two peoples never wanted to go to war with each other; and that the symbols of this desire were the Anglo–German Naval Agreement and the Munich Agreement. As early as November 1938, the German government was asserting that the declaration of September 30 had no significance for the conduct of the nation's foreign policy.[8]

The appointment of Joachim von Ribbentrop to the German Embassy in London in 1936 is still referred to by some as a reflection of German interest in a quasi-alliance with England.[9] Again, it would be wise to leave the superficial generalities and look at the specifics of the time. The German ambassador to London, Leopold von Hoesch, died on April 18, 1936. In the midst of the negotiations following upon Germany's breaking of the Locarno Treaty – ironically the first defensive alliance between England and Germany since 1871 – the German Embassy fell vacant. At first no one at all was appointed to replace von Hoesch. In the traditional framework of status in the diplomatic service of Germany, this was the highest post, but Hitler did not consider it worth filling; a chargé would have to do.

Where does von Ribbentrop come into the picture? On June 21, 1936, Bernhard Wilhelm von Bülow, the state secretary in the German Foreign Ministry, died suddenly; and von Ribbentrop expected to receive this position. The foreign minister, Constantin von Neurath, objected most vehemently. Hitler did not wish to dispense with von Neurath as yet, so von Ribbentrop received the post in London as a consolation prize. And

---

7 The text may be found in Max Domarus (ed.), *Hitler: Reden und Proklamationen, 1932–1945* (Neustadt a.d. Aisch: Verlagsdruckerei Schmidt, 1962), Vol. 1, p. 946.
8 See Gerhard L. Weinberg, *The Foreign Policy of Hitler's Germany: Starting World War II, 1937–1939* (Chicago: University of Chicago Press, 1980; Atlantic Highlands, N.J.: Humanities Press, 1994), (cited hereafter as Weinberg, *1937–1939*), p. 508. Herbert von Dirksen, then German ambassador to England, reports in his memoirs that he was told in the German Foreign Ministry a few days after the declaration was signed that it was of no importance for German policy. Herbert von Dirksen, *Moskau, Tokio, London* (Stuttgart: Kohlhammer, 1949), p. 235.
9 See e.g., Andreas Hillgruber, *Deutsche Grossmacht – und Weltpolitik im 19. und 20. Jahrhundert* (Düsseldorf: Droste, 1977), p. 188. No one reading this reference to "die Entsendung v. Ribbentrops als Botschafter nach London" (the dispatch of von Ribbentrop as ambassador to London) would ever guess that the ambassador remained in Germany for many months after this appointment.

since von Ribbentrop did not want that position, he accepted it on the agreed terms that he did not have to go there right away and need not spend much time so far away from his beloved Führer.[10] He finally showed up in London to present his credentials on October 25, 1936 – after the post had been empty for more than half a year – only to return immediately to Germany. And for the rest of the year and a half as nominal ambassador to the Court of St. James, he spent most of his time elsewhere.[11] If von Ribbentrop's reports to Hitler on the abdication crisis of early December 1936 border on the lunatic, this reflected not only their author's general level of intelligence but also his rather tenuous connection with his official post.[12] When one asks, what was von Ribbentrop actually doing with his time while nominally accredited to London, the answer can be found by examining not his memoirs but his activities in Berlin and Rome during 1936 and 1937: he was negotiating with the Japanese and the Italians for an alliance *against* England.[13]

The reality of 1936–37, as shown elsewhere,[14] is that the German government had no interest in a replacement for the Locarno Treaty, that it rejected all attempts by the British to get negotiations for a new agreement with Germany under way, that it found a pretext to call off the planned visit of von Neurath to London, tried to do the same thing to the visit of Lord Halifax to Germany, and waved off the last British attempt to initiate talks on a general settlement in Hitler's meeting with Nevile Henderson, the British ambassador, of March 3, 1938. Henderson did get Hitler to promise to think over the British offer and to respond to it in writing. In the year and a half which separate that meeting from the British declaration of war on September 3, 1939, Hitler never could find

---

10 On this matter, see John L. Heineman, *Hitler's First Foreign Minister: Constantin Freiherr von Neurath* (Berkeley: University of California Press, 1979), pp. 140–44; Paul Seabury, *The Wilhelmstrasse: A Study of German Diplomats under the Nazi Regime* (Berkeley: University of California Press, 1954), pp. 54–55.

11 Wolfgang Michalka, *Ribbentrop und die deutsche Weltpolitik, 1933–1940* (Munich: Wilhelm Fink 1980), pp. 112–13, claims that von Ribbentrop was convinced that there was no hope of an Anglo–German agreement at the beginning of his mission. For an itinerary of von Ribbentrop for the period February 1937 to March 1938 which shows his travels, see National Archives Microcopy, T-120, Cont. 778, serial 1562, frames 378076–77. For British Foreign Secretary Anthony Eden's suggestion to von Ribbentrop that the British government would appreciate his spending some time in London, see his letter to Henderson, No. 1288 of October 27, 1937, C 7451/270/18, Public Record Office, FO 371/20736.

12 See Weinberg, *1937–1939*, p. 62, n. 36.

13 These negotiations are covered in ibid.; Gerhard L. Weinberg, *The Foreign Policy of Hitler's Germany: Diplomatic Revolution in Europe, 1933–1936* (Chicago: University of Chicago Press, 1970; Atlantic Highlands, N.J.: Humanities Press, 1994) (cited hereafter as Weinberg, *1933–1936*); John P. Fox, *Germany and the Far Eastern Crisis, 1931–1939* (Oxford: Oxford University Press, 1982).

14 Weinberg, *1933–1936*, chs. 10, 11, 13; Weinberg, *1937–1939*, chs. 3, 4.

time to write the promised letter to the country with which he supposedly wanted good relations.[15]

When the German government really wanted to reach agreement with another power, it went about the process rather differently. Whether their attempts were successful or not, the authorities in Berlin always understood that agreements are not negotiated by leaving embassies unfilled, questions unanswered, and proposals without replies. When Germany wanted agreements with Italy, emissaries were sent to Rome in such numbers as to embarrass their hosts. When agreements were desired with Turkey and the Soviet Union in 1939, the Embassy in Ankara was filled by Franz von Papen, who proceeded to engage in negotiations there, and similarly, the ambassador in Moscow, Count von der Schulenburg, was regularly provided with the instructions he needed to move forward the negotiations in the Soviet capital. When an agreement with Japan was wanted in 1940, a special envoy was dispatched to Tokyo in order to speed up the negotiating process. If Hitler early in 1938 appointed as foreign minister von Ribbentrop, who had just explained to him at great length that war with England, and as soon as possible, was called for, and then appointed as von Ribbentrop's new state secretary, Ernst von Weizsäcker, who saw nothing in this concept to object to, one might consider the possibility that these appointments reflect Hitler's true preference in regard to the policy to be followed toward Britain now that he was pushing out the last of the high officials wished upon him by the late President Paul von Hindenburg.

A third example to be scrutinized is the alliance offer Hitler sent to London through Ambassador Henderson on August 25, 1936.[16] The fact that this offer was described by Hitler himself as merely a notice of a future offer which Germany intended to make "immediately after the solution of the German–Polish question" ought to alert the careful observer. This promise of an offer to be made in the future was sent *after* Hitler had ordered the attack on Poland to begin on the following day, August 26. The message was sent on the same day as he informed Benito Mussolini of his plans, urged the Soviet Union to fill the vacancy in the Soviet Embassy in Berlin as well as to send a military representative, gave French Ambassador Robert Coulondre a special and urgent message for

---

15 Henderson would comment in his memoirs that "though Hitler was constantly talking of the hand which he had held out to England and complaining that England had rejected it, whenever definite advances were made to him, he always found some way of withdrawing and of refusing to meet us half-way. It is impossible today to believe that this was fortuitous." Nevile Henderson, *Failure of a Mission: Berlin 1937–1939* (New York: G. P. Putnam's Sons, 1949), p. 110.

16 The text may be found in *Documents on British Foreign Policy, 1919–1939*, Third Series, Vol, 7, *1939* (London: H.M. Stationery Office, 1954), No. 283 (English) and No. 310 (German).

French Prime Minister Edouard Daladier that Germany did not want war with France and had no claims on the country, and had the German ministers in Holland, Belgium, Luxembourg, and Switzerland instructed to promise those countries respect for their neutrality along with assurances of war and destruction if they sided with the Western Powers.[17] Is it not curious that the only portion of this array of measures taken the day before war was to start which is subsequently cited as evidence of Hitler's supposed real views is the "offer" to England – and even then without any reference to a key portion of it which might make readers skeptical: "Agreement with Russia was unconditional and signified a change in foreign policy of the Reich destined to last a very long time. Russia and Germany would never again take up arms against each other."[18]

It seems obvious that with these measures, all taken between the order to attack Poland and the recall of that order, Hitler hoped to isolate his war on Poland by simultaneously reassuring and scaring Britain and France as well as the neutrals – with *none* of the assurances to be taken seriously. This is the way German State Secretary von Weizsäcker interpreted the offer to England in his diary at the time;[19] this is the way the offer was read in London. There the authorities had had plenty of experience with Hitler's prior generous offers, like the one to return to the League of Nations at the time of the remilitarization of the Rhineland. If the Chamberlain government did not take seriously a promise of Hitler to send at a later date an offer to defend the British Empire against Germany's Italian ally, Germany's Japanese partner in the Anti-Comintern Pact, and Germany's newly proclaimed "unconditional" Soviet friend, that may serve to show that the British prime minister and his associates were more perceptive than some have been willing to believe. If so, they could only be reinforced in their views by the receipt on August 29 of a full report on Hitler's notorious secret speech to the generals on August 22 in which he had expressed his original preference for attacking the Western Powers first, had explained his reversal of the sequence, announced his intention to attack Poland whether or not the Western Pow-

---

17 Weinberg, *1937–1939*, pp. 629 ff.
18   An example in Klaus Hildebrand, *Das Dritte Reich* (Munich: Oldenbourg, 1979), p. 43, where the offer is cited as demonstrating Hitler's "Lieblingsidee" (favorite concept). Similarly Hillgruber, *Deutsche Grossmacht*, p. 191. Quite preposterous is the account in Josef Henke, *England in Hitler's politischem Kalkül 1935–1939* (Boppard: Boldt, 1973), pp. 287 ff., where the chronology is altered to fit the author's thesis. The works of Dietrich Aigner, Oswald Hauser, Fritz Hesse, and David Hoggan on German–English relations are not cited since, unlike the works that are mentioned, these do not merit serious consideration.
19 Leonidas E. Hill (ed.), *Die Weizsäcker-Papiere, 1933–1950* (Frankfurt/M: Propyläen, 1974), diary entry for August 25, 1939, p. 160.

ers intervened, and asserted that his only worry was that Chamberlain might try to find a way to cheat him out of war as he had in 1938.[20]

The fact that Hitler, after learning of Mussolini's defection and the British signing of the formal treaty with Poland, postponed hostilities for a few days meant, of course, that the British considered his offer and the French his special message not in the originally intended context – the same time that they were to have learned of the German invasion of Poland – but on a day of continued diplomatic activity. But again, in this instance as in the others, one should look at the circumstances under which initiatives are undertaken, not later developments, to understand them. The fact that in the hectic moments before war these circumstances are measured in days and hours, not months and years, in no way alters the need for precision in perspective.

I come now to a fourth example, the touching story of the reaction in Berlin to the British ultimatum of September 3, 1939. It is based on the memoirs of Paul Schmidt, the famous interpreter.[21] In his dramatic account, Schmidt has Hitler, on being informed of the British ultimatum, angrily asking von Ribbentrop: "What now?" and Göring turning to Schmidt to say: "If we should lose this war, then heaven have mercy on us!" It is a nice story, but it cannot be trusted. We know that Göring was not there at all,[22] so that this part at least of Schmidt's account is certainly a fake. Given the other examples of errors and fabrications in a book of memoirs written a decade later and under very different circumstances, those who study the beginning of World War II would be well advised to ignore the unsubstantiated account of Schmidt and turn instead to *contemporary* evidence on Hitler's views.[23]

In August 1939 Hitler preferred to attack Poland as a preliminary to attacking France and England, but he was quite willing to face war with the Western Powers earlier if that was their choice.[24] And he believed himself well on the way to being ready for it. This is clearest in the air. As in the case of the navy, the armaments program had been pushed forward

20 Weinberg, *1937–1939*, pp. 610–11, 643, n. 80.
21 Paul Schmidt, *Statist auf diplomatischer Bühne, 1923–1945* (Bonn: Athenäum, 1950), pp. 463–64.
22 Ernst Meyer-Hermann, "Göring und die englische Kriegserklärung am 3.9.1939," *Geschichte in Wissenschaft und Unterricht*, 9 (1958): 375–76.
23 Some other examples of errors were pointed out in his review of the book by Lewis Namier, *In the Nazi Era* (London: Macmillan, 1952), pp. 104–108. David Wingeate Pike has shown that Schmidt faked his account of the Hitler–Franco meeting at Hendaye – at which Schmidt was *not* present – in "Franco and the Axis Stigma," *Journal of Contemporary History*, 17 (1982): 377–79.
24 Weinberg, *1937–1939*, chs. 13, 14.

for military, not aesthetic, purposes. The dive bombers, like the battleships, were built for effectiveness, not appearance. And the single-engine
short-range JU-87, built with France in mind – and appropriate for
Poland when that country refused to subordinate itself to Germany – was
by 1939 being supplemented by the new "wonder bomber," the JU-88.
This was a two-engine dive bomber, designed primarily for use against
England, with production levels vastly increased early in 1939.[25] It is no
coincidence that Hitler ordered production of the JU-88 doubled on
August 31, 1939.[26] This seems to be a better clue to Hitler's thinking
three days later than Schmidt's account. A further three days later, on
September 6, Hermann Göring, the commander-in-chief of the German
air force, informed the General Army Office (Allgemeine Heeresamt)
that Hitler had decided that the main effort against England would be
with the JU-88; there would be 1,500 available by the summer of 1940
and a death blow, the *tödliche Schlag*, against England would follow in
1941.[27] Surely the 1939 diary of the chief-of-staff of the General Army
Office is more dependable than postwar memoirs and apologias.

The evidence does indicate that Hitler's expectations of his air force
were exaggerated, in part because of excessive optimism by Göring, in
part because Hitler believed the new models shown him at an air force
demonstration at Rechlin in July 1939 were ready for immediate mass
production when in fact they were nothing of the sort.[28] But to analyze
policy choices, one must look at contemporary perceptions and expectations, not subsequent rationalizations.

The massive allocation of resources to weapons is perhaps a more
useful guide to our understanding of German policy than the chitchat
with which Hitler entertained – or more often put to sleep – his evening
companions during World War II. Carefully selected passages from
Hitler's "table talk" are sometimes quoted as evidence for his views on
England. But as the JU-88 had been his favorite device for expressing his
attitude toward England in 1939–41, so the *Vergeltungswaffen*, the "V"
weapons, would illustrate his views in the middle and last years of World
War II. Because it does not fit well with interpretations which have
become fashionable since 1945, it has not been sufficiently noted that at
Hitler's personal insistence, enormous human, scientific, and material

25 Ibid., pp. 513–14. Note Göring's comments to Mussolini on April 15, 1939, in *Documents on
   German Foreign Policy, 1918–1945*, Series D, Vol. 6, No. 205.
26 Edward L. Homze, *Arming the Luftwaffe: The Reich Air Ministry and the German Aircraft
   Industry, 1919–1939* (Lincoln: University of Nebraska Press, 1976), p. 231.
27 Chef des Stabes AHA, "Tagebuch V, 10.8–9.10.39," September 6 and 7 1939; London
   Imperial War Museum, MI 14/981.
28 Homze, *Arming the Luftwaffe*, pp. 248–49.

resources were allocated to these weapons in the very years that the German war machine was most strained.

The new weapons, the V-1, V-2, V-3, and V-4, were not only designed with England in mind, they were originally *all* to be launched from *fixed* sites constructed through additional considerable allocation of resources. And these fixed sites were all exclusively aimed at England, presumably as a special sign of the kindly regard in which Hitler held the island kingdom. Again it is true that the subsequent employment was not quite what the Germans had originally intended. When they came to be used, a high proportion, especially of the V-2s, ended up being fired at Belgium, and the only V-3s ever in action were aimed, of all places, against Luxembourg.[29] Here too one must look at clearly demonstrated initial intent to comprehend the nature and thrust of German policy. Does anyone believe that in 1943 and 1944 Hitler was greatly concerned with dangers that Luxembourg might pose for the Third Reich?

Let us go back then and see whether it is not possible to find some pattern which fits the evidence a little better. In the first, formative years of his movement, Hitler anticipated a new war against France *and* England. It was only after 1923 that he began to consider the possibility that the two powers might be separated. For the balance of the time until 1933 he argued for a war in the West which would enable Germany to seize vast stretches of land in the East. Wider aspirations could be realized later. The difficult war in the West would be easier if England and Italy helped or stood aside; the seizure of land in the East was assumed to be a simple matter anyway since by what Hitler considered a stroke of good fortune for Germany, that land of what he believed were inferior beings was now ruled by incompetents.

Once in power, Hitler recognized rather quickly that England, unlike Italy, could *not* be separated from France. And since war in the West was the primary prerequisite for grabbing living space in the East, that meant that war with England would almost automatically be part of the fight in the West as he had originally anticipated. Since the Poles, unlike the Hungarians, would not subordinate themselves to Germany in the winter of 1938–39, so that Germany would have a quiet eastern border while fighting France and England, Poland had to be crushed before the Western campaign. But if France and England joined in right away, that made

29 Olaf Groehler, "Die 'Hochdruckpumpe' (V–3)–Entwicklung und Misere einer 'Wunderwaffe'," *Militärgeschichte*, 5 (1977), p. 743. For wartime intelligence on the V-3 site at Mimoyecques, see Francis H. Hinsley et al., *British Intelligence in the Second World War: Its Influence on Strategy and Operations*, Vol. 3, Part I (Cambridge: Cambridge University Press, 1984), pp. 405, 413, 435–36, 439, 595–96; its location is noted on the map facing p. 593.

for a difference in timing but not in essence. When the 1940 campaign in the West brought about the defeat of France but not that of England, the latter automatically moved from being one of several enemies to being enemy Number One.

If German policy is viewed from this perspective, it becomes possible to obtain a better understanding not only of the way the resources of that country were used during World War II, but also of some major policy decisions, or at least the timing of those decisions. The decision to attack the Soviet Union, for example, was made in the late summer of 1940 in part because it was Hitler's view that beginning such an operation then – and he originally planned to attack in the East still in the fall of 1940 – would assist in knocking England out of the war. He thought that among the factors keeping England in the war was hope for assistance from the Soviet Union and the United States. By launching the attack on Russia he had always planned, he could remove both hopes, as the quick defeat he expected to administer the Soviets would free Japan from concern about her back door and thus encourage that power to move southward in East Asia, thereby tying up the United States in the Pacific.

Similarly, the willingness of Germany to go to war with the United States alongside Japan if that was what it took to get Japan into the war with England shows how Berlin saw the priorities. Here too Hitler would have preferred war later when he would have been able to make additional preparations; but he subordinated such considerations to the preference for gaining an ally against Great Britain. And he was willing to do so before or after the German invasion of the Soviet Union.[30]

If the calculations and anticipations of Germany's leadership proved wrong on many points, it is still their premises and intentions which must be analyzed if we are to understand them. And that requires that the primary focus be on what was planned and what was done when the policies were first adopted, not what was said to mislead at the time or to explain miscalculation and disaster afterward.

The evolution of new alignments and alliances since 1945 may have led some to see the past through glasses which screen out certain unpleasant elements. This makes for neither good history nor good policy. Sound construction had best be based on the hard rock of reality, not the shifting sands of myths, however comforting or satisfying they might temporarily appear to be. And there are few countries whose future has been more seriously compromised by myths and legends about its past than Germany.

---

30 Gerhard L. Weinberg, *World in the Balance: Behind the Scenes of World War II* (Hanover, N.H.: University Press of New England, 1981), pp. 75–95.

7

———— • ————

GERMAN FOREIGN POLICY
AND AUSTRIA

In the years that followed the end of the First World War successive German governments toyed in principle with the idea of annexing Austria. Long-standing concerns about increasing the Catholic proportion of the population, which had persisted as a deterrent during the Second Empire, now appeared less important.[1] The concept of annexation acquired additional and to some extent new perspectives in the wake of Adolf Hitler's appointment as chancellor of Germany in 1933. Hitler was an advocate of the annexation of Austria, had called for it on the first page of his book *Mein Kampf,* and had consistently urged such a step – although neither because he felt an overriding affection for his native land nor because many Austrians were suffering economic hardship in the postwar years. He set his sights on annexation because he wished to increase the national substance of the German Reich as a preparatory step to implementing his plans for territorial aggrandizement.

Long before he came to power he had realized that Italy's concerns with regard to the Brenner frontier posed a serious impediment to the annexation; in *Mein Kampf* he called for South Tyrol to be abandoned and had the relevant chapter reprinted as a separate pamphlet with a preface dated February 12, 1926, obviously hoping thereby to acquaint a larger reading public with his view that an alliance with Italy, entailing the abandonment of South Tyrol, was a desirable objective.[2] Today we know

This is a revised translation of a talk at an international conference in Vienna on the fiftieth anniversary of the annexation of Austria. It was published in Gerald Stourzh and Birgitta Zaar (eds.), *Österreich, Deutschland und die Mächte: Internationale und österreichische Aspekte des "Anschlusses" vom März 1938* (Vienna: Österreichische Akademie der Wissenschaften, 1990), pp. 61–74. The book also contains commentary on and discussion about the theses advanced in the paper.

1 See Alfred D. Low, *The Anschluss Movement 1918–1919 and the Paris Peace Conference* (Philadelphia: American Philosophical Society, 1974); Stanley Suval, *The Anschluss Question in the Weimar Era: A Study of Nationalism in Germany and Austria, 1918–1932* (Baltimore: Johns Hopkins University Press, 1974).
2 Adolf Hitler, *Die Südtiroler Frage und das deutsche Bündnisproblem* (Munich: Eher, 1926).

that he also went into this question in some detail in his second book, written in 1928 but not published at the time.[3] A few weeks later he had communicated his ideas on the subject of the South Tyrol to Benito Mussolini through Ettore Tolomei, the most prominent advocate of an Italianizing policy in South Tyrol.[4]

During the first months of National Socialist rule in Germany, Berlin regarded the annexation of Austria as just another step in the process of imposing Nazi rule on the domestic political front.[5] It was assumed that a combination of pressure from within and from without would achieve very much the same effect in Vienna as in Munich and in Danzig (Gdansk), with Theo Habicht assuming the role in Austria which had been played by Ritter von Epp in Bavaria and Albert Forster in the Free City of Danzig. The Austrian National Socialists generated the pressure from within, the tourist boycott that from without. But the plan failed. The Austrian government of Chancellor Engelbert Dollfuss resisted energetically, secured the support of Italy by openly fighting against the Social Democratic Party in the country, and maintained itself in power. Not that this fact deterred the German government from continuing to pursue its goal. It simply necessitated a slight change of approach: if the type of low-gear subversion which had proved effective elsewhere did not achieve the desired results in Austria, Berlin would simply have to shift into a higher gear. The summer of 1934 brought an attempted putsch.

It is generally agreed today that the putsch of July 25, 1934, was orchestrated by Berlin.[6] The personal and extensive involvement of Counsellor of Legation Günther Altenburg, who was assigned to the German Legation in Vienna from February to September 1934, in the preparations of the coup is simply inconceivable without high-level authorization.[7] True, some of the details of the takeover were worked out in Austria; and it is equally evident that Hitler's assessment of some of the

---

3 Gerhard L. Weinberg (ed.), *Hitlers zweites Buch: Ein Dokumen aus dem Jahr 1928* (Stuttgart: Deutsche Verlags-Anstalt, 1961). A new edition of Hitler's second book with a revised introduction has been refused publication by the Bavarian government.

4 Karl-Heinz Ritschel, *Diplomatie um Südtirol: Politische Hintergründe eines europäischen Versagens* (Stuttgart: Seewald, 1966), pp. 133–37.

5 Gerhard L. Weinberg, *The Foreign Policy of Hitler's Germany: Diplomatic Revolution in Europe, 1933–1936* (Chicago: University of Chicago Press, 1970; Atlantic Highlands, N.J.: Humanities Press, 1993) (cited hereafter as Weinberg, *1933–1936*), pp. 87–94.

6 See Bruce F. Pauley, *Der Weg in den Nationalsozialismus: Ursprünge und Entwicklung der NSDAP in Österreich* (Vienna: Österreichischer Bundesverlag, 1988), chs. 5–7; Gottfried-Karl Kindermann, *Hitlers Niederlage in Österreich: Bewaffneter NS-Putsch, Kanzlermord und Österreichs Abwehrsieg 1934* (Hamburg: 1984), chs. 3–5.

7 Weinberg, *1933–1936*, pp. 102f. Kindermann (*Hitlers Niederlage in Österreich*, pp. 151f.) has understood this point; on the other hand, Gerhard Jagschitz in *Der Putsch: Die Nationalsozialisten 1934 in Österreich* (Graz: Verlag Styria 1976) has failed to do so in spite of his knowing (p. 85) of the prior notification of the German Foreign Ministry.

important factors pertaining to the situation in Vienna – like the way the Austrian armed forces were likely to react – was flawed. But it was Berlin which gave the go-ahead for the putsch. The most recently available sources demonstrate beyond any doubt that Hitler knew of the planned coup beforehand, even if some of the initiative originated from National Socialists within Austria.[8] It was in Berlin that the decision had been taken to murder Chancellor Dollfuss and install a new government under the subservient Anton Rintelen.[9] The murder of Hitler's predecessor as German chancellor, Kurt von Schleicher, had just been enthusiastically acclaimed by the Reichstag. In the present case the victim's wife had of necessity to be spared, since Frau Dollfuss happened to be in Italy at the time. But Dollfuss was duly shot, albeit a day later than planned. Nevertheless, the attempted takeover failed. The Nazis both in Berlin and in Vienna had miscalculated.[10]

Without recapitulating the events of July 25, 1934, in detail, suffice it to say that the insurgents had been inaccurate in their assessment of the situation in Vienna as it related to the government, the police force, and the army, and that in the prevailing circumstances the coup did not result in a Nazi takeover. This was not the only miscalculation. The implications in terms of foreign policy had also been erroneously forecast, this time in Berlin rather than in Vienna. Prior to the National Socialist takeover by Forster in Danzig, Hitler had carefully and in detail sounded out the possible repercussions with regard to Poland. I shall at a later juncture return to the subject of the parallels between the Danzig and the Austrian issues as seen through the eyes of the German government.

Here I cite the analogy in order to point out the world of difference

8 Note esp. the comments of the commander of Military District VII (Befehlshaber im Wehrkreis VII, München), in Anton Hoch and Hermann Weiss, "Die Erinnerungen des Generalobersten Wilhelm Adam," in Wolfgang Benz (ed.), *Miscellanea: Festschrift für Helmut Krausnick zum 75. Geburtstag* (Stuttgart: Deutsche Verlags-Anstalt, 1980), pp. 47f.

9 Although certain questions remain open, and may well remain so, other matters are entirely clear. In the preceding October a National Socialist had wounded Dollfuss with two shots from a pistol. Shortly before the fatal July 25 a hand grenade assassination of the chancellor had been planned. On July 25 the chancellor, already lying wounded from one shot and unable to move, was shot a second time at the closest possible range. Not one other person of all those in the chancellory who were loyal to him was wounded; Dollfuss on the other hand was long considered a sworn enemy of the Nazis. How could the conspirators be certain that the Austrian president would appoint Rintelen chancellor as long as Dollfuss, though wounded, was still alive? When Pauley wonders (p. 131) why Dollfuss was allowed to bleed to death without a doctor or a priest, the explanation is surely that only the death of Dollfuss could guarantee the appointment of a new chancellor. Jagschitz (*Der Putsch* pp. 93, 119) has failed to understand the evidence he himself has found on this subject.

10 Weinberg, *1933–1935*, pp. 98–105. One should also recall the killing of the former prime minister of Bavaria, Gustav von Kahr, in connection with the murders of June 30, 1934. The killing of chancellors and similar officials was very much a part of daily life in Nazi circles in the summer of 1934.

which lay between a correct and an incorrect assessment of the most important foreign government for the Nazis in these two cases. Hitler had failed to grasp Mussolini's standpoint; in part presumably because he had not fully confided in the Italian primer minister during their meeting in Venice the preceding month, and in part because he either could not or would not understand that the Duce did not share his perception of the German and Italian quests for *Lebensraum*, that is, territorial aggrandizement, as being complementary – notably in the context of southeastern Europe.

Italy's response to the attempted coup of July 25 forced Hitler to realize that the annexation of Austria was even more a foreign policy matter than he had supposed. If the course which the German government now began to follow was new, the objective remained the same; and it must be pointed out that, in this case as in many others, a temporary modification of tactics did not imply a radical change of overall policy.

With a view to further preparing the domestic political ground in Austria for annexation, Hitler dispatched Franz von Papen to Vienna.[11] It was by an oversight that von Papen had not also been a victim of the murders of June 30, and Hitler wanted him out of Berlin at all costs. In the previous year he had banished Hans Luther from the Reichsbank to the Embassy in Washington. Now von Papen was to put the subversive tactics he had rehearsed in the United States during the First World War to good use in Vienna.

Von Papen went to work. The tasks originally allotted to Habicht and Rintelen were now assigned to others. Edmund von Glaise-Horstenau, Carl von Bardolff, and Ritter von Srbik were given the opportunity to prepare themselves for their seats in the National Socialist Reichstag by mounting von Papen's Trojan horse. The conclusion of the German–Austrian agreement of July 11, 1936, developed out of this strategy and at the same time facilitated its continuation.[12]

But the main work of paving the way for the annexation was being carried out elsewhere. On January 19, 1935, Hitler explained to some Austrian Nazis that such preparatory measures would require between three and five years.[13] The most important was the rearming of Germany. Within a relatively short space of time, Germany's rearmament program would give it a significant edge over the other European powers in the context of a world which had disarmed. The remilitarization of the Rhineland would in its turn enhance Germany's military headstart. That this step would effectively terminate Germany's only defensive alliance

11 Weinberg, *1933–1936*, pp. 106f.
12 Ibid., pp. 267–71.   13 Ibid., pp. 232f.

with Britain since 1871 left Hitler cold. I mention this, first, because there are still people who take Hitler's purported desire for an alliance with Britain seriously and, second, because we shall return to the subject of German–British relations in connection with the annexation of Austria.[14]

The second major thrust of Berlin's preparations for annexation consisted in the strengthening of ties between Germany and Italy. As in the case of the rearmament program, this policy was obviously designed to pursue far broader goals than just the annexation of Austria, but it needs to be examined here in connection with the Austrian question. In terms of Italian foreign policy we need to recall Rome's actions in Ethiopia and Spain, which alienated Paris and London but effected a rapprochement with Berlin, and made any significant Italian protest against the remilitarization of the Rhineland impossible. Mussolini's ability to protect the independence of Austria had thus been greatly reduced, and the whole question of the Brenner frontier now had to be seen in a new perspective.

Two factors accounted for this new perspective. On the one hand Fulvio Suvich, whose importance has generally been overlooked by historians, relinquished the post of foreign minister under Mussolini in the summer of 1936, and was replaced by Galeazzo Ciano. I mention this because when he first took office, Ciano used his influence with Mussolini to advocate closer ties with Germany – it was only later that he was to adopt his more widely publicized contrary stance (which had also been that of his predecessor). On the other hand, Hermann Göring's visit to Rome in January 1937 had an enormous impact on subsequent developments. All the evidence suggests that Göring's remarks on the South Tyrol question led the Italian government to believe Berlin favored the idea of resettling South Tyrol's ethnic Germans who wished to live elsewhere. We do not know whether Göring spoke of a comprehensive resettlement program at that stage, but in my view the source material adequately justifies the supposition that he used the term "resettlement" (*Umsiedlung*) during the deliberations in Rome.[15] The possibility of a population transfer not only would safeguard the Italian government against any German measures on the South Tyrol question if Germany annexed Austria but would also alleviate any fears of a German effort to seize the previously Austrian Adriatic harbor city of Trieste. If Germany were in fact prepared to write off the German-inhabited area of the

14 See Gerhard L. Weinberg, "Hitler and England, 1933–1945: Pretense and Reality," reprinted as Chapter 6 in this book.
15 Gerhard L. Weinberg, *The Foreign Policy of Hitler's Germany: Starting World War II, 1937–1939* (Chicago: University of Chicago Press, 1980; Atlantic Highlands, N.J.: Humanities Press, 1993) (cited hereafter as Weinberg, *1937–1939*), pp. 270, n. 41, and 286–87.

South Tyrol, it would hardly look toward taking over a Trieste with its Italian and Slovene population.

Equal significance attached to another, very different outcome of the visit. Göring passed on Hitler's invitation to the Duce to visit Germany. That visit took place in the autumn of 1937 and finally convinced Mussolini that the Third Reich, to all appearances so powerful, had a glorious future ahead of it. Henceforth Mussolini would under no circumstances place Italy in open opposition to Germany. It very soon became apparent what impact all this was to have on Berlin's policy toward Austria.[16]

In the autumn of 1937 Hitler felt that the time would soon be ripe to launch cross-border operations. He was planning to take the initial steps soon, anticipating that these would in turn facilitate the implementation of subsequent moves. The overall strategy, which envisaged a major war on the western front as a necessary prelude to the seizure of vast territories in the East, would have to be carried out in a relatively short time span in order to safeguard Germany's lead in armaments. In this context the annexation of Austria and Czechoslovakia would serve to strengthen Germany's military and strategic position for the great war in the West, as he explained to his most important advisors on November 5, 1937.[17] Once both countries had been annexed, Germany would have a shorter and more readily defensible military border to secure, while – according to Hitler's estimates – the German population of the new territories would provide approximately twelve new divisions. Although some of Hitler's most important advisors had misgivings about an invasion of Czechoslovakia, predicting that it would in all probability unleash a world war which Germany would lose, there was full agreement that Germany should and could annex Austria without running a risk of war. The questions that remained to be settled related to the timing of the annexation and the methods to be applied. These two questions need to be considered, but first some broader issues must be examined.

The timing of the invasion of Austria was closely bound up with Hitler's assessment of the prevailing political conditions in general. The exact date was determined by specific domestic factors both in Germany and in Austria and by developments in Berlin's attempt to mediate in the war between Japan and China. But Hitler arrived at his choice of the first half of 1938 as the right time to launch his attack on Austria by an assessment of the interrelation of two broad factors: the progress of Germany's rearmament program and the diplomatic situation. This point must be made absolutely clear to avoid confusing cause and effect. The

16 Ibid., pp. 279–83.
17 The meeting generally referred to after the author of a key source on it as the "Hossbach Conference" is reviewed in ibid., pp. 34–41.

economic advantages which the annexation of Austria brought were applauded in the same measure as the economic disadvantages resulting
from Germany's concurrent new policy in the Far East were deplored.
But the former undertaking was no more the outcome of any economic
problems Germany was encountering than the latter policy stemmed
from the belief that the strength of the domestic economy would easily
make amends for the predicted setbacks.

It must also be said quite unequivocally that with regard to the annexation of Austria, the German government was no more fastidious in its
choice of methods than it had been in the early years of National Socialist
rule, when the whole issue was still regarded as a matter of Austrian
domestic politics. While the various steps and developments leading up
to annexation were partly the products of numerous individual events and
personalities within Germany and Austria, the initial decision to terminate the independence of Austria remained unaltered. Pointing this out is
not designed to divert attention from such events and personalities; but in
observing events we must never lose sight of the crucial decisions in the
background as we study the details of the foreground. The timing decided upon in Berlin and the choice of individuals for preordained roles
were to be modified or changed completely by the actual course of
events. But a brief outline of these details will shed an interesting light on
the decision-making process in Berlin and the direction of German
policy at the time.

In January 1938 Hitler took one domestic and one foreign political
occurrence as pretexts for reshuffling personnel in the fields of military
and foreign policy. The domestic occurrence was the marriage of War
Minister Werner von Blomberg. Hitler seized this opportunity to make
sweeping changes in the upper echelons of the military high command:
Hitler himself took over von Blomberg's portfolio, while key positions in
the command structure were assigned to individuals of unswerving loyalty to and personal dependence on the Führer. The following detail
sheds an interesting light on the rationale behind these changes. The
new commander-in-chief of the army, Walther von Brauchitsch, received
regular personal monetary allowances from Hitler which enabled him to
divorce his wife and marry a woman whose past differed in no significant
way from that of von Blomberg's new spouse. It seems clear, then, that
the personnel changes were not motivated by moral scruples. Rather,
Hitler was installing a new military command structure composed of men
on whose sycophantic compliance with his wishes he could rely.[18]

The foreign political occurrence happened by chance to coincide with

18 Ibid., pp. 43–51.

the developments just outlined. On January 16 Japan provoked the termination of Germany's efforts to mediate in the Sino–Japanese conflict. In light of the breakdown of the negotiations, Hitler felt that Germany could abandon its more or less neutral stance on the East Asian war. He was now free to work toward his goal of a German–Japanese alliance against Britain. On the diplomatic front he hoped to bring this about with the help of concessions to and preferential treatment for Japan. Hitler's aspirations again gave rise to personnel changes. Foreign Minister Constantin von Neurath, who had argued in favor of neutrality toward or friendship with China, was replaced by Joachim von Ribbentrop, an advocate of siding with Japan as an ally against Britain.[19] It is no coincidence that Hitler's speech of February 20, 1938, contained not only his account of these personnel changes but also the public proclamation of the new German policy in the Far East.[20]

By the end of January at the very latest Hitler had made up his mind to step up the pressure on Austria, partly in order to divert attention at home and abroad away from the crisis in the German high command. He had in fact made the same decision the previous November, envisaging January as the time for its implementation.[21] Why did he feel that the time had come for this step, and what measures was Hitler planning as a way of initiating the annexation?

Hitler regarded France – his most formidable continental opponent in the forthcoming European war – as being at the time too weak and divided to pose the slightest threat. He was aware that the British government was in the process of formulating a new offer covering European and African affairs which would provide concessions to Germany.[22] Although some historians continue to imagine that Hitler wanted a comprehensive treaty with Britain, this is entirely untrue. The published diaries of Joseph Goebbels illuminate the absolutely negative attitude of Hitler toward England and its proposals and offers as it really was at the time and not as some have portrayed it subsequently. His initial preference was not to discuss issues with the English at all.[23] When on March 3

19 Ibid., and pp. 174–78. The first important concession to Japan, German diplomatic recognition of the puppet state of Manchukuo, was announced in this speech; see Gerhard L. Weinberg, "German Recognition of Manchoukuo," *World Affairs Quarterly* 28 (1957): 149–62.
20 Text of the speech in Max Domarus (ed.), *Hitler: Reden und Proklamationen, 1932–1945* (Neustadt a.d. Aisch: Verlagsdruckerei Schmidt, 1962), Vol. 1, pp. 792–804.
21 See Weinberg, *1937–1939*, p. 291.
22 Ibid., ch. 4.
23 Elke Fröhlich (ed.), *Die Tagebücher von Joseph Goebbels: Sämtliche Fragmente*, Part 1, Vol. 3 (Munich: Saur, 1987), Nov. 15, 1937 (p. 336), November 16, 1937 (p. 337), November 27, 1937 (p. 348).

the British ambassador, Sir Nevile Henderson, presented him with the first official notification of the offer, Hitler dismissed it out of court. Henderson had a difficult time persuading Hitler even to promise a written reply – and the Führer never did find the time to commit his response to paper. As in questions of personnel policy, Hitler did exactly the opposite of what might be expected of a responsible head of state. He interpreted the British government's desire for an overall settlement with Germany as an indication that he could afford simply to ignore any communication from London and that Britain, like France, would not imperil his plans to annex Austria.[24]

The third country whose response was of concern to Hitler was Poland. In theory at least it was conceivable that the government in Warsaw might take some initiative over Danzig at the time Germany had chosen to take action against Austria.[25] In November 1937 Hitler had sought to forestall this, flouting the recommendations of his foreign policy advisers.[26] He had given his consent to a new declaration on the Danzig and minority issues and had instructed Forster to ensure that the city remained calm from January onward so that Berlin could devote all its attention to Austria.[27] In this light we can more readily appreciate the true significance of a section of Hitler's previously cited speech of February 20, 1938. He lavished fulsome praise on the excellent relations between Germany and Poland, apotheosized them as a shining example of dealings between nations, and emphasized how the potentially dangerous Danzig question was now completely stripped of its dangers.[28]

The country which figured most prominently in Hitler's deliberations was Italy. In view of the recent rapprochement between the two countries it appeared very unlikely that Rome would intervene. Precisely because Hitler himself was prepared to accept a total abandonment of South Tyrol, he was in a position to reassure the Italian government on this score. As we shall see, Hitler originally envisaged a lengthy process of annexation for Austria which would last for several months and would allow Rome time to accustom itself to the new conditions rather than being confronted by a fait accompli overnight. Certainly, Hitler could be sure of two things: first, that Mussolini, having committed large numbers of troops to the Spanish Civil War, would on no account intervene mil-

---

24 Weinberg, *1937–1939*, pp. 122f.

25 The Polish government instead utilized the crisis over the Anschluss to take diplomatic action against Lithuania; see ibid., pp. 204–6.

26 Ibid., pp. 196–202.

27 My source for the Hitler–Forster conversation of November 10, 1937, is a report of the American consul-general in Danzig of November 16, 1937, ibid., p. 288.

28 Domarus, *Hitler*, Vol. 1, p. 802.

itarily on behalf of Austria;[29] and second, once Austria's independence
had been terminated, neither Italy nor any other country could restore it
against the will of the Austrian people.

How was the Berlin government planning the annexation of Austria in
practice? As far as we can tell, Hitler had the following scenario in mind.
In the course of the general diplomatic reshuffle, Ambassador von Papen
would be posted to Spain as the right man to replace Eberhard von
Stohrer as envoy to Franco.[30] Von Stohrer for his part was to succeed von
Ribbentrop in London. The vacancy in Vienna left by von Papen was at
first to be filled by Hitler's long-standing political friend Hermann
Kriebel. One of the old guard, Kriebel had as consul general in Shanghai
been involved in Germany's attempts to mediate in the Far East; but now
that that operation had ended, he was free for new duties. In the light of
Kriebel's performance in Munich in the postwar years Hitler must have
felt that he was the right man for the job in Vienna. For reasons we do not
know, Hitler changed his mind and appointed Kriebel head of the personnel and administrative section of the Foreign Ministry the next year.[31]
Gauleiter Albert Forster was then designated for the post of ambassador
in Vienna. A comrade of Hitler in the struggles for power, he had demonstrated his talent for subjugating a territory outside Germany in Danzig, and Hitler could rely on this loyal and unscrupulous henchman to
carry out his orders to the letter. The idea of using the same approach
toward Austria as had been applied to Danzig had been put forward
several times in the past. There was clearly nobody better suited to
performing the second task than the man who had already carried out the
first.

Forster's instructions from the Führer involved ensuring that the local
National Socialists caused havoc for the first few months, until some
extraordinary occurrence in June or July provided the pretext for a putsch
which would radically alter the course of events.[32] Hitler, not at his most
original, initially planned to arrange for the murder of the German military attaché in Vienna, General Wolfgang Muff. But developments took a
different turn from that predicted by Hitler and von Papen remained at
his post in the Austrian capital. He now emerged as a far more suitable
target for assassination. Of course we shall never know, but it is conceivable that a smile passed across Hitler's face when this thought occurred
to him: the murder of von Papen would kill two birds with one stone. Yet

29 John F. Coverdale, *Italian Intervention in the Spanish Civil War* (Princeton, N.J.: Princeton
University Press, 1975).
30 Because von Papen remained In Vienna, von Stohrer was not moved, and the former
German Ambassador in Tokyo, Herbert von Dirksen, was shifted to London.
31 Weinberg, *1937–1939*, p. 46.   32 Ibid., pp. 46f., 288f.

once again developments took a slightly different turn. Von Papen was not assassinated by German agents (the Soviets tried to kill him in Ankara some years later); and in the end Hitler posted another member of the old guard to Vienna: Josef Bürckel, who had proved his worth in the Saarland. This solution, too, had been mentioned earlier.[33]

The detailed planning outlined here had to be abandoned as circumstances changed. But it is worth studying if only because it provides an insight into the thought processes that led to the final decisions. A carefully orchestrated assassination leading to a putsch, and both following a succession of domestic upheavals, would help to prepare the world – first and foremost Italy – for the demise of Austria's independence. As we know from countless remarks of Hitler's, he intended to invade immediately after any assassination, unlike Vienna which had waited for weeks in 1914. The individuals whom he had selected to run the military execution of the operation would have no scruples whatsoever. The members of the old guard who had been assigned the task of supervising the political implementation of the annexation could be relied upon to acquit themselves with ferocious thoroughness. Complete and immediate incorporation in the Third Reich had been envisaged from the very start; in his choice of methods and the people to apply them Hitler could afford to take his cue from the course of events.

These events will not be reviewed here in detail, but it is important to pick out a few specific aspects which were of major significance in terms of the strategy of the German government. Austrian Chancellor Kurt von Schuschnigg, as it later transpired, was in the habit of confiding in his interior minister, Arthur Seyss-Inquart, although the latter – like many National Socialist Party members – promptly relayed any information entrusted to him straight to Berlin. Like the Norwegian fascist leader Vidkun Quisling, who only later lent his name to this form of treachery, Seyss-Inquart pulled the wool over Schuschnigg's eyes at the German government's behest. Consequently Hitler was well informed as to the policies and stances adopted by the Austrian government and was able to plan his strategy of increasing the internal and external pressure on Schuschnigg accordingly.[34] At the Berchtesgaden meeting between Hitler and Schuschnigg, the Führer applied massive pressure on the Austrian chancellor; it was the first time since 1933 that Berlin had threatened another government with military intervention.[35] The concession which Hitler held out to soften the impact of Schuschnigg's enforced capitulation was an undertaking to reiterate in public German recognition of Austria's independence, but this pledge was promptly and

33 Ibid., p. 300.   34 Ibid., pp. 290f.   35 Ibid., pp. 291–93.

unilaterally revoked. The speech on February 20 contains not a single reference to the promised declaration.[36]

It was this breach of the Berchtesgaden agreement that led Schuschnigg to the idea of holding a plebiscite. A ballot in which the people of Austria were to be given even the slightest scope to voice a personal preference was, of course, anathema to Berlin's style of totalitarian government.[37] The German army would occupy Austria, and in the subsequent plebiscite the electorate would be allowed only to vote Yes.

From the course of events that followed, only four specific aspects will be mentioned here. First, Hermann Göring played an important part in the running of the German operation – he had done so on June 30, 1934 – and he was also partly responsible for appeasing the Italians, a subject elaborated below. Second, as we have already seen, the man who had imposed Nazi rule on the Saarland was posted to Austria; and just as the name of the Saarland ceased to exist, so the name of Austria disappeared from the map. Third, Bürckel, the "Scourge of Catholics," was enthusiastically welcomed by Austrian Cardinal Theodor Innitzer, an incredible step given the cardinal's prior behavior.[38] Innitzer issued an appeal to the populace to vote for Hitler – an act which earned Innitzer an extremely angry rebuke from Pope Pius XI, a rebuke about which the Pope informed President Roosevelt through American Ambassador Joseph Kennedy in London.[39]

Fourth, Hitler sought to invest the annexation of Austria with the appearance of legality – as he had done with his seizure of power in Germany. Before the National Socialist plebiscite, on the very day of the annexation, the German government published a bogus request for the assistance of German troops purporting to have been sent by the Austrian government. The logistics of this scheme were considerably facilitated by the fact that the official request – supposedly sent by Seyss-Inquart – was in fact written and made public in Berlin.[40] Since the unification of the German empire in January 1871 had been heralded by an "imperial letter" contrived by means of bribery, it was only logical that the founding

---

36 Domarus, *Hitler*, Vol. 1, pp. 802f.
37 Weinberg, *1937–1939*, pp. 293–96.
38 Herbert Rosenkranz, "Bemerkungen zu neueren Arbeiten über das Problem der Judenverfolgung und des Antisemitismus in Österreich," *Österreich in Geschichte und Literatur* 20/2 (1978); 90f.
39 Weinberg, *1937–1939*, p. 301. At the time of the publication of this document by the American government (1955), Cardinal Pacelli was Pope (Pius XII). It is highly improbable that the Vatican would have agreed to publication without the personal approval of the Pope.
40 Ibid., p. 299. The idea of a fake request for German troops may well have originated with the then state secretary in the German Foreign Ministry, Ernst von Weizsäcker. See the entry for March 10, 1938 in Leonidas E. Hill (ed.), *Die Weizsäcker-Papiere, 1933–1950* (Frankfurt/M: Propyläen, 1974), pp. 122f.

of the "Greater German Reich" should have been accompanied by a similar piece of skullduggery.

Hitler's attempt to invest his annexation of Austria with the trappings of legality was to some extent caused by considerations of foreign policy. Events moved at such a pace that a barrage of lies was required to forestall foreign protest – particularly by the Italian government, which had not been prepared for such precipitate action on Berlin's part. Today it is perhaps easier to understand Hitler's gratitude and relief at Mussolini's acquiescence if we remember that he himself had until only a short time previously planned a rather slower procedure.[41] The annexation effectively put an end to British efforts to bring about a comprehensive settlement of British–German differences; but Berlin did not view this side-effect of the annexation as a drawback – particularly since, as far as we know, not a single official in the German government supported any kind of settlement which might have been acceptable to London.[42]

In terms of foreign policy, the annexation of Austria brought only advantages for Berlin. With the borders of the Third Reich now extending to Hungary and Yugoslavia, it was easier for Germany to exert pressure on these two countries, while at the same time both countries were increasingly drawn into economic dependence on Germany now that Austria was part of the Reich.[43] The annexation of Austria by the Reich was of considerably more far-reaching consequence for Czechoslovakia, which was now even more cut off from the outside world than hitherto and also more vulnerable to a two-pronged German attack.[44] The new resources of manpower acquired by the annexation of Austria would be useful as reinforcements for the planned pincer strategy against Czechoslovakia. Hitler's conciliatory visit to Italy in early May 1938 convinced him that the time was now ripe for the attack on Czechoslovakia.[45] On his return to Berlin, in the second week of May, he made up his mind to carry it out before the end of the year.[46]

Within Germany itself the annexation of Austria proved to be of immediate economic and financial advantage to the regime. But the political advantages were more significant yet. In negative terms the appearance of a major success eliminated any possible misgivings in the armed forces about Hitler's handling of the Blomberg–Fritsch affair. On the positive side, it earned the government a great deal of popularity and trust[47] – although still not enough to generate as much enthusiasm for war among the German populace as Hitler would have wished. He was not to recognize this until the crisis in September.

41 Weinberg, *1937–1939*, p. 299.
42 Ibid., pp. 136–41, 301f.
43 Ibid., pp. 219, 227.
44 Ibid., p. 302.
45 Ibid., pp. 303–12.
46 Ibid., pp. 364–66.
47 Ibid., pp. 302f.

Within what had been Austria the annexation was followed by radical upheavals, but these belong in the domain of internal rather than international affairs. Only one event of the months after March 1938 needs to be mentioned here, because it says a great deal about the self-image of the National Socialists. In November of each year the Nazis paraded through the streets of Munich with Hitler leading the procession. The parade commemorated the Nazis' first abortive attempt to seize power in Germany in 1923. On July 25, 1938, the fourth anniversary of the failed putsch in Vienna, the Austrian Nazis arranged similar rites. In a major speech in Klagenfurt Rudolf Hess expatiated on the marvelous advantages of the annexation of Austria for all concerned and on Hitler's desire for nothing but peace. In Vienna the surviving members of the SS unit 89 marched down the route they had used in 1934 to the Ballhausplatz.[48] On this occasion they could not shoot anybody, but their Führer would soon give them ample opportunity to do so.

48 A photograph of the processional march may be found in Jagschitz, *Der Putsch*, as illustration No. 64; see also ibid., pp. 195f.

8

═══════ • ═══════

GERMANY, MUNICH,
AND APPEASEMENT

The term "appeasement" was originally a term of approval. It had the positive connotation of peaceful change in a world not recovered, and perhaps never to recover, from the ravages of a conflict always referred to either as "the war" or the "Great War," what is now referred to as World War I. It was increasingly believed by both the public and those in government in most European countries that the terrible disaster which that war had been for all European peoples had come about more by inadvertence than design and that assuredly no one would intentionally start once again such a chain of horrors.

If this was one generally held set of beliefs, there was another, more dimly perceived but nevertheless of great significance. The war had started in Europe and had, to a very large extent been fought in Europe and by Europeans, but it had required the participation of non-European states for the Allies to defeat the Central Powers, as Germany and its associates were called. The monument on Parliament Hill in Ottawa to the Canadians who fought at Vimy Ridge, the commemoration by Australia of Anzac Day, the day the Australian and New Zealand Expeditionary Corps landed at Gallipoli; these and other symbols reminded the British government that in a reversal of the prior pattern of British forces struggling with others for the control of territories outside of Europe, on this occasion it had been troops from all over the Empire and Commonwealth that had had to come to the aid of the United Kingdom. Similarly, the French were very much aware of the fact that great numbers of soldiers from their African possessions had fought and died alongside their own soldiers on the battlefields of northern France and would have to be drawn upon in any future effort to defend the country that had

A slightly different version appeared in *Appeasing Fascism: Articles form the Wayne State University Conference on Munich after Fifty Years*, edited by Melvin Small and Otto Feinstein (Lanham, Md.: University Press of America, 1991), pp. 9–18.

suffered the highest percentage of casualties of any of the belligerents in that war. And whether or not everyone recalled that Japan had participated in the war on the side of the Allies, they most assuredly did remember the essential contribution of the United States. That nation, as most Europeans knew in the 1930s, had decided to stop the world and get off; a posture guaranteed to discourage those facing a reviving Germany and to encourage the latter.

It was in this context that the prospect of another war looked not only terrifying but in some sense hopeless to those in charge in England and France in the 1930s. They had scraped through by the skin of their teeth the last time; what were the prospects of doing so again? Were there any conceivable causes for which they could call on their peoples to fight and die once again? They had seen first Russia, then the Ottoman Empire, then Austria-Hungary, then Germany, and – though after the formal ending of the war – finally Italy come apart under the strains of conflict. If they were to summon their own people to take up arms once again, and if they were to have even the slightest hope of any non-European countries participating, the issues would have to be clear not merely to a few initiated observers but to the mass of the population that would be called upon to make the sacrifices a modern war, as recent experience had shown, necessarily involved.

If, therefore, there were outstanding problems in international affairs, surely the best thing to do was to try to solve those differences by peaceful negotiation and adjustments. Whatever the costs and sacrifices involved in such new arrangements, they were almost certainly going to be a great deal less than the costs of another world war, not only for the British and French, but for everybody.

Both Great Britain and France made numerous efforts, sometimes independently of each other and sometimes jointly, but generally in consultation with each other, to try to work out a peaceful accommodation with Hitler's Germany as they had tried to do since 1923 with Weimar Germany. In all of these cases, whatever the specific details and circumstances, their efforts were designed to accommodate Germany within a peaceful Europe that might be changed in some details but would remain essentially the Europe of nation-states that had emerged from the settlements of 1919. There could be this adjustment and that change, and they were prepared to extend those changes to such extra-European issues as colonial possessions and international trade; but just as in 1919 they had not done away with the new German nation-state – in spite of the fact that the appearance of the latest of the great powers had hardly proved a great blessing for the continent – so they were not about to go back to what most of them considered a major cause of the Great War: the suppression of one nationality by another. The issue of Austria's enforced independence was thought by some to lie on the margins of what might or might not be subject to change, but there was no inclination to allow any major reordering of Europe, least of all the unlimited expansion of Germany eastward, which would automatically assure Germany complete domination of the continent.

It was precisely because the German government of the 1930s understood both the hope for peaceful settlement of disputes and the unwillingness of Britain and France to acquiesce in the kind of massive reordering of the continent that Germany intended, that Berlin always waved off the British and French efforts at what was occasionally referred to as a "general settlement." Germany would take advantage of the hopes for peace, but it would do so in a manner designed to prepare the way for war, first against Czechoslovakia, then against England and France. That second war would be the big one; and once it had been won, then Germany could easily and quickly seize from the inferior and disorganized peoples of Eastern Europe, especially the Soviet Union, the vast reaches of *Lebensraum,* living space, that Hitler coveted for his nation. And even while these wars were in preparation and progress, Germany would build the "blue-water" navy, and seize the intended bases for it, so that thereafter she could fight the United States.

As we look back on German policy toward Czechoslovakia in 1938, we can see some aspects of that policy more clearly than in the past. Here it is important first to summarize what recent research on German foreign policy and the outbreak of World War II shows about certain critical questions in regard to the background and nature of the Munich agreement, then to indicate what of the recently revealed information the German government did *not* know about at the time, and finally to describe the lessons which the German government, and particularly Adolf Hitler himself, drew from what others then and since have considered a great German triumph but which he regretted at the time and came to believe was his greatest mistake.[1]

The German government from the beginning contemplated the destruction of Czechoslovakia as a whole. Even those civilian and military officials who argued with Hitler about his plans at the famous "Hossbach Conference" of November 1937 and on subsequent occasions invariably concentrated on the risks, not the merits, of such a policy. The national principle, that is, the belief that a self-defined national minority in a state dominated by people of a different nationality was entitled to a firmly

---

[1] Gerhard L. Weinberg, *The Foreign Policy of Hitler's Germany: Starting World War II, 1937–1939* (Chicago: University of Chicago Press, 1980; Atlantic Highlands, N.J.: Humanities Press, 1994) (cited hereafter as Weinberg, *1937–1939*), pp. 461–62.

anchored system of protection of special rights, was at *no* time a serious concern. The Sudeten Germans were perceived from first to last as instrumentalities which might help Germany in destroying Czechoslovakia, never as people in need of assistance. The noise made by German propaganda and diplomats about the Sudeten Germans was designed to weaken resolution in the West, harden resolve in Germany itself, and provide an excuse for military action at the appropriate moment. It was aimed at the public abroad and at home, designed to obscure rather than to emphasize the real interest of Germany.

The secret instruction which Hitler gave to Konrad Henlein, the leader of the Sudeten Germans, on March 28, 1938, to raise demands of the Prague government which could not possibly be granted, has often been quoted as a clear sign that Hitler did not want an agreement between Germany and Czechoslovakia or between the latter and its German-speaking citizens; what has too frequently been ignored has been the simultaneous instruction given Henlein to use his contacts in England to work for the nonintervention of that country. This portion of Henlein's directives from Berlin points to a war against Czechoslovakia which Hitler already at that time expected to wage but hoped to isolate from any wider conflict – just the opposite of any German interest in international pressure to be exerted on a continuing Czechoslovak state in favor of its Sudeten German citizens.

The literature dealing with Munich has always cited the diary of Alfred Jodl, already a central figure in the military planning of the Third Reich, as a key source for German policy in the spring and summer of 1938 without regard to the fact that the entries for April, May, and June about Hitler's plans are *not* contemporaneous entries at all but are in reality a subsequent reconstruction and insertion, prepared by Jodl himself, almost certainly after July 24, 1938 – by which time a great many things had changed. These reconstructed entries, accordingly, cannot be quoted, as they often are, as proof of what Hitler and his advisors thought on the dates to which they are attributed. Instead these entries reflect the way in which the events were perceived by Jodl weeks and even months later, a distinction of very great importance indeed. Once this fact is recognized, a number of apparent discrepancies in the sources, and the way they have been interpreted, quickly resolve themselves.[2]

We can now accept as correct the accounts of Hitler explaining to the newly appointed German ambassador to Italy, Hans Georg von Mackensen, at the beginning of April 1938 that the Czechoslovak issue would

2 Ibid., p. 337, n. 87, and p. 370, n. 219.

be settled in a few months; his instructions on military planning for General Keitel, the then recently appointed head of the high command of the armed forces and thus Hitler's immediate military assistant, on April 21, instructions which assume the complete and permanent military occupation of Czechoslovakia; and his deduction from his trip to Italy in early May that the attack on Czechoslovakia could come safely in that year.

In his memoirs, German State Secretary Ernst von Weizsäcker carefully omitted passages now to be found in his published papers which deal with this critical point of sequence and causation. The omission was designed to maintain in postwar retrospect the misleading impression that the decision to go to war against Czechoslovakia was reached *after* and as a result of the May Crisis of 1938 – when in reality the decision predated that event and hence cannot be attributed to it. Hitler returned from this Italian visit on May 10 confident that Italy would provide the *diplomatic* support which alone he then wanted, certain of Germany's military headstart over all others, and having been reminded of his own mortality by the fear of cancer which had induced him to write his last will on May 2.[3] His rejection of the contrary position of the chief of staff of the German army, General Ludwig Beck, whose warning against the decision to attack Czechoslovakia that year was presented to Hitler by the new commander-in-chief of the German army on or about May 12, thus reflects quite accurately Hitler's *prior* conclusion that the first of his wars, that against Czechoslovakia, was to be started in 1938.

The crisis on the weekend of May 19–22, 1938, in which rumors of an imminent German invasion of Czechoslovakia precipitated a partial mobilization of reserves inside Czechoslovakia and warnings of possible complications from London to Berlin if Germany did move, can therefore now be seen as playing a role entirely different from that assigned to it by miscellaneous past and present apologists for German policy as well as that ascribed to it by those who still believe in the driven rather than the driving Hitler. The German dictator had already made up his mind to launch an invasion later that year, and he was in fact working on the details of that attack when the weekend crisis temporarily disturbed his planning. The technical implications were promptly taken into account by the German plans for the invasion. The major long-term significance of the crisis was the way in which it may well have misled the government in Prague into believing that it could count permanently on support from

3 Gerhard L. Weinberg (ed.), "Hitler's Private Testament of May 2, 1938," *Journal of Modern History* 27 (1955): 415–19.

England and France, not only in case of a sudden and unprovoked German invasion but also in the face of apparently more limited German demands.

Whatever the reason, the Czechoslovak government failed to seize the diplomatic initiative from a position of strength by offering concessions to the Sudeten Germans, concessions which would have exposed the negotiating strategy of the latter and thereby clarified the real as opposed to the pretended aims of German policy. Instead, the authorities in Prague inadvertently played into German hands by leaving the initiative to Henlein and his masters in Berlin.

The unofficial Anglo–German contacts in the summer of 1938 can now be seen as underlining the rigidity of Hitler's determination for war. The visits to London of Albert Forster, the leader of the Nazis in the Free City of Danzig, and of Fritz Wiedemann, Hitler's military adjutant, left Hitler entirely unmoved; and the warnings about German intentions conveyed to London and Paris by German opponents of Hitler served to confuse rather than enlighten the recipients.

As for the truly critical problem of the potential role of the German armed forces, here too we can now see the issues considerably more clearly. The German air force and the navy presented no problems. Hermann Göring, the commander-in-chief of the air force, was pushing forward as rapidly as possible, conscious of the very risks of a wider war that would make him hesitant in the fall. Admiral Erich Raeder, the commander-in-chief of the navy, exiled to a post of no significance the one high-ranking naval officer who warned against the precipitation of war that year. The new commander-in-chief of the German army, Walther von Brauchitsch, was in a very different position. On the one hand, his chief of staff, General Ludwig Beck, was warning against war, as has already been mentioned, and there were obvious signs of widespread concern on the part of other high-ranking military officers. Von Brauchitsch himself, however, had sold himself and the army to Hitler for financial subventions to enable him to move from his prior into a new marriage; he had promised to open the army wider to National Socialist influence; and as a man without either moral courage or standards could on all occasions be relied upon to defer to Hitler's preferences. His disastrous role in German history has not received the attention it deserves; assuredly his first major action was that of rallying many skeptics within the military hierarchy to Hitler's side in the summer of 1938.[4]

4 A related subject that surely merits research is the connection between Hitler's successful utilization of bribery in the case of von Brauchitsch and earlier instances of such corruption at the highest levels of the German government on the one hand, and Hitler's subsequent

With von Brauchitsch on his side, Hitler could, or thought he could, disregard the more cautious and skeptical within his own government. Very sensitive to what he believed was an extremely poor public relations arrangement by the German government of 1914 in staging Germany's entrance into that war, he now planned to do very much better himself by having incidents staged inside Czechoslovakia to provide an excuse for the invasion. At one time – under the obvious influence of the Sarajevo assassination – he had mentioned the cheerful idea of arranging the murder of the German minister in Prague (as he had once toyed with the idea of having the German ambassador or military attaché in Vienna murdered to excuse the occupation of Austria), but he turned to the German minority inside Czechoslovakia for the staging of incidents instead. As for prospective allies, the parallel policy of Poland, the possibility of closer relations with Japan, and the presumed willingness of Italy to join Germany outweighed the hesitations of Hungary – hesitations which the German government tried hard to overcome and never forgave.

As for the Soviet Union, its role was perceived as negligible in any case, and that country played no significant role in German planning in 1938. In the throes of the great purges, which had begun to affect the Soviet armed forces seriously in 1937, the Soviet Union was busy decapitating its own military mechanism. While the German government knew better than anyone that the charges of collusion with themselves leveled by Stalin's secret police against the leaders of the Red Army were false, they could only rejoice at a double benefit for themselves: the Soviet government would be incapable of any serious projection of military power beyond that country's own borders, and the charges were guaranteed to discourage any and all foreign powers which might think of allying themselves with the Soviet Union against Germany by the prospect of having to deal with Soviet officers who would be shot as German agents the following week. No wonder State Secretary Ernst von Weizsäcker could write: "As long as Stalin makes himself as useful as he is doing at present, we really need not have any special military worries about him."[5]

Startled by Chamberlain's offer to come to Germany, Hitler immediately feared that the war he intended might somehow be averted – that he might by circumstances be forced to settle for what was propagandistically defensible but designed only to shield from Western interference what he actually intended: the destruction of Czechoslovakia. He could not afford the domestic and the international repercussions of

---

extraordinarily extensive secret handing out of huge sums to practically all his highest military, naval, and air commanders during World War II on the other.

5 See the reference in Weinberg, *1937–1939*, p. 190.

refusing to see the British prime minister, but all the evidence shows that a military, not a diplomatic, resolution of the crisis remained his goal. He therefore utilized the interval between his two meetings with the British prime minister at Berchtesgaden and Bad Godesberg for a series of steps designed to avert what he considered the danger of a peaceful settlement. At first this approach appeared to succeed, and he was ready to go to war. Even if the Hungarians were still unwilling to move, the Poles seemed eager to act against Czechoslovakia for a piece of the booty, and his newly organized squad of Sudeten German hoodlums could arrange the incidents he thought necessary as a pretext for war. All appeared to be ready for war when Hitler himself decided to back off.

Not only were most of Hitler's military and diplomatic advisors doubtful because they feared the wider war which they saw developing out of a German invasion of Czechoslovakia, but his own political associates Joseph Goebbels and Hermann Göring had reservations which they expressed to him, and the German public appeared to be unprepared for the ordeal of what seemed likely to be a general war as Britain and France looked more and more certain to intervene rather than stand aside. It would appear that a critical turn came when at the last moment his one prospective major ally – Benito Mussolini – revealed his doubts. With Italian forces in Spain, where the Civil War was still continuing, a hostage to fortune, no direct interest in the question at hand, and some recognition of Italian unpreparedness, Mussolini at the last moment suggested that the diplomatic triumph for Germany implicit in the cession to Germany of the German-inhabited border areas of Czechoslovakia – a cession already agreed to by both the Western Powers and Czechoslovakia itself – would be better for Germany than the all-out war which now seemed to be at hand. As surprised by this latest turn in Italian policy as he had been by Chamberlain's original offer to fly to Germany, Hitler abandoned his plan for immediate war and grudgingly agreed to a settlement by conference at Munich. Trapped to some extent by his own strategy of pretending to be concerned about the fate of the Sudeten Germans, he would settle for what Germany had publicly demanded rather than for the immediate attainment by war of the real aims of German policy.

If this is the way the sequence of events leading up to Munich with a focus on Berlin looks at this time, there were some things either not known or not understood then which can now be clarified. While the Germans recognized that a France still reeling from the enormous casualties and other sacrifices of World War I and preoccupied with the most extreme internal difficulties was reluctant to fight another war for almost any cause, and while Hitler was until the last moment more confident of

French abstention than most of his associates, *no* evidence has come to light of any German knowledge that the French government had informed Prague officially in July 1938 that France would not fight over the Sudeten issue under any circumstances.[6] For once the proverbial sieve in Paris did not leak: what we now know from the published French diplomatic documents had been kept secret from Berlin as successfully as it had been concealed from London – to say nothing of historians of the Munich crisis.[7]

On the other hand, Hitler had not until the last moment, if ever, recognized the real probability that an attack on Czechoslovakia would bring on a general war, because neither he nor his new foreign minister, Joachim von Ribbentrop, understood a key implication of London's perceiving as a *real* issue that which for them was purely a propaganda pretext: the fate of the Sudeten Germans. That implication, of course, was that if the fate of the Sudeten Germans was to be decisively affected by their German cultural identity as contrasted with their formal citizenship, then in London's eyes the Czechs ought to have a fate determined by their most definitely *not* being Germans. In other words, the converse of reluctance to fight on the issue of the Sudeten Germans – if there really were such an issue – was a willingness to fight if the issue were that of a German invasion of Czechoslovakia clearly designed to annex that country's *non-German* inhabitants to the Third Reich.

This divergence of perspective not only contributed to Hitler's last minute reversal of September 28, 1938, when it became evident that an invasion after Czechoslovakia had already agreed to concede the border areas to Germany would precipitate a general war. The difference between the use of alleged nationality grievances as a pretext for expansionist ambitions on the one hand, and the belief that negotiated concessions to improve the degree to which state and nationality lines coincided might promote the peace of all peoples of Europe on the other, also continued after Munich and therefore precluded a German–British accommodation in subsequent years. After the German tearing up of the Munich Agreement in March 1939, the British would not negotiate with the Germans unless they first restored an independent Czechoslovakia, and after the German attack on Poland in 1939 they would not negotiate

---

6 The relevant French documents are cited ibid., p. 398.

7 One can still find accounts which take at face value the assertion that French reluctance to support Czechoslovakia was due to the uncertainty of British assistance, when we now know that the French government deliberately hid behind the reluctance of London and became positively hysterical the moment they learned that the British government was in fact prepared to go to war in case of a German invasion of Czechoslovakia – and that they could therefore no longer pretend to be holding back out of fear of being let down by the British. See ibid., pp. 423, 428.

until both Czechoslovakia and Poland had regained their independence. Since the German government was never willing to give the slightest thought to either of these possibilities, there could be no new Anglo–German agreement: if the nationality issue was a serious one, it had to be one for Czechs or Poles as well as for Germans; if it was a fake, there could be no basis for negotiations. Nothing has come to light to suggest that anyone in Berlin ever grasped this point after Munich.

Upset as he was over having been cheated of war in 1938, Hitler drew four conclusions from this setback to his projects. First, he was more determined than ever that the Czechs must be deprived of their independence; they would be punished rather than rewarded for having given in to the public German demands, thus escaping for a moment the fate Germany actually had in store for them. Second, while such an operation against a helpless Czechoslovakia would not now require a war at all, the doubts about any war among the German public which had surfaced during the 1938 crisis would have to be removed by a deliberate internal propaganda campaign designed to whip up stronger resolution for military action on the home front. Third, Hitler determined that he would now secure his eastern flank for a campaign against the British and French who, he now insisted, had bluffed him out of war in 1938. Fourth, he would in the course of preparing for a campaign in the future not allow himself to be trapped in negotiations again as he believed had happened in 1938.

When Hitler's effort to secure his eastern front for an attack on the West foundered on Poland's unwillingness to subordinate herself to Germany, he accordingly conducted his diplomatic preparations for a preliminary war against Poland in such a manner as to avoid any possibility of a peaceful settlement. There would be no negotiations all summer in 1939 as there had been in 1938; and to prevent any resumption, in the critical final weeks of the crisis in 1939 the German ambassadors in London and Warsaw were recalled from their posts and forbidden to return. This time the creation of incidents which would provide the pretext for war was entrusted, not to the German minority in Poland – the special organization of Sudeten German hoodlums had run out of steam at the last moment – but instead to the newly formed Reich Security Main Office in Berlin under its leader Reinhard Heydrich in person. As for Hitler's one great worry in 1939 – that some SOB would try to arrange a compromise, as he phrased it[8] – he would go to great lengths to avoid that pitfall.

8 On this comment, see Winfried Baumgart, "Zur Ansprache Hitlers vor den Führern der Wehrmacht am 22. August 1939," *Vierteljahrshefte für Zeitgeschichte* 16 (1968): 120–40; 19 (1971): 294–304.

Never again would Hitler change his mind about attacking another country once he had formed and expressed a decision to that effect.[9] The way in which he projected his own weakness onto others, claiming after Munich that his advisors were weaklings because of their warnings – when he himself was the one who had held back rather than test the accuracy of their prediction that an attack would lead to a general war Germany was likely to lose – may well help us to understand why none of his subsequent decisions to initiate hostilities against another country was ever reversed. Circumstances might require postponements, but he was careful not to repeat what he considered a terrible mistake. In the North, the West, the Southeast, the East, and against the United States across the Atlantic; every extension of the war was carried through once Hitler had determined on it.

Germany accordingly drew one country after another into the war, but the conflict took a course Hitler had not anticipated. When looking back over the disastrous development of the war from the ruins of Berlin in February 1945 he tried to discern what had gone wrong; how and where the spectacular ascent of Germany to world domination had been derailed. Munich was the explanation: "I ought to have seized the initiative in 1938" he asserted on February 14, 1945.[10] "We ought to have gone to war in 1938" he repeated a week later.[11] "September 1938 would have been the most favorable date . . . . We ought then and there to have settled our disputes by force of arms." It was all the fault of that "arch capitalist bourgeois, Chamberlain, with his deceptive umbrella in his hand."

Whether this retrospective analysis of Hitler's is correct or not, it is essential for an understanding of German policy from October 1938 until the end of World War II that that country's leader quite consistently held such a view. He drew his conclusions from these alleged "lessons of Munich," and if they differ from those drawn by others, they are not therefore any the less important. On the contrary, they must be assimilated into any examination of subsequent developments if one is ever to understand those events and the impact of Munich upon them.

9 It might be argued that the German project for an invasion of Switzerland in the summer of 1940 constituted the one exception to this rule, but the available evidence on this plan for operation "Christmas Tree" (*Tannenbaum*) does not include any indication of an actual decision by Hitler to go forward with the attack. No precise date was ever set, and hence no postponement took place either.

10 Hugh R. Trevor-Roper (ed.), *The Testament of Adolf Hitler: The Hitler-Bormann Documents February–April 1945* (London: Cassell, 1961), p. 58. It should be noted that some questions have been raised, but not resolved, about the authenticity of this collection of documents, especially by Professor Werner Jochmann of Hamburg. The comments on the Munich crisis in them are consistent with other known utterances of Hitler, but a caveat is in order.

11 Ibid., p. 84.

In his speech of September 26, 1938, Hitler had proclaimed to the world: "Wir wollen gar keine Tschechen," We really don't want any Czechs.[12] As we now know, by that he meant not what most listeners assumed, namely that he wanted only the portion of Czechoslovakia inhabited by Germans, but rather that he expected to seize all of Bohemia and expel its Czech population. As we also now know, the hope of the Sudeten Germans expressed in their slogan: "Heim ins Reich," home into Germany, would also be fulfilled after World War II in a manner few could have anticipated – by their expulsion from Czechoslovakia. As one looks back upon the disasters that those years brought upon both the Czechs and the Germans, it should become increasingly clear that peoples who have difficulties in living side by side would be well advised to beware of even greater tragedies than having unpleasant neighbors that could so easily befall them.

12 Max Domarus (ed.), *Hitler: Reden und Proklamationen, 1932–1945* (Neustadt a.d. Aisch: Verlagsdruckerei Schmidt, 1962), p. 932.

9

A PROPOSED COMPROMISE
OVER DANZIG IN 1939?

Although the general outlines of German–Polish relations in the last year before the outbreak of World War II have been known for some time, a number of important details came to light only slowly, and some of these have never been properly integrated into the generally accepted picture of either the final crisis or the personalities who played major roles in it. As additional documents have been published and some of the archives opened, it has become possible to trace the development of German–Polish relations with increasing precision. One of the problems which needs investigation as new material becomes available is the question of whether and under what conditions either country might have been willing to compromise on any of the issues which arose. The positions actually assumed by the two counties and the outcome of the negotiations will be understandable only when the various possibilities considered during the period from October 1938 to August 1939 have been clarified.

The problems raised in the negotiations ranged from the intended issuance of certain Polish stamps considered offensive by the Germans to the German demand that Poland adhere to the Anti-Comintern Pact. The question raised first and the one most in the public eye at the time and frequently also in retrospect is the issue of Danzig, as it was then called, now Gdansk. This city, together with its environs, had been made a Free City under the protection of the League of Nations by the Treaty of Versailles.[1] By the end of 1938, its status as a territory separate from Germany was still intact. Shortly after Hitler's statement that the Sudetenland portion of Czechoslovakia was Germany's last territorial demand, the Germans on October 24, 1938, asked Poland to agree to the incor-

Revised from the version which appeared originally in the *Journal of Central European Affairs* 14, no. 4 (1955); 334–38.
1 For the relevant provisions of the treaty, together with a summary of developments between 1920 and 1939, see U.S. Department of State, *Foreign Relations of the United States: 1919, The Paris Peace Conference*, Vol. XII (Washington D.C.: Government Printing Office, 1947), pp. 241–62.

poration of Danzig into Germany.[2] Jozef Lipski, the Polish ambassador, immediately warned German Foreign Minister Joachim von Ribbentrop that Poland could not be expected to agree to this, but he acceded to von Ribbentrop's request that he go to Warsaw to discuss the matter with Polish Foreign Minister Jozef Beck.[3]

The instructions which Lipski obtained from Beck for his reply to the German foreign minister contained a lengthy exposition of the Polish attitude toward some of the demands made by von Ribbentrop. The instructions included proposals for a number of technical changes in the status of Danzig but also contained the statement that the "Polish Government must state that . . . any attempt to incorporate the Free City into the Reich, must inevitably lead to a conflict."[4] The term "conflict" in the context of the document did not necessarily mean war, but the implication was still there. Accordingly, when Lipski saw von Ribbentrop again on November 19, he warned the German foreign minister of the danger of an annexation of Danzig for good German–Polish relations.[5] In the subsequent discussions, the Germans nevertheless continued to insist that the Free City must be incorporated into Germany, while the Poles continued to object to this as inadmissible.[6] Was any effort made to find a middle way?

From the available material, there is no evidence to indicate that any thought was ever given by the German government to plans for a possible compromise of the Danzig question. When von Ribbentrop was in War-

2 Lipski to Beck, October 25, 1938, *The Polish White Book* (New York, 1940), No. 44, p. 47; Memorandum of Hewel, *Akten zur deutschen auswärtigen Politik, 1918–1945*, Series D, Vol. V (Baden-Baden: Imprimerie Nationale, 1953), No. 81, p, 88. A cut and doctored version of Hewel's memorandum was published by the German government as No. 197 in *Zweites Weissbuch der deutschen Regierung* (Basel: Birkhäuser, 1940) (cited hereafter as *German White Book*).

3 Lipski appears to have thought at first that Ribbentrop was acting to some extent on his own initiative and without specific instructions from Hitler (Jean Szembek, *Journal 1933–1939* [Paris: Plon, 1952], October 29, 1938, p. 366; November 22, 1938, p.379). This is definitely proved wrong by a document which shows that at that time Hitler discussed the demands being made on Poland with at least one of his ministers (Todt to Ribbentrop, October 27, 1938, *Akten zur deutschen auswärtigen Politik*, Series D, V, No. 86, p.95).

4 Beck to Lipski, October 31, 1938, *Polish White Book* (Basel: Birkhäuser, 1940), No. 45, p. 50. A number of the Polish documents cited in this article, though not this particular one, are printed in Waclaw Jedrzejewicz (ed.), *Diplomat in Berlin, 1933–1939: Papers and Memoirs of Jozef Lipski, Ambassador of Poland* (New York: Columbia University Press, 1968).

5 Lipski to Beck, November 19, 1938, *Polish White Book*, No 46, p. 50; Memorandum of Ribbentrop, November 19, 1938, *Akten zur deutschen auswärtigen Politik*, D, V, No. 101, p. 107. Because German propaganda wanted to associate the Polish attitude on Danzig with the guarantee given Poland by Great Britain more than four months later, the passage containing Lipski's warning and Ribbentrop's answer to it were cut out of Ribbentrop's memorandum as published in the *German White Book* (No. 198).

6 *Polish White Book*, Nos. 47–49, 52, 61–64; Szembek, pp. 385, 404–06, 411, 414–17; *Akten zur deutschen auswärtigen Politik*, D, V, Nos. 112, 119–20, 126; *German White Book*, Nos. 203, 208, 211.

saw at the end of January 1939, an agreement was reached to the effect that Germany and Poland would consult with each other in case the League of Nations withdrew from Danzig, and would respect the status quo until a new arrangement had been agreed upon.[7] This agreement was not considered a compromise solution by the Germans, who continued to demand Polish agreement to the annexation of Danzig.

In the published material there are signs that within the Polish government some thought was given to a possible compromise. Although the proposals considered were never *formally* presented to the Germans by the Polish government, a brief examination of them may help illuminate Polish policy in the last months before the war and indicate some avenues for exploring whatever additional evidence on this period may yet be made available now that the communist regime in Poland has been terminated, the passions surrounding the events of 1939 have abated, and real attempts have been made from both sides to alleviate those attitudes which have poisoned German–Polish relations in the past.

In the period immediately after the Ribbentrop–Lipski conversation of November 19, some consideration was given to the possibility of a compromise on the question of a road across the Corridor which had also been raised by the Germans.[8] It was arranged that Beck should meet Hitler and von Ribbentrop at the beginning of January 1939, while the German foreign minister himself was to visit Warsaw later in the same month.[9] Beck appears to have though that there was some chance of a settlement as a result of these conferences,[10] but he was thoroughly disillusioned by his meetings with Hitler and von Ribbentrop on January 5 and 6, 1939, when the demand for Danzig (and the "Corridor across

---

7 *Polish White Book* Nos. 52–53; Memorandum of Ribbentrop, February 1, 1939, *Akten zur deutschen auswärtigen Politik*, D, V, No. 126 p. 140. See also Szembek, pp. 411–15; Paul Otto Schmidt, *Statist auf diplomatischer Bühne* (Bonn: Athenäum, 1949), pp. 425–427; Bruno Peter Kleist, *Zwischen Hitler und Stalin* (Bonn: Athenäum, 1950), pp. 17–23.

8 Szembek, *Journal 1933–1939*, November 22, 1938, p. 380; December 6, 1938, p. 383; December 7, 1938, p. 385; Memorandum of Hewel, December 15, 1938, *Akten zur deutschen auswärtigen Politik*, D, V, No. 112, pp. 119–20.

9 See the letter of Moltke to Ribbentrop, December 20, 1938, *Akten zur deutschen auswärtigen Politik*, D, V, No. 115, p. 122.

10 See Beck's statement to the under-secretary of state in the Polish Foreign Ministry on December 21 that he had worked out a plan for future conversations with the Germans and had discussed it with Marshal Smigly-Rydz, the inspector general of the Polish army (Szembek, *Journal 1933–1939*, p.396), and his statement to the British ambassador on December 20 that he expected a settlement of the Danzig question by late January 1939 (Kennard to Halifax, December 20, 1938, *Documents on British Foreign Policy, 1919–1939*, Third Series [London: HMSO, 1949–1953] [cited hereafter as *British Documents*] Vol. III, No. 437, p. 439). It should be noted that Beck avoided informing the British about the details of the German-Polish negotiations; the British government did not learn the exact German demands until February 24, 1939, and then from the *German* Ambassador to Poland (Kennard to Halifax, February 24, 1939, *British Documetns*, Vol. IV, No. 144, p. 147).

the Corridor") was made again in imperious tones.[11] After this, Beck did not believe that any basic agreement could be reached when the German foreign minister came to Warsaw later that month, but for the first time he seems to have seriously considered the possibility of a compromise solution of the Danzig question.[12] Sometime in the period between Beck's return from the conversations in Germany and the German occupation of the rest of Czechoslovakia on March 15, 1939, a plan for such a compromise was worked out in the Polish Ministry of Foreign Affairs.

The proposal which was prepared provided that the territory of the Free City would be partitioned between Germany and Poland. According to a report from Sir Howard Kennard, the British ambassador to Poland, the plan specified that "the Poles would have the railway and the western part of the Free City Territory, running up between Oliva and Zoppot with some loop system in Danzig itself and a new canal connection with the Vistula."[13] The existence of such a plan, which had, however, not been officially communicated to the Germans, was confirmed to Kennard by Miroslaw Arciszewski, general secretary of the Polish Foreign Ministry.[14] While even the possibility of such a project being seriously considered by the Polish government at the time has been doubted,[15] it seems inconceivable to me that its existence would have been admitted to the British ambassador had not Beck authorized its preparation.

Although the quoted report is not entirely clear, its general meaning can be derived from a study of the territory involved and the later plan which is referred to below.[16] The railway mentioned must be the Tczew (Dirschau)-Danzig-Zoppot line, which runs through the territory of the Free City from south to north, parallel to and slightly west of the Mottlau River. The rest of the sentence is clearly garbled in some manner because the railway passes through both Oliva and Zoppot, two towns northwest of Danzig. Apparently what is meant is that the western part of the Free City area, including the railway, Oliva, and Zoppot, would go to Poland; while the eastern part, including the city of Danzig itself and about two-thirds of the total area of the Free City, would go to Germany.

11 Szembek, January 8, 1939, pp. 405, 407; January 10, 1939, pp. 407–8.
12 See Under-Secretary of State Szembek's account of his conversation with Beck on January 10, 1939, ibid., pp. 407–8.
13 Kennard to Sargent, June 28, 1939, *British Documetns*, Vol. VI, No. 164, p. 186.
14 Ibid.
15 One of the major scholars who holds a different view is Professor Anna Cienciala; among the publications in which the differences between us are explored is Alexander Korczynski and Tadeusz Swietochowski (eds.), *Poland between Germany and Russia, 1926–1939: The Theory of Two Enemies* (New York: Pilsudski Institute of America, 1975).
16 For the geography of the Free City of Danzig, see Nikolaus Creutzberg, *Atlas der Freien Stadt Danzig* (Danzig: Danziger Verlagsgesellschaft, 1936).

The "loop system in Danzig itself and a new canal connection with the Vistula" probably refers to Polish retention of the Westerplatte, a Polish-controlled area at the mouth of the Dead Vistula, and/or some way of building a branch of the Tczew-Danzig-Zoppot railway line to bypass Danzig. In any case, partition along the general lines indicated would have returned to Germany the major part of both the area and the population of the Free City of Danzig.

The German occupation of the rest of Czechoslovakia on March 15, 1939 – after that country had yielded its German-speaking areas to Germany in October 1938, and had given the Germans permission for the construction of an extraterritorial road across its territory in November 1938 – no doubt deterred the Poles from advancing the compromise plan after Ribbentrop again raised the German demands in his conversation with Lipski on March 21, 1939.[17] The Poles offered to make concessions on the question of transit across the corridor but insisted that Danzig must remain independent.[18] Hitler took this reply as indicating that Poland would not subordinate herself to Germany and decided to attack Poland as a necessary preliminary to his war with the Western Powers, a war for which he wanted to make certain of a subservient row of states on Germany's eastern border.[19]

From the published Italian and German documents it appears that the idea of partitioning Danzig was again raised in August 1939, in the last weeks before the outbreak of war. On August 7, Pietro Arone, Italian ambassador to Poland, reported to Italian Minister of Foreign Affairs Galeazzo Ciano about a partition plan. The outline of the plan as included in the report is essentially identical with the aforementioned one. The territory of the Free City would be divided along the Mottlau River; Danzig itself and the territory between the Mottlau and East Prussia would go to Germany; Poland would acquire the area west of the Mottlau (which would include the railway, Zoppot, and Oliva). Poland would also retain the Westerplatte. According to Arone, the author of the project had contacts with the Polish Ministry of Foreign Affairs; and though there were conflicting reports about the attitude of the Ministry toward him, Arone thought that the plan could be considered a discreet sound-

---

17 *Polish White Book*, No. 61, pp. 61–64; *German White Book*, No. 203, pp. 229–32.
18 *Polish White Book*, No. 62.
19 See Hitler's order cited by the chief of the high command of the German armed forces in a note of April 3, 1939, in Nuremberg document No. C-120, *Trial of the Major War Criminals* (Nuremberg: Tribunal, 1946–48), Vol. 34, p. 381. The whole development is covered in more detail in my book, *The Foreign Policy of Hitler's Germany: Starting World War II, 1937–1939* (Chicago: University of Chicago Press, 1980; Atlantic Highlands, N.J.: Humanities Press, 1994), chs. 12–14.

ing. Arone therefore asked Ciano for permission to continue to investigate this possible compromise.[20] Ciano telegraphed authorization.[21]

In subsequent reports Arone identified the author of the project as Wladyslaw Studnicki and summarized an interview he had given the latter.[22] Studnicki was an old follower of the Polish leader Jozef Pilsudski who had repeatedly been in trouble because of his pro-German attitude. He was strongly anti-Russian, anti-Ukrainian, and anti-Semitic. He favored a policy of collaboration with Germany and had repeatedly urged such a policy on the Polish government in 1939, even recommending that Poland agree to the German annexation of Danzig.[23] Later, when he continued to advocate some cooperative arrangement with Germany even after the German invasion and occupation of Poland, German Minister of Propaganda Joseph Goebbels thought it appropriate to have him committed to a mental institution.[24]

Arone, who evidently did not know that a partition plan had earlier been developed in the Polish Ministry of Foreign Affairs, tried to sound out the attitude of the Polish government to such a proposal at that time.[25] At his request, Monsignor Cortesi, the papal nuncio in Warsaw, hinted at the existence of a compromise proposal to both Beck and Arciszewski. The nuncio's impression was that both were maintaining a reserved attitude without excluding the possibility of negotiating a peaceful solution. He thought that before a compromise of the Danzig question could be effected, it would be necessary to establish whether this would in fact be the last German demand or merely an opening for new ones.[26]

What was the attitude of Germany toward such a proposal in August 1939? According to Arone, the German ambassador to Poland had heard about the plan and could be expected to discuss it with his superiors during his stay in Berlin in the second week of August.[27] No further

20 Arone to Ciano, August 7, 1939, *I documenti diplomatici italiani*, 8th Series (Rome: Libreria dello stato, 1952–1953) (cited hereafter as *Italian Documents*), Vol. XII, No. 794, pp. 592–93. For a detailed discussion of the Italian document publication, see Ferdinand Siebert's review in *Historische Zeitschrift* 176 (1953): 376–90.
21 Ciano to Arone, August 9, 1939, *Italian Documents*, Vol. XIII, No. 816, p. 609.
22 Arone to Ciano, August 10, 1939, ibid., No 822, pp. 613–14; Arone to Ciano, August 18, 1939, ibid., Vol. XIII, No 97, p. 65.
23 Some of Studnicki's suggestions were published by the Germans from captured Polish archives in Werner Frauendienst, "Ein ungehörter Warner," *Monatshefte für Auswärtige Politik* 7 (1940): 5–14. For the general views of Studnicki, see his *Polen im politischen System Europas*, (German) ed. Johannes Maass (Berlin: Mittler, 1936) and *Das östliche Polen*, trans. W. von Harpe (Kitzingen-Main: Hölzner, 1953).
24 Elke Fröhlich (ed.), *Die Tagebücher von Joseph Goebbels: Sämtliche Fragmente*, Part I, Vol. 4 (Munich: Saur, 1987), pp. 38, 41, 50, 52.
25 Arone to Ciano, August 10, 1939, *Italian Documents*, Vol. XII, No. 822. p. 614.
26 Arone to Ciano, August 18, 1939, ibid., Vol. XIII, No. 97, pp. 65–66. Arone commented that Szembek had recently told him the same thing.
27 Arone to Ciano, August 10, 1939, ibid. Vol. XII, No. 823, p. 614.

direct evidence on this aspect of the question is available. On the other hand, there is some interesting indirect evidence on the German position. Studnicki had given Arone a detailed memorandum on the partition proposal; and the latter had sent it to Italian Foreign Minister Count Galeazzo Ciano by special courier to Salzburg, where Ciano was conferring with Hitler and von Ribbentrop from August 11 to 13.[28]

There is nothing in the records of the Salzburg conversations to indicate that Ciano passed on any information about the compromise plan, presumably because the trend of the conversation convinced him that the Germans had already decided on war and that nothing would deter them.[29] He commented in his diary: "The decision to fight is implacable. He [Ribbentrop] rejects any solution which might give satisfaction to Germany and avert the struggle. I am certain that even if the Germans were given more than they ask for they would attack just the same, because they are possessed by the demon of destruction."[30]

In spite of this pessimistic – but accurate – assessment of his German hosts, Ciano forwarded a copy of the proposal he had received from Arone to the Italian ambassador in Berlin with instructions to hand it to the Germans. The ambassador, Bernardo Attolico, was a determined advocate of a peaceful resolution of the crisis – an orientation for which his German hosts would subsequently demand his recall – and gave a copy of the project on August 14 to State Secretary Ernst von Weizsäcker, the second man in the German Foreign Ministry.[31] The latter neither commented on the project to Attolico nor mentioned it in his diary.[32] Perhaps, though, this project was in his mind when on August 19 he endorsed the proposal that in the face of Polish willingness to make concessions in the then noisy dispute over customs inspectors in Danzig, Germany simply keep raising its demands though leaving the responsibility for a final break with Poland.[33]

If one asks the question, What does all this add up to?, the answer

28 Arone to Ciano, August 10, 1939, ibid., Vol. XII, No. 822, p. 613; Arone to Ciano, August 18, 1939, ibid., Vol. XIII, No. 97, p. 65 and n. 2. The memorandum of Studnicki has not been found.
29 The Italian records of the conversations are in ibid., Vol. XIII, Nos. 1, 4, 21; for the German records, see Nuremberg documents PS-1871 and TC-77.
30 Galeazzo Ciano, *The Ciano Diaries, 1939–1943*, ed. Hugh Gibson (Garden City, N.Y., Doubleday, 1946), August 11, 1939, p. 119. For Ciano's statement that Ribbentrop told him outright that Germany wanted war, see ibid., p. 582, and Ernst von Weizsäcker, *Erinnerungen* (Munich: Paul List, 1950), p. 246.
31 Memorandum by Weizsäcker, August 14, 1939, *Akten zur deutschen auswärtigen Politik*, D, 7, No. 58.
32 Leonidas E. Hill (ed.), *Die Weizsäcker-Papiere, 1933–1950* (Frankfurt/M: Propyläen, 1974), p. 158.
33 Weizsäcker to Ribbentrop, August 19, 1939, *Akten zur deutschen auswärtigen Politik*, D, 7, No. 119.

seems to me to be quite clear. Beck's policy of trying to work out some sort of accommodation with Germany had clearly been thwarted by Germany's aggressive insistence on massive concessions after the Munich conference had satisfied the publicly proclaimed final demands of the Third Reich. But Beck was aware of the enormous danger to Poland, and if there were any alternatives to war – short of yielding Poland's independence – he was prepared to explore them. It was, however, the end of Poland's independence that Germany was insisting upon; the demand that the anti-Communist government of Poland join the Anti-Comintern Pact was the most obvious sign of a demand for ritual submission to Berlin.

From the perspective of some in the government in Warsaw, a partition of the territory of the Free City, which would turn over the bulk of the population and territory to Germany but improve the borders of the Corridor and facilitate a direct, entirely Polish, railway connection to the Polish port of Gdynia, could theoretically be made acceptable to a people proud of their regained independence; and it might actually lead to better relations with a difficult neighbor. But from the perspective of those in charge in Germany, this was precisely what was not wanted. Ciano had it right: the Germans wanted not Danzig, but war.

10

———— • ————

THE GERMAN GENERALS AND THE
OUTBREAK OF WAR, 1938–1939

While imprisoned along with other German generals and admirals after
the Second World War, Field Marshal Ritter von Leeb wrote in his diary
on December 10, 1945: "After the experiences of this war, we shall, in view
of the enormous numerical superiority of the English fleet, have to give
priority in a future naval construction program to U-boats, destroyers,
mine layers . . . above all to the strongest naval air arm in order to be able to
search out and destroy the English fleet in its hidden bases."[1]

Here is a conservative and generally moderate German military leader
so fastened to perceptions of a world which had vanished that he quite
automatically assumes that World War II will be followed after an appropriate interval by World War III in which Germany will fight essentially
the same enemies as in the two preceding struggles but will, of course,
attempt to do better by applying the lessons learned in the war that had
just ended.

If one of those whose reputation as a skeptic about National Socialism
was strong enough for him to be rudely retired in the housecleaning of
February 4, 1938, could express himself in the manner quoted after
World War II, it should be easier to understand how completely a new
conflict was thought likely, perhaps assumed inevitable, during World
War I. The great debate about war aims in World War I Germany, which
was almost as heated as the controversy on that subject inaugurated by
Fritz Fischer in the 1960s, had revolved around several issues; but unquestionably one key element had been the anticipation of a later war
against at least some of the same enemies, England in particular, and the

This is a lightly revised version of a talk originally published in Adrian Preston (ed.), *General
Staffs and Diplomacy before the Second World War* (London: Croom Helm and Rowman &
Littlefield, 1978), pp. 24–40.

1 Georg Meyer (ed.), *Generalfeldmarschall Ritter von Leeb: Tagebuchaufzeichnungen und Lagebeurteilungen aus zwei Weltkriegen* (Stuttgart: Deutsche Verlag-Anstalt, 1976) (hereafter cited as
   Leeb Papers), p. 80, n. 195.

need to secure in any peace settlement territories and arrangements that would assure an advantageous starting situation for Germany in the next war. Certainly the discussion about the future of Belgium cannot be understood without regard for this factor.

The war, of course, ended in a manner very different from the expectations of those Germans who had confidently discussed new maps of Europe in the years 1914–18. The peace settlement both limited German military strength and reduced her territory. Of the territorial losses, none was perceived as more horrendous than the losses to Poland. Here was a double indignity. The victors had had the effrontery to reverse Frederick the Great's corridor construction: instead of an east-west corridor connecting Prussia with Brandenburg and separating the main territory of Poland from her port of Danzig, the new settlement established a north-south corridor connecting Poland with the Baltic and separating the main territory of Germany from what had come to be called East Prussia. As if this were not bad enough, the lands Germany had lost were not handed over to a respectable state like Russia, with which Prussia had in the past traded Polish territory in very much the way children trade marbles; but adding insult to injury, the area was turned over to Poles, a group of beings perceived as hardly human, surely undeserving of the proud title of nation, and in any case thought incapable of establishing and running a country.[2]

Although German military activities in the Weimar years were concentrated on the reconstruction of military power, domestic turmoil, and concern about possible foreign attack, there was some military planning that went beyond these preoccupations. The critical priority of all German military leaders after 1919 was the hope for recovery of lands lost to Poland; and the major line of thinking and planning was directed toward that end. The most likely prospect was thought to be a new war between Poland and the Soviet Union which would open the opportunity for joint German–Soviet efforts to make the hated country once again disappear from the map. The more remote possibility was a situation in which assurance of security to France and the worldwide preoccupations of England might free Germany from the danger of a two-front war if she attacked Poland by herself.[3]

---

2 A useful study of German attitudes and images is Harry K. Rosenthal, *German and Pole: National Conflict and Modern Myth* (Gainesville: University Press of Florida, 1976).

3 There is as yet no comprehensive study of German military planning in the Weimar years. The best summary available is in Gaines Post, Jr., *The Civil-Military Fabric of Weimar Foreign Policy* (Princeton, N.J.: Princeton University Press, 1973). Very helpful is Michael Geyer, *Aufrüstung oder Sicherheit: Die Reichswehr in der Krise der Machtpolitik, 1924–1936* (Wiesbaden: Steiner, 1982). Important on the naval side is Carl-Axel Gemzell, *Raeder, Hitler und Skandinavien: Der Kampf für einen maritimen Operationsplan* (Lund: Gleerup, 1965).

Three aspects of this military thought need to be underlined since all played key roles in the perceptions of German generals in the 1930s as in the 1920s. The first, of course, is the fundamental assumption that war would continue to be an accepted instrument of national policy for Germany as well as for other countries. The second was the concern that Germany in the future should avoid a two-front war. Surely every effort had to be made to avoid a situation like that of 1914 where Germany had fought in the East and West simultaneously. It was assumed that if Germany were ever involved in a war in the West, Poland would try to take advantage of the situation to seize additional territory from Germany; but there was at least a slight possibility of a quiescent West if Germany attacked Poland – and if that were seen by all to be the situation, fighting might not be necessary. The third factor was the importance of cooperation with the Soviet Union against Poland, a cooperation that seemed to be based on national interest entirely separate from and independent of the differing social systems of the two countries, and that therefore could be expected to become operative at the appropriate moment whether or not there had been prior formal agreement.

It was into such a framework of assumptions and expectations that the National Socialist regime was subsumed by the leaders of the German army. When Hitler explained to them a few days after assuming the chancellorship that his government would crush democracy, pacifism, and Marxism at home, build up a vast military establishment, and then use the new army for the conquest and Germanization of living space in Eastern Europe, the generals were on the whole not unfavorably impressed.[4] There was not much in Hitler's domestic policies as explained to them to which the military leaders objected: the idea of rebuilding German military might appealed to them greatly, and they associated the idea of conquering living space in the East with the recapture of lands lost to Poland together with perhaps such additional parts of Poland as might be obtainable in the next partition of that degenerate country. It must be recalled in this connection that Prussia had once held substantial Polish territories *beyond* the 1914 border, even if only briefly, and there had been much discussion of the need to annex smaller or larger pieces beyond the 1914 border during the First World War.[5]

In this alignment of the military leaders with Hitler there were several miscalculations, mostly on the side of the soldiers; and it would take

4 See Gerhard L. Weinberg, *The Foreign Policy of Hitler's Germany: Diplomatic Revolution in Europe, 1933–1936* (Chicago: University of Chicago Press, 1970; Atlantic Highlands, N.J.: Humanities Press, 1994), pp. 26–27.
5 On this subject, see Imanuel Geiss, *Der Polnische Grenzstreifen, 1914–1918* (Lübeck/ Hamburg: Matthiesen, 1960).

some of them years to recognize those miscalculations – while the rest never figured them out at all. The first misunderstanding was about the location of the living space in the East that Hitler intended to conquer. While the generals assumed Poland, Hitler wanted such vast stretches that they could only be taken from Russia. Since in Hitler's view, Poland was only a subsidiary element in the picture, he could contemplate and actually sign a temporary agreement with that country – an idea repugnant to his military (and diplomatic) advisers in whose thinking hostility to Poland was a central and fixed, not a minor and subordinate consideration. They could only grit their teeth over the German–Polish agreement of January 1934, but they certainly did not alter their beliefs. (It was not until Hitler decided to attack Russia that they learned that he had not changed *his* beliefs either.)

A second misunderstanding arose from Hitler's attitude toward the Reichswehr. As became dramatically evident in June 1934, Hitler decided to forestall any idea of a politicized party army of the sort Ernst Röhm and some other Sturm-Abteilung leaders preferred by quite literally beheading that organization. The highest leaders of the army were implicated in these murders, prepared to pay the price of criminal complicity for what they imagined was their own and their country's advantage. In reality this was a complete miscalculation. Hitler was in a hurry, needed an army to fight soon, and therefore wanted to keep and use the existing leadership – while looking forward to doing slowly and with precision what Röhm had hoped to accomplish swiftly and with boisterous celebrations. In this regard, as in the closely related sphere of economic and social structure, Hitler's triumph over what *others* perceived as the radicals among the Nazis was in reality the victory of the most extreme radical concepts over ideas of change that were still essentially within a traditional framework.[6] Hitler's preparations for *his* kind of army were quite small in peacetime and only accelerated once war had started; in the meantime he was as voluble in his assurances to the soldiers as to the Poles, and equally sincere.

The appearance of a maintained traditional military structure and leadership served to reconcile the military commanders even if some had qualms about the methods used. The murder of the wife of General von Schleicher caused hardly a stir – in POW camps after the war Field Marshals von Leeb and von List were still hysterical about the shame von Blomberg had allegedly brought on the army by his marriage to a woman

---

6 For a clear statement on the nature of National Socialism and the extreme radicalism of Hitler as opposed to the far less revolutionary character of the National Socialist "left-wing," see Henry A. Turner, Jr., "Fascism and Modernisation," in H. A. Turner (ed.), *Reappraisals of Fascism* (New York: Franklin Watts, 1975), pp. 120–22.

they considered inappropriate for a man in von Blomberg's position.[7] In the early years of the National Socialist regime, therefore, real enthusiasm, cautious professionalism, and determined blindness reigned supreme among the generals. Officers who began by turning their "non-Aryan" comrades out of the army in 1934 would end up by turning their politically compromised comrades over to the hangman ten years later.[8] In the mid-1930s, the first of these processes had been completed, but there were as yet no candidates for the second.

With the one-war contingency that German military men had been concerned about – a war with Poland – temporarily removed from the scene by diplomacy, the build-up of the German armed forces moved forward along lines most of the soldiers favored. There were arguments over the proper speed of expansion as well as over problems of equipment, personnel assignment, and tactical doctrine; but none of this went beyond the usual daily frictions that accompany major change in the size of a military establishment. More severe friction, and friction having a bearing on the contingency of war, would grow out of the conflict over the respective roles of the army general staff and the staff of the war minister and commander-in-chief of the armed forces.

During the years of the Weimar Republic, the problem of how Germany's military forces were to be directed as a whole was never satisfactorily solved, but the issue was not of great importance. The navy had managed to secure considerable independence for itself; and personal continuity on the inside as well as diffidence about naval matters on the outside protected some of this status in the National Socialist period. Personal and political factors performed the same role for the new air force. Hermann Göring was made air minister as well as commander-in-chief of the air force, and his personal closeness to Hitler guaranteed that the air force would be effectively independent of any military command structure below the chief of state himself.

The importance of the independence of the navy and air force will be seen in the impact of the attempt to establish a central, overall command structure upon the relationship between that structure and the command and general staff of the army.[9] As first General Walther von Reichenau and, after October 1, 1935, General Wilhelm Keitel, together with his chief assistant Alfred Jodl, attempted to create an armed forces command structure in the office of the minister of war, there was a direct clash

7 *Leeb Papers*, pp. 78–79.
8 A thoughtful analysis of the application of the "Aryan Paragraph" to the army is in Klaus-Jürgen Müler, *Das Heer und Hitler, Armee und national-sozialistisches Regime 1933–1940* (Stuttgart: Deutsche Verlags-Anstalt, 1969), pp. 78–86.
9 For the best survey, see ibid., ch.5.

between them and the commander-in-chief and the chief-of-staff of the army. Given the independence of the navy and the air force, the developing Armed Forces Office (*Wehrmachtamt*) with its National Defense Section (*Abteilung Landesverteidigung*) threatened to become a sort of competing army general staff at a higher level. In von Reichenau's time, the conflict was muted; but his successors, the team of Keitel and Jodl, moved forward rapidly, enthusiastically, and abrasively.[10]

They not only wanted to assume the role of staff planners for all the armed forces in theory and for the army in practice, but they saw the role of such a staff in a new and different way. The general staff tradition of the Prussian and then German army had insisted on a major advisory role in broad strategic-political matters. The risks to be run, the basic nature of military deployment, and at times even the details of foreign policy had been considered within the proper sphere of general staff advice, if not direction.[11] If there had at times been a tendency, most recently personified by Erich Ludendorff, toward military control of decisions that were properly political, the orientation of Keitel and Jodl was in the opposite direction. Personally fascinated by Hitler and impressed by the dynamism of his movement, they now wanted the military to operate as a purely executive arm of the Führer; they would merely translate his commands as transmitted by the minister of war into formal military directives, the more detailed elaboration of which could then be left to the separate general staffs of the branches of the armed forces. No one along the route, neither they themselves nor most assuredly the staffs of the army, navy, or air force, had any business giving advice about the wisdom or unwisdom of the orders given. If Hitler with the *Führerprinzip*, the leadership principle, had transferred the rule of absolute obedience to superior orders from the infantry company to the political arena, they now wanted it returned to the military establishment at the very top. That in this attempt they would clash with an army leadership insisting on its own responsibility to give advice and weigh risks, and that they would find themselves in full accord with Hitler's preferences, should not be surprising.[12]

When the first outline for a German surprise attack on Czechoslovakia had gone in 1935 from the Armed Forces Office over War Minister von Blomberg's signature to the high command of the army, the army chief-

---

10 The first author to recognize the relationship of this organizational issue to policy questions was Gemzell, but the matter is most clearly discussed by Müller.

11 Gordon Craig, *The Politics of the Prussian Army, 1940–1945* (New York: Oxford University Press, 1956).

12 It should be noted that although there was a short clash between Hitler and Jodl in the autumn of 1942, Keitel and Jodl both retained Hitler's confidence until 1945, a confidence they more than fully reciprocated.

of-staff, General Ludwig Beck, had rejected the whole idea and simply refused to work on it.[13] It was then, and continued to be, his judgment that any such attack would lead to a general war which Germany must lose. In June 1937 the Armed Forces Office once again prepared and von Blomberg issued an over-all plan for the employment of Germany's armed forces, and once again this caused difficulties.[14] Since von Blomberg and his staff had not consulted the army on the basic issue of the risks involved, Beck once again disregarded much of the new directive,[15] and the commander-in-chief of the army, General von Fritsch, went in person to the Armed Forces Office to complain.[16]

The arguments continued through the summer and autumn of 1937. Though he made a friendly visit to Paris in June 1937, Beck thought of France as Germany's most likely and most dangerous enemy.[17] He was, however, opposed to Germany's taking the risk of any war which was likely to become general, and this meant in effect though not in theory to practically any war started by Germany at all. The problem of those risks and the probability of incurring them was, of course, in the background of the controversy as Keitel and Jodl argued for their position of unquestioning implementation of whatever inspiration the leader of Germany might pass on to his soldiers. While the argument among the latter over command structure was still in progress, Hitler summoned the highest figures in the Reich to a conference at which he voiced the inspirations he wanted implemented.

When Hitler met the minister of war, the foreign minister, and the chiefs of the three branches of the armed forces on November 5, 1937, he gave his assessment of the current situation and his plans for the future as far as he cared to reveal them.[18] Germany, he asserted, needed space for her population which could not be fed from her present space. Dependence on world trade would not do; it limited independence and

13 Weinberg, *Foreign Policy, 1933–1936*, p. 224.
14 The "Weisung 1937/38" of June 1937 is in International Military Tribunal, *Trial of the Major War Criminals* (Nuremberg: IMT, 1946–48) (hereafter cited as *TMWC*), Vol. 34, 733–45.
15 Wolfgang Foerster, *Ein General kämpft gegen den Krieg: Aus den nachgelassenen Papieren des Generalstabschefs Ludwig Beck* (Munich: Münchener-Dom Verlag, 1949), p. 63.
16 Nuremberg document 1781-PS, National Archives.
17 On Beck's visit to Paris, see Müller, *Das Heer und Hitler*, pp. 634–5; Foerster, *Ein General kämpft gegen den Krieg*, pp. 47–49, Hans Speidel (ed.), *Ludwig Beck, Studien* (Stuttgart: K. F. Koehler, 1955), pp. 295–302.
18 The memorandum of Friedrich Hossbach on the meeting is printed in *Documents on German Foreign Policy, 1918–1945*, Series D, No. 19, and in *TMWC*, Vol. 25, 403–13; a supplementary statement by Hossbach is in *TMWC*, Vol. 42, 222–30. An important source is Hossbach's memoirs, *Zwischen Wehrmacht und Hitler* (Wolfenbüttel: Wolfenbütteler Verlagsanstalt, 1949). For a full and final authentication of the text, see Bradley F. Smith, "Die Überlieferung der Hossbach-Niederschrift im Lichte neuer Quellen," *Vierteljahrshefte für Zeitgeschichte* 38 (1990), 329–36.

was in any case dubious in a world in which all countries were indus-
trializing.[19] Germany would have to expand by seizing agriculturally useful land. This would involve war, and Germany had to decide where to
seize the most with the least risk. Force alone could solve Germany's
problem, and the only questions to be answered were "where and how?"

In his discussion of the possible answers to these questions, Hitler
threw together two types of consideration: the short-term one of "im-
proving our military-political situation," which required the conquest of
Austria and Czechoslovakia, and the long-term one of "solving the German space problem." The short-term task would help with the bigger
one: troops freed by better borders and the additional divisions recruited
in the annexed territories as well as the economic resources of the seized
lands would strengthen Germany for its subsequent war.

Hitler argued that the effort to reach the long-term goal would have to
be launched by 1943–45. Thereafter the odds would shift against Germany; but the short-term goal might be reached much earlier, and Hitler
gave a great deal of attention to the prospects for that. In the discussion
which followed, von Blomberg and von Fritsch argued that Britain and
France might not stay out of a war Germany started in Central Europe,
and that Germany was not ready to face them. Von Neurath expressed
doubts about Hitler's expectation of a war between Italy and the Western
Powers in the Mediterranean. Hitler maintained his own position; but
when von Fritsch suggested that in view of what had been said he ought
not to go through with intended leave, Hitler responded that the probability of war was not that close.

No one argued at the meeting with the Führer's long-term aims. With
his short-term aims, no one argued either; all the objections dealt with
his calculations as to the risks involved. What Beck in his subsequent
analysis of the record of this meeting, as well as von Blomberg, von
Fritsch, and von Neurath, criticized was the assessment by Hitler that
England and France would stay out of a war Germany might start in
Central Europe.[20] Beck, furthermore, was appalled at the whole line of
reasoning which led Hitler to conclude that war was necessary, but this
view was not shared by any of those present.[21]

There have been efforts to interpret away the record of this meeting or
to pretend that Hitler's comments were unimportant or meaningless.

19 This was an old theme of Hitler's; see Gerhard L. Weinberg (ed.), *Hitlers zweites Buch*
    (Stuttgart: Deutsche Verlags-Anstalt, 1961), p. 60 n. 1.
20 Beck was shown the memorandum by Hossbach since he was acting in von Fritsch's place
    during the latter's leave. Beck's memorandum is in Bundesarchiv, H 08-28/4, item 52.
21 Admiral Raeder said nothing in the first part of the meeting of November 5. Since his
    memoirs and his testimony at Nürnberg are wholly unreliable, one can only assume that he
    was – as usual – in general agreement with Hitler.

Such efforts are irrelevant for understanding German military planning since none of those present at the meeting or immediately informed of Hitler's wishes could possibly know that there ever would be such a literature; they were too busy trying to carry out what they took to be the dictator's orders.

Göring immediately gave some new directives to the general staff of the air force. A new general construction plan for the navy reflecting the decisions of November 5 took a few weeks to prepare; it was issued on December 21.[22] Both to assure a uniform approach by all branches of the armed forces – when each was working on its own implementing procedures – and in accordance with their concept of the military being purely an instrument and never an adviser of the political leader, Keitel and Jodl now prepared a supplement to the general war directive of June 24.[23] Von Blomberg's agreement to this approach, in spite of his reservations at the November 5 meeting, may well have been caused by his eagerness to utilize an expression of Hitler's will to override all objections in the high command of the army to such general directives. They might object to them when issued on von Blomberg's own authority; once the revision of his order had been approved by Hitler, it could not be resisted without an open break with the Führer himself.[24] The revision was accordingly prepared in the Armed Forces Office, approved by Hitler, and issued like the navy's new program on December 21, 1937.[25]

The prior directive of June had left open the possibility of "military exploitation of politically favorable opportunities"; the new formulation called for an "aggressive war against Czechoslovakia." Hitler had picked his immediate goal and alerted his generals, but he would move forward as opportunity offered.

While Hitler watched for opportunities, and nudged the process a bit too, the occasion to make drastic changes among his military and diplomatic advisers arose, with at least some help from Hitler himself, early in 1938. On January 12 the German minister of war and commander-in-chief of the armed forces, Field Marshal Werner von Blomberg, married a young woman who turned out to have a record of moral offenses. Hitler seized the opportunity to rid himself of a whole series of generals and diplomats and to take over the position of commander-in-chief of the armed forces himself. The details of what has come to be known as the

22 Jost Dülffer, *Weimar, Hitler und die Marine: Reichspolitik und Flottenbau 1920–1939* (Düsseldorf: Droste, 1973), p. 455.
23 Müller, *Das Heer und Hitler*, pp. 246–47.
24 This probably explains the absence of a reaction by Beck; he was not yet psychologically ready for an open break with Hitler.
25 *TMWC*, Vol. 28, 356, 745–47; *Documents on German Foreign Policy*, D, 7, 547–51.

Fritsch-Blomberg crisis need not be recounted here, but one aspect of it would have a most important bearing on the situation of Germany's military leadership: the succession at the top.[26]

Almost as soon as von Blomberg's "fault" was called to Hitler's attention, and before anyone had an opportunity to discuss the matter with him, he decided to dismiss von Blomberg and also to use trumped-up charges of homosexuality, that he knew to be false, to dismiss von Fritsch as commander-in-chief of the army. What has often been ignored in the literature on this crisis is that Hitler was perfectly willing to tolerate in his associates and officials all sorts of defects far more serious than the real or imagined ones of the two general officers, and that the man appointed to succeed one of them was known by Hitler to be vulnerable to questions about *his* marriage.

If Hitler acted so quickly in the cases of von Blomberg and von Fritsch, therefore, it makes no sense to attribute those hurried actions to the Führer's disappointment in von Blomberg or his initial belief in the charges against von Fritsch. Quite the contrary, Hitler promptly utilized what looked like wonderful excuses to get rid of these two under circumstances almost guaranteed to weaken any independence left to the military and to strengthen his own position. The peculiar advantage of the supposed faults of the two generals, from Hitler's point of view, was that a strong reaction from the army leadership was practically precluded as long as the sordid circumstances of the whole operation could be kept concealed, a problem Hitler dealt with by arranging for a succession with a vested interest in keeping it concealed. Before the succession is examined, some further aspects of the dismissals must be mentioned.

Von Blomberg's marriage left him without support from his colleagues; he had enjoyed little enough before because he was seen as an advocate of National Socialist influence in the army. In any case, as a devoted admirer of Hitler, he could be depended upon to go quietly. Von Fritsch, though not uncritical, was equally unwilling to do anything himself or to encourage those among the military who were inclined to act forcefully on behalf of a leader they admired and in whose downfall they sensed, even before they fully understood, a foul maneuver. In October 1926, when General Hans von Seeckt had been removed quite legally from a position equivalent to the one von Fritsch held now, the latter, then a lieutenant-colonel, had urged von Seeckt to use force against the govern-

26 Müller, *Das Heer und Hitler*, ch. 6, is useful, but the author has been misled by too narrow a focus on the details without proper regard for the general pattern of Hitler's conduct. The account of Harold C. Deutsch, *Hitler and His Generals: The Hidden Crisis, January–June 1938* (Minneapolis: University of Minnesota Press, 1974), is both the most detailed and the most reliable.

ment of the Weimar Republic in order to maintain himself in office.[27] He would not move himself now. In a way, von Fritsch continued to believe in Hitler as he had never been willing to support the Republic.

Given this loyalty to Hitler of the men removed, why did he drop them? It is too often forgotten that von Blomberg had not originally been chosen by Hitler himself, but by President Paul von Hindenburg.[28] Though the appointment had been acceptable to Hitler, and though von Blomberg had proved himself a willing and capable instrument of Hitler's will, he retained some independence, a quality he had shown in the conference of November 5. Von Fritsch was even more obviously a man out of tune with Hitler's preferences. Like von Blomberg, he had been the choice of von Hindenburg when Hitler and von Blomberg himself would have preferred to appoint von Reichenau.[29] Unlike von Blomberg, he had demonstrated a certain rigidity in resisting accommodation to the regime, and this had been recalled to Hitler not only on November 5 but also at a subsequent meeting of von Fritsch with Hitler on November 9.[30] Now that Hitler felt ready to begin implementing the aggressive policies he intended to pursue, he wanted not just willing instruments but totally dependent and pliant tools.

This raises the key issue of the succession to von Blomberg and von Fritsch. Hitler decided to take the position of commander-in-chief of the armed forces himself and to use as his staff in that capacity the staff Keitel had been building up.[31] Hitler's daily contacts with Keitel during the crisis convinced him that here was a man he could depend on, a judgment that correctly assessed an officer who would remain in the same position until 1945. In this case, as in so many others, Hitler displayed an almost uncanny ability to sense the presence (or absence) of absolute devotion to himself. As a replacement for von Fritsch Hitler wanted to appoint his favorite among the generals, Walther von Reichenau. Keitel managed to dissuade Hitler by pointing to von Reichenau's failings in the one and only field where Keitel could detect mortal sin: von Reichenau was neither hard working nor thorough. Furthermore, Keitel – whose objections to von Reichenau were supported for entirely different reasons by others – had a candidate who was likely to meet Hitler's needs even if Hitler did not know him well as yet.

Walther von Brauchitsch was technically competent, had enough seniority to calm the army leadership, and was politically pliable. Before

27 Friedrich von Rabenau, *Seeckt: Aus seinem Leben, 1918–1936* (Leipzig: Hase and Koehler, 1940), p. 536.
28 Müller, *Das Heer und Hitler*, pp. 49–50; Deutsch, *Hitler and His Generals*, pp. 8–10.
29 Deutsch, *Hitler and His Generals*, pp. 11–13.
30 Ibid., pp. 29–30, 71, 74–75.   31 Ibid., p. 119.

receiving the appointment – which a man of minimal decency would have refused except on an acting basis at a time when the charges against von Fritsch were still to be tried – von Brauchitsch had to promise to bring the army "closer to the state and its ideology"; to make a host of personnel changes, and a string of other concessions.[32]

Hitler was quickly, and correctly, convinced that in von Brauchitsch he had found the man he needed. Here was an individual so hopelessly compromised that Hitler would always be able to bend him to his will. About to resign from the army because of marital problems when the big prize dangled before his eyes, von Brauchitsch needed and received the assurance of financial support from Hitler to enable him to get out of his first into a second marriage.[33] If the dependence on Hitler created by this secret subvention was not enough, the new commander-in-chief of the army turned out to be an anatomical marvel, a man totally without a backbone, who would be the despair of all who hoped for some sign of strength and leadership from him in the crisis ahead. In the critical years when Hitler wanted to attack Czechoslovakia, when he attacked Poland, and when he expanded the war in the North, the West, and the Southeast, and finally the East, the commander-in-chief of the German army was a slavish servant of the Führer. Here is perhaps the single most important factor in the internal German military situation before the war and during its critical first years.[34]

An instructive comparison might be made between King Edward VIII and von Brauchitsch: to marry the woman he loved one gave up his throne, the other sold his soul to the devil. And on the installment plan. The down-payment had been a condition of von Brauchitsch's initial appointment and has already been discussed, but there were to be further installments, more or less parallel to the monthly payments to von Brauchitsch's now divorced first wife. As Hitler diverted attention from the domestic crisis to foreign affairs by speeding up the annexation of Austria, he did *not* have to worry about the army; with no danger of foreign intervention, even Beck was quite willing to throw together a quick plan for the occupation of that country. As Hitler moved toward war on Czechoslovakia, however, the situation changed.

Although the work on new draft directives for the German army in

---

32 Müller, *Das Heer und Hitler*, pp. 263–64. For an example of how the promise of von Brauchitsch to dismiss inconvenient generals was implemented, see *Leeb Papers*, pp. 41–42.
33 Deutsch, *Hitler and His Generals*, ch. 7, has a full account. I am indebted to Professor Deutsch for personal explanations supplementing his book.
34 See Hildegard von Kotze (ed.), *Heeresadjutant bei Hitler, 1938–1943: Aufzeichnungen des Majors Engel* (Stuttgart: Deutsche Verlags-Anstalt, 1974), March 28, 1938, p. 19; October 18, 1938, p. 42; and August 20, 1941, pp. 109–10, where Hitler berated von Brauchitsch about his marriage problems in front of subordinate officers.

early May 1938 was deliberately kept secret from the army general staff,[35] there was enough discussion of the intent to attack within the highest levels of the German government to alert Beck.[36] On May 7 he handed von Brauchitsch a memorandum for Hitler arguing that an attack on Czechoslovakia would start a general war that Germany must lose and accurately predicting the strategy Britain and France would follow.[37] Von Brauchitsch took this to Keitel before showing it to Hitler; and since Keitel was actually working on new plans for an attack on Czechoslovakia on Hitler's instructions, he advised von Brauchitsch to present only the strictly military portion of Beck's memorandum to Hitler.[38] Von Brauchitsch followed this advice when he saw Hitler on or about May 12. Hitler rejected all Beck's views; he was himself already determined to attack Czechoslovakia that year and was confident that there would be an isolated war in which the Western Powers would not intervene.[39] Later that month, he explained his views to this effect to an assemblage of military leaders.

The difference in assessment between Hitler and many of the generals would continue from early May to late September 1938. Hitler operated on the assumption that extensive construction and noise about the construction of fortifications in the West would isolate Czechoslovakia militarily, while propaganda about the Sudeten Germans would isolate her diplomatically so that there could be a localized war. A number of the generals were skeptical about the military adequacy of the former and the political adequacy of the latter procedure. In the event, neither was put to the test.[40]

The errors both in Hitler's political calculation of an isolated war and in the tactical directives for such an operation were pointed out by Beck in several memoranda.[41] The attempt to enlist von Brauchitsch in holding Hitler back failed completely; when Hitler needed his new minion to

35 Walter Görlitz (ed.), *Generalfeldmarschall Keitel: Verbrecher oder Offizier?* (Göttingen: Musterschmidt, 1961) (hereafter cited as *Keitel Papers*), p. 183; Müller, *Das Heer und Hitler*, p. 300.
36 Müller, *Das Heer und Hitler*, p. 301; *TMWC*, Vol. 37, 443–60.
37 Müller, *Das Heer und Hitler*, pp. 302–5; Foerster, *Ein General kämpft gegen den Krieg*, pp. 81–87.
38 *Keitel Papers*, p. 184.
39 The events in April–May 1938 are reviewed in Gerhard L. Weinberg, *The Foreign Policy of Hitler's Germany: Starting World War II, 1937–1939* (Chicago: University of Chicago Press, 1980; Atlantic Highlands, N.J.: Humanities Press, 1994), chap. 10.
40 As for the fortifications, Hitler simply transferred control of that work to his favorite builder of the day, Fritz Todt. In September, he would boast about the great accomplishments in this regard in public right after he had been warned privately of their inadequacy by General Wilhelm Adam.
41 The text of the May 29 memorandum is in Bundesarchiv, H 08-28/3, parts published in Foerster, *Ein General kämpft gegen den Krieg*, pp. 90–94; cf. Müller, *Das Heer und Hitler*, pp. 309–13. The June 3 memorandum is in Müller, pp. 651–54.

restore confidence in himself among the generals after the foul treatment accorded the revered von Fritsch and also to rally them for the projected war against Czechoslovakia, von Brauchitsch readily complied. At the meeting of Hitler and von Brauchitsch with many of the generals on June 13, von Brauchitsch told those assembled of the forthcoming attack on Czechoslovakia, with which he fully identified himself, as an introduction to Hitler's presentation of a carefully doctored account of the Fritsch case.[42] Having thus expressed his own support for Hitler's handling of both the internal and the foreign policy issues facing the regime, von Brauchitsch turned a deaf ear to Beck's further pleadings. Instead of the general strike of the generals that Beck recommended, these efforts merely led to Beck's own resignation.[43] As Sir Lewis Namier has commented, "Sense, courage, and character cannot be transmitted from him who has them to him who has not."[44] If von Brauchitsch sided with Hitler out of a combination of cowardice and inclination, Keitel and Jodl took the same view out of enthusiastic conviction.[45]

In these circumstances, military planning for the attack on Czechoslovakia went forward. If Hitler had his ideas for isolating the war, some of his generals had theirs for preventing it. They would urge the British to remain firm, operating on the widely held view of the time that a clear British warning might have averted war in 1914. On the other hand, they also prepared a coup against Hitler if he ordered the attack all the same. The details of these contacts and projects cannot be reviewed here.[46] Four aspects are, however, important for our understanding of the German generals in the face of a possible war. First, the whole idea of a war against and about Czechoslovakia, and one in which Poland might even be on Germany's side, was entirely outside the military tradition of the Prussian and German general staff.[47] Second, there was a widely held view, shared by the new chief of staff of the army, General Franz Halder, that a general war would develop out of any German attack on Czechoslovakia; that such a general war would see the reconstitution of the world alliance against Germany of World War I – including eventually the United States and the Soviet Union – and that Germany was certain to lose such

42 Deutsch, *Hitler and His Generals*, pp. 401–6.
43 Müller, *Das Heer und Hitler*, pp. 317–33.
44 *In the Nazi Era* (London: Macmillan, 1952), p. 32.
45 Note Jodl's comment in his diary, *TMWC*, Vol. 28, 373.
46 There is an account in Müller, *Das Heer und Hitler*, ch. 8. Professor Deutsch is preparing a volume devoted to the subject. It is treated in ch. 11 of Weinberg, *Foreign Policy 1937–1939*.
47 Fighting in Bohemia in the Napoleonic and the German civil wars was always a part of wider conflicts, with the location a purely coincidental element. In the Weimar years, concern about Czechoslovakia was always subsidiary to worries about France and Poland; see, in addition to the book by Post, F. Gregory Campbell, *Confrontation in Central Europe: Weimar Germany and Czechoslovakia* (Chicago: University of Chicago Press, 1975).

a war. Third, that if Hitler was warned of this contingency by both his military advisers and the British, he might desist from ordering the attack; but fourth, that if he ordered it anyway in the face of such warnings, an attempt to overthrow his government should be prepared.

In the final evolution of the crisis over Czechoslovakia, in the face of a British warning delivered at the last moment, in view of clear signs of a reluctant German public, and with Mussolini urging a conference, Hitler backed off, settling at the Munich Conference for his ostensible and propagandistically defensible rather than his real aims.

Speculation on what would have happened had Hitler gone forward with the order to attack Czechoslovakia is not especially profitable; my reading of the evidence suggests that Britain and France would have gone to war but that in the face of von Brauchitsch's dubious position,[48] the planned coup either would have been called off or would have misfired. More important than such theoretical constructs are the real effects of the September crisis on Hitler and his generals. Hitler had backed down; he not only regretted having done so to the last days of his life, but in the immediately following months combined a projection of the show of weakness on his own part with a determination to avoid any repetition.

The first of these was simple enough: he would berate those military and diplomatic advisers who had warned of a general war for showing a despicable and unwarranted weakness of will. Not a single one among them appears to have mustered the nerve to respond that it was Hitler who had backed down and funked putting their dire predictions to the test of action. On the contrary, in their relief over the avoidance of the predicted disasters, they meekly accepted the charge of cowardice and resolved not to expose themselves to such charges next time.

Since Hitler was determined not to be cheated out of a war, that next time was not to be long in coming. He assured a group of high-ranking officers to this effect on February 10, 1939,[49] and discussed the whole subject at length in his famous talk to the generals on May 23.[50] In that speech he also alluded to the two points which, combined with von Brauchitsch's subservience and the distorted impressions of the 1938 crisis, would make the generals willing to move without much question

---

48 Professor Deutsch speculates that von Brauchitsch would "conceivably" have gone along with a coup: *The Conspiracy against Hitler in the Twilight War* (Minneapolis: University of Minnesota Press, 1968), p. 38. On the general problem of the diffidence of the opposition to Hitler, George K. Romoser's article, "The Politics of Uncertainty: The German Resistance Movement," *Social Research* 31, no.1 (Spring, 1964): 73–93, is still very useful.

49 Helmut Krausnick and Harold C. Deutsch (eds.), *Helmuth Grosscurth: Tagebücher eines Abwehroffiziers 1938–1940* (Stuttgart: Deutsche Verlags-Anstalt, 1970), p. 166.

50 *Documents on German Foreign Policy*, D 6, No. 433.

and even with a little enthusiasm in 1939. In the first place, the enemy now was to be Poland. Here was a country that deserved invasion; as Quartermaster-General Eduard Wagner – who would commit suicide in July 1944 lest he betray the names of associates in the July 20 plot – wrote to his wife on August 31, 1939: "wir freuen uns offen gestanden darauf" – we admit to looking forward to it gladly.[51] Secondly, Hitler hinted at a possible agreement with the Soviet Union.[52] Here was a perspective that to the highest military leaders of Germany looked positively dazzling: Hitler coming back after five years to the very view they had held since 1920, namely cooperation with Russia to destroy Poland, and all this with the lovely prospect of a one-front war.

It is in this context that one must, in my judgment, examine the reaction of most German generals to Hitler's explanation to them on August 22 not only of his decision to attack Poland after signing an agreement with the Soviet Union, but his determination not to allow a repetition of 1938 under any circumstances.[53] Those present were clear in their own minds – even if some pretended otherwise under oath later – that Hitler wanted war.[54]

The ever faithful von Brauchitsch would not even reply to a warning letter from Beck;[55] Halder agreed to see his predecessor, but would not budge either.[56] That General George Thomas's last-minute attempts to discourage *his* superior, General Keitel, would produce no effect on that devotee of the Führer will surprise no one.[57] Only within the Abwehr, the military intelligence apparatus, were there doubts; the critical command positions in the German army, however, were filled by men who were either satisfied with the developments or not sufficiently worried to do anything other than play their part in launching the war that would destroy so much. They were not all as confident as Hitler that the West would stay out,[58] though the evidence suggests that Hitler was himself

---

51 Elisabeth Wagner (ed.), *Der Generalquartiermeister* (Munich: Olzog, 1963) (hereafter cited as *Wagner Papers*), p. 109.

52 The author has reviewed this subject in *Germany and the Soviet Union, 1939–1941* (Leyden: Brill, 1954 and 1972), chs. 2–4.

53 Wagner, ironically, thought that this might be possible: first an agreement truncating Poland under German threats, and then a second stage in the spring of 1940 when Germany and the Soviet Union would jointly crush the remaining Polish state: Wagner diary, August 29, 1939, *Wagner Papers*, p. 105.

54 See von Leeb's October 3, 1939, diary entry on a conversation with von Brauchitsch: "We soldiers know from the conference at the Obersalzberg that Hitler wanted this war." *Leeb Papers*, p. 184.

55 Hans Bernd Gisevius, *Bis zum bittern Ende* (Zurich: Fretz and Wasmuth, 1946), 2, 116.

56 Ibid., p. 117.

57 An account is included in Thomas's short memoirs, "Gedanken und Ereignisse," *Schweizer Monatshefte* (25 December 1945): 537–58.

58 Note Wagner diary for August 24, 1939 *(Wagner Papers*, p. 93) with its report on Halder's talk to the staff officers stressing that it was Hitler who did not believe that the attack on Poland would lead to a two-front war.

fully prepared to risk Western intervention at the end; but eagerness for war on Poland and relief over the agreement with Russia were strong enough to still most doubts. There was no German public rejoicing in September 1939 to match that of August 1914, but the *Burgfrieden*, the harmony within, that had quieted political debate in 1914 did indeed return, if only for a short time, to the one place where it counted in the Germany of 1939: the high command of the German army.

11

———— • ————

HITLER'S DECISION FOR WAR

If one compares the publications on the beginning of World War II with the vast literature on the outbreak of war in 1914, a significant difference immediately becomes apparent. A substantial proportion of the latter works concerns itself with questions of detail about the various mobilization measurers and declarations of war in 1914 and attempts to arrive at a most precise reconstruction of the course of events at the time. With very few exceptions, there is nothing similar in the literature about 1939.[1]

This difference is easy to explain. The interest in the most minute details of the crisis of July 1914 is connected with the controversy over the responsibility for the outbreak of the First World War; there is, on the other hand, no sensible person who today disputes the fact that the Third Reich initiated World War II. There are, nevertheless, details of the developments of August 1939 which merit closer examination because they spotlight important aspects of German foreign policy at the time.

It is generally known that the German government in 1939 arranged a number of measures in order to surprise Poland while simultaneously blaming the Poles for the outbreak of war. The quiet, publicly unannounced mobilization, now described in detail in the first part of the fifth volume of the series "Germany in the Second World War"[2] was expected to contribute to the element of surprise, while the provocative incidents fabricated on German soil at the Gleiwitz radio station and near the

This is a revised translation of a short paper delivered at the international conference in Berlin on the fiftieth anniversary of the German attack on Poland which began World War II. It was published in Klaus Hildebrand et al. (eds.), *An der Schwelle zum Weltkrieg: Die Entfesselung des Zweiten Weltkrieges und das internationale System* (Berlin: de Gruyter, 1992), pp. 31–36.

1 The first attempt at a systematic reconstruction was that of Lewis B. Namier, *Diplomatic Prelude, 1938–1939* (London: Macmillan, 1947). Still important, and providing the title for the conference in August 1989, at which this paper was given: Walther Hofer, *Die Entfesselung des Zweiten Weltkrieges, Darstellung und Dokumente*, rev. ed. (Düsseldorf: Droste, 1984).
2 Militärgeschichtliches Forschungsamt, *Das Deutsche Reich und der Zweite Weltkrieg*, Vol. 5/1 (Stuttgart: Deutsche Verlags-Anstalt, 1988), pp. 364–69, 707–58.

villages of Hochlinden and Pitschen were supposed to prove that it was the Poles who had attacked Germany.[3]

Here two other matters of detail in regard to the German timing of the attack on Poland will be examined because they provide important insights into the foreign policy of Nazi Germany. After Hitler had withdrawn the original order for the attack on August 25, he had to set a new timetable. Hitler had originally ordered the beginning of the attack for August 26. When the highest military leaders answered affirmatively to his question as to whether a recall was still possible, the then effective date for the invasion of Poland was canceled.[4] Hitler wanted to have a few more days for another attempt to separate the Western Powers from Poland. But since he wanted to finish the campaign in Poland before the beginning of the fall rainy season there, his calculations did not leave him much time because so few roads in Poland were paved and most airfields had grass runways. The fall weather, therefore, would make any rapid German advance and a speedy completion of the campaign extremely difficult.[5]

Under these circumstances Hitler worked out the following timetable, which he explained to the commander-in-chief of the army, Walther von Brauchitsch, and the chief-of-staff, Franz Halder. By August 28 he had established September 1 as the probable date for the invasion.[6] But since he could not know precisely how long the British government would take to answer his ultimatum that a Polish plenipotentiary appear in Berlin, he explained to von Brauchitsch and Halder that if necessary he would postpone the invasion until September 2. In his judgment, however, that was the latest possible date; thereafter the invasion would have to be called off.[7] Because Hitler had already once recalled the order to attack, it was especially important on this occasion that there be a precise scheduling of the hour by which the troops would be notified of the decision to move. A detailed schedule was worked out and communicated to the

3 Jürgen Runzheimer, "Die Grenzzwischenfälle am Abend vor dem deutschen Angriff auf Polen," in Wolfgang Benz and Hermann Graml (eds.), *Sommer 1939: Die Grossmächte und der Europäische Krieg* (Stuttgart: Deutsche Verlags-Anstalt, 1979), pp. 107–47.
4 Gerhard L. Weinberg, *The Foreign Policy of Hitler's Germany: Starting World War II, 1937– 1939* (Chicago: University of Chicago Press, 1980; Atlantic Highlands, N.J.: Humanities Press, 1993) (cited hereafter as Weinberg, *1937–1939*), p. 638.
5 Consideration of the impact of the weather on the possible speed of operations repeatedly influenced important decisions of Hitler during World War II. A striking example is the postponement of the attack on the Soviet Union from the fall of 1940, which Hitler originally preferred, to the early summer of 1941 in order to avoid any interruption in the winter which might be caused by the weather.
6 Weinberg, *1937–1939*, p. 644.
7 The diary of Halder for August 30, 1939: "The Führer: either 1.9. or 2.9., after 2. not any longer." Hans-Adolf Jacobsen (ed.), *Generaloberst Halder: Kriegstagebuch*, Vol. 1 (Stuttgart: Kohlhammer, 1962), p. 46.

military leaders; this schedule provided the time by which the decision as to whether the extra day for negotiations was needed would have to be made and also specified when the final attack order would need to be handed out.

All this reveals two significant findings. In the first place, Hitler did not utilize the last day and the last hours available according to his own schedule, but instead started the war earlier than the schedule required. In the second place, there is not the slightest evidence to show that his military advisors urged Hitler to take full advantage of the time which his own timetable, which he had given to them, indicated as available for negotiations.

Precisely because the British government, hoping to the last for a peaceful resolution of the crisis, hastened to reply to the German government as quickly as possible that German–Polish negotiations ought to be undertaken – but on an equal basis and not under the threat of an ultimatum – Hitler decided *not* to wait the extra available day. War was not the *ultima ratio* of his policy but the *prima ratio*. Under these circumstances, furthermore, he did not wait until the last minute allowed by his timetable for ordering the attack on September 1 but instead gave it eight and a half hours prior to the time he had originally set as the last possible moment.[8]

If one asks, why this manic haste, this fear of any peaceful resolution, one must, in my opinion, turn for an answer to Hitler's annoyance over the peaceful settlement of the crisis of September 1938.[9] Already at that time he had wanted war but had drawn back at the last moment. He had attained the propagandistically proclaimed but not the real aims of German policy, and he was very embittered over this outcome. He blamed the alleged weakness of his advisors for his own pulling back, although it was he who had been unwilling to take the risk of seeing whether their warnings were justified. This time he was under no circumstances going to risk becoming involved in negotiations and then once again not finding the path to a war he had wanted from the beginning. His fear of a peaceful resolution makes it easier to understand why there were no negotiations with Poland in the summer of 1939 and why the German ambassadors in London and Warsaw were ordered *not* to be at their posts during the August crisis. As Hitler had explained to his generals on August 22, 1939: "My only fear is that at the last moment some SOB (*Schweinehund*) might offer a compromise plan."[10]

---

8 Weinberg, *1937–1939*, pp. 645–47.
9 Details ibid., chs. 10 and 11; a summary in Weinberg, "Munich after 50 Years," *Foreign Affairs* 67, No. 1 (Fall 1988): 165–78.
10 Notes by Admiral Canaris on Hitler's speech to the commanders in chief in the morning of August 22, 1939, quoted in Klaus-Jürgen Müller, *Armee und Drittes Reich 1933–1939*

This explanation of Hitler's manner of operating as well as his reference to the events of the preceding year also explain his prohibition against handing to the British or to the Poles the demands on Poland which he had formulated to utilize with the German people as an alibi for going to war. Hitler explicitly instructed Foreign Minister Joachim von Ribbentrop not to hand these demands over under any circumstances, an instruction which almost led to blows between von Ribbentrop and the British ambassador.[11] The now fully published diary of Ulrich von Hassell, the long-time former German ambassador in Rome who was close to the scene in August of 1939, reminds us that von Ribbentrop on August 31 twice reminded his state secretary, Ernst von Weizsäcker, that the text of the demands was absolutely not to be handed to the British or to the Poles;[12] if demands are formally raised, there is the "danger" that they might be accepted. Hitler and von Ribbentrop were afraid of peace, not of war.

Both in 1938 and subsequently, before the attack in the West and before the invasion of the Soviet Union, important military leaders had voiced doubts about plans for war. Why did not a single one of them speak up in August of 1939 against the attack on Poland, or at least in favor of using every last possible hour for negotiations? Why was there in 1939 a repetition of the internal solidarity (*Burgfrieden*) of 1914, this time among the highest military commanders? Here one must point to the widespread anti-Polish sentiments. The concept of trading pieces of Poland back and forth with Russia, the way children trade marbles, had a long tradition. The possibility that an independent Poland between Germany and the Soviet Union had advantages for both was not perceived by anyone. Similarly no one wanted to recall that for centuries Germans had lived on both sides of Poles, even though this was shown in every historical atlas. The idea of a corridor was considered a good one when Frederick the Great had connected his Prussian and Brandenburgian territories by one going east-west, thereby separating Poland from its harbor in Danzig; but it was held to be an outrage when a corridor was developed to implement the right of Poland to a secure outlet to the sea as promised in Wilson's Fourteen Points.

The diary of one of the generals who was opposed to Hitler, Quarter-

(Paderborn: Schöningh, 1987), pp. 389–90. A similar text, also probably derived from Canaris's version, in *Akten zur deutschen auswärtigen Politik 1918–1945*, Series D, Vol. 7 (Baden-Baden: Imprimerie Nationale, 1956), p. 172. On the expression of Hitler, see the textual analysis in Winfried Baumgart, "Zur Ansprache Hitlers vor den Führern der Wehrmacht am 22. August 1939," *Vierteljahrshefte für Zeitgeschichte* 16 (1968): 133–34, 138, 146.

11 Weinberg, *1937–1939*, pp. 647–48.
12 Friedrich Freiherr Hiller von Gaertringen (ed.), *Die Hassell-Tagebücher 1938–1944* (Berlin: Siedler, 1988), p. 121.

master General Eduard Wagner, who committed suicide on July 23, 1944, lest he be forced to implicate others involved in the July 20 coup attempt, shows at several points that he too favored an attack on Poland. He even held the postponement of a few days to have been a mistake.[13] On August 31, 1939, after the final invasion order had been issued, he wrote to his wife: "So arms will decide, and it will all probably have started by the time you receive this letter. We hope to finish with the Poles quickly, and I have to admit that we look forward to it [wir freuen uns offen gestanden darauf]."[14]

It is one of the ironies of history that at this point Hitler's policy and the hopes of Germany's military leaders coincided: it was here that the war designed to expand Germany's "living space" would end up causing a reduction of the portion of Europe on which Germans live. The millions of all countries who lost their lives after September 1, 1939, should serve as a warning for all survivors and those yet to be born.

13 Elizabeth Wagner (ed.), *Dir Generalquartiermeister: Briefe und Tagebuchaufzeichnungen des Generalquartiermeisters des Heeres, General der Artillerie Eduard Wagner* (Munich: Olzog, 1963), pp. 98, 101.
14 Ibid., p. 109.

Part IV

WORLD WAR II

12

GERMAN DIPLOMACY TOWARD
THE SOVIET UNION

This analysis is designed to deal with four aspects of a broad topic: the general aims of Hitler which required a war with Russia for their implementation; his policy toward that country during the years 1933–39; the circumstances under which Hitler decided to invade the Soviet Union and the factors which led to his adhering to that decision; and finally the attack itself and its failure on the field of battle as that relates to earlier German policy choices.

In Vienna, in pre- and postwar Munich, during World War I, and in jail after the failed coup attempt of November 1923 Hitler developed ideas of which only those dealing with foreign relations will be touched on. Convinced that Germany needed more space to feed its population, he rejected a return to the frontiers of 1914 as a sound goal for his movement. He was certain that it would take at least one war and perhaps several to secure the return of the lost territories; in Hitler's eyes that was not worthwhile – if you were going to fight, then you should fight for territorial aims that were worthy of the sacrifices that would be required, and that meant huge stretches of land. The 1914 borders had been inadequate for the old Germany, so the new Germany should formulate its territorial ambitions without reference to them. A notorious American robber was once asked why he robbed banks. His response was, because that's where the money is. Similarly, Hitler argued on the basis of the most obvious geographic considerations that Germany should seize land in Eastern Europe because that's where the land is. There would be no Germanizing of the people there; in Hitler's racist views that was impossible anyway. The inhabitants would be expelled or exterminated – their appropriate punishment for being inferior. The *soil* would be Germanized and would provide the basis for German world power.

Slightly revised from *The Soviet and Post-Soviet Review* (formerly *Soviet Union/Union Soviétique*), 18, Nos. 1–3 (1991), 317–33.

In the more elaborate presentation of these views which Hitler dictated in the summer of 1928 but did not publish (until I arranged it for him in 1961), he explained all this in very great detail, adding that only the continental empire Germany would acquire by land conquest could enable her to face the United States.[1] Expansion eastward in Hitler's eyes referred primarily to the seizure of *Russian* territory; Poland was considered by Hitler as by most other German political figures of the time as a despicable but fleeting evil and, in any case, neither large enough nor rich enough to satisfy the requirements of German expansion.

Hitler never expected that the lands he wanted could be secured without conflict. As his aims implied a war of conquest, the fact that Russia had come under the control of the Communist Party was, from his standpoint, a stroke of unusual good fortune. It meant that in his eyes all those of real ability in Russia had been eliminated and replaced by inferior beings, thus weakening the future enemy at the same time that the theme of anti-Communist crusading could be added to the German store of propaganda weapons.

It was thus Hitler's view that the seizure of living space in the East would by itself be quite easy because the land there was inhabited by inferior Slavs ruled by even less competent Jews, but the prerequisite was a rear in the West made safe by the prior defeat of France. At one time he had hoped to separate England from France, but by 1935 he had given up on that prospect and assumed that the war in the West which he saw as the prerequisite to the quick seizure of land in the East would be against both the Western Powers.

By 1935, of course, Hitler was already chancellor of Germany. As few need to be reminded, the road between the pronouncement of programs by those desiring high office and the implementation of such programs after the attainment of office is often very long. This discrepancy between the proclamation of objectives and their fulfillment is not necessarily a sign of either bad faith or changed opinions; all sorts of factors beyond the control of any individual can intervene to force abandonment or postponement of the most cherished ambitions. Hitler's *views* certainly did not change after he became chancellor. On February 3, 1933, a few days after coming to power, he had his first opportunity to explain to the generals of the German army the military plans of the new government. He asserted that the building up of the armed forces was the most important prerequisite for his aim of restoring Germany's political might. Universal military service would be reinstituted. As for the utilization of the new army, he was quite explicit as is known from two contemporary

---

1 Gerhard L. Weinberg (ed.), *Hitlers zweites Buch: Ein Dokument aus dem Jahr 1928* (Stuttgart: Deutsche Verlags-Anstalt, 1961). There is no reliable English language edition.

accounts. After insisting that Germany's living space was inadequate, Hitler told his listeners that the new might of Germany would be used "for the conquest and ruthless Germanization of new living space in the East."[2]

At various times during the following years Hitler expressed similar sentiments, but such harangues neither inaugurated hostilities nor increased the size of the Reich. It is, therefore, necessary to examine how and why the desire for additional territory in the East was translated into a policy decision to launch an attack on the Soviet Union. The years of Hitler's chancellorship must, accordingly, be examined with the question of policy toward the Soviet Union in mind. There is a curious irony in the fact that the first major diplomatic action of the new regime Hitler installed in Germany was the extension, approved by the cabinet on May 5, 1933, of the Berlin Treaty of 1926 with the Soviet Union.[3] This, however, no more signified an abandonment of his earlier aims than the signature of the Concordat with the Vatican in July of the same year meant that he had become a devout Catholic. For the time being, there were quite different things which in German eyes needed doing. Destruction of all other parties and the building up of Germany's armed forces were at the top of the agenda. The first aim was accomplished by the summer of 1933; the other was the primary preoccupation of the regime in subsequent years.

As Germany built up her armaments, that program was conditioned by the assumption that the difficult wars Germany would have to fight were against the Western Powers. Single-engine dive bombers would be appropriate for France; two-engine dive bombers were believed appropriate for England. By 1937 specifications for the "New York Bomber" showed what was next.[4] Similarly, in the naval sphere, the big battleships designed and ordered in 1935 (in violation of the Anglo–German Naval Agreement of that year) were for the intended conflict with England, while the 56,200 ton superbattleships which were designed thereafter and laid down beginning in the spring of 1939 were supposed to cope with the American navy.[5] No specific armaments projects were developed with the Soviet Union in mind because it was always assumed that that

2 The quotation is from General Liebmann's notes on Hitler's talk. For a full discussion with references to the surviving accounts of this meeting, see Gerhard L. Weinberg, *The Foreign Policy of Hitler's Germany: Diplomatic Revolution in Europe, 1933–1936* (Chicago: University of Chicago Press, 1970; Atlantic Highlands, N.J.: Humanities Press, 1994) (cited hereafter as Weinberg, *1933–1936*), pp. 26–27.
3 Ibid., p. 78.
4 Jochen Thies, *Architekt der Weltherrschaft: Die "Endziele" Hitlers* (Düsseldorf: Droste, 1976), pp. 136ff.
5 Jost Dülffer, *Weimar, Hitler und die Marine: Reichspolitik und Flottenbau 1920 bis 1939* (Düsseldorf: Droste, 1973), pp. 384–85.

war would be quick and easy, a perception which, it should be noted, continued to be characteristic of German weapons designs until the confrontation with reality in 1941 when the appearance of the T-34 and KV tanks led the Germans for the first time to create weapons (the Mark V and Mark VI tanks, the "Panther" and "Tiger") for use against the Red Army.[6]

Just as the Germans did not think it important to adapt their weapons systems to the needs of an eastern campaign, so they disregarded all approaches from the Soviet Union during the mid-1930s which looked to some German–Soviet association. Stalin clearly wanted a new form of alignment with Germany and repeatedly attempted to obtain it, at times trying to do so through the economic elites which, as an orthodox Marxist-Leninist, he imagined were running Germany.[7] Those elites might well have been very interested in better relations with the Soviet Union, especially in the economic field, but they had practically no influence on the formation and direction, as distinct from the implementation, of German policy. From the perspective of the Berlin government, there was nothing that the Soviet Union could do for them. It would hardly help them inside the country – as it once had in the assault on the Weimar government – and it could not assist the first foreign policy moves: there was nothing the Soviets could do to help them remilitarize the Rhineland and there was similarly nothing they could do to help them seize Austria. By the time Germany turned to Czechoslovakia, the Soviet Union not only could do nothing much to help Germany directly; it was already doing all it could indirectly without Germany having to pay anything for that assistance. Stalin was busy decimating the officer corps of the Red Army, encouraging others to fight Germany, and turning aside, as the publication of new evidence has shown, Romanian offers of an avenue for aid to Czechoslovakia.[8] Under these circumstances, the German waving aside of all offers from Moscow should not be difficult to understand.[9]

6 F.M. von Senger und Etterlin, *German Tanks of World War II* (New York: Galahad Books, 1969), pp. 6off.
7 See Weinberg, *1933–1936*, pp. 220–23, 310–12; Gerhard L. Weinberg, *The Foreign Policy of Hitler's Germany: Starting World War II, 1937–1939* (Chicago: University of Chicago Press, 1980; Atlantic Highlands, N.J.: Humanities Press, 1994) (hereafter cited as Weinberg, *1937–1939*), pp. 214–15. For a reference to the earliest Soviet published mention of these soundings, see Jaroslav Valenta, "Addenda et Corrigenda zur Rolle Prags im Falle Tuchatschewski," *Vierteljahrshefte für Zeitgeschichte* 39 (1991); 444.
8 Jiri Hochmann, *The Soviet Union and the Failure of Collective Security, 1934–1938* (Ithaca, N.Y.: Cornell University Press, 1984), pp. 149, 164, 194–201.
9 Ingeborg Fleischhauer in her book, *Der Pakt: Hitler, Stalin und die Initiative der deutschen Diplomaten 1938–1939* (Frankfurt/M.: Ullstein, 1990), dismisses all these approaches as imaginary. The evidence on them, however, is too substantial, even if fragmentary, to make this an acceptable reading.

In early May of 1938 Hitler had decided to have the first of his wars later that year against Czechoslovakia, but he had drawn back from war at the last moment for reasons we need not examine here. Unable or unwilling to make the exit from negotiations to war on that occasion, he was certainly determined not to have such a development ever occur again. He had hoped that his next war, now the first in the sequence, would come against the Western Powers, who had so recently thwarted him, and he wanted to make his eastern flank secure beforehand. In the winter of 1938–39, Hungary agreed to subordinate herself to Berlin, and it was obvious that Lithuania would present no difficulty, but the Polish government was under no circumstances prepared to give up a portion of that nation's so recently regained independence. The sequence, therefore, had to be reversed. If pressure could not change the minds in Warsaw, then war would encompass Poland's defeat, thereby clearing the way for the attack in the West which remained the prerequisite for the seizure of land in the East. A recognition of these priorities from the perspective of Berlin should make it easier to understand Hitler's willingness to risk war with Britain and France sooner – when it was coming in his plans anyway.[10]

It is also in this context that it should be easier to understand first, Hitler's dread of a compromise and rush to war in 1939, his insistence in the negotiations with Japan that any alliance be directed against the Western Powers, *not* against the Soviet Union as Japan preferred. The Germans wanted Japan to assist in either deterring the Western Powers from aiding Poland or in fighting those powers if and when Germany was at war with them; the Japanese who had been engaged in border fighting with the Soviet Union in 1938 and would be again in 1939 wanted an ally against that country and were not yet ready to fight Britain and France, countries behind which they saw the United States. In the face of Japan's hesitations and with his determination to have a war with Poland and then, preferably separately, war with France and Britain, Hitler was willing to change his prior disregard of offers from Moscow in favor of agreement with Stalin. To obtain such an agreement, he was prepared to offer even more concessions than Stalin thought to ask for. Once the Soviet Union had assisted him by calming domestic fears of a two-front war, breaking any blockade of Germany even before it could be instituted, and enabling Germany to concentrate all its forces on the defeat of the Western Powers, the following conquest of Russia would be a simple matter and whatever had been yielded in the negotiations could easily and quickly be seized by a German army freed from any concern in the

---

10 These issues are reviewed in detail in Weinberg, *1937–1939*, chs. 12, 13.

West. If in this willingness to make concessions Hitler was influenced by the vast publicity attending on the Soviet negotiations with the Western Powers, it was because of the *prior* German decision to go to war with Poland and the Western Powers, a subject which will come up again in the discussion of his refusal to be influenced in the least by Stalin's desperate attempts to join the Tripartite Pact in the winter of 1940–41.

By the early summer of 1940 the bargain with Stalin had paid off. With only four regular and nine territorial divisions left to occupy the German portion of Poland and to guard the eastern frontier, Germany could concentrate her main force in the West, the only time in World War II that Germany could so concentrate her armed might on one front. A series of hard blows and a daring thrust to the English Channel so weakened Germany's enemies that the offensive southward against General Weygand's new line quickly brought a collapse of French resistance. The surrender of France left Germany the undisputed master of Western and Central Europe, while the renown of the victorious Wehrmacht would terrorize any potential opposition into a discreet acceptance of the new hegemonic power. The United States might well make unpleasant clucking noises about all this, but her response to French appeals for help had certainly shown that for the time being no danger need be feared from that quarter. In any case, the resumption of Germany's huge battleship and aircraft carrier construction program, ordered on July 11, 1940, when victory in the West appeared to have been attained, would provide the means for dealing with that country. Mussolini had decided to enter the war lest Italy be overlooked in the distribution of booty, and Franco was ready, even eager, to join in, provided he was assured of the colonial gains to which he considered Spain entitled.[11]

Under these delightful circumstances, Hitler assumed that the war in the West was over. Since he had always considered that campaign the necessary preliminary to the seizure of land in the East, the fact that the Soviet Union had helped him sweep the Allies first out of Northern Europe and now out of Western Europe would only facilitate the in any case less difficult conquering of territory in the East; and he had begun consideration of that project even while the fighting against France was still under way.

Hitler assumed that England would quit now that no one was fighting her battles for her any longer. Parts of the German army could be demo-

11   The thesis that Franco really did intend to enter the war and in fact preferred to do so if only his colonial ambitions were met, is fully supported by the works of Denis Smyth, *Diplomacy and Strategy of Survival: British Policy and Franco's Spain, 1940–41* (Cambridge: Cambridge University Press, 1986), and Norman J. Goda, "Germany and Northwest Africa in the Second World War: Politics and Strategy of Global Hegemony," unpublished Ph.D. dissertation, University of North Carolina at Chapel Hill, 1991.

bilized and soldiers from other units furloughed to help with the harvest. If the English should fail to draw the obvious conclusion from their hopeless position, a good hard knock on the head would bring them to their senses; and if their skulls proved too thick to register the facts properly, an invading army would quickly terminate the struggle. The arrest lists for the United Kingdom, at least, had already been compiled.

The developments of July 1940 failed to bear out the confident predictions of the German leaders. The British would not acknowledge the fact of defeat that seemed self-evident to everybody else. Would an invasion be necessary after all? The squabbles among German military and naval leaders over the invasion plans and preparations only pointed up the significance of a basic question – why were the English still fighting? In 1925 Hitler had correctly analyzed the likelihood of England's fighting through to the end any war she might enter regardless of the state of her armaments at the beginning. In 1939 the British government itself had told Hitler: "It would be a dangerous illusion to think that, if war once starts, it will come to an early end even if a success on any one of the several fronts on which it will be engaged should have been secured."[12] The reference then had been to a possible German victory over Poland, but there was no reason to suppose that a Churchill would weaken a Chamberlain's warning. Now, however, in the flush of victory, Hitler examined the continuing resistance of Britain without the counsels of other days.

While some of Hitler's military advisors urged that Germany strike at Britain's position in the Middle East and others argued for a concentration on the war against English shipping, Hitler preferred to analyze the basis of England's remaining in the war in very different terms.[13] Unwilling or unable to comprehend the determination of an aroused people for what it really was, the Führer searched for other explanations compatible with his own image of the world. The diagnosis seemed obvious. If England had always let *others* fight for her in the past, she must have reason to hope that even the defeat of France had not eliminated the prospect for such an arrangement in the future. But whom had Churchill cast for the role of defenders of the British Empire? From Hitler's perspective, the answer seemed obvious: Russia and the United States (ironically two states which for quite different reasons wanted that empire dissolved). True, Stalin had just rejected a British approach (a subject to

---

12 *Documents on British Foreign Policy, 1919–1939*, Third Series, Vol. 7, *1939* (London: H.M. Stationery Office, 1954), No. 145.

13 I covered these matters in my *Germany and the Soviet Union, 1939–1941* (Leyden: Brill, 1954, 1972) (cited hereafter as Weinberg, *1939–1941*), chs. 6–7; and in greater detail in *A World at Arms: A Global History of World War II* (Cambridge: Cambridge University Press, 1994), ch. 4.

be reviewed subsequently), and the United States was both unprepared and, in Hitler's eyes, inherently feeble because of its racial and nationality policy. But somehow the hope in London must be based on the expectation of future aid – grasping at straws, to be sure; but since England was obviously sinking, that would be only appropriate. If these hopes, be they real or illusory, could be shattered, then the most obdurate Englishman would admit defeat.

Once the puzzle of British resistance was explained in these terms, Hitler knew what to do. He would destroy Russia. That would take only a few weeks – originally he hoped to take care of the whole operation in the fall of 1940 – and it would serve a double purpose in the dilemma before him. The stone thrown at the Soviet vulture would also bring down the American eagle. As Hitler phrased it: "Russia is the Far Eastern sword of Britain and the United States, pointed at Japan."[14] The elimination of Russia would free Japan to carry out her program of expansion in the Pacific. This, in turn, would immobilize the United States. Bereft of hope, the English would hasten to emulate the French. The enormous resources seized in Russia, would, furthermore, make it possible first to speed up construction and thereafter to support the huge navy which would be needed for the war with the Americans.

If these speculations of Hitler, reconstructed on the basis of excellent contemporary evidence, look farfetched and even ludicrous in the glare of hindsight, one should recall some other aspects of the situation which help explain the paradox of Hitler's deciding to attack the Soviet Union to bring the war to a speedy and victorious end. The supposition that Japan might keep the United States sufficiently occupied in the Far East to prevent any effective American aid to Hitler's enemies in Europe was not only a Hitlerian illusion; it was the constant fear of American planners in 1940 and 1941 and affected the American outlook up to, and even after, Pearl Harbor. The idea that the Soviet Union could be defeated in a few weeks also did not seem so farfetched. It certainly fitted in with Hitler's worldview as explained previously. And now in *days* the German armies had moved victoriously over terrain where they had once struggled and bled more than four years in vain. The impression of this contrast on men who had almost without exception toiled in the trenches themselves cannot be overestimated. Even in the First World War, Germany had been victorious on the *Eastern* Front; now that the German

---

14 The relevant portion of the diary of the Chief of Staff of the German Army, General Franz Halder, for July 31, 1940, is quoted in Weinberg, *1939–1941*, p. 115. The German text has been published in Hans-Adolf Jacobsen (ed.), *Generaloberst Halder Kriegstagebuch*, Vol. 2 (Stuttgart: Kohlhammer, 1963), p. 49.

army had shown its superiority over the most formidable continental foe, there seemed to be no limit to its potential continental successes.[15]

The prospects of an invasion of England, on the other hand, looked far more doubtful. Why risk a setback with all its attendant loss of prestige after an unbroken run of victories? In spite of his high opinion of himself, Hitler did not trust himself – to say nothing of his army – to walk across the Channel. But an invasion of the Soviet Union, that was another matter. There one *could* walk, or, better still, one could let the soldiers walk and come riding behind in a staff car. Since an attack on Russia was in any case intended, and since both Hitler and a number of the generals had already begun thinking about that project during and right after the last days of fighting in the West, it is not too surprising that this project should have appealed to Hitler at the pinnacle of triumph, and that he should have told his military advisors on July 31, 1940, that "Russia's destruction must therefore be made a part of this struggle."[16] Because the technical obstacles to an attack later that year had by this time been explained to him, Hitler regretfully set the date for the spring of 1941. Not all his advisors were entirely convinced; a few still preferred continued concentration on England and even fewer did not share Hitler's boundless optimism. But this was not a time for outspoken objections: the German army had just demonstrated its great striking power, and the German generals had each just received another promotion.

Again, however, one should note that there is a big gap between the decision to attack a neighbor in about ten months and actually launching such an operation. Major operations of war are sometimes planned but then canceled. Thus the German operation to attack Switzerland and divide it with Italy, being devised in the same days that the first detailed plans for an invasion of the Soviet Union were being developed, was postponed indefinitely. The German attack on the Soviet Union, though postponed slightly from its tentative launching date, was actually carried out. There are several reasons for this; two of them will be touched on here. In the first place, some steps taken by Germany in preparation for the attack were likely to antagonize the Soviets, thereby evoking hostile reactions which would strengthen Hitler in his resolve. Immediately after the decision had been made, the first preparatory steps were taken. Some of these, such as the reversal of certain demobilization measures, were unlikely to attract immediate attention. The transfer to the East of sub-

15 There is a fine analysis by Andreas Hillgruber, "Das Russlandbild der führenden deutschen Militärs vor Beginn des Angriffs auf die Sowjetunion," in his *Die Zerstörung Europas: Beiträge zur Weltkriegsepoche 1914 bis 1945* (Berlin: Propyläen, 1988), pp. 256–72.
16 See n. 14.

stantial military forces, however – a whole army group in September and October 1940 – was likely to arouse Soviet suspicions. Even more important, the change in German policy toward Finland and Romania led to serious complications.[17]

These two countries had both suffered from Soviet aggression; and although Germany had been responsible for facilitating and even encouraging that aggression, she now hoped to profit from the resentment aroused by it to recruit the two countries as allies on the flanks of the attack on Russia and as bases for her own operations. Early in August 1940, therefore, Germany reversed her policy toward Finland. By August 18, an arms delivery agreement had been worked out with Finnish Marshal Mannerheim; military transit agreements followed on September 12 and 22; and staff conversations for joint military operations against the Soviet Union were inaugurated in December. Finland had been assigned to the Soviet sphere by the secret protocol to the Nazi–Soviet Pact of August 23, 1939, and up to August 1940 the Germans had scrupulously observed their promise. Not surprisingly, the sudden violation of the agreement brought strong Soviet protests.

Similarly, at the same conference of July 31, 1940, in which Hitler announced his determination to attack Russia, he had also decided to guarantee Romania. The guarantee of Romania was quickly followed by a German occupation of that country, simultaneously providing a base for future German operations and closing the door to Soviet expansion into the Balkans. The Russian government was, of course, perturbed by these moves, but their protests only confirmed Hitler in his intention to destroy that troublesome power once and for all.

The will to attack in the East was strengthened not only by the repercussions of the preparations undertaken by Germany but also by the growing preoccupation with the putative advantages of an invasion among the planners themselves. All kinds of glorious prospects seemed to lie within the grasp of the confident schemers. Here would be an opportunity to carry into practice the wildest dreams of the racial enthusiasts. The extermination of so-called undesirables could begin with the prisoners of war. Commissars, other Communists, intellectuals, Jews, men with Asiatic features (whatever that meant) were to be killed on capture. Afterwards, special slaughter commandos attached to the armies would kill off some groups in the occupied territories, while still later mass settlement and resettlement programs would turn the demographic map

17 Weinberg, *1939–1941*, ch. 8; Gerd R. Ueberschär, *Hitler und Finnland 1939–1941: Die Deutsch-Finnischen Beziehungen während des Hitler–Stalin Paktes* (Wiesbaden: Steiner, 1979), pp. 196ff.

of Eastern Europe upside down.[18] Furthermore, there were the fabled riches of Russia's farms and mines. A stupendous looting organization was established and equipped with volumes of instructions. The Germans would exploit the area, starving millions to death and simultaneously providing thousands of plush jobs for the National Socialist Party's faithful. The natural resources of the land to be conquered would supply all the necessary materials for German industry; in fact, Hitler estimated that the campaign would cost no more men than were required to operate the synthetics industries that would then no longer be needed.[19] We secure some insight into Hitler's thinking from the fact that the difference between a German worker and a German casualty was assumed not to matter.

Stalin's turning away a British approach in the summer of 1940 has already been mentioned. In the following months, the Soviet government attempted to repeat its 1939 ploy of negotiating with the British and leaking information about those talks in order to entice the Germans into making a better offer. This time the tactic did not work.[20] Every attempt on the part of Stalin to obtain German approval for the Soviet Union to join the Tripartite Pact of Germany, Italy, and Japan was rebuffed by Berlin; frequently there was not even an answer. The tried and true 1939 technique of using an economic agreement favorable to Germany as a means of paving the way for a new political deal similarly failed. When Foreign Commissar Molotov suggested to the German ambassador after a whole series of new agreements favorable to Germany had been signed in early 1941 that perhaps the time had now come to return to the negotiations for Soviet adhesion to the Tripartite Pact, there was no response from Berlin. If Stalin imagined, as he appears to have, that a clearly implied willingness to join Germany in war with Britain and the United States would influence Berlin, he was completely mistaken.

The Germans were certainly happy to receive all the economic benefits, including lots of extra oil, grain and nonferrous metals from the Soviet Union and plenty of tin, rubber, and soybeans transshipped from the Far East on Soviet freight trains, but they were not the least bit interested in political negotiations since these, as they knew better than anyone, would only muddy the waters and might interfere with the

18 Czeslaw Madajczyk (ed.), "Generalplan Ost," *Polish Western Affairs*, 3 (1962), 391–442; Helmut Krausnick and Hans-Heinrich Wilhelm, *Die Truppe des Weltanschauungskrieges: Die Einsatzgruppen der Sicherheitspolizei und des SD* (Stuttgart: Deutsche Verlags-Anstalt, 1981).

19 See the documentation on this statement in Weinberg, *1939–1941*, p. 165, n. 31.

20 The efforts of the Soviet Union to join the Tripartite Pact and the utilization of talks with Britain and economic concessions to Germany to support those efforts are reviewed in ch. 4 of my *A World at Arms*.

stream of supplies. This time they had already decided on war with the Soviet Union, as in 1939 they had decided on war with Poland and later or simultaneously with the West. Then the prior rejection of all approaches from Moscow had given way to a willingness to make a deal; this time there was nothing to make a deal about from the German point of view. The Soviet government was now treated to the exact procedure which Germany had followed toward Britain and France in 1936 and 1937 when those countries had proposed a series of substitutes for the Locarno Treaty Germany had broken; no answer is itself an answer of sorts. As the state secretary in the German Foreign Ministry put it, the German regime was moving on a one-way street against Russia.[21]

On June 22, 1941, the Germans attacked with 3 million men, 3,500 tanks, 2,700 planes, and over 600,000 horses.[22] The Soviet forces, still underestimated by the Germans but not as wildly as in 1940, were more numerous in each category. The Germans therefore faced the problem of attacking the greater forces of a huge country on a front that would lengthen as they moved eastward. Their plans called for solving this difficulty, of which they were at least partially aware, by cutting off and destroying such large portions of the Red Army in the initial enveloping thrusts that organized resistance would come to a quick end and the whole structure thereupon come crashing down. There was much to be said for this concept from the military point of view. After all, any effort to push the Red Army back through the whole USSR would founder on the wearing out of the German tank treads, if nothing else. Furthermore, according to the German plans, Soviet resistance was supposed to cease when the Wehrmacht reached a line stretching from Archangel to Astrakhan. Although they had kept this brilliant idea secret from the Russians, the German staff maps did not go much beyond this mythical divide – and were in reality quite inaccurate even short of it. The *first* blows would be the decisive ones, and in this analysis the Germans were perhaps more right than they ever realized.

The concept that the campaign would be decided in a few weeks was always assumed to operate only for the Germans – they would win in that period. But in fact the first blows did not destroy the Red Army and topple the Soviet system. The German victories were stupendous, the booty huge, the prisoners numberless; but the war continued along an ever lengthening front. Did this not imply something else: that if the Germans did not win in six weeks, they would not win at all? What would

21 Ernst von Weizsäcker, *Erinnerungen* (Munich: Paul List, 1960), p. 313.
22 An excellent recent account in Horst Boog et al., *Das Deutsche Reich und der Zweite Weltkrieg*, Vol. 4, *Der Angriff auf die Sowjetunion* (Stuttgart: Deutsche Verlags-Anstalt, 1983), pp. 451–712.

have happened to David if Goliath had not toppled after the first hit from the sling? This was an aspect of the "few weeks' war" concept which none at the top and few at the bottom of the German military hierarchy had pondered. The postwar debate about the possible alternative moves of the Germans after the end of July 1941 similarly ignored the realities of a campaign fought by an army with few reserves in a vast country against a strong foe; more recently, a very careful study of logistics has shown that there was in any case no possibility of an early resumption of German attacks on the central portion of the front.[23]

The German army suffered increasingly heavy losses, especially in the forward units, and was eventually stopped. That halt was administered by the Red Army. Too frequently people have been misled by stories about the winter. Contrary to the fairy tales in some German memoirs, they have a winter in Russia every year, not just when there are invaders around, so the Germans could hardly assert surprise. And curiously enough, it gets about as cold and the snow is about as deep for the Russians as for the Germans, or anyone else for that matter. It had been precisely the anticipation that an attack on Russia launched in the fall of 1940 would have had to be interrupted by the winter which had led Hitler to accept the view of his military advisors that the attack had best be postponed until the early summer of 1941 so that it could be completed in one campaign season. Although the December counteroffensive of the Red Army did not result in a total German rout, the defeat inflicted on the Germans was such that the latter were thereafter unable to launch an offensive on more than one limited sector of the front at any one time, a certain recipe for defeat if the alliance against Germany held together.

Hitler had had all sorts of elaborate plans for the reduction of the army and a shift to air and sea warfare after the quick defeat of the Soviet Union, and much of the planning work in the German high command in the last weeks before the attack was actually devoted to these post-Barbarossa concerns. After the defeat of France in 1940, the Germans had been caught without a set of plans for follow-up operations against England if that country remained in the war, or against other countries like Switzerland, which were on the list of states destined to disappear from the map. The Germans did not want to be caught short in this way again and therefore prepared all manner of projects to follow on the great victory in the East which was anticipated with confident certainty. Most of those plans were never realized as the Eastern Front swallowed Ger-

23 Klaus A. F. Schüler, *Logistik im Russlandfeldzug: Die Rolle der Eisenbahnen bei Planung, Vorbereitung und Durchführung des deutschen Angriffs auf die Sowjetunion bis zur Krise vor Moskau im Winter 1941/42* (Frankfurt/M: Lang, 1987).

man manpower and matériel in increasing quantities. For Hitler, this meant delay and eventual failure in the realization of great dreams of great conquests. For his soldiers, it meant bitter fighting that ended in death for many and never seemed to end at all for the rest.

As one looks back over this extraordinary series of events, and the terrible cost in lives and treasure they imposed on the peoples involved, one further interpretive concept may be worth putting forward. The two dictators who dealt with and faced each other in peace and in war appear to have been in some ways equally blinded by their own ideological preconceptions. Hitler did not only preach the most preposterous racial nonsense, he actually believed in it and founded policies on that belief. The supposed need for living space motivated a policy that required war; the assumption of Slavic racial inferiority conditioned preposterously erroneous military plans and preparations.

Perhaps Stalin's policies can be more easily understood if one is prepared to recognize that he too believed at least some of the equally ridiculous notions which he preached. If National Socialism was indeed primarily the tool of the monopoly capitalist elite of Germany in the struggle for markets and investments, and not an independent movement looking toward agricultural expansionist settlement, then Soviet policy based on that erroneous analysis becomes much easier to understand. The approaches to such people as Hjalmar Schacht in the 1930s and the belief that it would be wise to turn Germany against the imagined rivals for markets and investments and raw materials in 1939; the willingness to assist Germany in its war against Britain and France; the unwillingness to believe that a Germany which had open to her the colonial possessions and markets of the countries she had defeated with Soviet help would thereafter turn east to seize farmland; all these perceptions of Stalin can be understood more readily if one is prepared to see him as equally misled by ideology as Hitler. In 1927 there was a war scare in the Soviet Union at a time when there were no real signs of significant preparations for an attack on the country; in 1941 when there was certainly plenty of evidence of such preparations, it was assumed that these were a provocation, extortion, or bluff. The Soviet Union under the leadership of Stalin had helped Hitler drive the Western Powers out of Northern, Western, and Southern Europe. If at the end of this development it found itself facing Germany on the European continent by itself, that was not the result of some evil plot by the capitalist-imperialists; it was the product of mistaken policies based on erroneous assumptions which would cost millions of Soviet citizens their lives.

In the spring of 1939, President Roosevelt had tried to caution Hitler against attacking a long list of countries, most of which Hitler subsequently invaded; the German dictator responded by making fun of the president. He might have done better to pay attention. In the summer of 1939 Roosevelt, who did not share the general belief in the strength of the French army, had tried to warn Stalin of the danger of siding with a Germany which, once it dominated Western and Central Europe, would be a mortal threat to both Russia and America.[24] That warning, conveyed through both the Soviet ambassador in Washington and the American ambassador in Moscow, had been ignored by Stalin. As one looks back on the great disaster of World War II, it would be well to examine closely the extent to which policies based on fundamental misconceptions contributed to the terrible suffering that war brought to so many people.

24 Weinberg, *1937–1939*, pp. 578, 608.

13

———— • ————

THE NAZI–SOVIET PACTS OF 1939:
A HALF CENTURY LATER

Early on August 22, 1939, the world was startled to learn from an announcement in the Soviet press that German Foreign Minister Joachim von Ribbentrop would arrive in Moscow on the following day to sign a nonaggression pact. Equipped with instructions from Adolf Hitler authorizing him to sign both a treaty and secret protocol which would enter into force as soon as signed (rather than when ratified later), von Ribbentrop left for Moscow that evening. At the airport, the German delegation was met by Deputy Commissar for Foreign Affairs, Vladimir P. Potemkin, who had earlier that year declined an invitation to meet with British Foreign Secretary Lord Halifax.

In the Kremlin, there were several conversations between von Ribbentrop and other German diplomats, Josef Stalin, and Vyacheslav Molotov, the Commissar for Foreign Affairs. During the night of August 23–24, agreement was reached on all points, the pact and a secret protocol were signed; and there followed a celebration party in which the participants drank toasts to each other, to German–Soviet friendship, and to the absent Adolf Hitler.

The pact, which was published, provided that neither country would attack the other or assist any third power at war with the other, thereby assuring each of the neutrality of the other party if it should decide to attack anyone else. They promised not to join in groups of powers directed against the other and to settle by peaceful means all differences that might arise between themselves. The pact was to last for ten years and an additional five unless notice of termination were given a year before its expiration. The treaty was to enter into effect immediately.

The same immediate effectiveness applied to a secret protocol attached to the treaty and governed by a special agreement to ensure its

Originally published in *Foreign Affairs* 68, No. 4 (Fall 1989): 175–89.

secrecy, an agreement which the Germans maintained until the end of the Third Reich and which Moscow only broke at the end of the existence of the Soviet Union. This protocol provided that Finland, Estonia, and Latvia were to be in the Soviet sphere of interest; Lithuania enlarged by the Vilna area then in Poland was assigned to Germany. In the initial German concept, Latvia was to have been divided between the two powers at the Daugava (Dvina) River, but on Soviet insistence that country was quickly turned over entirely to the Soviet Union. Poland, with the exception of the Vilna area, was to be partitioned along the line of the rivers Pissa, Narev, Vistula, and San. This line divided the core area of Polish settlement within prewar Poland, and the two powers agreed to review later the question of whether or not a rump Poland would suit their convenience. In the event, the Soviet Union subsequently proposed, and the Germans accepted, an arrangement agreed to during von Ribbentrop's second visit to Moscow on September 28, 1939, that the territory between the Bug and Vistula rivers together with a small piece of Polish territory in the north would be traded to the Germans in exchange for most of Lithuania now to be Soviet. In effect this left the question of a rump Polish state in the tender hands of the Germans.

Further south, the partition scheme provided that the Soviet Union called attention to its interest in Bessarabia (which Russia had taken from its ally Romania in 1878 only to lose it after World War I), while the Germans declared their complete political disinterest in Southeast Europe. It is now known that von Ribbentrop was authorized to go even further and agree to Soviet control of Istanbul and the Straits, but Stalin evidently did not ask.

The new arrangements worked out on September 28 also included a friendship treaty between Germany and the Soviet Union later supplemented by a boundary protocol, a confidential agreement on the exchange of populations across the borders separating the Soviet and German spheres in Eastern Europe, a secret protocol to the effect that neither would tolerate Polish agitation concerning territory seized by the other, and several exchanges covering major extensions of the economic agreement which had been signed between the two countries on August 19. The latter were designed to help Germany break the British blockade by assisting her in acquiring raw and war materials which could then be shipped across the USSR. While these arrangements to support the German war effort were kept secret, in public the two powers called for an end to the war which, now that they had divided Poland between them, served no further purpose in the opinion of Berlin and Moscow. It is, of course, essential to recall that between the two trips of von Ribbentrop to the Soviet capital, the partners of the Nazi–Soviet Pact had both attacked Poland; and, in Stalin's phraseology, their friendship had been "cemented with blood."[1]

As is already clear from the description of the text of the August agreements, the pact provided the Germans with a green light for an attack on Poland and was so interpreted by all at the time. Unlike prior nonaggression pacts signed by the Soviet Union, this one contained no provision that it would be invalid if either party attacked a third country. Furthermore, the agreements assured the Germans that if England and France honored their promise to go to war if Germany attacked Poland, the disappearance of the hated Polish state would once again assure Germany a common border with Russia, who would be a friendly neighbor committed to helping her break the British blockade. From the Soviet Union itself, Germany could draw on supplies of oil, grain, and nonferrous metals which she needed to conduct war against the Western Powers; and across the Soviet Union she would be able to obtain other important raw materials from the Near East, East Asia, and possibly also from the Western Hemisphere. Above all, she could concentrate all her forces after the quick defeat of Poland on the Western Front.

For the Soviet Union, well informed by its espionage network that the German attack on Poland, when it came, would be a preliminary to an attack by Germany in the West, the agreement appeared to provide insulation from what was already being referred to as the "Second Imperialist War," great accretions of territory, the disappearance of the Polish state, which it hated about as much as did the Germans, and an encouragement to Germany, which had drawn back from war in 1938, to launch herself into a war with the Western Powers which Stalin assumed would weaken both parties equally by satisfying Soviet belief in "the need for a war in Europe."[2] In addition, the pact assured the leaders in Moscow that Japan, whose troops had just been defeated by the Red Army in clashes at Nomohan on the border between Manchuria and Mongolia,[3] would not dare attempt a new attack on East Asian territories belonging to or controlled by the Soviet Union.

For Poland, the pact clearly meant total isolation in the face of what looked like an imminent German attack. Though not immediately apparent to the Polish government, it also meant that any hope of holding out

1 Stalin to von Ribbentrop, December 22, 1939, quoted in R. Umiastowski, *Russia and the Polish Republic, 1918–1941* (London: Aquafondata, 1945), p. 182.
2 Soviet Commissariat for Foreign Affairs to the Ambassador in Tokyo, July 1, 1940, in James W. Morley (ed.), *The Fateful Choice: Japan's Road to the Pacific War* (New York: Columbia University Press, 1980), pp. 311–12.
3 See Alvin D. Coox, *Nomonhan: Japan against Russia, 1939*, 2 vols. (Stanford, Calif.: Stanford University Press, 1985).

against German troops in eastern Poland during the winter of 1939–40 could not be realized because the Soviet Union would invade Poland from the east and seize the territory allocated to it by the secret German–Soviet agreements.

For Great Britain and France, the pact meant that all their hopes of a multifront war against Germany had been dashed. In pursuit of those hopes, drawn from a belief that a powerful Germany could most likely be defeated only by a combination of allies, they had made a long series of concessions to the Soviet Union in lengthy negotiations during the summer of 1939, and London had postponed signing an alliance with Poland in the hope that one with Moscow could be arranged. Now that this possibility was clearly excluded, the treaty with Poland was rushed to signature. Determined to go to war at the next step of German aggression if it were resisted, the British government hoped that an obvious and public stand might still deter Germany from war. But, as Neville Chamberlain warned Berlin in a special letter, Britain would go to war with or without allies, and as he warned both Hitler and Italian dictator Benito Mussolini, the war once started would not end after any defeat of Poland but would be continued.

For the French, as for the British, the pact meant dashed hopes of assistance against the German menace. The various French schemes advanced in the winter of 1939–40 for attacking the Caucasus oil fields and aiding the Finns in their defense against Soviet attack while occupying the Swedish iron mines along the way can be seen in part as a reflection of the disappointment and anger in Paris.

For Japan, the pact was a traumatic experience, partly because the Japanese had been involved in fighting with the Soviet Union and wanted help from their German Anti-Comintern Pact partner which would now obviously not be forthcoming from that supposed opponent of international Communism, and partly because they imagined themselves still involved in negotiations with Berlin and Rome for an alliance against the Soviet Union. The government in Tokyo fell in the face of what looked from their perspective like a humiliating diplomatic reversal, but successor cabinets in Japan failed to draw long-term conclusions from the way Germany had treated them.

For fascist Italy, which had been among the first of the major powers to develop good relations with the Soviet Union, the German step appeared to have gone rather far, but Mussolini was not prepared to argue the point at the time. Like the Germans, Italy's leaders had considered the Anti-Comintern Pact as directed primarily against England, and this reinforcement of the anti-British forces could only be welcome to Rome.

The United States had been the last of the major powers to recognize the Soviet regime, and had done so in part as a counterweight against possible aggressors in Asia or Europe. President Roosevelt, who did not share the then common belief in the great strength of the French army, had tried hard to warn Stalin of the dangers of aligning the Soviet Union with Germany, pointing out in the summer of 1939 that a Germany victorious in Western Europe would then menace all other countries, including the Soviet Union and the United States. As these warnings fell on deaf ears in Moscow, Washington could only observe the outbreak of war in Europe in sadness; it would adopt a policy for keeping out of that war opposite from the one followed by the Soviet Union. Instead of helping Hitler, the United States would assist his foes.

How had the agreement between Germany and the Soviet Union come about? Why had the two powers which had made the nastiest comments about each other in public for years worked out in secret agreements to partition Eastern Europe between them and to call jointly upon the other nations of the world to accept this situation with its ending of the independence of Poland as well as Czechoslovakia, most of which Germany had swallowed and whose permanent demise the Soviet Union had recognized legally just before invading Poland? The motives of the two partners were different, and we are far better informed on those of the Germans; the two must therefore be examined separately.

Germany had since 1933 been following a policy which called for the establishment of a dictatorship inside the country, massive rearmament of a population governed by a racist regime, and thereafter a series of wars which would enable the country to seize territories on which the German population could feed itself and grow ever larger. It was obvious from a look at the map that most of Europe's agricultural land lay in the East, primarily in the Soviet Union. In the official doctrine of the Nazi state, the peoples living there, most of them of Slavic stock, were inferior racial types who, by what Hitler considered an extraordinary stroke of good fortune for the Germans, were now ruled by even more inferior and incapable Jews who had come to power as a result of the Bolshevik Revolution, a revolution in which the at least minimally capable old Germanic ruling class of Russia had been replaced by total incompetents. The seizure of vast land masses from such dolts would be a simple matter, and the inhabitants of the conquered area could easily be displaced or murdered; but before that could be done, Germany's position in Europe had to be strengthened. In particular, the French, whose army stood perilously close to Germany's most important industrial area, the Ruhr, had to be crushed, and the British, who could obviously not be separated from them, had to be driven off the continent. The war against the West could, it was believed, be won most easily from a base which included Austria and Czechoslovakia under German control, and these had accordingly been absorbed as preliminary steps.

During the years when the Germans were engaged in preparing for these measures, as they rearmed and as they moved against first Austria and then Czechoslovakia, all soundings from the Soviet Union had been waved aside. There was, from the perspective of Berlin, nothing that the Soviet Union could do for them under these circumstances. In internal German affairs, the Communist Party had once assisted the Nazis in destroying the Weimar Republic by targeting the Social Democratic Party as its main enemy, but now the Communist Party was itself the target of the regime's destructive fury. In the field of rearmament, the Soviet Union had provided the German Republic with the opportunity for secret work in the areas prohibited to Germany by the peace treaty of 1919: armored warfare, poison gases, and air warfare. The new government in Berlin, however, was carrying out its rearmament program on a vastly greater scale and increasingly in the open so that secret facilities in the Soviet Union were no longer of any special use. As for the building up of a huge blue-water navy, now underway or being planned for war against Britain and the United States, that was a field in which the Soviet Union had never been of assistance to Germany.

In the diplomatic field, there was similarly nothing that in Berlin's eyes the Russians could do to help in the years 1933–38. Neither Austria nor Czechoslovakia had a common border with the Soviet Union; and in its preparations for seizing Austria and attacking Czechoslovakia, Germany ignored Russia entirely. Under these circumstances, the repeated soundings made in Berlin by special representatives sent by Stalin for that purpose were invariably ignored. In the winter of 1938–39 this situation began to change.

Germany had planned to attack Czechoslovakia in 1938, expecting to annex that country as a result of an isolated war. That project had not worked out as Hitler had intended; the very device by which he had hoped to isolate his victim from outside support, the presence in it of over 3 million Germans, had ended up by getting him engaged in negotiations from which he had emerged with the territory on which they lived. To his subsequent regret, he had drawn back from war and had settled for the ostensible rather than the real aims of German policy (see Chapter 8). Thereafter, he had plotted to seize the rest of Czechoslovakia after a "decent interval" while preparing for the war with the Western Powers which he now intended to launch in the near future. Such a war in his opinion required a quiet eastern border; and such a quiet border in his judgment meant the subordination to Germany of her eastern neighbors: Hungary and Poland.

In the winter of 1938–39, this aim was attained with regard to Hungary but not in regard to Poland. The litmus test was joining the Anti-Comintern Pact. After much hesitation, Hungary took this symbolic step of obeisance to Berlin, but the Poles simply would not do so. The leaders of the revived independent Poland were as anti-Communist as anyone in Europe, but they were not about to give up the independence of their country without a fight. On all other questions they were prepared to make some compromises, but formal obeisance to Berlin was out of the question. It took Hitler a while to recognize that Warsaw meant what it said; but once he realized that the Polish regime would not subordinate itself to the whim of Berlin, he decided that a preliminary war against Poland would be needed before he attacked the West, unless, of course, the Western Powers joined Poland.

It was in this context that the German picture of relations with the Soviet Union changed. The Soviet Union had a long common border with Poland; Russia had a long tradition of hostility to Poland; and a partition of Poland with the Soviet Union appeared to offer a number of advantages to Germany. It would isolate Poland for a quick attack; it might deter Britain and France from aiding Poland and going to war with Germany until the latter picked its own time to attack them; and it would open the way for Germany to acquire much needed materials from and across the Soviet Union, thereby invalidating any blockade of Germany even before it was instituted.

The prospect of an alignment with the Soviet Union looked even more attractive to Berlin in a situation where it was having difficulty recruiting other allies for the coming war with Britain and France. The Italians eventually agreed to sign an alliance, the so-called Pact of Steel of May 1939, but the Germans recalled that Italy had urged a compromise in 1938 and had, at the time of signing the alliance, made it clear that several years of peace were needed to prepare Italy for the confrontation with the West. The other major prospective ally, Japan, had not wanted an alliance against the West at all. Tokyo, engaged in prior years and again during 1939 in border clashes with the Soviet Union, wanted an alliance against that country, not against Britain and France who, in their eyes, were likely to be supported by the United States. Here was an ally who wanted to march in the wrong direction; the Soviet Union looked like a much better prospect to Hitler.

Since in Hitler's eyes, the attack on the West was the *difficult but necessary* prelude for the subsequent *simple and fast* attack on the Soviet Union, concessions could easily be made to Moscow. Whatever the Soviets wanted, they could get, including a few things they did not even ask for, on the assumption that once Germany had won her big war in the West, she could take back everything given away in the East – and lots more besides. The real question was not, therefore, the terms on which an agreement might be reached but whether the Soviet Union was prepared to arrive at an agreement in the time frame with which the Germans were working and would provide assurance of economic support as well as the diplomatic aid Germany wanted.

It was from this position that the Germans examined the soundings from Moscow in 1939 and took the speech of Stalin of March 10, 1939, and the replacement of Foreign Commissar Maxim Litvinov by Molotov in early May as signs of Soviet seriousness. The vast publicity attendant upon the negotiations by the Soviets with Britain and France long left the Germans in some doubt as to whether their secret talks with the Soviet Union really would produce an agreement, but the very fact that their own negotiations were being kept secret and that an economic agreement was being worked out combined to made the prospects look good. In order to get at the Soviet Union directly, the disappearance of the smaller countries between the two powers was an inviting prospect for Berlin, and accordingly ending the independence of these countries by partition with Moscow was just fine, with the exact terms and lines of no special importance. Here was the chance to secure Germany's eastern border while fighting in the West, and if the Soviet Union provided that, all the better. But of course, once the agreement with the Russians had served its purpose of shielding a German victory over Britain and France, then the campaign in the East against Russia could follow, hampered neither by the paper barrier of the nonaggression pact nor by the need to keep large forces in the West.

If this was the perception of Hitler, it was one which in its essentials was supported enthusiastically by others in the upper levels of Germany. Many of the diplomats had long believed that good relations with Russia, whatever her government, would be good for Germany (though a few were sufficiently alarmed by the prospect of a German–Soviet agreement to warn the United States). The military leaders could hardly contain their eagerness for war against Poland and welcomed anything that looked likely to lead to that happy event. And the prospect of what they now believed could be a one-front war made the agreement with the Soviet Union all the more welcome.[4] A few old Nazi Party members were affronted by the tie to the center of Communism, which their propaganda

4 On this point, see esp. Eberhard Jäckel, "Hitlers Kriegspolitik und ihre nationalen Voraussetzungen," in Klaus Hildebrand et al. (eds.), *1939: An der Schwelle zum Weltkrieg* (Berlin: de Gruyter, 1990), pp. 21–29.

had long pictured as the great enemy, but such rumblings had no impact on policy. For a short time, the German government was willing to sign with Moscow.

On the Soviet side, a different ideology led by a different route to the same result. Assuming that the capitalist world would continue to unite against the Soviet state, and incapable for ideological reasons of comprehending the special nature of the Nazi state, Stalin had repeatedly approached the Germans for some agreement which would assist them in turning against what he perceived to be the capitalist imperialist rivals of the Third Reich. A war between Germany and the Western Powers looked to the Soviet leader like the best prospect for both the safety and the future expansion of Soviet power. The repeated refusals of his approaches by Berlin did not discourage him from making more. In 1938, when it looked as if war might break out over a German attack on Czechoslovakia, a country with which the Soviet Union had a defensive alliance contingent on France honoring her alliance with that country, the Soviet Union took a *public* stance in support of Czechoslovakia while privately declining any opportunity to assist that country. The fact that the Germans funked at war – by contrast with the Japanese who had thrown themselves into war with China without encouragement from anyone – made it look in 1939 as if an agreement with Germany might have the effect of encouraging that country to take the plunge.[5]

In this context, negotiations with the Western Powers for an agreement with them, accompanied with plenty of publicity, might induce the Germans to come to a settlement and to go forward with their plan for war against Poland and the West simultaneously or in sequence. From what evidence we have, it would appear that three factors required clarification in Soviet eyes. First was the question of whether the Germans were serious about an agreement with them, an issue all the more important to Moscow because in January 1939 the Germans had aborted an economic mission to them under circumstances which left the Soviets both mystified and annoyed. Second was whether or not the Germans were prepared to make the concessions which Stalin wanted in terms of territory in Poland. And third was whether the Germans saw the need for the disappearance of the independent states of Eastern Europe in essentially the same way as he did. Stalin subsequently explained to the British ambassador that "the U.S.S.R. had wanted to change the old equilibrium

---

5 Vjaceslav Dashichev, "Planungen und Fehlschläge Stalins am Vorabend des Krieges – der XVIII. Parteitag der KPdSU(B) und der sowjet-deutsche Nichtangriffspakt," in ibid., pp. 303–14, argues that Stalin had decided to sign with the Germans before the Communist Party congress of March 10–21, 1939.

... but that England and France had wanted to preserve it. Germany had also wanted to make a change in the equilibrium, and this common desire to get rid of the old equilibrium had created the basis for the rapprochement with Germany."[6]

The negotiations showed the Russians that the Germans were indeed serious about sharing Eastern Europe by division with them, just the opposite of the position of the Western Powers, who hoped to preserve the independence of the countries there. From Stalin's point of view, therefore, it was a matter of stringing along the Western Powers with steadily increasing demands in public in order to put pressure on the Germans to raise their offers in private. When Hitler wrote Stalin a personal letter asking him to receive von Ribbentrop promptly, the Soviet leader realized that the time to take final action had come. Further stalling would force the Germans to postpone an attack on Poland because the good campaign weather in Eastern Europe was coming to an end. He had by that time already signed a long-term economic agreement with Berlin – a clear sign that he had no intention of joining Britain and France. Now was the moment to receive the German foreign minister and hammer out the details of an agreement. The "old equilibrium" would indeed disappear.

Once the agreement of August 23, 1939, and its secret protocol had been signed, Germany felt free to go to war with Poland, and after some last-minute efforts to separate that country from its Western Allies, Germany did attack. Since Hitler intended to strike in the West after beating Poland, it did not appear to him especially important whether the war with France and England came immediately or was postponed. The key point for him was to obtain the quiet border in the East for a subsequent campaign in the West, and here was the chance to get it. Once it became certain that the Western Powers would stand by Poland, he did not even wait out the extra day his own timetable allowed. Acting in part under the impact of the lessons *he* had drawn from the Munich Agreement, he was most worried that someone might arrange a compromise at the last minute and cheat him of war, as had happened in 1938. Now was the time to strike – and the sooner the better.

As an immediate follow-up to their own attack on Poland, the Germans urged the Soviet Union to seize the territories assigned to it, and they were somewhat unhappy that Russia did not move sooner. But once the Soviets had signed a truce with Japan, they moved quickly, both against Poland and against the Baltic states. Since the Lithuanians had refused

6 Sir Stafford Cripps to the Foreign Office, July 16, 1940, Public Record Office, FO 371/24846, f. 10, N 6526/30/38. The document is quoted with the permission of the Controller of Her Majesty's Stationery Office.

German pressure to join in the war against Poland, their country was traded to the Soviet Union for portions of central Poland, as already mentioned; and the two partners of the pact worked out the details of applying their division of Eastern Europe. When the Soviets ran into trouble in their attempt to impose their will on Finland, Germany supported the Soviet position, while Communist parties in Western Europe were ordered by Moscow to do what they could to undermine resistance to the Germans. Vast quantities of raw materials were provided to Germany under the trade agreement with the Soviet Union, which also did what it could to support the German navy's war against Allied shipping. In exchange, the Germans delivered some machinery and naval equipment to Russia.

As the war continued in 1940, the cooperation between the two partners appeared to go well.[7] The Soviet Union assisted the Germans in their strike at Narvik in the Norwegian campaign and were delighted by the German victory there. The German triumph in the West in May and June of 1940 was, on the one hand, made possible by the Russians, who had enabled Germany to concentrate its forces on one front in the war at a time when Germany was not yet exhausted as it had been by the time the Soviets had signed a separate peace with them in 1918. On the other hand, it enabled the Soviet Union to end the vestiges of independence still left to the Baltic states,[8] to put renewed pressure on Finland, and to annex not only Bessarabia but a substantial additional piece of Romania as well.

What Stalin did not realize or would not believe was that by this time the Germans were already planning an attack on the Soviet Union, an attack Hitler originally scheduled for the fall of 1940 and for which Soviet action against Finland and Romania provided Germany with allies at the two flanks of the coming front. As friction developed out of this and other issues, the Soviet Union expressed a willingness to join the Tripartite Pact signed by Germany, Italy, and Japan in September 1940, but the Germans were not interested. Neither Soviet growling nor Soviet pleading had any influence on Berlin; and the acceleration of Soviet

7 See Sergei Slutsch, "Warum brauchte Hitler einen Nichtangriffspakt mit Stalin?" in Roland G. Foerster (ed.), *"Unternehmen Barbarossa": Zum historischen Ort der deutsch-sowjetischen Beziehungen von 1933 bis Herbst 1941* (Munich: Oldenbourg, 1993), pp. 69–87.
8 The Red Army occupied the portion of Lithuania assigned to Germany by the secret agreement of September 28, 1939, when it entered that country on June 15, 1940. There followed lengthy negotiations which ended with a new secret agreement, signed on January 10, 1941, by which the Soviet Union compensated Germany for its annexation of this territory with $ (gold) 7.5 million. There is an account in Bronis J. Kaslas, "The Lithuanian Strip in Soviet–German Secret Diplomacy, 1939–1941," *Journal of Baltic Studies* 4, no. 3 (1973): 211–25. Related documents and a map are included in the 1980 reprint prepared by Professor Kaslas.

deliveries of supplies to Germany from its own stocks or across its territory from the Far East had no more effect on German policy than the simultaneous acceleration of American deliveries to Britain with the passage of the Lend-Lease Act had on Hitler's assurance to Japan that Germany would go to war with the United States if Japan got into such a war as a result of its attacking Great Britain. The German government made policy and went to war with others on the basis of its calculations, not the policies of those it planned to strike.

The bloody fighting which began with the German attack on the Soviet Union on June 22, 1941, pointed up the terrible miscalculations made by both parties to the Nazi–Soviet Pact. The Germans would discover that heading to the East before finishing the war in the West was a dangerous step. They would learn the hard way that their beliefs about the inferiority of Slavs and the weakness of the Soviet Union were delusions derived from the false doctrines of racial determinism. At least a few Germans would also begin to learn that the establishment of a tier of independent states between Germany and the Soviet Union at the end of World War I had been an enormous advantage, not a disadvantage for Germany; but that along with another great blessing of the Treaty of Versailles for Germany, the maintenance of German unity, it had been destroyed by the Germans themselves.

The Soviet leadership was similarly deluded by its own ideology. Just as many Germans believed in the racial inferiority of the peoples of Eastern Europe, so Stalin appears to have believed in the Marxist-Leninist nonsense about fascism as the tool of monopoly capitalism which would engage in the struggle for markets, investments, and raw materials, with no room for an independent Nazi ideology of racial agrarian expansionism. The shocked surprise with which the Soviet leadership met the German attack when their own intelligence had warned them, when the British had warned them, and when the Americans had provided them with the outlines of the German invasion plan, has to be understood as the triumph of preconceptions over reality. In 1927, when there had been no signs of serious preparations for an invasion of the Soviet Union, there was something of a war panic in Moscow. Now that all the signs were in place and innumerable warnings provided, what should not be could not be.

What made the Soviet miscalculation so terrible was, of course, that by the time Stalin realized that Chamberlain and Roosevelt had been correct in their belief that Germany could be defeated best by an alliance of powers, Germany had with Soviet help driven the Allies out of Northern, Western, and Southern Europe, leaving the Soviet Union alone with the

Germans on the continent in the East. Millions and millions of Soviet citizens would lose their lives over this disastrous miscalculation; only the incredible endurance of a suffering civilian population, the bravery of the Red Army's officers and soldiers, and the diversion of German man-power and resources to an escalating war against the Western Powers could bring survival to the regime.

During and after the war, various new explanations were offered for the Soviet Union's signing the pact. An effort was originally made in official Soviet statements to depict the pact as an instrument of peace, but this line was abandoned after June 1941. It was also asserted that the Western Powers were about to make a Munich-type agreement with Germany, a somewhat curious line of argument which had to be aban-doned when the Soviet Union in the fall of 1939 urged them to make peace with Germany on the assumption that both Poland and Czechoslo-vakia were to disappear.[9] Other arguments advanced in public then and later have asserted that the Western Powers would not make sufficient concessions to the Soviet Union, a point which has to be interpreted in terms of Stalin's own belief that ending the independence of the coun-tries of Eastern Europe was in Soviet as well as German interest. It was also claimed afterward that the expansion of the Soviet Union westward provided an additional buffer against a German invasion, though the events of 1941 would show that the shift from the old defended border to a new one weakened rather than strengthened the ability of the Red Army to hold off the Germans.[10]

There cannot be any doubt whatever that the documents which record the partition of Eastern Europe into spheres of influence between Nazi Germany and the Soviet Union are authentic. The originals were delib-erately destroyed by the Germans, but only after they had been micro-filmed along with a great number of other important documents. A new perception of the past has enabled scholars of the former Soviet Union to see the secret protocol as part of a mistaken and adventurous policy by Stalin which helped bring on a war which cost their people the most terrible losses and for which the country had not been properly prepared. As Europe moves into a new phase, perhaps Russians as well as Germans

9 It has at times been suggested that the Soviet Union reacted to the news of talks in London between a German official, Helmuth Wohlthat, and Robert S. Hudson, Secretary of the Department of Overseas Trade. Since we now know that the Soviet decision to sign a long-term trade agreement with Germany preceded those talks, that theory must be discarded regardless of how the Hudson–Wohlthat talks are interpreted. In view of the information available by that time, I called attention to this point in the preface to the second printing of my *Germany and the Soviet Union, 1939–1941* (Leyden: Brill, 1972), p. vi.
10 The piece cited in n. 7 is especially precise on this point.

may come to see that allowing the peoples between them to enjoy a real independence can contribute to the security of all.

Now that this stage is being reached, scholars of the former Soviet Union can interpret the Nazi–Soviet Pact of 1939 in the light of a speech Maxim Litvinov gave at the League of Nations on September 14, 1935:

> We know of another political conception that is fighting the idea of collective security and advocating bilateral pacts, and this not even between all States, but only between States arbitrarily chosen for this purpose. This conception can have nothing to do with peaceful intentions. Not every pact of non-aggression is concluded with a view to strengthening general peace. While non-aggression pacts concluded by the Soviet Union with its neighbours include a special clause for suspending the pact in cases of aggression committed by one of the parties against any third State, we know of other pacts of non-aggression which have no such clause. This means that a State which has secured by such a pact of non-aggression its rear or its flank obtains the facility of attacking with impunity third States.[11]

Litvinov's description of "other pacts" may serve as a particularly apt characterization of the Nazi–Soviet Pact.

11 Jane Degras (ed.), *Soviet Documents on Foreign Policy*, Vol. 3, *1933–1941* (London: Oxford University Press, 1953), p. 145.

14

·

FROM CONFRONTATION
TO COOPERATION: GERMANY
AND THE UNITED STATES, 1917–1949

Over the years from 1933 to 1949 German–American relations fluctuated more violently than before or since. The inheritance of those fluctuations is still with us. In tracing the dramatic events of those years, I shall combine two approaches: broad interpretive generalization and specific details of recent scholarship.

From a low point in World War I, as well as at and after the peace conference, German–American relations improved steadily in the 1920s. At the beginning of the 1930s, it could be said that no two major powers had fewer difficulties and worked better with each other than the United States and Germany. In the United States, reaction against participation in the war, doubts about the peace settlement, hopes for the success of Germany's experiment in democracy, growing economic ties, and interest in some circles in the cultural experimentation identified with Weimar Germany made for a generally pro-German view of European affairs. In Germany, appreciation of past support for revisions of the peace settlement, hope for more of the same, and less friction than in Germany's relations with most other countries made the United States appear as a benevolent if distant associate in world affairs. This situation would change rapidly after Hitler came to power in Germany.[1]

The economic crisis in the United States kept most Americans from following the details of the last years of the Weimar Republic, a neglect that contributed to the shock produced by the widely reported, extraordinary events surrounding the advent of the new regime in Germany. The American public reacted with astonishment and indignation to the end of democratic institutions and rights in Germany, the interference with the

Slightly revised from my essay in Frank Trommler and Joseph McVeigh (eds.), *America and the Germans: An Assessment of a Three-Hundred-Year History* (Philadelphia: University of Pennsylvania Press, 1985), Vol. 2, pp. 45–58.
1 The subject is reviewed in detail in Gerhard L. Weinberg, *The Foreign Policy of Hitler's Germany*, 2 vols. (Chicago: University of Chicago Press, 1970, 1980; Atlantic Highlands, N.J.: Humanities Press, 1994), esp. Vol. 1, ch. 6, and Vol. 2, ch. 8.

universities, the burning of books, the attacks on the churches, and the discrimination against Jews. Although in America practice – as most knew – often fell short of ideals, the public proclamation in Germany of ideals diametrically opposed to the American ones aroused disgust and distrust. This reaction was accentuated by the conduct of Nazi organizations in the United States, the Friends of the New Germany and the German-American Volksbund, and in a way unrelated to the small size of those formations.[2] The repercussions of a movement looking to foreign political models on a country of immigrants would be hard to exaggerate.

It is, of course, true that groups of immigrants into the United States have maintained and cherished an ethnic identity, but their motives have always been a combination of the desire to preserve their cultural heritage in a new land and continuing interest in the fate of the former homeland. No Polish-Americans, Irish-Americans, or Italian-Americans ever suggested that the political institutions of their prior home should be brought to the United States and substituted for those established in the formative years of the republic. The overwhelming majority of German-Americans fit into this well-established, practically universal pattern. The apparently excessive alarm of the American public at the antics of the Nazi Bund should be seen as an understandable reaction to a unique development that was intuitively and correctly perceived as being novel and dangerous. And if this new movement was described in a term that came to have other connotations – "un-American" – there was in fact a muddled accuracy in that label.[3]

Two additional characteristics of the new Germany contributed to its estrangement from the United States. In both, the policies of Germany and America were moving in opposite directions. While the 1930s saw pacifism reach its greatest strength in this country in the twentieth century, Germany was engaged in a vast rearmament program. Contrary to the German propaganda fables of the 1920s about a highly armed world, the United States like the other victors of World War I had disarmed extensively and had reduced its army voluntarily almost to the 100,000 troop level specified for Germany. It would be years before the United States began to rearm, but in the meantime, the rearmament of Germany – still alleged today by some historians to be among the successes of the Third Reich – made a fatal impression on the American public. And German propagandistic boasting about rearmament only reinforced the impres-

2 A good description in Sander A. Diamond, *The Nazi Movement in the United States, 1924–1941* (Ithaca, N.Y.: Cornell University Press, 1974).

3 What came to be known as the House Committee on Un-American Activities was originally established in March 1934 to investigate *German* activities in the United States. See Walter Goodmen, *The Committee: The Extraordinary Career of the House Committee on Un-American Activities* (New York: Farrar, Straus and Giroux, 1968).

sion that any danger of a new war in Europe stemmed primarily from Germany.

A second alienating issue was to be found in economic policy. Those who were brought to power in this country by the election of 1932 were identified with the policy of tariff reduction in American politics, and they had fought for years against the protectionist policies of Republican opponents and their supporters in trade, industry, and finance. Among those who had long believed in the importance of freeing world trade from barriers both to preserve peace and to promote prosperity was a man whose position in the new administration gave special weight to such views: Cordell Hull, the secretary of state from 1933 to the end of 1944. Hull's role in the years when President Roosevelt was necessarily preoccupied with domestic affairs made his devotion to the cause of freeing the channels of world trade especially significant for American policy at the same time that Germany's trade policies were moving in an opposite direction. The German attempt in 1934 to pressure the United States into a new treaty by terminating the German–American Friendship and Trade Treaty of 1923 was a total failure. In spite of the desperate situation during the Depression, the State Department could resist all efforts at new forms of trade with Germany urged by some inside and outside the administration; the American public's view of Germany had changed too drastically. Hjalmar Schacht, appointed in 1933 to head Germany's central bank, had made his own contribution to this process by his procedures, cheered on by Hitler, for defrauding American holders of German bonds in order to subsidize German foreign trade. The man who could pick out of a nation of 125 million inhabitants precisely those whose funds as buyers of German bonds had helped Germany so that they might be turned against the Third Reich surely deserved his reputation as a wizard.

The German government hardly reacted to the deterioration in German–American relations. Hitler had long anticipated a war against the United States as a necessary part of Germany's future, and initiated important preparations for such a war in the 1930s.[4] The negative reaction of the American public to the new developments in Germany – developments of which he was exceedingly proud – only showed what dolts they were. His racial views made the United States out to be a country incapable of serious effort on the international scene.[5] And his belief, shared by most of those around him, in the truth of the stab-in-

---

4 A preliminary summary in Jochen Thies, *Architekt der Weltherrschaft: Die "Endziele" Hitlers* (Düsseldorf; Droste, 1976), pp. 136–48.
5 See Gerhard L. Weinberg, *World in the Balance: Behind the Scenes of World War II* (Hanover, N.H.: University Press of New England, 1981), pp. 53–95.

the-back legend made the military role of the United States in World War I appear unimportant. The use of Germany's last reserves in World War II in the Ardennes offensive, the Battle of the Bulge, shows that until the end of his career, America would remain in Hitler's eyes the land of unlimited incompetence.

In Washington, on the other hand, the obvious dangers posed by Germany caused increasing alarm, even if the isolationist preferences of the population meant that no active steps were taken in the international arena. President Roosevelt was a tireless collector of information and impressions, and the materials and details he received increasingly pointed toward a new war initiated by Germany. As this danger appeared to grow in the years 1936–38, the president considered a number of nebulous projects designed to awaken the American public to the problems and to alleviate the danger through new forms of international negotiations. All of these fell by the wayside, which gave greater impetus to the one aspect of international policy that appeared capable of implementation: efforts at revival of world trade through multilateral trade concessions and arrangements. It is in this context that one should, in my judgment, see the Tripartite Stabilization Agreement with France and England of September 25, 1936, and the Trade Agreement with England of November 17, 1938.

Roosevelt sympathized in general with the attempts of the British and French governments to reconcile the new Germany by concessions in Europe and Africa to a world order unchanged in its essential nature, but he also gave what support he could to their rearmament projects against the possibility of a new war. He hoped to avert war in 1939 by altering America's neutrality legislation and by advising Stalin to align himself with the Western Powers against the dangers that would be posed for all by Germany if she triumphed in the West. The American Congress, however, left the neutrality laws unamended, and Stalin – as he himself expressed it   preferred to demolish the old equilibrium in Europe with Hitler rather than maintain it against him.[6]

When the war was begun by Germany in September 1939, the American government wanted to remain neutral and hoped that assistance to the Allies would make it possible to stay out of hostilities. The minute size of the American army – in May 1940 less than a third the size of Belgium's – the almost total absence of an air force, and the fact that the navy was smaller than twenty years earlier both reflected and reinforced a strong preference for continued neutrality. The German victories in Scandinavia and in the West in the spring of 1940 brought about some-

6 Ibid., p. 7.

thing like a political revolution in the United States. Roosevelt decided to run for a third term, and Hull's predecessor as Republican secretary of state, Henry Stimson, as well as Frank Knox, the most recent Republican candidate for vice-president, joined the Roosevelt cabinet (after the Republican candidate for president, Alfred Landon, refused to do so) – events without precedent in the history of the United Sates. A massive rearmament program was inaugurated, the most dramatic steps being the bill for the two-ocean navy and the country's first peacetime draft. The direct alliance with Canada created by the Ogdensburg Agreement and the sale, however reluctant, of some of the World War I equipment in American storage to Britain may be seen as the external portions of this reaction to the German triumphs of April, May, and June 1940.

How did Roosevelt see German–American relations in this world turned upside down? There has been endless argument over the issue, and I would like to suggest an interpretation strongly supported by the evidence that has come to light in the last two decades. Roosevelt hoped that aid to Britain would enable that power to survive and fight on. Convinced of the danger to all posed by Germany – as he had warned Stalin – he wanted to rearm the United States, as he had once tried to help France build up its air force, against the possibility that it would be involved in war against its wishes; but he retained a strong preference for avoiding involvement in the war. Britain's success in resisting German attack, and in the following year Russia's ability after initial disasters also to hold out, suggested the possibility that Germany could be defeated by others. Too many have imagined that countries can only be either at peace or at war with each other. A knowledgeable Roosevelt, however, was aware that the American navy had taken its main origins from the Undeclared War with France, a limited struggle of naval engagements without general hostilities between the two former allies; and he was equally aware that Japan and the Soviet Union had in 1938 and 1939 engaged in bloody but limited hostilities at flash points in East Asia without becoming involved in general conflict with each other.

Roosevelt's September 11, 1941, "shoot-on-sight" order to the U.S. navy and the incidents attendant on the flow of American supplies first to England and later to Russia have been interpreted by some as indicating a search for pretexts for war, but they can also be seen as a return to prior American naval policy. This view is reinforced by what we now know about the way the United States put to use in 1941 the knowledge of German naval signals derived from Britain's breaking German naval codes. Far from using this intelligence to arrange for a maximum number of incidents in the Atlantic, as would have been possible, the United

States used the knowledge to minimize incidents and as far as possible avoid them altogether.[7]

This picture of Roosevelt trying to keep the United States from becoming embroiled in general war with Germany has been reinforced by the discovery of recordings of comments he made in the fall of 1940 which were captured by a recording machine that was not turned off at the end of a press conference.[8] Roosevelt explained to the Democratic leaders of the House that if Germany, Italy, or Japan threatened to declare war on the United States if it did not cease aiding Britain, he would reply that that was their problem; the United States would not declare war on them. They could consider themselves belligerents if they wished, but the Americans would defend themselves only if others attacked them. This view of Roosevelt's coincides with extraordinary precision with events when Hungary, Bulgaria, and Romania declared war on the United States in December of 1941: for half a year the American government, at Roosevelt's personal direction, tried unsuccessfully to persuade those countries that their people could manage without a war with the United States before finally declaring war in return on June 5, 1942.[9] A similar policy was followed – with almost the precise words used by Roosevelt on October 4, 1940 – when Thailand declared war on the United States in January 1942.[10] But all such hopes were shattered by German policy.

The German navy had been pushing for war with the United States since fall 1939, but at first Hitler wanted to postpone hostilities until he had been able to build the blue-water navy Germany lacked and to provide it with bases to operate against the Western Hemisphere. Work on such a navy had been started in the mid-1930s but had been interrupted by the outbreak of war in 1939. When the war seemed to be over in the summer of 1940, work on that program was resumed, but again had to be postponed in favor of the buildup for the attack on Russia. When that appeared to be going well in the summer of 1941, the battleship and aircraft carrier projects were again reactivated, only to have to be postponed once more because of the bitter fighting in the East. But by that time, Hitler had found a ready substitute for his own navy in that of Japan.

The German government had been trying to secure the support of

---

7 See Jürgen Rohwer, "Die USA and die Schlacht im Atlantik," Jürgen Rohwer and Eberhard Jäckel (eds.), *Kriegswende Dezember 1941* (Koblenz: Bernard & Graefe, 1984), pp. 81–103, esp. 97, 99, 101.
8 Robert J.C. Butow, "The FDR Tapes," *American Heritage* 33 (February–March 1982): 16–17.
9 *Foreign Relations of the United States; 1942*, Vol. 2, pp. 833–42.
10 Ibid., Vol. 1, p. 916.

Japan against the Western Powers since 1938; in the summer of 1940 it became increasingly insistent that Japan join the war against England and attack toward Singapore. When the Japanese hesitated, Hitler tried to spur them on. Recognizing that in the view of Tokyo, a move south either would have to come after the Americans had left the Philippines in 1946 as existing U.S. legislation specified, or would require a war with the United States, Hitler pressured the Japanese to move quickly. In early April 1941 he promised to join in war against the United States if required by Tokyo as a necessary part of an attack on Britain. If Japan joined in, there would be a blue-water navy on the Axis side right away, and the German navy was straining at the leash. Unlike all previous steps to expand the war, German moves toward war with the United States found practically no opposition within the German government. Blind ignorance, devout belief in the truth of the stab-in-the-back legend, and enthusiasm at the prospect of an open season on Americans combined to make the German official declaration of war on the United States (preceded by several days by the orders to open hostilities), the one occasion in the history of the Third Reich when the cheering of the Reichstag reflected unanimity within the government. For the second time Germany entered war with the United States so as to win more quickly an ongoing war with Britain (see Chapter 15).

The tremendous victories of Japan in East Asia and of the German U-boats off the North American coast in the Atlantic in the first half of 1942 appeared to substantiate the calculations of those in Tokyo, Berlin, and Rome who had gambled on war. But contrary to the expectations of the Germans and the Japanese, the American government was not only determined to conclude with a total victory the war into which the country had been forced, but it was backed by a united public and the necessary human and material resources, even if several years might be required to mobilize them for battle. The American leadership was well aware that such a long delay carried with it the danger of a breakup in the Allied coalition, and it knew from bitter personal experience the debate inside and outside the United States concerning the armistice of 1918 as opposed to demanding Germany's surrender, and the legends subsequently spread about it in Germany; it was therefore firmly convinced that this time the enemies should be forced to capitulate.[11] What Germany had required of Belgium on May 27, 1940 – unconditional surrender[12] – would be Germany's fate. Whatever the difficulties at the front,

---

11 Raymond G. O'Connor, *Diplomacy for Victory: FDR and Unconditional Surrender* (New York: Norton, 1971).

12 Franz Halder, *Kriegstagebuch*, ed. Hans-Adolf Jacobsen, Vol. 1 (Stuttgart: Kohlhammer, 1962), p. 322.

at home, or with the Allies, there were no substantial divergences within the United States on this issue. The picture which the Third Reich presented to the world by its hopes and ambitions left the Americans no alternatives, and what became known about German-dominated Europe in the later years of the war could only reinforce that view within the American government and public.

Expectations for the postwar world within the American government were imprecise on many points until very late in the war and fluctuated considerably. Conscious of the experience of the "secret treaties" of World War I and of the slow unfolding of American military power, President Roosevelt preferred to postpone decisions about such matters as long as possible. He resisted British preference for recognizing and accepting Soviet aspirations in Eastern Europe; knowing this reluctance, the British government without prior consultation with the United States proposed its scheme for the zones of occupation in Germany and joined the Soviets in urging this solution on the Americans. On only one point was Roosevelt, like Winston Churchill, ready to commit the United States in advance to a specific position at the forthcoming peace conference, which all then anticipated would take place soon after the war: East Prussia would never be returned to Germany. On this point the German propaganda about the alleged deficiencies of the peace settlement of 1919 could record one delayed, if unanticipated, final "success."[13]

American strategy in the final phase of the war in Europe was subordinated to the requirements of the war in the Pacific, which was then expected to last an additional eighteen months and which, in the months that the fighting in Europe was ending, was in its bloodiest phase. When the first important American headquarters was pulled out of the European front on May 1, 1945, for transfer to the Pacific, the Third Reich already lay in ruins. At the last minute, the British government tried to get the Americans to revise the occupation zone arrangement which they had persuaded a reluctant Roosevelt to accept a few months before, but Roosevelt's successor, Harry S Truman, was not to be persuaded. I suspect that the internal American comments on this proposal were considerably less polite than Truman's firm refusal. The American troops withdrew or entered into the areas assigned to them by Allied agreement, and an entirely new period of German–American relations began.

The situation in which Americans and Germans faced each other at

13 The formal approval for turning over part of East Prussia to the Soviet Union was given by Truman at Potsdam, but Roosevelt had earlier agreed that East Prussia would not remain a part of Germany.

the end of the European portion of World War II was new for both. There had been an American occupation of parts of Germany after World War I, but it had differed not only geographically but, more important, in purpose and political nature. The American occupation forces of 1918–23 were to demonstrate the contribution of the United States to the victory over Germany; they were also to make certain that the peace treaty was accepted by Germany and not broken by a new war. But the United States then had to deal not only with other occupying powers but with a German central government and an administrative apparatus more or less subordinated to it. The situation in occupied Germany in 1945 was entirely different.

The developments following 1945 cannot be reviewed in detail here, but I would like to set forth some theses concerning events up to 1949. In answering the questions how Germany came to be divided for decades between East and West, how the three Western zones came to be joined into one unit – a far less likely event than is now often assumed – and how German–American relations came to turn around once more, I emphasize four aspects of the situation in those years as being decisive.

In the first place, the conceptions of Germany's future held by the Soviets and by the Americans were diametrically opposed from the start in one most important area. Whatever a new Germany might look like, and whatever its borders might be, Stalin wanted to start the new German system from the top, whereas the Americans wanted to start from the bottom. The Soviet government flew the Ulbricht group to Berlin before the German surrender of May 1945 and attempted to erect a building under this roof during the following years. The major steps and the main difficulties of this process can be understood only if seen from such a perspective.[14] In the years between 1945 and 1948 that meant primarily the creation of the SED, the Socialist Unity Party. Recognizing that the new roof could never be supported by the thin walls of the German Communist Party, the Soviet leadership quickly concluded that only a forced union of the Communist and Socialist parties combined with a ban on the formation of any other workers' party could sustain the new construction.[15] During the period under discussion here, this process produced the party that dominated the German Democratic Republic until its demise, and it also had major repercussions on the other zones of occupation. After 1949, and until its collapse, this birthmark of

14 Alexander Fischer, *Sowjetische Deutschlandpolitik im Zweiten Weltkrieg, 1941–1945* (Stuttgart: Deutsche Verlags-Anstalt, 1975), pp. 156–58, reaches the same conclusion.
15 See Henry Krisch, *German Politics under Soviet Occupation* (New York: Columbia University Press, 1974); Jan Foitzik, "Kadertransfer: Der organisierte Einsatz sudetendeutscher Kommunisten in der SBZ 1945/46," *Vierteljahrshefte für Zeitgeschichte* 31 (1983): 308–34.

the system would leave it permanently in search of internal and external supports to hold up a roof constantly in danger of falling in.

The Americans, operating on their political and ideological perspectives, did the exact opposite. They began at the bottom. Not always very carefully or consistently, and with much confusion and many errors, they built, or encouraged, or kicked the Germans into building, from the local to the regional and wider levels. Those Germans who believed this policy was mistaken and complained, for example, about the delays in the licensing of political parties, would get their chance eventually. Seen from a subsequent perspective, "later" is indeed very different from "never." It was fashionable for a while to pontificate on the alleged interference of the American occupation forces with a real reorganization of German society; what all speculations overlook is that the extreme Right was far stronger and had the potential for far greater support in post-1945 Germany and that the American occupation forces hindered the unreconstructed nationalists and Nazis far more than any other elements in the population from affecting developments in a country where great privation was much more a postwar than a wartime phenomenon as compared with World War I.[16] The development of the American zone of occupation was not only entirely different from that in the Soviet zone, but it was to be far more influential than might have been expected. This brings me to the second and third aspects of the postwar situation.

The British government had insisted that England get the northwest zone. Until late in the fall of 1944 President Roosevelt had opposed this allocation and had insisted for reasons intertwining political and transportation factors that the northwest should go to the United States. Only the united advice of his associates had finally persuaded him to accept a division according to which the Russians got the agriculture, the British the industry, and the Americans the scenery, as the allocation was described at the time. It quickly became evident that the London government had miscalculated badly. At the time when American occupation policy was greatly affected by pressure to reduce the extent to which costs weighed on the American taxpayer, the obvious and rapid decline of British power in the postwar years was decisive for England's policy in Germany. London simply could not afford a policy of its own: the poorest of the great victors had selected for itself the zone of occupation which under the circumstances of the time was by far the most expensive. New decisions would certainly be needed.

16 Hans Woller, "Zur Demokratiebereitschaft in der Provinz des amerikanischen Besatzungsgebiets," *Vierteljahrshefte für Zeitgeschichte* 31 (1983), 343; Daniel E. Rogers, "Transforming the German Party System: The United States and the Origins of Political Moderation, 1945–1949," *Journal of Modern History* 65 (1993): 512–41.

The government of France had been the most consistent of the occupying powers in opposing any larger units or central governmental apparatus in Germany. Under the influence of the national idea as the basis for state formation – which was itself largely of French origin – and of the perceived impossibility of occupying all of Germany, the French government of 1919 had accepted the continued existence of a Germany then less than fifty years old (see Chapter 1). The French would strive to avoid such a settlement in the future. It is difficult to describe with precision what future the French visualized for Germany, but it was definitely not to include any larger units or centralized institutions. In this regard the combination of French colonial wars and the Soviet threat would lead to new decisions. The first – the colonial wars – undermined the position of France in Europe, the second pushed the French government in new directions in its German policy.

The fourth element was pressure from the East. Whether understood correctly or not, the policies of Stalin in the second half of the 1940s led to new choices in the West; and each time difficulties arose among the Western Powers, Soviet action pushed them aside. The blockade of Berlin played a special role in this process. It must be emphasized that this was universally seen and understood as a highly dramatic event. On the German side – including the people of Berlin and the simultaneously convening founders of the Federal Republic – the time had arrived when Germans themselves for the first time since 1945 played a major role in deciding significant aspects of their own fate. And at this time the daily deliveries of the airlift were not only conspicuous at three-minute intervals over Berlin but were everywhere on the radio, in the newspapers, in the newsreels, at the center of both sight and thought. Suddenly one looked at the swarms of large American and British planes in the sky with hope rather than fear. More was turning than the new radar equipment at the Berlin airports.

It was a new beginning for the American public as well. Whatever people might think about the details of American occupation policy – if they thought about the subject at all – they saw the Germans as the recently defeated enemy. This attitude changed in the year of the airlift, and one should recall that it lasted for practically a full year. A new chapter began, and not only for pilots who had perhaps once carried bombs to Berlin and now learned in Montana how to land at Tempelhof airport in the winter. The critical point is that this was a development which took place in full view of the public. It would be difficult to imagine anything more likely to attract attention and influence the average American. The challenge to the technical competence of a proud people combined with the possibility of starvation and enslavement for many who had chosen the American side – no one could have dreamed up a scenario more shrewdly designed for an American audience. Only the Soviet government could conceive of such an effective way of forcing masses of people to rethink their own perceptions and preconceptions. A new state was founded in Germany, and this state would have a new relationship with the United States. Whether or not this chapter in German–American relations is now moving toward an end, it surely began over Berlin in 1948–49.

15

———— • ————

PEARL HARBOR:
THE GERMAN PERSPECTIVE

When news of the Japanese attack on Pearl Harbor reached Germany, that nation's leadership was absorbed by the crisis in its war with the Soviet Union, begun by the German attack earlier that year. In view of a serious defeat administered to the German forces by the Red Army at the southern end of the front, Adolf Hitler had relieved the commander-in-chief of the German army group fighting there, Field Marshal Gerd von Rundstedt, on December 1 and flew to the army group and army headquarters in the southern Ukraine on December 2. Late on December 3, he flew back to his headquarters in East Prussia, only to be greeted by more bad news: the German army group at the northern end of the main front was also being pushed back by Red Army counterattacks; and, most ominous of all, the German offensive in the center toward Moscow was not only exhausted but was itself in danger of being overwhelmed by a Soviet counteroffensive of which the first major effects were beginning to be noted in German headquarters on December 5 and 6.[1] Not yet recognizing the extent of the defeat at the front, and imagining that there would merely be a temporary halt in German offensive operations, Hitler and the German Army Chief of Staff, General Franz Halder, as well as the head of operations in the high command of the armed forces, General Alfred Jodl, prepared a general directive for winter operations which was signed by Hitler, issued on December 8, and quickly overtaken by the reality of Red Army victories on the Eastern Front.[2]

It was in this context of crisis in the land fighting in the East that the German leaders, geographically divided between the East Prussian head-

A revised and documented version of a piece which appeared in *MHQ: The Quarterly Journal of Military History* 4, no. 3 (Spring 1992): 18–23.

1 See Klaus Reinhardt, *Moscow – The Turning Point: The Failure of Hitler's Strategy in the Winter of 1941–42*, trans. K. B. Keenan (Oxford: Berg, 1992).
2 Full text in Walther Hubatsch (ed.), *Hitlers Weisungen für die Kriegführung 1939–1945* (Frankfurt/M: Bernard & Graefe, 1962), pp. 171–74.

quarters and Berlin, heard the news of Japan's attack on Pearl Harbor. Immediately, in the night of December 8, Hitler ordered the German navy to sink at any opportunity the ships of the United States and those Central and South American countries which had declared their solidarity with the United States. That evening he also left East Prussia by train for Berlin, summons having been sent out to the members of the German parliament, the Reichstag, to meet there so that they could hear and acclaim Germany's declaration of war on the United States in a formal session that would be broadcast to the whole country.[3]

Why this eagerness to go to war with the United States, and at a time when Germany already had what its own leaders recognized as a serious situation on the Eastern Front? Why the rush to declare war with only the worry, as both Hitler and his Foreign Minister Joachim von Ribbentrop put it, that the Americans might get their declaration of war in ahead of Germany?[4] Some have argued that this was an irrational reaction designed by Hitler as an escape from worries over the failure of the effort to take Moscow; some have confused the delay of a few days due to the fact that Japan's initiative surprised the Germans with reluctance on Hitler's part; still others imagine that Germany was reacting to American policies of aid to Britain, completely ignoring the fact that in all prior declarations of war on other countries Hitler had disregarded the course of those countries' policies, most recently in the case of the Soviet Union, which had been providing important supplies to Germany until literally minutes before the German attack of June 22, 1941. The reality is that war with the United States had been included in Hitler's program for years, that he had deferred hostilities only because he wanted to begin them at a time and under circumstances of his own choosing, and that the Japanese attack fitted his requirements so precisely that he was positively enthusiastic both at the time and retrospectively.

It had been an assumption of Hitler's since the 1920s that Germany would at some point fight the United States. As early as the summer of 1928 he asserted in his second book (not published until I did it for him in 1961) that strengthening and preparing Germany for war with the United States was one of the tasks of the National Socialist movement.[5] Both because his aims for Germany's future entailed an unlimited expansionism of global proportions and because he thought of the United States as a country which with its population and size might at some time

3 The text of Hitler's speech is in Max Domarus (ed.), *Hitler: Reden und Proklamationen, 1932–1945* (Neustadt a. d. Aisch: Verlagsdruckerei Schmidt, 1963), pp. 1794–1811.
4 Ernst von Weizsäcker, *Erinnerungen* (Munich: Paul List, 1950), p. 328.
5 Gerhard L. Weinberg (ed.), *Hitlers zweites Buch: Ein Dokument aus dem Jahr 1928* (Stuttgart: Deutsche Verlags–Anstalt, 1961), p. 130.

constitute a challenge to German domination of the globe, a war with the United States had long been a part of the future he envisioned for Germany either during this own rule of it or thereafter.

During the years of his chancellorship before 1939, German policies designed to implement the project of a war with the United States had been conditioned by two factors: belief in the truth of the stab-in-the-back legend on the one hand and the practical problems of engaging American military power on the other. The belief in the concept that Germany had lost the First World War because of the collapse at home – the stab in the back of the German army – rather than defeat at the front automatically carried with it a converse of enormous significance which has generally been ignored. It made the military role of the United States in that conflict into a legend. Believing that the German army had not been beaten in the fighting, Hitler and many others in the country disbelieved that it had been American participation which had enabled the Western Powers to hold on in 1918 and then move toward victory over Germany. They perceived that to be a foolish fable, not a reasonable explication of the events of that year. Only those Germans who remained unenlightened by nationalist euphoria could believe that American forces had played any significant role in the past or could do so in the future. A solid German home front, which National Socialism would ensure, could preclude defeat next time; the problem of fighting the United States was *not* that the inherently weak and divided Americans could create, field, and support effective fighting forces, but rather that they were so far away and that the intervening ocean could be blocked by a large American fleet. Here were the practical problems of fighting America: distance and the size of the American navy. Three facets of this issue will be reviewed here: first, how Hitler planned and tried to deal with these two practical problems, second, how Japan fitted into these efforts, and finally why there was such unanimity, even enthusiasm, for war with the United States in the Germany of 1941.

Unlike the German government of the pre-1914 era, in which the discussion over war with the United States took the form of debates about the relative merits of landing on the beaches of Cape Cod versus landing on the beaches of Long Island, debates Holger Herwig has described in some detail, the German government of the 1930s went at the matter from a more practical side.[6] In line with its emphasis on the building up of the German air force, specifications were issued in 1937 and 1938 for what became the ME-264 and was soon referred to inside

6 A summary in Holger H. Herwig, *Politics of Frustration: The United States in German Naval Planning, 1889–1941* (Boston: Little Brown, 1976), ch. 2.

the government as the "America-Bomber" or the "New York Bomber."[7] Capable of carrying a five-ton load of bombs to New York, a smaller load to the Middle West, or reconnaissance missions over the West Coast and then returning to Germany without intermediate bases, such long-range planes would bring Germany's new air force directly into the skies over America. Several types and models were experimented with, the first prototype flying in December 1940, but none of these advanced beyond preliminary models. Instead, Hitler and his advisors came to concentrate ever more on an alternative means of approach to the Western Hemisphere: acquiring bases for the German air force on the coast of Northwest Africa as well as on the Spanish and Portuguese islands off that coast after the defeat of France. Since these efforts, and the discussion of Hitler with his naval advisors and with Japanese diplomats about bombing the United States from the Azores, took place in 1940 and 1941, that is, during the war, they will be reviewed in that context; we must look at the prewar, naval planning first.

The Germans, like the Japanese, faced in the 1930s the question of how to cope with the American navy in the furtherance of their respective expansionist ambitions. Without the slightest consultation on this point – in fact, as far as is known today, in complete ignorance of each other's projects – the two powers came to exactly the same conclusion. In both countries the decision was to trump American quantity with quality, to build superbattleships which by their vastly greater size could carry far heavier armament firing over greater distances and thus able to destroy the American battleships at ranges these could not match. As an article in *The Journal of Military History* explains in detail, the Japanese began constructing three such superbattleships in great secrecy, one subsequently being converted into an aircraft carrier.[8] The Germans hoped to engage the same problem by the construction of six superbattleships, plans being worked out in 1937 and 1938, with the keels of the first ones being laid down in April and May of 1939.[9] These 56,200 ton monsters would outclass not only the new American battleships of the "North Carolina" class then beginning to be built, but even the successor "Iowa" class of which the *Missouri* was to become especially famous. The precise details of how a war with the United States would actually be conducted

---

7 Jochen Thies, *Architekt der Weltherrschaft: Die "Endziele" Hitlers* (Düsseldorf: Droste, 1976), pp. 136ff.

8 Malcolm Muir, Jr., "Rearming in a Vacuum: United States Naval Intelligence and the Japanese Capital Ship Threat, 1936–1945," *Journal of Military History* 54 (1990): 473–85. The original Japanese plan called for four such ships, but one was scrapped while still under construction.

9 Jost Dülffer, *Weimar, Hitler und die Marine: Reichspolitik und Flottenbau 1920 bis 1939* (Düsseldorf: Droste, 1973), pp. 384–85.

was not a subject to which it seemed to Hitler or his associates it made much sense to devote a great deal of attention. When the time came, something could always still be worked out; what was important was to prepare the prerequisites for success.

The beginning of World War II in September of 1939 led to a cessation of work on those portions of the blue-water navy not near completion, and that included the superbattleships. The immediate exigencies of the war took precedence over projects that could not be finished in the near future. Almost immediately, however, the German navy, starting in October 1939, urged steps by Germany that would bring the United States into the war.[10] Admiral Raeder, the navy's commander-in-chief, could hardly wait to go to war with the United States, hoping that the increase in sinkings of merchant shipping that would result from a completely unrestricted submarine campaign against American as well as other ships would have a major impact on a Britain whose surface navy Germany could not yet defeat; but Hitler held back. From the latter's point of view, what was the point of getting a marginal increase in U-boat sinkings when Germany had neither a major surface navy as yet nor bases for it to operate from? The spring of 1940 appeared to provide the opportunity to remedy both deficiencies.

The conquest of Norway in April 1940 produced two immediate decisions related to our topic: first, Norway would be incorporated into the Third Reich, and second, a major permanent naval base for Germany's new navy would be built on the former Norwegian, now German, coast at Trondheim with a large entirely German city being added, all of it connected directly to mainland Germany by special roads, bridges, and railways. This colossal project was worked on until the spring of 1943.[11] The conquest of the Low Countries and France which followed soon after that of Norway appeared to open further prospects. In the eyes of Hitler and his associates, the war in the West was over; they had won and could turn to their next objectives. On land that meant an invasion of the Soviet Union, a simple task that Hitler originally hoped to complete in the fall of 1940 but was persuaded to postpone until the spring of 1941. (See Chapter 12 of this volume.) At sea, it meant that both sea and air deficiencies for war with the United States could now be tackled.

On July 11, 1940, Hitler ordered the resumption of the naval con-

---

10 The arguments can be followed in the published records of the conferences of Hitler and
    Raeder which exist in various English and German language editions.
11 Some references to the Trondheim project will be found in my *A World at Arms: A Global
    History of World War II* (Cambridge: Cambridge University Press, 1994), see esp. p. 982, n.
    233.

struction program.[12] The superbattleships together with large numbers of aircraft carriers, cruisers, and hundreds of other warships could now be built. While that program went forward, there would be not only naval base construction at Trondheim and a taking over of the French naval bases on the Atlantic coast, but the land connection across German-occupied France to Spain and then across Spain to North Africa could now be utilized for the acquisition and development of air and sea bases in French and Spanish northwest Africa as well as the Spanish and Portuguese islands in the Atlantic.[13] Here would be the perfect bases for war with the United States on which the new fleet could be based and from which airplanes that did not yet quite meet the earlier extravagant specifications could deal with the Americans.

These rosy prospects did not work out the way the Germans had expected. Whatever Francisco Franco's enthusiasm for joining the war on the side of Germany and whatever his willingness to assist his friend in Berlin, the Spanish dictator was a nationalist who was not about to yield Spanish sovereignty to anyone else, in either old Spanish territory or the new, formerly French, perhaps British, and even former German colonial territory he expected as a reward for joining the Axis. The fact that the Germans in 1940 were willing to sacrifice the participation of Spain in the war on their side rather than give up on their project for bases on and off the coast of Northwest Africa is an excellent indication of the priority which the German leaders at the time assigned to their concept of war with the United States. Franco's offer of the use of Spanish bases was not enough for them; German sovereignty was what they believed their schemes required. When the Spanish foreign minister went to Berlin in September and when Hitler and Franco met in October 1940, it was the issue of German bases in present and anticipated Spanish territory that caused a fundamental rift between the prospective partners in war.

But not only the bases proved elusive. As the preparations for war with the Soviet Union made another reallocation of armament resources necessary, the construction of the blue-water navy was once again halted in the late fall of 1940. Under these circumstances Hitler once again had to restrain the enthusiasm of the German navy for war with the United States. But why was the navy so enthusiastic? This was because it be-

12 Some of the figures then considered in German naval headquarters are reviewed in Michael Salewski, *Die deutsche Seekriegsleitung 1935–1945*, Vol. 1 (Frankfurt/M: Bernard & Graefe, 1970), p. 238.
13 Details in Norman J. Goda, "Germany and Northwest Africa: Politics and Strategy of Global Hegemony," unpublished Ph.D. dissertation, University of North Carolina, 1991.

lieved in World War II as in World War I that the way to defeat England
lay in unrestricted submarine warfare even if that meant war with the
United States. But Hitler was doubtful that what had not worked the last
time would work this time; he had other ideas for coping with England. It
was in this context that Japan came into the picture.

Since the Germans had long looked toward a war with the Western
Powers as the major and difficult prerequisite for the easy conquest of the
Soviet Union, and since it appeared to them that Japan's ambition in East
Asia clashed with British, French, and American interests, Berlin had
tried for years to obtain Japanese participation in an alliance directed
against the West.[14] The authorities in Tokyo had been happy to work
with Germany, but major elements in the government there had been
reluctant about war with Britain and France. Some preferred a war with
the Soviet Union, others were worried about a war with the United States
which they saw as a likely concomitant of war with Britain and France,
some thought that it would be best to settle the war with China first, and
still others held some combination of the preceding views. In any case, all
German efforts to rope Japan into an alliance directed against the West
had failed; and the German reaction to this failure, their signing of a
nonaggression pact with the Soviet Union in 1939, had served to alienate
some of their best friends in a Japan which was then engaged in open
hostilities with the Soviet Union on the border between their respective
East Asian puppet states of Manchukuo and Mongolia. From the perspective of both Berlin and Tokyo, these issues appeared to be trans-
formed in 1940 by the German victories in the West.[15]

From the view of Tokyo, the defeat of the Netherlands and France and
the need of the English to concentrate on defense of the home islands
appeared to open the colonial empires of Southeast Asia to easy conquest. From the perspective of Berlin, the same lovely prospects lay in
front of the Japanese, but there was no reason to let the latter have all this
without some military contribution to the common cause of maximum
looting. That contribution would lie in pouncing on the British Empire in
Southeast Asia, especially Singapore, *before*, not after England had followed France and Holland into defeat. Such a Japanese step would at one
stroke solve the problem of how to deal with the United States.

In the short run, Japanese participation in the war would divert American attention and resources from the Atlantic to the Pacific. In the long
run, and of even greater importance, was that in this fashion the Axis

14 These issues are reviewed in the author's *The Foreign Policy of Hitler's Germany: Starting
World War II, 1937–1939* (Chicago: University of Chicago Press, 1980; Atlantic Highlands,
N.J.: Humanities Press, 1994), chs. 12–13.
15 For details and sources, see my *A World at Arms*, pp. 166–86 and ch. 4.

would acquire a huge and effective navy. At a time when the United States had a navy barely adequate for one ocean, and assumed that the Panama Canal made it possible to move that navy from one ocean to the other, no one had figured out a way to employ the same navy in two oceans at the same time. If this was the basic concern behind the American project for a two-ocean navy, authorized by Congress in July 1940 but obviously not likely to be completed for years, its converse was a lengthy interval when any major American involvement in a Pacific conflict would make substantial support of Britain in the Atlantic impossible. After all, the obvious at least temporary alternative to building your own navy was to find an ally who already had one. The Germans believed that Japan's navy in 1940–41 was the strongest and best on the globe (and it is quite possible that this assessment was correct). It is in this framework of expectations that one can perhaps more easily understand the two, apparently contradictory policies toward the United States followed by the Germans in 1941.

On the one hand, Hitler repeatedly ordered restraint on the German navy to avoid incidents in the Atlantic which might bring the United States into the war against Germany. Whatever steps the United States might take in its policy of aiding Great Britain, Hitler would not take these as a pretext to go to war with America until *he* thought the time proper: American Lend-Lease legislation no more affected his policy toward the United States than the simultaneous vast increase in Soviet assistance to Germany influenced his decision on war with the Soviet Union. If in this manner he appeared to be avoiding open hostilities with the United States, on the other hand, he repeatedly promised the Japanese that if they believed that war with the United States was an essential part of any entrance into the war against England, Germany would join them in such a conflict. Hitler personally made this pledge to Japanese Foreign Minister Matsuoka Yosuke when the latter visited Germany in early April 1941,[16] and it was repeated on various occasions thereafter.

The apparent contradiction between trying to avoid submarine-caused incidents with the United States on the one hand, and promising to join Japan in war on the United States on the other, is easily resolved if one keeps in mind what was central in the thinking of the German leader and very quickly became generally understood in the German government of the time. As long as Germany had to face the United States essentially by herself, she needed time to build her own blue-water navy; it therefore made sense to postpone hostilities with the Americans until Germany had been able to remedy this deficiency. If, on the other hand, Japan

---

16 *Akten zur deutschen auswärtigen Politik, 1918–1945*, Series D, Vol. XII/1, No. 286, p. 376.

would come into the war on Germany's side, then that problem was automatically solved.

This approach as seen from Berlin will also make it easier to understand why the Germans were not particular about the sequence. If Japan would go to war in the spring or summer of 1941, even before the German invasion of the Soviet Union, that was just fine and Germany would immediately join in. When it appeared that Japanese–American negotiations might lead to some agreement – during the Japanese–American negotiations of the spring and summer of 1941 unraveled by Professor Robert Butow – the Germans tried hard to torpedo those talks.[17] One way that Berlin then tried to preclude a Japanese–American agreement of any sort was by drawing Japan into the war through the back door by getting them into the war with the Soviet Union at a time when the Germans were still certain that war was headed for a quick and victorious ending,[18] but Tokyo preferred to continue with its emphasis on the strike southward rather than in the opposite direction.

In the summer of 1941, while the Japanese seemed to the Germans to be hesitating, the German campaign in the East appeared to be going just perfectly. As in the preceding year, when Berlin thought that the war in the West had been won, so now when it was believed that the war with the Soviet Union was going according to plan, the first and most immediate reaction was a return to the program of naval construction. In the weapons technology of the 1930s and 1940s, big warships were the system with the longest lead time from orders to completion. The German leaders were entirely aware of this and highly sensitive to its implications. Whenever the opportunity appeared to be there, they turned first to the naval construction program. Once again, in 1941 as in 1940, the prospect of prompt victory over the immediate foe faded from view, and once again work on the big warships had to be halted. This renewed postponement only reinforced the German hope that Japan would move and the enthusiasm with which her action would be greeted.

Just as the Germans had not kept the Japanese informed of their plans to attack other countries, so the Japanese kept the Germans in the dark about their plans. When Tokyo was ready to move, it only had to check with the Germans (and Italians) again to make sure that they were as willing to go to war against the United States alongside Japan as they had repeatedly asserted they were. As the Germans quickly reassured them in late November and again at the beginning of December, the Japanese had nothing to worry about. Germany, like Italy, was eager to go to war with the United States provided only that Japan took the plunge.[19] There

17 Weinberg, *A World at Arms*, pp. 250–51.
18 Ibid., p. 252.   19 Ibid., pp. 262–63.

were, however, two ways in which the German declaration of war on the United States differed from her going to war with other countries: the timing and the absence of opposition. In all other cases, the timing of war had been essentially in Germany's own hands. This time the date was selected by an ally who moved at a time of his own choosing and had kept the Germans uninformed. Hitler had not known the first time he promised Japanese Foreign Minister Matsuoka Yosuke on April 4, 1941, a German entrance into the war that Japan would dither for months; he also did not know the last time Tokyo checked that this time the Japanese intended to move immediately, something they concealed from the Germans (as from their own diplomats) to assure total surprise. As a result, Hitler was caught out of town at the time of Pearl Harbor and had to get back to Berlin and summon the Reichstag to acclaim war. His great worry, and that of his foreign minister, was that the Americans might get their declaration of war in ahead of his own. As von Ribbentrop explained it, "A great power does not allow itself to be declared war upon; it declares war on others." He did not need to lose much sleep; the Roosevelt administration was quite willing to let the Germans take the lead. Just to make sure, however, that hostilities started immediately, Hitler had already issued orders to his navy, straining at the leash since October 1939, to begin sinking American ships forthwith, even before the formalities of declaring war.[20] Now that Germany had a big navy on its side, there was no need to wait even an hour. The very fact that the Japanese had started hostilities the way Germany had begun its attack on Yugoslavia earlier that year, by a Sunday morning attack in peacetime, showed what a delightful and appropriate ally Japan would be.

The second way in which this German declaration of war differed from most which had preceded was in the absence of opposition. Practically every time Germany had gone to war up to this point, there had been a substantial degree of argument within the government and the military. Most recently, Hitler's intention of invading the Soviet Union had drawn oral and written objections from some in the German military, diplomatic, and administrative hierarchy. With the sole exception of the last German ambassador to the United States, Hans-Heinrich Dieckhoff, no one had any objections this time. When the Germans repeatedly promised Japan that they would join in war with the United States, no one had suggested caution. For once the frenetic applause of the unanimous Reichstag, the German parliament last elected in 1938, reflected a unanimous government and military leadership. Germany had not been

---

20 The order is recorded in the diary of the German navy command for December 9, 1941 (Germany, Seekriegsleitung, Kriegstagebuch Teil A, Vol. 28, pp. 135–36, Bundesarchiv/ Militärarchiv, RM 7/31).

defeated at the front in World War I but had succumbed to the home front's collapse when that home front had been deluded by Woodrow Wilson's siren songs from across the Atlantic. There was now no danger of anything like that happening again. The opponents of the regime at home had been silenced; its imagined Jewish enemies were already being slaughtered with hundreds of thousands killed by the time of Hitler's speech of December 11, 1941. With a strong navy at Germany's side, victory *this* time was certain. But as a German saying puts it: in the first place it turns out differently, in the second place from what one expects.

From the perspective of half a century, one can see an additional unintended consequence of Pearl Harbor for the Germans. It not only meant that they would most certainly be defeated. It also meant that the active coalition against them would include the United States as well as Great Britain, its Dominions (except for Ireland), the Free French, various governments in exile, and the Soviet Union. This would mean that there could be a major cross-Channel invasion of Europe, based on the United Kingdom, to drive into Germany itself as it was crushed by the coalition the Germans had arrayed against themselves. The most likely alternative would have been a Germany eventually completely occupied by the Red Army. If the Germans today enjoy both their freedom and their unity in a country aligned and allied with what their leaders of 1941 considered the degenerate Western democracies, they owe it in part to the disastrous cupidity and stupidity of their Japanese friends.

16

―――――――― • ――――――――

GLOBAL CONFLICT:
THE INTERACTION BETWEEN THE
EUROPEAN AND PACIFIC THEATERS
OF WAR IN WORLD WAR II

The concept of an earth that is round rather than flat is supposed to be generally accepted, but is implications for history – as opposed to navigation – are not always recognized. The Second World War is all too often looked at as if the world were a cube. One side of the globe is examined after another, one theater is reviewed after the next, and in the process the interrelations between them are all too often overlooked. This is particularly true of the European and Pacific theaters, which are usually dealt with quite separately, only the barest mention being made of the interconnected character of global war. But when we do this, treating war on one side of the globe as a sort of appendix to the other or alternating mechanically between them, we hide from our vision key aspects of all theaters of war and make it impossible to understand significant features of the conflict. What I would like to do here is to point toward a different view of the war by examining the interrelation of the European with the Pacific theater of war at critical points: the initiation of war in the Pacific with its great Japanese victories, the possibility of a German–Japanese meeting in the Indian Ocean and the elimination of this possibility by Allied arms, the inability of the Axis powers to coordinate their submarine campaigns in the middle of the war, the failure of the Axis powers to coordinate their political strategy in the war, and, finally, the way in which developments in Europe determined the ending of the war in the Pacific even as the last stages of the war in the Pacific shaped the Europe that was already emerging into a new era.

The willingness of Japan to expand her local East Asian conflict with China into a portion of the general war which Germany had initiated in

This is a slightly revised translation of an essay originally published in Karl Dietrich Bracher et al. (eds.), *Deutschland zwischen Krieg und Frieden* (Düsseldorf: Droste, 1991), pp. 89–98. Only minimal references are provided; the details are more fully documented in my *A World at Arms: A Global History of World War II* (Cambridge: Cambridge University Press, 1994).

Europe was entirely dependent on both the existence of that war and the course it had taken. There would, in other words, have been no Pacific war at all had there not already been a European war. Furthermore, the actual development of that European war determined the direction of Japan's thrust as well as her decision to take the plunge. The victory of Germany over France and the Netherlands uncovered the colonial possessions of those powers in Southeast Asia which Japan coveted; the unwillingness of Great Britain to make peace with a Germany triumphant on the European continent meant that the military resources of the United Kingdom would continue to be needed for the defense of the home islands and the Middle East, thereby leaving the territories Britain controlled in South and Southeast Asia as well as the South Pacific almost as undefended as the French and Dutch ones; and the German attack on the Soviet Union provided the latter with every incentive to adhere for the time being to the Soviet–Japanese Neutrality Pact of April 1941, a point on which the Japanese reassured themselves before heading south. And they also checked to be sure that Germany and Italy would join them in war against the United States.

The outbreak of general war in the Pacific was thus essentially a function of the war in Europe. The decision for war in Tokyo was the result of an opportunity which it was believed Germany's initiative had created. The general direction of the Japanese advance was framed by the configuration of prior hostilities elsewhere; and Yamamoto appears to have been influenced by the British attack on the Italian navy at anchor in Taranto in November 1940 in making his plan for an attack on the American ships at Pearl Harbor.[1] Once they started their advance, however, the Japanese quickly lost sight of the preconditions for their great initial successes. Intoxicated by their early victories, they overlooked the derivative character of their great conquests. Not surprisingly they attributed the triumphs won over the American, British, and Dutch forces in the first five months of hostilities to their own daring, bravery, and planning, and in the process acquired an ever higher opinion of themselves and lower opinion of others, especially Americans and Europeans. Given the spectacular character of the Japanese advances and the fact that it was, of course, Japanese forces which really were carrying them out, such a result should be easy to understand. It produced, nevertheless, a false picture, since it ignored the crucial role of prior German victories in making the Japanese victories possible. As a result of the self-centered

---

1 The article by Hans Lengerer and Sumie Kobler-Edamatsu, "Die Entstehung des Operationsplanes für den Angriff auf die US-Pazifikflotte in Pearl Harbor," *Marine-Rundschau* 78, No. 12 (December 1981), brings some interesting details from Japanese sources but is also highly apologetic in tone and marred by numerous errors.

euphoria in Tokyo, German advice that the key aim of Axis policy in the spring and summer of 1942 should be a meeting in the Indian Ocean was ignored for too long.

The myopic inclinations of the Japanese in the spring of 1942 were reinforced by three factors. The prestige of Yamamoto gave added weight to his urgings of an offensive in the Central Pacific. The difficulties the Japanese were beginning to have in the South Pacific, symbolized by the check suffered at the Battle of the Coral Sea northeast of Australia in early May, contrasted with the continued victories in Burma and suggested to some a reinforcement at the point of troubles rather than a further push in the area of rapid advance. Finally, the bombing of Tokyo by Doolittle's raid in April undermined Japan's confidence in its inaccessibility to air attack which came from Soviet assurances that U.S. planes would not be allowed to fly from Soviet Far Eastern bases. The air raid, flown by army planes but from an aircraft carrier, at first suggested to the Japanese a *land* base, and that meant Midway Island. Instead of following up their victory off Ceylon in early April, the Japanese headed in the opposite direction. Not only did they meet disaster in this direction in the first week of June 1942, but their disregard for coordination with their main European ally contradicted the basis of their position in the broader conflict.

In the summer of 1942, even as they ran into difficulties on the periphery of their newly captured empire, the Japanese did begin to pay more serious attention to the possibility of linking up with their European associates. An Axis meeting across the Indian Ocean would disrupt the whole supply system of the Western Allies, would shift the oil resources of the Middle East to the powers of the Tripartite Pact, would cut the southern supply route to the Soviet Union, and would instead facilitate the exchange of critical materials between Germany and Japan, substituting a flow of goods for a trickle of blockade breakers.

The Germans and Italians had in prewar days talked of striking into the Indian Ocean from bases in Italian Somaliland, but those dreams had evaporated when the British conquered the area in early 1941. The defeats of Italy in Africa in the winter of 1940–41 had, however, brought the Germans onto the Libyan scene in the form of Rommel's Africa Corps. In the summer of 1942 Rommel had resumed the offensive and was moving toward the Suez Canal with extraordinary rapidity. Simultaneously, the German return to the offensive on the Eastern Front opened up the possibility of an expedition across the Caucasus into the Middle East from the north with the added prospect of a German thrust through Turkey. Here were indeed prospects of a drastic acceleration in the tide of Axis victories and Allied defeats.

When we ask the question, why did not the Japanese now resume the offensive in the Indian Ocean they had begun so auspiciously in April, only to hold back there while emphasizing other fronts, we cannot look for an answer to the troubled Japanese advance on New Guinea, for there the forces actually engaged remained extremely small. Nor can we simply point to the Japanese defeat at Midway; soon after the loss of four carriers in that battle, the large carrier damaged in the Coral Sea battle as well as the other such ship engaged there were again available for action. The rest of Japan's surface fleet had in any case hardly been touched during the course of hostilities up to the summer of 1942.[2] The focus of attention, therefore, must be on the campaign in the Solomon Islands.

The long and bitter struggle for Guadalcanal has generally been viewed in isolation or at most in terms of American strategy and Japan's response to the first serious American counteroffensive. There is another way to fit this campaign into the broader picture of World War II.

The Japanese reaction to the landing of American forces on Tulagi and Guadalcanal in the Solomon Islands on August 7, 1942, which crossed Japan's own offensive in the South Pacific, produced five months of continuing crisis as each side in turn reinforced the units already engaged, striving to offset losses and to turn definitively in its own favor the ever-changing tide of battle. If the Americans were unwilling to abandon their first major counteroffensive under circumstances certain to lead to further spectacular Japanese victories, Imperial Headquarters in Tokyo thought it had every reason to persist in its strategy of fighting hard on the periphery of the newly won – and hopefully still to be expanded – empire. And the great initial Japanese naval victory at Savo Island off the coast of Guadalcanal in the night of August 8–9 had confirmed both sides in their respective views.

The resulting desperate naval, air, and land struggle which continued for the remainder of 1942 has too often been looked at only on its own terms. If its broader ramifications have been considered at all, it has been in terms of a greater diversion of American forces from the Atlantic to the Pacific theater than had been contemplated by the Europe First strategy. The critical point I would like to stress is the fact that Japan's steady pouring of her naval air strength, her warships, and her ground combat assault troops into the struggle for the Solomons precluded a

2 According to the chronological listing, *Japanese Naval and Merchant Shipping Losses during World War II by All Causes,* issued by the Joint Army–Navy Assessment Committee (Washington, D.C.: GPO, 1947), the Japanese navy had lost up to the time of the American landings in the Solomons, in addition to the four carriers sunk in the Battle of Midway, altogether one heavy cruiser, one light carrier, eight destroyers, one frigate, and miscellaneous smaller warships. Additional ships had, of course, been damaged in the initial Japanese campaigns, but most had been repaired and others were newly commissioned.

return to the offensive in the Indian Ocean. The Japanese did come to anticipate such a return, and they so informed their German ally; but the naval and naval air units needed for that offensive were slowly but steadily headed for the bottom of the appropriately renamed "Iron-Bottom Bay" off the Guadalcanal coast. What did this diversion of *Japanese* attention and resources mean?

It meant that there would be no possibility of any major Japanese thrust into the Indian Ocean. In the very days of the initial American landings in the Solomons, the British Eighth Army was battling to hold the approaches to the Suez Canal as the Germans and Italians were within a couple of hours' drive of Cairo. The supplies lost by the British in their African disasters of the summer of 1942 could be replaced, and additional forces and equipment sent to Egypt, relatively safely because the Indian Ocean was still open to the Allies. The British had recognized the critical importance of Madagascar at about the same time as the Germans and the Japanese. For the first time in World War II, the Allies managed to get somewhere *before* the Axis when in early May – during the Battle of the Coral Sea – British forces landed on Madagascar, thereby making any Axis seizure of the key base at Diego Suarez extremely difficult. For the reason I have just discussed, the Japanese counter to this British response to the Japanese attack on Ceylon never took place. The Middle East remained in Allied hands, and by the time the Japanese had shifted their emphasis from Guadalcanal to the Northern Solomons at the beginning of 1943, the battle for control of North Africa had been decided, even if not yet finally concluded.

The fighting in the Solomons similarly coincided with the Soviet struggle to contain Germany's new offensive on the Eastern Front. The Red Army was holding at Stalingrad and in the Caucasus even as the American supply route across Iran was coming into full use: October 1942 was the first of two months of World War II in which that route carried the majority of American supplies to the Soviet Union. The Soviets would not have to be concerned about still another front on which they might be threatened; instead almost a quarter of the total supplies they would receive from the United States could come through the Indian Ocean and across Iran.

But these were not the only results of the riveting of Japanese power to the struggle in the South Pacific. The opportunity to topple British power in India at its weakest between 1857 and 1947 passed unutilized by the Axis. Here was Japan's land alternative to an oceanic thrust westward. It went unexploited at the critical moment. And with it also went the one real opportunity for Japan to cut major supply routes to Nationalist China: the air supply route over the Hump as it was called and the land supply route which came to be called the Ledo Road. The utilization of both routes had as a prerequisite the diversion of Japanese power from Northeast India, that is from Assam, to the campaigns in the South and Southwest Pacific.

In the middle period of the war, meaning primarily 1943, the main land front was the bloody struggle between German and Soviet forces on the Eastern Front. The contest dominating Allied strategy, however, was the Battle of the Atlantic. The very high level of sinkings threatened to immobilize Britain and the United States entirely, leaving them incapable of carrying the war effectively to Germany even if England should somehow survive. But the U-boat threat had implications for the war on the Eastern Front as well. The margin of mobility for the Red Army would have to be provided to a large extent by the delivery of American trucks, while the survival of much of the Russian civilian population depended on shipments of American grain – both vulnerable to the war against Allied tonnage waged by Germany.

It should not be surprising that the Germans tried their best to persuade the Japanese to join in this campaign and to use their substantial fleet of submarines, equipped with the best torpedoes of any belligerent, in the war on Allied shipping. The marginal increment in total sinkings that the numerous Japanese submarines might provide could well be that addition needed to sever the Allied supply routes, or at least to damage them even more severely. Why did this not happen?

The Japanese had developed their submarine force as an auxiliary to the surface fleet in the strictest sense, that is, as a means of aiding that fleet in combat against the navies of Japan's enemies, particularly the United States. Before Yamamoto pressured the Imperial Navy into his Pearl Harbor plan in the late fall of 1941, the Japanese had always intended to use their submarines for harrying the American navy, reducing its size by torpedo attacks as that navy moved across the Pacific, and leaving it smaller and damaged enough to be overwhelmed by the Japanese navy. When this strategy was scrapped in favor of Yamamoto's concept, however, there was no reorientation of Japanese submarine employment doctrine, a reorientation for which there was, in any case, only a few weeks' time.

Japanese submarines would still be used to engage warships, and the German urgings for redirecting emphasis toward the war on Allied shipping at first fell on deaf ears. Slowly, very slowly, the Japanese leaders came around to the German point of view. They had actually had considerable success against Allied shipping in the Indian Ocean in April 1942, but this had seemed to them an aberration in the employment of submarines. As Japanese naval officers began to grasp that the best hope for the Axis lay in paralyzing their enemies by a war on Allied shipping, they found, however, that new and entirely unanticipated developments in the Pacific War precluded their putting the newly adopted concept into practice.

The combination of U.S. attacks on Japanese shipping, primarily by submarine, with MacArthur's strategy of bypassing Japanese garrisons in the Southwest Pacific increasingly forced the Japanese navy into a new pattern of submarine employment. If the Japanese garrisons isolated by American and Australian advances were to remain even the least bit effective militarily, they had to be supplied with certain critical materials: ammunition, spare parts, and medicine. Increasingly submarine supply would become the only practical way to provide these items, and the very submarine commanders who had once disdained as unheroic any campaign against merchant ships now found themselves in the equally hazardous but even less heroic business of running sacks of rice and crates of ammunition to assorted remnants of Japan's outer garrisons.

To try to compensate for this diversion of submarines, the Japanese secured a German U-boat as a model for their own construction program and provided basing for a small squadron of German submarines on the Malay coast. Whatever results these operations provided, however, were too little and too late. The struggle over the oceanic supply routes was won by the Allies in 1943, and nothing the Japanese or the Germans tried to do could reverse this situation.

If the inability of the European Axis and Japan to coordinate their military strategy and to cooperate in naval operations contributed signally to their eventual defeat in spite of enormous initial victories, the divergence in their political strategy contributed toward the same end. The fact that Germany was at war with the Soviet Union while Japan was determined to keep peace with that country created a host of difficulties for both. It should not be difficult to understand how upset the Germans were over the sight of American supplies pouring into Vladivostok and the Soviet East Asian arctic ports. About half the total tonnage shipped to the Soviet Union was passing quite literally under the noses of the Japanese in the very years that Germany's military machine was bleeding to death on the Eastern Front.[3] Time and again the Germans urged their ally in East Asia to take steps to interrupt or at least to restrain the flow of supplies, only to be told that this was out of the question. The converse of Soviet assurances to Japan that U.S. planes could not use Soviet Far

---

3 The generally very useful work of Alexander Lensen, *The Strange Neutrality: Soviet–Japanese Relations during the Second World War, 1941–1945* (Tallahassee, Fla.: Diplomatic Press, 1972), rather neglects this issue.

Eastern bases to bomb the Japanese home islands was abstention by Japan from interfering with the aid the Soviet Union drew from the Western Hemisphere. Japan would do everything possible to assure Soviet neutrality in the Pacific War, and she would refrain with great care from any action that might provoke her powerful neighbor.

The always implicit and quite frequently explicit rejoinder of the Japanese to the Germans was to urge the latter to make peace with the Soviet Union so that the nations of the Tripartite Pact could concentrate all their energies on defeating their real enemies: Britain and the United States. From the fall of 1941 to the fall of 1944, the Japanese time and again made efforts to bring their European ally to negotiate a separate peace on the Eastern Front (while naturally watching anxiously for the slightest sign that Germany might think of a separate peace with the Western Powers). None of these Japanese attempts succeeded: in the face of German determination to expand into the agricultural areas of the Ukraine and beyond, there was no possibility of a negotiated German–Soviet peace in spite of many signs of Moscow's willingness to try. The very efforts of the Japanese were not, however, without some effect. They could not divert their German ally, but unwittingly they provided added strength to the Soviet position.

In the direct sense, all Japanese hints to the Soviet Union about the possibility of bringing the Soviet Union and Germany together again could only confirm the leaders in Moscow in their knowledge that Japan had no intention of attacking them in East Asia. Thus reassured by Tokyo, the Soviets could concentrate on the war in Europe until themselves ready to turn against Japan. In the indirect sense, the Soviet Union's bargaining position vis-à-vis Britain and the United States was strengthened because of the ability of the latter to read Japanese diplomatic telegrams. Having broken several Japanese machine code systems, the Americans (and also the British) were reading the Japanese exchanges about a possible German–Soviet separate peace; and not only were these generally more optimistic than reality warranted, but even if discounted they always reminded Washington and London that this alternative policy was open to Moscow. If Stalin wished to return to his program of 1939–41 of letting the Germans fight the Western Powers by themselves, he would not encounter insuperable obstacles – or at least so it seemed. In most of the post–World War II discussions about wartime diplomacy, attention has all too often been concentrated on the great difficulties of the Allies in working together effectively; that the powers of the Tripartite Pact were even less successful in this regard is often overlooked.

In the concluding as in the initial and middle stages of the conflict there were significant connections between Europe and the Pacific. There has been so much discussion of the Europe First strategy that little attention has been given to its corollary: the Pacific Second. The long and difficult fight to defeat Germany meant that all efforts to open up the supply lines to China always ended up at the bottom of the priority list; thus the August 1944 invasion of southern France eliminated a landing on the Burma coast. The collapse of the Chinese Nationalist armies in 1943 and 1944 in the face of major Japanese offensives was to have many significant repercussions later. Of more immediate concern was the interaction between the last stages of the war in Europe and the continuing war in East Asia.

It cannot be stressed often and heavily enough that as the war in Europe was winding down, that in the Pacific was escalating. This contrast is most dramatic if for a moment one places into strict chronological sequence the alternating high points of war in the first half of 1945. January was the month that the Red Army tore open the German Eastern Front and poured into Germany. February was the month of Iwo Jima. March saw the American capture of the bridge over the Rhine at Remagen. April, May, and June were months of bitter fighting on and around Okinawa in the bloodiest campaign of the war in the Pacific. This contrasting trend had major implications for the future of Europe and for American policy there.

In the years since 1945, there have been two schools of revisionist writings on the last stages of World War II and the immediate postwar period. The first argued that American leaders during those years were engaged in selling out American interests and Europe's future to the Soviets. The second has tried to show that those same leaders were actually doing the opposite of what the first school of revisionists had charged. Far from selling out to the Soviets, those leaders were supposedly challenging the Soviet Union and looking for ways to confront, weaken, threaten, and perhaps even fight that country. Whatever these diametrically opposed groups of writings may tell us about currents of thought within the United States in the late 1940s and early 1950s on the one hand and in the late 60s and early 70s on the other, they tell us extremely little about 1944–45. The major concern of American political and military leaders in the spring of 1945 was neither of the policies invented for them later but an entirely different set of issues.[4] Perhaps

---

4 A book which comes to similar conclusions by careful examination of new evidence on a highly controversial episode is Bradley F. Smith and Elena Agrossi, *Operation Sunrise: The Secret Surrender* (New York: Basic Books, 1979), pp. 6–7.

best described by one word often used at the time – redeployment – their policy focused on the need to move American military power from Europe to the Pacific as expeditiously as possible.

Operation Olympic, the invasion of the Japanese home island of Kyushu, was given the final go-ahead by President Truman in mid-June 1945. Scheduled for November 1 of that year, with preliminary actions and landings to occur in the interim, it could be mounted with forces already in the Pacific theater. But the climactic follow-up, Operation Coronet, the invasion of Japan's main island, Honshu, planned for March 1946, required the employment of units previously engaged in Europe. The American First Army, which had landed in Normandy in June 1944, was pulled out of line on May 1, 1945 – before the German surrender. Its headquarters was transferred to the Far East, being activated again in Manila on August 1, 1945, with the expectation that it would command one of the three armies that would carry out Operation Coronet the following year.[5]

The rapid evaporation of American military power in Europe in the spring and summer of 1945 was, to be sure, in part the result of agitation and war weariness, but those were by no means the only or even the main factors. As Okinawa showed all too vividly, the hardest fighting was still ahead. Soviet help against Japan was greatly desired, as MacArthur repeatedly reminded any in Washington who might think otherwise. If one wishes to understand what was probably President Truman's most significant single decision in U.S.–Soviet relations in 1945, the evacuation of American forces from a large part of what was scheduled to be the Soviet zone of occupation in Germany, one must emphasize as a major factor the need for America to move forces to the Pacific and to have the Red Army tie down Japanese forces in Manchuria while Americans stormed ashore on the home islands of Japan. In this sense the Europe of 1945 could see something comparable to what the Philippines had experienced in 1941–42. If the war in Europe had provided the occasion for war in the Pacific, the war in the Pacific in some ways overshadowed the final developments in Europe.

There was to be, moreover, still one more way in which events in Europe affected the Far East. The ending of the Pacific War had been envisioned as a repeat performance of the way Germany had been crushed. While the Red Army tied down a large part of Japan's army

---

5 D. Clayton James in his superb book, *The Years of MacArthur, 1941–1945* (Boston: Houghton Mifflin, 1975), pp. 770–71 and n. 35, refers to the second edition of the Coronet plan as the "final edition." Whether or not that would indeed have been the case, the reduction of the proposed army group from three to two armies involved dropping Tenth Army from the assault; First Army was to be included alongside Eighth Army.

elsewhere – just as had happened with the German army in Europe in 1944 – American forces augmented by contingents from the British Commonwealth would strike at the Tokyo plain. And not only would that operation include the very army which had landed in Normandy on D-Day, but it would also benefit from the extraordinary device which Allied ingenuity had devised to facilitate support of a mass amphibious assault in an area where no ports were likely to be seized quickly and intact. A huge Mulberry, an artificial harbor, would be towed to Tokyo Bay as two had once been dragged across the English Channel. But another outlandish device would serve instead.

German initiative had enabled Japan to start the Pacific War; the results of fear of another German initiative would induce Japan's leaders to end it. The terrifying prospect that Germany's scientific and technological capacity would first harness the power of the splitting atom into an explosive device had triggered a race by the British and Americans to do so before Hitler. As is now known, the Soviet Union and Japan were also working on the same problem, but neither was far along. When the Western Powers became certain in the fall of 1944 that Germany had decided to allocate its resources instead to other new weapons – jet airplanes, pilotless airplanes, rockets, and new models of submarines – they could see the possibility of actually having some atomic bombs themselves. By December 1944 the availability of the first ones was expected for the summer of 1945. Germany had by that time already surrendered. The Western Allies knew that Soviet spies were working to obtain as much American and British knowledge as possible. It was also known that the Japanese had been asking their German ally to provide them with radioactive materials for their experiments. But for a short time, the Western Allies alone had sufficient materials for a few A-bombs.

After testing one device to see whether the things were likely to work, the U.S. air force dropped the other two then available in a gigantic bluff designed to fool the Japanese into thinking the Allies had an indefinite supply. The hope was that the Japanese would be shocked out of their strategy of continued fighting into surrender. For the first time since 1895 the Emperor intervened directly and personally into government policy when the leaders of the country were evenly divided. Siding with those who advocated surrender, he enabled that faction to win out in the bitter internal struggle over policy.

As the war in East Asia ended, the suddenness of Allied victory, brought about by a weapon originally designed for the fight against Germany, was to continue the interaction between the European and the Pacific portions of the globe into the postwar years. The Japanese surrender came *after* the fighting return of the American army to the Philippines and Guam, but *before* the return of Allied armies to Indo-China. There Japan's enemies and America's allies had included Ho Chi Minh, who was accordingly being supported by the U.S. Office of Strategic Services. But here begins another story, which only shows that after as during World War II, developments in Europe and East Asia must be looked upon as an interrelated historical process.

17

———— • ————

THE "FINAL SOLUTION"
AND THE WAR IN 1943

The Nazis, who came to power in Germany in 1933, had promised for years in their speeches, leaflets, and in their published program that they would persecute the Jews as soon as they had the opportunity to do so. When attainment of power provided them with that opportunity, they proceeded rapidly with a long sequence of measures designed to deprive the Jewish population of the country of their rights as citizens, to hound them in all sorts of ways, and then to boast in public of all the steps they were taking to carry out the promises they had made on this subject. In a country where fully equal legal rights for Jews were as recent as the 1919 constitution and where anti-Semitism had a long and highly respected tradition, these actions actually helped the Nazis in their consolidation of power.

During the years 1933–39, as Germany prepared for a series of wars designed to provide its people with what was referred to as *Lebensraum*, "living space," ever harsher measures were taken against the less than 1 percent of the population which was Jewish. About half the approximately 550,000 Jews left Germany. However, many were reluctant to leave a place their ancestors had lived in for generations, and others who wanted to leave found the doors of possible lands of refuge closed at a time of worldwide economic depression, when countries were reluctant to accept refugees whose property had been confiscated by the land of their birth. The dramatic escalation of persecution in November 1938, when most Jewish houses of worship in Germany were deliberately destroyed and over 20,000 Jews were taken to concentration camps, both led more Jews to try to emigrate and induced some countries to relax their tight restrictions on immigration. But before another year had passed, the Germans had started World War II.

This piece originally appeared in *Fifty Years Ago: Revolt amid the Darkness* (Washington, D.C.: U.S. Holocaust Memorial Museum, 1993), pp. 1–15.

The war not only made it very much more difficult for individuals to flee German persecution, it enormously increased the numbers of Jews under German control as first large parts of Poland, then Denmark and Norway, later France and the smaller countries of Western Europe, and eventually much of Southeast Europe came under German control or influence. As Germany reached for global domination, it acquired control over the fate of a steadily increasing number of Jews. This process was most obvious to the Germans themselves as they began to plan in 1940 for an invasion of the Soviet Union which would mean taking over the eastern part of a Poland Germany and the Soviet Union had partitioned between them in 1939 as well as the territory of the pre-1939 Soviet Union itself with its large Jewish population. It was in the context of the planning for this stage of the war that the Germans decided that the time had come to shift from persecution to extermination: instead of depriving Jews of rights and property, they would systematically take their lives.

The Germans had initiated a program of systematic killing under the cover of the war in the fall of 1939; that program had been designed for people in mental institutions, old folks' homes, and children with allegedly incurable medical problems and handicaps. Temporarily reduced in scope in the face of public protests inside Germany during the summer of 1941, that first systematic project of isolating, killing, and disposing of the corpses of specific categories of persons provided precedents, techniques, and personnel for the new vast killing operation which began with the German invasion of the Soviet Union that same summer.

As described in more detail below, the mass killing soon proved to be beyond the capacity of the people and organizations first established to carry it out, and at a meeting of representatives of the major segments of the German government in January 1942, the bureaucratic apparatus of the Third Reich was drawn far more closely and directly into it. By the end of that year, well over 3 million Jews had been killed, but those in charge were by no means satisfied with the results attained. During 1943 they hoped that German victories in the war would further extend the reach of German power – and thus also the number of Jews who could be killed – and that they could kill both those Jews remaining alive in the areas Germany controlled directly and those whose lives were still shielded by the reluctance of Germany's allies and satellites to hand them over. Furthermore, as the operators of the mechanism for mass killing saw their program simultaneously restricted by checks at the fronts on which the war was being fought and by a possible exhaustion in the available number of prospective victims, they turned more and more to the inclusion of new categories of people to kill: the Roma and Sinti

(Gypsies) who were placed in a legal status identical to that of the Jews and those people who were descended in part from Jews who had been married to non-Jews.

The war Germany started in 1939 not only provided a framework within which the Germans initiated and developed systematic killing programs; it also provided them with the overwhelming majority of their victims. About 95 percent of those Jews killed in the "Final Solution" came within the reach of the Germans only because of the war; and had Germany won that war, as its leaders confidently expected, their extension of the killing to the rest of the globe would obviously have increased even that high figure. It is, therefore, within the context of the great conflict that the development of Germany's so-called Final Solution in 1943 must be examined.

At the beginning of 1943 both the military conflict raging in Europe and North Africa and that facet of the war now generally referred to as the Holocaust were in the process of dramatic change from earlier stages into a new mode, even though at the time this change was not readily obvious to all. In North Africa, the defeat of the German–Italian army at El Alamein at the end of October and early November 1942, and the successful invasion of French northwest Africa by American and British troops had, on the one hand, restricted Axis forces to Tunisia and a small piece of Libya. On the other hand, the French authorities in Tunisia had remained loyal to the French collaborationist regime in Vichy, allowing the buildup of a German–Italian force there, and thus enabling the Axis powers to halt the initial Anglo–American advance. The short-term effect was that the Axis forces were able to launch offensives from their Tunisian bridgehead, offensives designed to reconquer French northwest Africa as far as Casablanca[1] but halted (after an initial American defeat at Kasserine Pass) by American and British troops.

A longer term effect of the need for an Allied campaign to crush the Axis bridgehead in Tunisia was that it made any invasion of northwest Europe in 1943 impossible for the Allies, a fact sadly recognized in London and Washington during December 1943. The follow-up to the liberation of Tunisia therefore could not be a rapid switch to northwest Europe. Given the impossibility of such a switch after victory in Tunisia in time for an invasion of France later in the same year of 1943, landings first in Sicily and then on the Italian mainland were carried out in 1943 instead, while the invasion of Northwest France was postponed to 1944.

A by-product of these invasions, coming after the loss of Italy's colonial

---

1 See the Hitler–Rommel conversation of March 10, 1943, in B. H. Liddell Hart (ed.), *The Rommel Papers* (London: Arrow Books, 1953), p. 419.

empire, was the July 1943 collapse of the regime Benito Mussolini had installed in Italy in 1922. The new Italian government of Pietro Badoglio, which surrendered to the Allies, fled to southern Italy, abandoning the bulk of the country and the Italian-occupied portions of France, Yugoslavia, Albania, and Greece to the Germans.

The fighting in North Africa with its follow-up in Sicily and Italy had an ironically contradictory impact on Germany's hopes of killing the world's Jews. The final crushing of Axis forces in North Africa ended all prospects for a German occupation of the British mandate of Palestine and the slaughter of its Jewish community, an action an optimistic Adolf Hitler had once promised Haj Amin el-Husseine, the Grand Mufti of Jerusalem. British evacuation plans which had provided for leaving the Jewish inhabitants of the mandate to the Germans – who intended to kill them all – never had to be implemented. The survival of a Jewish presence in Palestine, certainly a prerequisite for the establishment of a Jewish state there, was thus one result of the Allied victory in North Africa.

On the other hand, the defeat and surrender of Italy led to the German occupation of the Italian zones in France, Yugoslavia, Albania, and Greece as well as most of Italy itself and the Italian islands in the Aegean. This process, in turn, opened up to Germany's program of killing Jews areas which had hitherto been relatively safe for their Jewish inhabitants as well as Jews who had fled to them because Italian military and diplomatic officials had refused to cooperate in what they considered a barbaric procedure unworthy of any civilized society.

The fighting between German and Soviet forces on the Eastern Front constituted the vast majority of combat in 1943 as it had in the two preceding years. The Germans, together with their Axis partners, had been checked and severely mauled in 1941; in the summer of 1942 they had once more gone on the offensive. The 1942 offensive, moving simultaneously into the Caucasus area as well as toward Stalingrad and Astrakhan on the lower Volga, had been halted by the Red Army in the fall of 1942. In late November a major Soviet offensive had cut off the German Sixth Army and parts of another German and two Romanian armies in the Stalingrad area. The defeat of a German relief effort in December and successful Soviet offensives against the front of Germany's Hungarian and Italian partners northwest of Stalingrad had opened up the possibility that the whole German army group stalled in the Caucasus might be cut off by Red Army thrusts. In the winter of 1942–43 the Germans therefore withdrew from the majority of the north Caucasus area they had seized earlier, holding only a small bridgehead as a basis for a future renewal of offensive operations. In late February the Germans launched a major counteroffensive at the southern part of the Eastern Front. The Red Army, which had crossed the Donets and was approaching the Dnepr River, was thrown back with heavy losses as the Germans retook the cities of Kharkov and Belgorod.

The great victory of the Red Army at Stalingrad, followed by a renewed successful German local counteroffensive, had major repercussions. The victory of Stalingrad marked a visible change in the configuration of the war, a change that struck fear into the German home front, which only now began to mobilize for total war. The catastrophe suffered by Germany's satellites Romania and Hungary, whose troops had been called upon for the 1942 offensive at German insistence, had never been properly armed, and had been crushed in the Red Army offensives, led the leadership of Hungary and Romania to begin looking for ways out of the war.[2] This new perspective in turn made them more reluctant to yield to German pressure to turn over to the Germans the Jews in their populations for slaughter.

The German counteroffensive, on the other hand, showed these satellites that Germany still had substantial military resources and restrained their willingness to take any chances in the effort to withdraw from the war. Furthermore, the Germans' maintenance of a solid Eastern Front both assured their continued control of the area where the major centers for killing Jews were located and provided them a basis for a new German summer offensive.

That 1943 offensive, code-named "Citadel" and aimed at the Kursk salient retained by the Red Army at the end of its 1942 winter offensive, was launched on July 5. In bitter fighting, the Soviets triumphed in World War II's largest tank battle, stopping the German advance and then driving forward in their own first summer offensive. Having to send reinforcements to Italy as Italian resistance crumbled upon the Allied invasion of Sicily on July 10, the Germans were now obliged to remain on the defensive in the East. They continued to limit the Red Army to slow advances on the central portion of the front, thereby retaining the still operational killing facilities in occupied Poland; but in the fall of 1943 and the winter of 1943–44 they lost the important industrial and agricultural parts of the Ukraine to a rapidly and energetically advancing Red Army.

The German recovery and counteroffensive after Stalingrad appears to have shocked the Soviet leadership into considering ways out of the

---

2 For an excellent survey, see Jürgen Förster, *Stalingrad: Risse im Bündnis* (Freiburg: Rombach, 1975).

war under circumstances in which no major landing by the Western Allies could be expected in northwest Europe in 1943. Soundings for a separate peace with the existing government in Germany ran parallel to efforts to develop an alternative government for that country out of German prisoners of war and political refugees in the Soviet Union, an effort publicly signaled by the creation of the National Committee for a Free Germany and the League of German Officers in Moscow. The German government – in spite of strong urgings from its Japanese ally – rejected all approaches from Moscow, and the new organizations created by Moscow had minimal resonance inside Germany.

Within Germany there were, however, real stirrings of opposition in 1943. A small group of students at the University of Munich, the "White Rose," vainly tried to urge students and other citizens to regain control of their country and establish a decent government; a number of high-ranking civilians met at an estate at Kreisau in Silesia to plan for a post-Hitler Germany; and the opponents of Hitler among the military made their first attempt to kill the Führer in March, an attempt which failed when the detonator on the bomb placed in his airplane malfunctioned. Germany would fight on.

For the Western Allies, the conference held at Casablanca from January 14 to 24, 1943, set the highest priority on the defeat of the German submarines. As Allied losses in shipping exceeded new construction, all strategic concepts were strangled until the oceanic supply routes could be made safe, or at least safer. Tremendous battles between German submarines and Allied convoys in March and April proved to be the prelude to a major Allied victory in May. Massive sinkings of U-boats forced Admiral Dönitz, the commander-in-chief of the German navy, to withdraw his "wolfpacks" of submarines from the main combat zone temporarily. In September the Allies' new ship construction exceeded losses – a trend that continued thereafter by ever greater margins. The way for an invasion of Western Europe in 1944 lay open; up to then the German submarines in the West had performed a function similar to that of the German army in the East in assuring German control of much of Europe. Indeed, it was only appropriate that U-boat crews were issued felt footwear utilizing human hair gathered in the extermination centers and were rewarded with watches stolen from Jewish victims.[3]

At Casablanca the British and Americans also decided that the Tunisian campaign would be followed by an invasion of Sicily with staff planning for other operations in the Mediterranean and northwest Europe to follow. Furthermore, the bombing of German-controlled Europe

3 Raul Hilberg, *The Destruction of the European Jews* (New York: Holmes & Meier, 1985), pp. 954, 957.

was to be stepped up according to an Allied directive of January 21, 1943, which called for "the progressive destruction and dislocation of the German military, industrial and economic system, and the undermining of the morale of the German people . . .".[4] The subsequent bombing, conducted by British and increasingly also by U.S. planes, included massive raids on German cities and factories, but it produced such great losses of planes and crews in 1943 that the offensive seemed in danger of breaking down. The use of long-range escort fighters would turn this situation around in the first months of 1944; the Allies gained control of the skies over Western and Central Europe and thereby assured the feasibility of an invasion in the West.

At the end of the Casablanca Conference, President Franklin Roosevelt and Prime Minister Winston Churchill announced publicly that their nations would fight on until their enemies surrendered unconditionally, something Italy did in September and Germany's other allies all subsequently either did or tried to do. Only Germany itself insisted on fighting until the bitter end. Certainly an important element in that determination to continue the war was the recognition of having committed enormous crimes combined with a grim insistence on continuing the program of killing all Jews within German reach, a program inaugurated in 1941 and pursued until the last days of the war.

In the spring of 1941, in anticipation of the invasion of the Soviet Union, arrangements had been made for special killing squads, called *Einsatzgruppen*, to accompany the invading armies and, with the support of the latter, to slaughter several groups of people: Communist Party officials, political officers in the Red Army, people in mental institutions and old folks' homes, and, as the most numerous category, the Jewish population in the areas overrun. That program had barely been initiated in the early days of the campaign when, in view of the apparent success of the German offensive and the minimal internal German opposition to the murder program, Hitler decided to expand the program from the killing of Jews in the newly occupied territory to those in all areas under German control or influence. The vast killing operation went forward with several transports of Jews from Central Europe, especially from Germany, being added in the fall of 1941 to those Jews being shot in and near the towns of the occupied USSR.

In this process it soon became clear that there were two related practical difficulties. In the first place, the endless rounds of shootings, carried out daily on a vast scale, were more and more demoralizing the men who

4 Combined Chiefs of Staff Directive of January 21, 1943, Michael Howard, *Grand Strategy,* Vol. IV, *August 1942–September 1943* (London: H.M. Stationery Office, 1970), p. 623.

carried them out, frequently close to being in a drunken stupor. Second, adding to the procedure of sending the killers to the territories of the victims in the Soviet Union the further operation of bringing enormous numbers of additional victims from all over Europe to the killers threatened to overwhelm the established apparatus of killing, and this in spite of the extensive recruitment of local auxiliaries (especially in Lithuania and the Ukraine). To cope with these impediments to the efficient operation of the killing program, two measures were adopted by the Germans in the winter of 1941–42. They substantially expanded the numbers and kinds of people involved in the killing of Jews, what might be referred to as human apparatus for killing, and also altered the mechanics employed in the killing itself, that is, the technical apparatus.

The increase in the human apparatus for killing Jews meant involvement by large portions of the German bureaucracy in a program that had the highest priority in the eyes of Germany's leaders. At a meeting on January 20, 1942, referred to after its location as the Wannsee Conference, the leaders of the SS, which had been charged with responsibility for the program, explained to the assembled representatives of Germany's most important ministries how Jews from all over German-controlled Europe, as well as such parts of Europe as England and Spain, expected soon to be under German control, were to be deported to the East and killed there. Each ministry and agency was to play its part in the operation, and for the rest of World War II this would be one of their major activities.

The second alteration, that in the mechanisms of killing, was designed in part to reduce the stress on the perpetrators. Although shooting was to remain a significant part of the murder program until May 1945, a large portion of the killing was to be done in new facilities especially created for this purpose. In these killing centers, built in occupied Poland, vast numbers were to be killed by gas, thereby both sparing the murderers so direct a part in the killing of each victim and simultaneously greatly increasing the capacity of the operation. Several such camps were established exclusively for the killing of people, much of the personnel being simply transferred from the earlier program of killing the inmates of Germany's mental institutions, old people's homes, and hospital wards for severely handicapped children. With two years of experience in the killing of people on a routine basis, these men not only continued to carry out this grisly process inside Germany (even if on a reduced scale), many of them were transferred to the East and now applied their talents, knowledge, and techniques to new groups of victims, primarily using carbon monoxide gas in vans and in fixed installations. A slightly different procedure was followed in the portion of the vast complex of concentration camp, slave labor center, industrial facility, and killing center that was Auschwitz (Oswiecem). There, and on a small scale experimentally elsewhere, a commercially produced poisonous gas called Zyklon B was used instead of carbon monoxide.

During the course of 1942 vast numbers of Jews had been taken to these special killing facilities from German-occupied areas in both Eastern and Western Europe. In addition, the Germans had begun to deport to the killing centers Jews from such areas as Slovakia and France where local authorities were willing to turn over at least some of the Jews. By the end of 1942, the program for killing the largest Jewish population in Europe, that in occupied Poland and adjacent parts of the USSR, was nearing a temporary end. This slowdown had occurred because those Jews still alive in this region had been forced into ghettos and camps where they labored in factories and workshops producing or repairing goods for Germany's war effort, hoping thereby to survive until an Allied victory ended the war. In the rest of Europe that was occupied, controlled, or influenced by Germany, Jews survived primarily because the local regimes had been either slow to cooperate with German requests to turn over Jews or had refused outright.

The major German focus during 1943 would be on the killing of these two groups of Jews: Jews still alive in the ghettos of Eastern Europe and Jews still protected by the reluctance of Germany's allies, satellites, and collaborator regimes to give them up to the Germans. Although the German efforts along these two lines moved forward simultaneously, it is easier to follow them if the two are reviewed separately.

Of the Jewish communities of Europe in 1939, that of Poland had been the largest, and within Poland, Warsaw with close to half a million Jews – one-third of the city's population – was the most important center of Jewish cultural and political activity. The Germans had first killed some Jews and driven others from surrounding communities into Warsaw where they established a ghetto surrounded by walls, making the Jews pay for the construction of these walls. Tens of thousands of residents of the Warsaw ghetto died of hunger and disease as a result of the crowded and unsanitary conditions which the Germans imposed on the ghetto, but the majority of the inhabitants, some 265,000, had been deported to the killing center of Treblinka between July 22 and September 12, 1942, and murdered there.[5]

The non-Jewish population of Warsaw barely reacted to these terrible

---

5 See Ysrael Gutman, *The Jews of Warsaw, 1939–1943: Ghetto, Underground, Revolt* (Bloomington: Indiana University Press, 1989), ch. 6.

events. The Polish Underground Army as well as the civilian population generally looked on apathetically. There were some who enthusiastically or venally aided the Germans, but there were others who, moved by the horrible treatment of their neighbors, did try to help. A Council for Aid to Jews, generally referred to by the name of *Zegota*, was established by portions of the Polish Underground and largely financed by the Polish Government-in-Exile. It was able to assist hundreds of Jews to hide and survive; more were aided by Poles acting individually and without any organizational affiliation or support.[6] The conditions of German occupation and the attitude of a large part of the Polish population, however, restricted such help to a small percentage of the Jewish inhabitants of Warsaw.

The Jewish community itself, insofar as it survived the great deportations of 1942, was greatly changed. In spite of German efforts to pretend otherwise, all now knew that death awaited them and that the possibility of survival, even if in the most wretched conditions, was gone. Under these circumstances the resistance organizations, already formed during the months of deportations in 1942, became more elaborate. There had been individual acts of resistance, efforts to escape, and an organized attempt to assure survival of the community on the part of its official leaders; but after the deportations, the advocates of resistance found far more ready listeners among the approximately 35,000 survivors who either were working for the German-owned factories or living in hiding. At the same time there were also stirrings in the other ghettos.[7]

The crisis on the Eastern Front had affected the struggle between the SS and the other German armed forces over the utilization of Jewish labor. On the one hand, the desperate need for equipment suggested that every worker was needed. This view was reinforced by the desire of the SS to expand its own armed units within Germany's military, an expansion which required greatly increased production and repair of equipment. On the other hand, the ideological fanaticism of Heinrich Himmler, the head of the SS, and of other SS leaders, always urged forward by Hitler himself, called for the killing of all remaining Jews regardless of the impact on war production.

On January 9, 1943, Himmler ordered the remaining production facilities of the Warsaw ghetto shifted to SS factories near Lublin; presumably that would have meant the end of the ghetto, but that decision was

6 A sympathetic account of the Zegota is in Richard C. Lukas, *The Forgotten Holocaust: The Poles under German Occupation, 1939–1944* (Lexington: University Press of Kentucky, 1985), pp. 147–51.
7 Yitzhak Arad, *Belzec, Sobibor, Treblinka: The Operation Reinhard Death Camps* (Bloomington: University of Indiana Press, 1987), pp. 246ff.

apparently not made until later. After the experience of the deportations of the preceding year, however, the Jewish workers did not believe that such a transfer meant anything other than death. When the Germans tried to force a transfer and to round up those living in the ghetto without proper papers, the ghetto resistance forces went into action, frustrating the German operation in street fighting on January 18–22, 1943. Unprepared for any resistance and unwilling to scour the ghetto for those in hiding, the Germans temporarily withdrew, leaving the resistance with greatly increased prestige and support in the ghetto until April.[8]

The Germans had not intended to kill all the remaining Jews in Warsaw in January – that decision came later – but no one in the ghetto then knew that, and so the effectiveness of the resistance appeared even greater than it had been. This small victory inspired the survivors to work harder at preparations to resist in the future, encouraged the vast majority who had no weapons to build hiding places and bunkers, and even induced the Polish Underground Army, the Armya Krajowa, to provide the resistance with a small number of weapons.

By April 18, 1943, the Germans had massed about two thousand SS, regular soldiers, armed police, and auxiliaries for what they believed would be a quick and simple operation to raze the ghetto and deport its surviving inhabitants to Treblinka. The Jewish resistance obtained some intelligence on the coming operation and was ready to fight on the morning of April 19 when the Germans began their action. Although they had minimal weapons for only about 750 fighters – most armed only with revolvers, a few with small automatic weapons and improvised Molotov cocktails – the initial resistance was so much stronger than the Germans had expected that they were forced to withdraw. In subsequent days of fighting, the Germans moved forward block by block, systematically setting fire to and destroying the houses, killing the inhabitants, dropping chlorine gas into the bunkers and sewers, and slowly crushing the resistance.[9]

Over a period of four weeks, the desperately embarrassed Germans had to cope with the first armed uprising – and by Jews at that – in any city in occupied Europe. They proclaimed an end to the fighting and the final destruction of the ghetto on May 16 in a proud report, "The Jewish Residential Area of Warsaw Is No More," issued by Jürgen Stroop, the SS officer in command for most of the battle.[10] In reality, small remnants

8 Gutman, *The Jews of Warsaw, 1939–43*, chs. 11–12.   9 Ibid., ch. 14.
10 The full text of the Stroop report was first published in *Trial of the Major War Criminals before the International Military Tribunal* [Blue Series], 42 vols. (Nuremberg Tribunal, 1947–49), Vol. 26, pp. 628–94. An English language version is Sybil Milton (ed. and trans.), *The Stroop Report: The Jewish Quarter of Warsaw Is No More* (New York: Pantheon, 1979).

of ghetto fighters and inhabitants remained in bunkers and sewers, and the last of these were not destroyed until July. A few survivors escaped, but with practically no help from the Polish underground and a generally hostile Polish population, most of the survivors were caught by or turned over to the Germans.

The uprising, however, had a major impact both on the Jewish communities elsewhere in Eastern Europe and on the Germans. There had been many instances of isolated Jewish resistance to the Germans earlier, but there had been nothing like the ghetto revolt. The move from despair to action now seemed easier in spite of the obstacles which were as enormous as ever: an almost total lack of weapons, a lack of military training, and inadequate means of communication, a largely indifferent or even hostile non-Jewish population, physical debilitation from malnutrition and disease, while facing a determined and relatively well-armed force of Germans with their Ukrainian and Polish auxiliaries. Nevertheless, there was a notable change in attitudes and perceptions: it made some sense at least to try to fight. It is hardly a coincidence that the major uprisings in the killing centers and coordinated resistance in other Polish, Baltic, and Soviet ghettos almost all took place after the Warsaw ghetto uprising.

The Germans were also strongly affected by the events of April–May 1943 in Warsaw. The length of time needed to complete the operation, the two hundred or more casualties they had suffered, and the concern over the loss of face in the eyes of the non-Jewish population in the occupied territories of Eastern Europe – all had an impact on German procedures though not German policies hereafter. Practically all of the remaining ghettos and German-owned workshops in occupied Eastern Europe were to be closed down by the end of 1943 and the Jews in them killed, but the procedure would have to be different. After the experience of having to fight for weeks to destroy the Warsaw ghetto, more substantial forces would be gathered beforehand and employed in any similar German operation in the future, and every effort would be made to carry out the killing with a maximum of surprise and in a minimum of time.

This changed approach is apparent in the German killing operations of the fall of 1943. A significant part of these operations was referred to by the Germans by the code name "Harvest Festival" (*Erntefest*), clearly a reference to this being seen as the killing of the last remnants of Jewish communities in central Poland.[11] When murdering 42,000 Jews in three

---

11 Leni Yahil, *The Holocaust: The Fate of European Jewry, 1932–1945* (New York: Oxford University Press, 1990), ch. 16, applies the term to the whole 1943 program, but it appears to have been used by the Germans at the time only for the killing of the workers in the factories at Majdanek, Trawniki, and Poniatowka – see Helge Grabitz and Wolfgang Schef-

massacres in the Lublin area during a few days in November 1943, the Germans made certain to catch their victims completely by surprise and returned to the procedure of mass shootings which had characterized the early stages of the killing program in 1941.

Originally the Germans had intended to kill all Jews in occupied Poland except for those in certain specified ghetto workshops by the end of 1942.[12] Most of the program had, as already mentioned, been completed by that deadline; and one of the killing centers, that of Belzec, ended operations in December 1942 (though the burning of corpses there continued into 1943).[13] Treblinka, Sobibor, and the killing facilities at Auschwitz-Birkenau and Majdanek were still functioning, and these camps received the bulk of the remnant ghetto populations in the Baltic states, near Minsk, and in Vilna for killing during 1943. The large ghetto of Bialystock was also emptied despite the considerable resistance there.[14]

By the time Himmler personally inspected the killing centers of Sobibor and Treblinka in late February 1943 these centers had killed over 1,600,000 of the approximately 1,700,000 who eventually perished there.[15] They were close to shutting down because the killing capacity of Auschwitz had by now been expanded sufficiently for the murder of those Jews who could be extricated from Germany's allies and satellites and who could be gassed either on arrival or after a short period of slave labor in the factories of IG Farben, also known as Buna (actually the name of Germany's synthetic rubber), and other German firms at Auschwitz III or Monowitz. The major remaining task at the killing centers was, as mentioned in connection with Belzec, the disposal of vast numbers of corpses as part of a large program of trying to conceal the evidence of mass murder. In his speech to the leaders of the German government and Nazi Party on October 6, 1943, Himmler boasted about the extermination of Europe's Jews, going so far as to allude to the forthcoming slaughter of the "Harvest Festival";[16] but he preferred that

fler, *Letzte Spuren* (Berlin: Hentrich, 1988), pp. 328ff. Christopher R. Browning, *Ordinary Men: Reserve Police Battalion 101 and the Final Solution in Poland* (New York: Harper Collins, 1992), ch. 15, follows the same application of the term and recounts the role played in it by the reserve police battalion that is the subject of his book. Wolfgang Benz (ed.), *Dimensionen des Völkermordes: Die Zahl der jüdischen Opfer des Nationalsozialismus* (Munich: Oldenbourg, 1991), p. 478, also confines the term to this action.

12 Himmler's order is translated in Arad, *Belzec, Sobibur, Treblinka*, p. 47.

13 Ibid., pp. 126–27, 177.

14 Ibid., pp. 134–37.

15 Ibid., ch. 22.

16 Himmler's speech from his files in National Archives T-175, roll 85, frames 0152-0200, is published in Bradley F. Smith and Agnes Peterson (eds.), *Heinrich Himmler: Geheimreden 1933 bis 1945* (Frankfurt/M: Propyläen, 1974); the discussion of the extermination of Jews is on pp. 169–71; his reference to Albert Speer (who was present) and himself in regard to

as little physical evidence as possible remain. A special unit of concentration camp prisoners under SS command had, therefore, been established in June 1942 to burn hundreds of thousands of corpses and later to erase other traces of what had occurred.[17]

The process of erasure was, ironically, hastened by the acts of Jewish resistance within the death camps themselves. In Treblinka resistance activity began to be organized in February–March 1943 as the special commandos of Jews forced to carry out the most horrendous tasks in the camp realized that it was likely to be closed down for lack of victims and that they themselves would then certainly be killed. They prepared an uprising which took place in early August. The revolt resulted in a few German and Ukrainian casualties and enabled several hundred inmates to escape with about a hundred surviving the following hunt.[18]

The situation at Sobibor was essentially similar. There had been isolated acts of resistance and attempts at escape earlier, but it was in the spring of 1943 that a minimal resistance organization was formed. A combination of factors – a drop in the number of transports and the killing at Sobibor of the last Jewish prisoners from Belzec when that camp was closed down – led the underground to undertake a series of operations. Members dug an escape tunnel, but it was discovered, with a majority of the prisoners in a part of the camp being shot.[19] A major uprising was later planned under the leadership of a Jewish Red Army officer, Lieutenant Alexander Pechersky, one of a group of prisoners of war sent to Sobibor in September. On October 14, 1943, Pechersky and others in the camp led an organized revolt. The majority of the SS staff in the camp was killed and about half of the six hundred prisoners in that section of the camp escaped, though many of them were subsequently killed by Germans and Poles.[20] The revolts served to hasten the shutting down and destruction of Treblinka and Sobibor. In the late fall of 1943 both were closed, the remaining facilities leveled, and the land partially planted over with trees and turned into farms. After the war memorials would be erected at these sites.[21]

By the end of 1943, therefore, only a few thousand Jews in German-occupied Eastern Europe remained alive in hiding, in partisan units, in the Lodz ghetto, and in a small number of work camps. Special "Jew

their roles in the near future in removing the remaining Jews out of the armaments factories is on p. 170. Himmler's speech to SS leaders two days earlier, in which he discussed the "Final Solution" at length in somewhat different words, is reviewed in Richard Breitman, *The Architect of Genocide: Himmler and the Final Solution* (New York: Knopf, 1991), pp. 242–43, 308 nn. 50–52.

17 Arad, *Belzec, Sobibur, Treblinka,* ch. 23.
18 Ibid., chs. 33–36.   19 Ibid., ch. 37.   20 Ibid., chs. 38–42.
21 Ibid., ch. 46; Benz, *Dimensionen des Völkermordes,* p. 479.

Hunts" had been mounted in occupied Poland to locate and kill as many of those not in work camps as possible.[22]

The Holocaust in 1943 also involved a second major effort: to send to their deaths in the killing centers as many Jews as the Germans could lay their hands on in Central, Western, and Southeast Europe. From prewar Germany itself, there were several transports of Jews to Auschwitz, reducing the remaining community from about 51,000 at the beginning of the year to at the most one-third of that number at the end. Only one major hitch developed during this process: when the numerous Jewish men who had hitherto been exempted because they were married to "Aryan" women were gathered for deportation, their wives staged what has to be called a major riot in the streets of Berlin on February 28. As a result, the police released the men.[23] On the other hand, many German Jews previously sent to the Theresienstadt (Terezin) concentration camp in the Protectorate of Bohemia and Moravia, German-controlled Czechoslovakia, either died there or were sent to Auschwitz for killing during 1943.[24]

In northern Europe, the Germans had found it expedient to leave the small number of Jews in Finland alone when they realized that the Finnish government was not about to give them up.[25] In Norway the deportation of Jews began in October 1942, assisted by the Norwegian police and the followers of Vidkun Quisling, the leader of Norway's National Socialists. About half of Norway's 1,800 Jews managed to flee to Sweden.[26] The Swedish government was willing to accept them all, but the State Secretary in the German Foreign Ministry, Ernst von Weizsäcker, made it clear that such a proposal could not be considered.[27] This rebuff appears to have influenced the Swedish government into

---

22 There is an excellent description of a portion of this in Browning, *Ordinary Men*, ch. 14.
23 Yahil, *The Holocaust*, p. 408. Always sensitive to home front morale, the National Socialist government repeatedly pulled back when there was serious public opposition to the implementation of policies. Other examples are the substantial reduction in the "euthanasia" program and the rescinding of orders to remove all crucifixes from schools.
24 Benz, *Dimensionen des Völkermordes*, pp. 50–52.
25 Yahil, *The Holocaust*, pp. 576–78. Finnish Jews served as officers and soldiers in the Finnish army. There is an account in Hannu Rautkallio, "'Cast into the Lion's Den': Finnish Jewish Soldiers in the Second World War," *Journal of Contemporary History* 29 (1994): 53–94.
26 Benz, *Dimensionen des Völkermordes*, pp. 187, 197.
27 In a memorandum of December 17, 1942, von Weizsäcker reported that the Swedish minister to Germany had that day told him that the Swedish government was prepared to take in the Jews of Norwegian nationality who were to be deported from Norway. Von Weizsäcker recorded that he had immediately declined to engage in any official conversation about this and stated: "If he [the Swedish minister] were commissioned by his government to make a communication of this sort, I believed that I could predict a failure for him beforehand." *Akten zur deutschen auswärtigen Politik, 1918–1945*, Series E, Vol. 4 (Göttingen: Vandenhoeck & Ruprecht, 1975), no. 297.

following a different procedure a year later when Denmark's Jews were threatened. From October 1942 until March 1943 almost all the other half of Norway's Jews were deported and killed.[28]

The decision of the German government in 1941 to work through the Danish government rather than replace it with an occupation administration or annex Denmark immediately to Germany (as planned for the future) had as one of its implications that restraint had to be exercised in regard to Denmark's six thousand Jews. The German efforts to persuade the Danish government to surrender its Jews failed in 1942 and made no real progress in the first half of 1943.[29] The complete change in German policy toward Denmark in August 1943, supposedly the result of disturbances in Denmark, led to a new attempt to kill the country's Jews. On August 29 Germany proclaimed martial law in Denmark and, in effect, replaced the Danish government with a military occupation regime. Although internal security was supposedly the motive for the German step, it immediately seemed to open the door for implementing Berlin's high-priority policy of deporting Denmark's Jewish citizens to Auschwitz, a step guaranteed to have just the opposite effect on internal security in light of the Danish people's views about their Jewish compatriots.

In September, the first month of martial law, arrangements were initiated for the collection and deportation of the Jews to begin on October 1. Ferdinand Georg Duckwitz, a member of the German plenipotentiary's staff, tipped off the Danish Social Democrats as well as the Swedish government. From inside Denmark, the underground warned the Jews and helped them get on boats to leave the country; from the outside, the Swedish government announced its willingness to accept Denmark's Jews, not in a quiet démarche in Berlin but over Stockholm radio. In the last days of September and first days of October 1943 almost all of Denmark's Jews were taken on boats to Sweden. The help of the Danish underground and population, the willingness of a nearby neutral country to accept the refugees, and a timely warning from inside the German bureaucracy had saved most of this Jewish community.[30]

In Western Europe the Germans tried hard during 1943 to complete the deportation of Jews to the killing centers they had constructed in Poland. Unlike the Jews of Eastern Europe, who had seen and heard of the earlier massacres and by 1943 understood the purpose of deportation, many of those in Western Europe were not yet fully aware about

28 Benz, *Dimensionen des Völkermordes*, pp. 193–96; Samuel Abrahamson, "The Holocaust in Norway," in Randolph L. Braham (ed.), *Contemporary Views on the Holocaust* (Boston and The Hague: Kluwer-Nijhoff, 1983), pp. 125–31, 135–36.
29 Benz, *Dimensionen des Völkermordes*, pp. 170–73.
30 Ibid., pp. 174–79; Yahil, *The Holocaust*, pp. 573–76.

what awaited them. During 1942 many had been sent East; there the great majority were killed in the gas chambers on arrival. From Holland, tens of thousands were collected at the Westerbork camp in 1943 and then taken by train to the killing centers. Large numbers were sent to Auschwitz; from March until July 1943 a series of nineteen trains was directed to Sobibor. Of the more than 33,000 on these trains, 19 survived.[31] From August on the trains were again sent to Auschwitz since Sobibor was being closed. The additional more than 30,000 sent to their deaths later in 1943 had been collected in massive hunts in the Netherlands in May, June, and September 1943. Few survived the deportations, but thousands of other Jews were hidden by sympathetic Dutch families and escaped deportation.[32]

The situation in Belgium was somewhat different. The large-scale deportations of 1942 had left only a small number of Jews behind, primarily those working in militarily important factories. To the Germans, killing Jews invariably had a higher priority than factory production, and during 1943 six transports with about 6,000 Jews were sent via the transit and assembly camp at Malines to Auschwitz.[33] One such transport, that of April 19, 1943, was disrupted by one of the very few instances of a local underground cooperating with the Jewish resistance to save deportees; it did succeed in enabling a few to escape. The vast majority were killed.[34]

Many Belgian Jews had fled to France during the German invasion of 1940; most of them were caught up in the deportations from France of those Jews who were not French citizens. The Vichy French government of Marshal Henri Philippe Pétain had adopted a policy of cooperating in the deportation to their death of Jews in France who were aliens but, especially after the German defeat at Stalingrad, of being uncooperative when it came to French citizens. There were substantial revocations of French citizenship to accommodate German demands, and several categories of Jews hitherto exempt from deportation were now included in the death trains which the French police helped the Germans fill. Some 20,000 Jews were sent from France to the killing centers in Poland during 1943, and transports continued thereafter until the liberation. The Vichy regime, however, would not surrender all the Jews who held French citizenship; and the Germans, who very much needed the Vichy administrative and police apparatus, were prepared to pressure them only

31 Benz, *Dimensionen des Völkermordes*, pp. 150–53.
32 Ibid., pp. 155–56, 162–63; Yahil, *The Holocaust*, pp. 437–38. A fine survey of the whole matter in Henry L. Mason, "Testing Human Bonds within Nations: Jews in the Occupied Netherlands," *Political Science Quarterly* 99 (1984): 315–43.
33 Benz, *Dimensionen des Völkermordes*, pp. 129–31, 135.
34 Yahil, *The Holocaust*, pp. 435–36.

so far.[35] Here, as elsewhere, the Germans anticipated that victory in the war would enable the thousand-year Reich to finish whatever had had to be postponed.

An important factor in restraining the Vichy government, and one that particularly annoyed the Germans, was the obstruction deliberately placed in the path of deportation by the Italian authorities in the portion of France under Italian occupation. This attitude, which made the Italian zone in southeast France something of a precarious haven for Jews until the Italian surrender of September 1943, affected Italy itself as well as the Italian-occupied portions of southeast Europe.[36]

The issue of deportations reinforced the distaste most German and Italian civilian and military leaders already felt for each other. In the eyes of the Germans, the stubborn refusal of the Italians to cooperate in their program to kill all the Jews in Europe, Africa, and Asia they could reach, and the frequent instances in which Italian officials deliberately obstructed the Germans by extending Italian citizenship to Jews whose claims to it were dubious at best and through a variety of other devices, only reinforced the view that the Italians were unreliable and inefficient allies.[37] To most of those in the Italian diplomatic, military, and administrative services, on the other hand, the German mania for killing Jews seemed to be just one more sign that their Axis partner had hardly progressed from the level of the Germanic barbarians who had invaded the Roman Empire centuries before. And Mussolini's occasional inclinations to accommodate the Germans on this issue only made his regime less popular in Italy – where this was seen as a distasteful form of subservience to the Germans – and less effective, as his own officials sidestepped whatever concessions their leader had made.

The conflict between German and Italian policy was so vehement that German Foreign Minister Joachim von Ribbentrop went to Rome in February 1943 to try to pressure the Italian government into a more cooperative posture on this critical matter. Mussolini waffled; the Germans pushed harder; but whatever concessions the Duce made were

35 See Robert O. Paxton and Michael Marrus, *Vichy France and the Jews* (New York: Columbia University Press, 1981); Benz, *Dimensionen des Völkermordes*, pp. 125–27, 132–33; Yahil, *The Holocaust*, pp. 431–34.
36 For a comprehensive treatment of this subject, see Jonathan Steinberg, *All or Nothing: The Axis and the Holocaust, 1941–1943* (New York: Routledge, 1990).
37 The African Jews the Germans still hoped to kill were those of Libya and Tunisia. Although subjected to persecution, almost all survived because of Italian policy; by the time Italy surrendered, Libya and Tunisia were already in Allied hands. The Jews of Asia whom the Germans expected to kill were those on the Italian island of Rhodes, off the coast of Turkey; these did fall into German hands after the surrender of Italy and were deported for killing in 1944. See Benz, *Dimensionen des Völkermordes*, pp. 213–15; Yahil, *The Holocaust*, pp. 420–21.

promptly evaded, possibly with his tacit agreement, by the Italian authorities on the spot in France, Yugoslavia, Greece, and Italy itself.[38]

After the surrender of Italy in September 1943, the Germans made a major effort to seize and deport to killing centers the Jews of Italy who had hitherto lived under restrictions but had remained alive. It is no coincidence that on the conclusion of "Operation Reinhard," the systematic killing of the Jews of the central part of German-occupied Poland, Odilo Globocnik, the obviously accomplished and experienced leader of this major portion of the Holocaust named by the Germans in honor of the assassinated Reinhard Heydrich, who had done so much to move that project forward, was sent in the fall of 1943 to Trieste, the city of his birth, to apply his talents and experience in Italy (just as earlier the "euthanasia" experts had been sent to the killing centers in Poland). In northern Italy the Germans now tried their best, or worst, to collect as many Jews as possible for transport to the killing center at Auschwitz or to a new one at San Sabba, just inside the Trieste city limits. There was even a round-up of Jews in Rome itself. The Germans found, however, that the population sheltered many Jews, that other Jews found refuge with the partisans, and that although the Pope took no public position, many Catholic clergymen aided the objects of German hunts. Thousands were deported and killed, but the majority of Italy's Jews survived, in part because of the obstruction of non-Jewish Italians, in part because the country was in the process of liberation.[39]

The most dramatic events in the first half of 1943 affected by the conflict between German and Italian policy took place in Greece. Because Greece after its defeat and occupation in 1941 had a collaborationist government operating in the whole country except for the small pieces annexed by Bulgaria and Italy, the Germans would have preferred a common series of steps leading to the killing of all Jews in both the German and the Italian zones of occupation. Although most of Greece was occupied by Italy, the German zone in northern Greece[40] included the majority of the approximately 70,000 Greek Jews. This was so because the city of Salonika in the German zone contained a Jewish community of more than 50,000, many of them descendants of refugees from the expulsion of Jews from Spain and Portugal centuries earlier. Hitler had expressly authorized Himmler to include the Jewish population of

38 Steinberg, *Axis and the Holocaust*, pp. 115ff.
39 Ibid., pp. 156ff.; Benz, *Dimensionen des Völkermordes*, pp. 201–7; Yahil, *The Holocaust*, pp. 424ff.
40 Maps of wartime Greece show the northeastern portion of Greece and an enclave near Athens, as well as portions of Crete, under German occupation.

Salonika in the program of exterminating Jews in early October 1941,[41] but the German hope of deporting *all* Greek Jews to their deaths in one large operation had, in the face of steady Italian opposition, led to a substantial delay.

Since the Jews directly accessible to the Germans in the portions of Europe they fully controlled had for the most part been killed by the end of 1942, with the largest remaining group, that in occupied Poland, scheduled to be killed in early 1943, there were actually few places where the practitioners of mass murder could still locate large numbers of victims. With increasing obstacles in the West and, as is discussed below, in the satellites of southeast Europe, the substantial Jewish community of Salonika stood out as an obvious target for those whose prospects of careers, promotions, and decorations in the Third Reich – as well as safety from more hazardous duty at the front – provided a strong vested interest in a high level of continuous killing of Jews. Under these circumstances, the Germans decided in the winter of 1942–43 to abandon their concept of a uniform procedure in Greece and to deport separately and immediately the Jewish population of Salonika and of the smaller Jewish communities in German-occupied Greece.

In a series of dramatic steps, the Germans rounded up the overwhelming majority of Salonika's Jewish community and others in their zone for deportation to the killing centers, primarily to Auschwitz. In March, April, and early May 1943 over 42,000 Jews, mainly from Salonika, were sent to Auschwitz, with some smaller transports sent in subsequent months.[42]

This terrible process was not without its problems for the Germans. Some Jews escaped, fleeing to Italian-occupied Greece, joining partisans, or hiding with the assistance of non-Jewish Greeks. Furthermore, Salonika had diplomatic representatives from Italy, Spain, and Turkey who worked hard to save Jews with any claim on citizenship in other countries. If one major function of the German Foreign Ministry during the war was to pressure Germany's allies and satellites into yielding up their Jews to be killed, another was to cope with the complaints of those governments and of neutrals like Sweden and Spain about the fate of Jews who could claim citizenship in countries which did not approve of their citizens being killed by the Germans. Indeed diplomatic representatives in German-controlled Europe at times tried to assist Jews by developing their claims to citizenship in neutral countries. It was in part as a result of German efforts to move such Jews out of Greece into or

---

41 Hildegard von Kotze (ed.), *Heeresadjutant bei Hitler, 1938–1943: Aufzeichnungen des Majors Engel* (Stuttgart: Deutsche Verlags-Anstalt, 1974), p. 11.
42 Benz, *Dimensionen des Völkermordes*, pp. 152–55; Yahil, *The Holocaust*, pp. 408–14.

through the countries which claimed them that Bergen-Belsen in north-west Germany was created in 1943 as a special transit camp for people who might be exchanged or ransomed – a very different type of camp from what it later became.[43]

It was the surrender of Italy in September 1943, one month after the last transport of Jews from Salonika had left for Auschwitz, that opened up to the Germans the possibility of seizing those Jews who lived in Athens, other portions of formerly Italian-occupied Greece, and the Dodecanese Islands, which Italy had seized in the Italo–Turkish War of 1912. Deportation of Jews became the principal function of the German occupying force once they had captured and shot or shipped off to slave labor in Germany their erstwhile colleagues of the Italian army of occupation. This process continued into 1944; a major start was made already in 1943. The Germans were, however, hampered by the opposition of Greek political and religious leaders as well as by the willingness of the Greek resistance and population at large to assist the victims. More than 8,000 Greek Jews would survive as a result of such aid.[44]

The German–Italian conflict over the killing of Jews also extended to Yugoslavia. Portions of that state had been annexed to Germany, Italy, Hungary, Bulgaria, and Albania in 1941, but the bulk of prewar Yugoslavia was divided between a German-controlled smaller Serbia and an allegedly independent state of Croatia, supposedly under Italian polit-ical influence but actually divided into a German and an Italian sphere of military activity.[45] In Serbia, the exceptional enthusiasm of the German military authorities for killing Jews had resulted in the virtual elimination of the Jewish community by 1943. In Croatia the savagery of the Croatian extremists who ran this puppet state and the cold efficiency of the Ger-mans had combined to accomplish the same result with the sole excep-tion of small numbers protected by the Italians. These Jews either lived in the Italian zone of military activity or had fled there from their pro-spective German and Croatian killers. The Italian military and diplo-matic officials absolutely refused to turn these people over.[46] The Italian

---

43 Eberhard Kolb, *Bergen-Belsen: Vom "Aufenthaltslager" zum Konzentrationslager, 1943–1945* (Göttingen: Vandenhoeck & Ruprecht, 1985), pp. 19–25; Benz, *Dimensionen des Völker-mordes*, pp. 255, 257ff.; Yahil, *The Holocaust*, pp. 414–19.

44 Benz, *Dimensionen des Völkermordes*, pp. 260–71; Yahil, *The Holocaust*, pp. 419–21. Helpful on the subject is Rainer Eckert, "Die Verfolgung griechischer Juden im deutschen Okkupa-tionsgebiet Saloniki-Agäis vom April 1941 bis zum Abschluss der Deportationen im August 1943," *Bulletin des Arbeitskreises "Zweiter Weltkrieg"* (1966): 41–69. Important documents from American archives in Alexander Kitroeff (ed.), "Documents: The Jews in Greece, 1941–1944 – Eyewitness Account," *Journal of the Hellenic Diaspora* 12, no. 3 (1985): 5–32.

45 The line dividing "Croatia" ran from northwest to southeast diagonally through the puppet state.

46 Benz, *Dimensionen des Völkermordes*, p. 325; Steinberg, *The Axis and the Holocaust*, passim.

surrender made it possible for the Germans and their enthusiastic Croatian collaborators to kill most of those who had survived. It also made it easier for the same Croatians to escalate their slaughter of great numbers of others whom they wanted to eliminate from the puppet state they had been given in 1941: Serbs, Gypsies, the handicapped, and Croatian political opponents.

The fate of those Jews who found themselves in portions of Yugoslavia annexed by Germany, Italy, Hungary, Bulgaria, and Albania was determined primarily by the policies of the governments that now ruled them. The Germans had included the few Jews in the area they had annexed in their killing program in 1942, while those in the Italian portion, like those in all Italy, were kept from deportation until the Italian surrender. The Jews in the lands transferred to Hungary shared the fate of Hungary's already large Jewish community, a fate that will be examined next.

In late July 1941, about the time the decision was made to extend the program of killing Jews in the newly occupied portions of the Soviet Union to all parts of the globe accessible to German might, Hitler had predicted to Marshal Sladko Kvaternik, the commander-in-chief of the Croatian armed forces, that Hungary would be the last state in Europe to yield up its Jewish population for deportation.[47] This was the only one of the predictions Hitler made in the euphoric first weeks of the campaign in the Soviet Union which would prove to be correct. The Hungarian government of regent Miklós Horthy was quite willing to enact all sorts of anti-Semitic laws and to indulge in various forms of persecution, but it shied away from participation in the mass murder of Hungary's more than 700,000 Jews.

The intransigence of the Hungarian government was strengthened by an increasing inclination after Stalingrad to sound out possible ways to leave the war, preferably through a deal with the Western Powers, with whom the leaders of Hungary, like many others in Europe, erroneously imagined that Jews had great influence. Under these circumstances, neither the bullying of lower level German officials nor even the pressure personally applied by Hitler and von Ribbentrop themselves could budge the regent or his prime minister, Miklós Kállay, during 1943.[48] Further-

47 Memorandum on the Hitler–Kvaternik conversation of July 21 or 22, 1941, *Akten zur deutschen auswärtigen Politik, 1918–1945*, Series D, Vol. 13, pt. 2 (Göttingen: Vandenhoeck & Ruprecht, 1970), p. 838.

48 Benz, *Dimensionen des Völkermordes*, pp. 335–40. For the personal pressure of Hitler and von Ribbentrop, see the material on the conversations with Horthy on April 16–17, 1943, in *Akten zur deutschen auswärtigen Politik, 1918–1945*, Series E, Vol. 5 (Göttingen: Vandenhoek & Ruprecht, 1979), nos. 215–16; and a summary in Hilberg, *Destruction of the European Jews*, pp. 816–17. The full text of the conversation on the morning of April 17 is in Randolph L. Braham (ed.), *The Destruction of Hungarian Jewry: A Documentary Account* (New York: World Federation of Hungarian Jews, 1963), No. 103.

more, the refusal of Hungary's leaders to deliver the Jewish population of the country up for slaughter extended to the Jews in the part of Yugoslavia annexed to Hungary.

The Bulgarian government, however, followed a different policy with respect to Jews under its control. As with Hungary, the Germans applied pressure for the transfer to German custody of all Jews in areas under Bulgarian authority. The Bulgarian government decided that it would surrender to the Germans for killing those Jews living in the areas of Yugoslavia and of Greece assigned to it, and these were accordingly turned over and killed during 1943.[49] In view of massive opposition in the Bulgarian parliament, from religious leaders, and from much of the population, however, the government of King Boris decided to meet German pressure for the deportation of Jews from prewar Bulgaria by a very different tactic. The majority of these Jews lived in the capital of Sofia: in May 1943 they were forced to leave the city for other parts of the country, but they were *not* turned over to the Germans. In this unique case, deportation meant survival rather than death. With the Germans reluctant to pressure Bulgaria too much, the majority of the country's Jewish population survived to the great disappointment of German officials, who had originally seen in the banishment from Sofia the first stage on the road to Auschwitz.[50]

In 1943 the Germans also pressed the Romanians to surrender their remaining Jewish population for deportation. The Romanians had certainly been more than willing to persecute Jews, to drive many out of the country, and to slaughter large numbers of Jews in the areas ceded to the Soviet Union in 1940 when those areas were retaken in 1941 as well as in the region beyond the old border which was allocated to them under the name of Transnistria. The Romanian massacre of 50,000 Jews in Odessa in October 1941 was the single largest massacre of Jews in Europe during World War II. But the government of Marshal Ion Antonescu preferred to rob and persecute Jews with Romanian citizenship; the government would not turn them over to the Germans for killing.[51] A mixture of motives, including calculations about a possible exit from the war, countered the pressure of the Germans, who practically gave up on Romania in 1943.[52]

In part to offset or perhaps erase memories of their earlier conduct – and, they hoped, pick up some cash in the bargain – Romanian govern-

49 Benz, *Dimensionen des Völkermordes*, pp. 291–98, 327.
50 Ibid., pp. 282–91; Yahil, *The Holocaust*, pp. 579–87.
51 The Jews in the part of Romania transferred to Hungary in 1940 were treated like the Jews in other lands newly annexed by Hungary.
52 Benz, *Dimensionen des Völkermordes*, p. 382; Yahil, *The Holocaust*, pp. 347–48.

ment officials in 1943 toyed with a number of schemes for the shipment of Jews, and especially of Jewish children, out of the country to Palestine. Little came of these projects – which may well become clearer as Romanian archives on the subject become available – but they certainly show the futility of German attempts to obtain more victims here. On the contrary, the main thrust of German diplomacy had to be on preventing all such rescue efforts from taking prospective victims to havens which by 1943 were safe from the reach of German power.[53]

There was a third element in the German implementation of their killing of Europe's Jews in 1943 which must be mentioned. A subject which had already exercised the Nazis in the years before the war and to which they devoted a great deal of attention during the fighting was that of persons descended from marriages between Jews and non-Jews, people to whom they referred as *Mischlinge*, a term that can perhaps be translated as "mixed-ancestry," and who were categorized by degrees depending on the percentage of Jewish ancestry. Their policies toward this group underwent numerous changes and was a favorite topic for the endless debates of which German bureaucrats and ideologues were especially fond.

At the Wannsee Conference of January 1942 the question of what to do about the *Mischlinge* had taken up a very substantial proportion of the total time, but no decisions had been reached. Further debate followed, but no general policy decisions were arrived at in these either. The subject remained one of those not actually resolved with a clear decision by the end of the war, but the direction in which German policy was moving may be illuminated by steps taken during 1943.

It was in this year that, as far as is now known, the Germans began to send children in the *Mischling* category to at least one, and probably more, of the institutions originally established in 1939 for the so-called euthanasia program. There these children were literally and deliberately starved to death or killed by injections.[54] Although the numbers involved in this procedure appear to have been small, the very fact of the inclusion of healthy children in a program of killing that had been initiated for rather different purposes in 1939 probably shows what was in store for all those of "mixed ancestry" once victory in war had relieved the German government of any need for concern about the reactions of the public to its policies.

53 Jürgen Rohwer, *Die Versenkung der jüdischen Flüchtlingstransporter Struma und Mefkure im Schwarzen Meer, Februar 1942, August 1944* (Frankfurt/M: Bernard & Graefe, 1965), pp. 31–45.
54 Bettina Winter (ed.), *Verlegt nach Hadamar: Die Geschichte einer NS-"Euthanasie"-Anstalt* (Kassel: Landeswohlfahrtsverband Hessen, 1991).

Jews were the most numerous but by no means the only victims of National Socialist racial policies during 1943. There was continued persecution of Poles, Belorussians, Ukrainians, and other Slavic peoples whom the Germans considered racially inferior. Tens of thousands were killed, often in what were nominally antipartisan or reprisal operations, but in reality such operations focused primarily on civilians who happened to be around when German regular troops and police and SS formations came upon them. The gruesome medical experiments in concentration camps which looked toward the development of means of mass sterilization must, in my opinion, be seen in this context. Since it was assumed that there would be no Jews left alive in the area controlled directly or indirectly by Germany after it had finally won the war, it follows that any such methods that might be developed, were destined, had Germany won, to be applied to other racial groups considered inferior but whose labor on farms, in industry, or in mines was still needed for a time until they could be replaced by Germans. It seems reasonable to conclude that the Slavic peoples of Poland, Bohemia, Serbia, and the Soviet Union were at the top of the list of prospective victims.

By the time such techniques could be applied to Slavic peoples, one group in addition to the Jews was expected to have been eliminated from Europe by extermination: the Gypsies, or Sinti and Roma. Discriminated against for years, both before and after the Nazis came to power, the Gypsies were increasingly placed by the National Socialist government into the same legal category as Jews, at first in respect to restrictions and forced labor, eventually as candidates for death. The shift to this final position took place in December 1942 and January 1943, the same months as the decision to kill the Jews remaining in ghettos and labor camps in Poland and in German-occupied Greece; it should perhaps be seen as a part of the general push to complete the "racial cleansing" of German-controlled Europe that the Nazis hoped to accomplish during 1943. The first transport of Gypsies from Germany arrived in Auschwitz at the end of February 1943; the first from occupied Europe in early March; and the first gassings of Gypsies took place that month. By the end of 1943 many thousands had been killed at Auschwitz and many thousands had died under the terrible conditions in the camps to which they had been sent. Others were killed in Croatia by Germany's puppets there.[55]

---

55 Several articles by Sybil Milton cover the subject: "The Context of the Holocaust," *German Studies Review* 13 (1990): 269–83; "Gypsies and the Holocaust," *The History Teacher* 24 (1991): 375–87; "Nazi Policies toward Roma and Sinti, 1933–1945," *Journal of the Gypsy Lore Society* (February 1992): 1–18. See also Michael Zimmermann, *Verfolgt, vertrieben, vernichtet: Die nationalsozialistische Vernichtungspolitik gegen Sinti und Roma* (Essen: Klartext, 1989).

What, if anything, was done and could be done by others as this horrifying program of mass murder went forward during 1943? By this time all Allied and European neutral governments and most of the people in those countries had heard, at least in general terms, what was going on. Hitler himself repeatedly boasted about the extermination of the Jews in public speeches broadcast over the radio and printed in all German newspapers.[56] Reports of mass killings, primarily from occupied Poland, had led the governments of the United Nations publicly to condemn the program in the St. James Declaration of December 1942. As already mentioned, some in Germany opposed the Nazi regime, though not necessarily for this reason, and many in the occupied territories as well as countries allied with Germany hid or otherwise aided the victims. Small numbers of Jews escaped as a result of special exchanges, and a few were able to emigrate illegally. But on the whole, outside intervention remained minimal in 1943.

The Soviet government had never recognized the special character of National Socialist racial ideology as a driving force for anti-Semitism and never changed its line of complete disinterest in the subject. The governments of Britain and the United States expressed repeated concern in public but would take few or no practical steps to help. This was due in part to a continued inability to believe that what they knew was happening was indeed taking place – something perhaps not so difficult to comprehend when many find it difficult to credit fifty years afterwards – but probably most of all by the driving exigencies of a terrible war which was just beginning to turn in favor of the Allies. Two other factors operated to restrain any impulses to help. Both Britain and the United States did not want to give any semblance of truth to the major propaganda theme of the Germans, namely that the war was being waged for the benefit of and at the instigation of the Jews – a line which might well resonate with substantial anti-Semitic sentiments among their public. The British were also concerned about repercussions in the Muslim world over any further substantial Jewish immigration into Palestine.

Under these circumstances, the Allied conference held at Bermuda in the spring of 1943 – in the very days of the Warsaw ghetto uprising – to review the possibilities of aiding the Jewish victims of persecution came to no practical results whatever. There were public expressions of concern, especially by church groups. Although these began to show the way to what would prove to be a long-delayed confrontation with the reality of multimillion mass murder, words alone could not save any of the victims

---

56 On this issue, see Hans-Heinrich Wilhelm, "Wie geheim war die 'Endlösung'?" in Wolfgang Benz et al. (eds.), *Miscellanea: Festschrift für Helmut Krausnick* (Stuttgart: Deutsche Verlags-Anstalt, 1980), pp. 131–48.

at the time. Jewish organizations and prominent individuals who were horrified by what was going on made a number of attempts to arouse public opinion and thereby, it was hoped, put pressure on the governments of both Britain and the United States – but with little effect. The great influence that anti-Semites everywhere always attributed to Jews had proved to be as imaginary as the other constructs sick minds projected onto a group without help or power in its hour of supreme peril.

The Pope, having declined to denounce publicly the mass killing of Catholic priests in Poland in the winter of 1939–40, at a time when Germany and the Soviet Union were aligned with each other, was not about to voice any explicit public disapproval of the mass killing of non-Catholics. Though such a statement would hardly have had any effect on the German leadership, it might well have made the choice much easier for those many Catholic clergy who did help Jews, encouraged others to do so, and discouraged those who participated in the persecutions, especially in Croatia. Pope Pius XII was urged in this direction by high princes of the church, including Cardinal Roncalli, later Pope John XXIII; but while he quietly offered help in specific circumstances, nothing could move the Pope to a different posture in public.

The Allies did hope to limit the extent of terror by including in their first major meeting of the war, that in Moscow in October 1943 in preparation for the Big Three meeting at Teheran later that year, a warning that war criminals would be tried and punished after the war. Whatever some in Germany may have thought about this, there is no evidence that it affected their behavior during the rest of 1943.

The conference of the major Allies at Teheran from November 28 to December 1, 1943, symbolized and assured that having turned the tide of battle, they would stick together thereafter, thereby making German victory in the war impossible. This combination of a reversal of the Axis string of victories early in the war with a determination to remain allied into 1944 meant that by the end of 1943 about two-thirds of the world's approximately 19 million Jews had been spared from the death the Germans intended for the "extinct race" about which they were assembling artifacts for a museum in Prague. Of the third who before 1939 lived in what had come to be German-controlled Europe, the vast majority had already been killed.

The largest single remaining Jewish community within possible German grasp, that of Hungary, was in greater danger than most realized, for by the end of September 1943 the Germans were starting to plan an occupation of Hungary lest that country follow Italy's example and leave the war. The Germans were also examining the possibility of occupying

Romania, the Axis satellite with the second largest surviving Jewish community possibly within German reach. The Germans eventually decided to concentrate on Hungary, and their swift occupation of that country in March 1944 was to initiate a new and terrible chapter in the history of the "Final Solution." Romania, on the other hand, managed to leave the Axis side in August 1944 *before* the Germans could seize total control of the country.

The fate of Hungarian Jews and of other remnant Jewish communities, and the efforts to save them as the war was more and more obviously coming to an end in an Allied victory in Europe, would provide the focus for developments in the "Final Solution" during the remaining year and a half of conflict. These developments would be greatly complicated by two closely related aspects of the collapsing Third Reich. In the first place, the advance of the Allies was met by a German determination not only to hold on to as much territory as possible, but also to evacuate to other camps still under German control the surviving prisoners in the various types of camps being approached by Allied troops. In this process of hurried evacuation, vast numbers of Jews were deliberately killed because they were not strong enough to keep up in the forced marches and thousands died of exhaustion and cold. Second, the very process of collapse meant that the supply system of the Germans could not provide even the minimal rations and medical supplies which the camp inmates were supposed to get. As a result, additional tens of thousands – already terribly debilitated from the privations imposed on them by the Germans – died in the camps to which they had been moved.

The still pictures and newsreel films of the killing centers and camps liberated by the Allies in 1944 and 1945 first brought the shocking reality to the public, especially in the West, and in many ways came to frame the way in which the whole development of the "Final Solution" was viewed in the postwar years. The year 1943 had seen both the imposition of limits on that program by the turning tide of the war and also two major new developments during its application within the area German power still reached: massive and concerted German efforts to kill any remaining Jews who had survived the killing of over 3 million in 1941 and 1942, and a shift from isolated efforts at Jewish escape and opposition to significant attempts at organized and open Jewish resistance.

18

———— • ————

JULY 20, 1944: THE GERMAN RESISTANCE TO HITLER

It is fifty years since D-Day, the invasion of Western Europe on June 6, 1944. Two days before that famous date, in the South, the Allies had taken Rome; two weeks later, the great Soviet offensive tore open Germany's Eastern Front. Those coordinated attacks would squeeze the life out of Hitler's empire. But for a moment, it looked as if the war might end much more quickly. On July 20, 1944, a bomb exploded in Hitler's headquarters, a few feet from the dictator himself, and a broadly based opposition attempted, primarily in Berlin and Paris, to take power away from the Nazis and reestablish decency inside and peace outside Germany. But the explosion did not kill Hitler, and the attempted coup was quickly and successfully throttled. The war ground on. What had happened?

Opposition to the government of a totalitarian police state is no easy matter. If you make your disapproval of the government's policies known, you do not appear on the eleven o'clock news, you disappear forever. And you disappear quietly. Only a few friends and relatives learn that you are not around anymore; the controlled mass media make no reference to the event, unless the government itself decides to use the matter in a context of its own choosing – with no provision of equal time for the inmate of camp or tomb. The same media will have broadcast an almost impenetrable fog of propaganda in the first place, making everyone incredulous of any who have seen some light and who try to persuade others that they are indeed in a fog. As in the parable of Plato, the prisoners still chained in the cave who have seen only the passing shadows assume *them* to be reality, reject as preposterous and unreal the visions of those who have left the cave to look at the world in the light of truth.

Slightly revised from its first publication in the *Michigan Quarterly Review* 10, no. 2 (Spring 1971): 125–30.

Nevertheless, overthrowing a totalitarian regime is not impossible. As in East Germany in June 1953 and in Hungary in October 1956, sufficient mass dissatisfaction can topple an unpopular police state from below. In both those cases, only outside military intervention could reinstate a tottering tyranny. Obviously, no outside power would ever have saved Hitler as the Red Army saved Walter Ulbricht and Janos Kadar; and the events in Hungary in 1988–89 and in East Germany in 1989 demonstrated very clearly that once the Red Army's orders had changed, the local armies and police systems of these states could not save their regimes from the pressures from below. The German people's massive support of Hitler closed this road, however, in Nazi Germany. A successor government might have secured support by dispelling the fog and revealing the Third Reich in all its hideous reality, but this presupposed a thoroughly successful coup that could change the role of the mass media. The National Socialist regime, which was popular in peacetime, became, if not more popular, certainly less vulnerable in the early years of World War II when Germany's spectacular victories combined with the pressures of wartime to consolidate the population behind its rulers.

If the government could not be toppled from below, then the only alternative was from above, that is, from the inside. Individuals in important positions within the government might, precisely because of their positions, gain greater insight into the true nature of the regime. They might then try to persuade other officials of their insight and, joining with sympathetic individuals outside the government, attempt to seize power from within the governmental structure. The opposition in Germany necessarily took this direction. But the moral dilemma inherent in this situation must be noted. If you quit your position, you could disclaim any connection with the policies you opposed, but you would give up any chance to help in a major and active way in the effort to topple the regime. If you remained in office to stay close to the levers of power for the day of decision, you would have to participate in a regime you believed to be evil. Such a dilemma is necessarily most difficult for precisely those most sensitive to moral questions.

A few such people were in the German government, their numbers varying, their views differing, and their motives not always pure nor therefore entirely opportunistic either. Some came to be horrified at the excesses that accompanied victories; others, to be appalled at the unwillingness to react constructively to the onrush of defeat. Different straws break the backs of different camels: Carl Goerdeler, mayor of Leipzig, quit when the Party removed the statue of the great composer Mendelssohn from the city square; Helmuth Stieff, the chief of "Organization" for the German army general staff, when atrocities in Poland and the Soviet Union made him, as he wrote his wife, ashamed to be a German.[1] Diplomats and generals, labor leaders and clergymen, politicians of the old parties and disillusioned National Socialists, formed a loose association of kindred spirits about whom we know a good deal, but not as much as we might like, because conspiracies in a police state do not keep extensive files (and much of the little they kept was destroyed).

Ludwig Beck, for instance, had been chief of staff of the German army since 1934. He objected vehemently to suggestions of aggressive war in 1935; he became increasingly alarmed at the reckless drive toward war, and at certain domestic policies. Opposed to attacking Germany's neighbors, Beck attempted to rally the other German generals for a united opposition, a sort of general strike of the generals, against what he considered a foolhardy, dangerous, and immoral policy. He felt that a military man in a high position cannot restrict himself to purely technical details in the face of an imminent disaster, clearly perceived. Unable to move the commander-in-chief or other senior generals to a collective stand against Hitler, he resigned and worked with others in the opposition. Beck gave some of his key papers, warnings against the policies of Hitler, to an associate who had helped him draft some of them; many were destroyed in the war; but some survive to enable us to trace his views.

Julius Leber was a socialist from Lübeck, a labor leader who had worked hard to infuse some life and enthusiasm into German democracy in the Weimar years. When the Nazis attempted to murder him in the night after Hitler's appointment as chancellor, he was arrested, released, and arrested again, and spent four years in a concentration camp. After his release, although under constant surveillance, he did his best to keep in touch with like-minded men among former trade unionists. He was, in effect, the opposition's intermediary between labor and some generals, and many of both groups looked to him for a key role in any post-Hitler Germany.

Ulrich von Hassell, a professional diplomat, had served as ambassador to Italy in the 1930s. Hitler's dangerous foreign policy alarmed him, a conservative nationalist. The trend toward an alliance between Germany and Italy worried him as much as the hostility of prior years – either seemed dangerous. Dismissed in 1938, von Hassell could only observe the trend to disaster, but he made contact with other opponents, tried to recruit additional ones, and kept a diary that survived his arrest and

---

1 Hellmuth Stieff to his wife, November 21, 1939, in Horst Mühleisen (ed.), *Hellmuth Stieff: Briefe* (Berlin: Siegler, 1991), p. 108. See also Mühleisen's article, "Hellmuth Stieff und der deutsche Widerstand," *Vierteljahrshefte für Zeitgeschichte*, 39 (1991), 339–77.

execution to become one of our most important firsthand sources for the history of the opposition to Hitler.[2]

Since in National Socialist Germany only organized insiders could hope to overthrow the regime, this account like most must set aside the many ordinary people from all walks of life who refused to conform, who helped the persecuted, who passed on news they had heard on forbidden radio stations, with high moral courage. But sporadic individual acts of defiance, however heroic, could count for little.

The only possible exception to this generalization would be an attempted assassination; and it was precisely such an attempt in November 1939, planned for many months by the individual who carried it out and paid for it with his life, that almost worked. But even that project, though very intelligently conceived and executed, could look only to Hitler's death, not to the establishment of anything differently structured thereafter.[3] Any effort that was to include a seizure of power and not only the removal of Hitler necessarily called for planning by insiders.

The opposition at first tried to get the highest men in the army to use their authority against the regime. But the obtuseness of the first, and the weakness of the second commander-in-chief blocked all prospects of success along this route. When Hitler himself assumed command of the army in December 1941, assassination followed by seizure of control seemed the only possible avenue. With Hitler removed, the doubters would rally to the determined among the military, and together they would overawe, or crush, those still loyal to the swastika. But such a scheme was immensely difficult.

The first problem was finding someone with access to Hitler willing to try to kill him. Most of those around Hitler were personal friends. If any were doubters, finding them out was not easy. One could not take a poll. Furthermore, Hitler himself took increasing precautions against assassination, changing his schedule, declining visits near the front, and increasing his escort. In March 1943 the conspirators put a bomb on Hitler's plane, but the detonator failed, leaving the conspirators the ticklish task of recovering the unexploded bomb. One conspirator planned to blow himself up right next to Hitler and then had to disconnect his own fuse when the Führer left before the device was timed to explode. Other schemes came to naught for different reasons. And some of the conspirators had doubts. As long as Hitler was winning, an assassination followed by defeat in war would lead to another stab-in-the-back legend among

---

2 Friedrich Freiherr Hiller von Gaertringen (ed.), *Die Hassell-Tagebücher: Ulrich von Hassel, Aufzeichnungen vom Andern Deutschland* (Berlin: Siegler, 1988).
3 Lothar Gruchmann (ed.), *Autobiographie eines Attentäters: Johann Georg Elser* (Stuttgart: Deutsche Verlags-Anstalt, 1970).

the German people; not a very firm basis for creating a democratic order. Once Hitler was losing, on the other hand, a coup would look to the outside world like a last minute attempt to avert the consequences of defeat. Furthermore, what could then be saved anyway?

After the invasion of Normandy, the problem became acute. Should they go ahead? One of the key conspirators answered: "The assassination must be attempted, at any cost. Even should that fail, the attempt to seize power in the capital must be undertaken. We must prove to the world and to future generations that the men of the German Resistance movement dared to take the decisive step and to hazard their lives upon it. Compared with this object, nothing else matters."[4]

Plans to seize power in the capital immediately upon the assassination were, of course, essential. These plans were developed in the Replacement Army under the cover of contingency planning to cope with any revolt by foreign workers inside Germany or commando raids. This plan, called "Valkyrie," was partly regularized and deposited in sealed envelopes in all military district headquarters, to be opened only when the code word was given, and was partly to be supplemented by secret additions calling for a complete takeover.

In World War I, Germany had transferred executive and police powers to the military districts covering all Germany. In each district, the local military leader gave orders to civilian as well as military agencies. In World War II, Hitler refused to allow this; the Party and the police remained superior. But Valkyrie planned to transfer executive power to the military, along with authority to mobilize all reserves, thereby enabling them to dominate the situation at home at a time when the active units were at the front. With a concept familiar to the German public and military from the previous war, this plan offered real promise. And, in view of the millions of forced laborers inside Germany and the frequency of commando raids on the coasts of German-occupied Europe, a project ostensibly designed to cope with contingencies tied to these potential dangers could be formulated without arousing suspicion.

Separate plans were made to seize radio and telegraph facilities, to initiate local liaison officers into at least parts of the plot, and to explain to the German people and army what was going on. Utmost secrecy was, of course, imperative. Claus von Stauffenberg, a man who combined remarkable ability with decisiveness, played an increasingly important part in this planning. With some conspirators arrested and others hesitating, he infused energy into the group and recruited additional men. His organizational talents simultaneously assured him a key part in the con-

---

4 Henning von Tresckow quoted in Fabian von Schlabrendorff, *They Almost Killed Hitler*, ed. Gero v. s. Gaevernitz (New York: Macmillan, 1947), p. 103.

World War II

spiracy, and earned him the post of chief of staff of the Replacement Army, a position that gave him access to the Führer's headquarters. Though he had lost one eye, one hand, and three fingers of the other hand in the war, Stauffenberg had become the motor of the conspiracy.

After several postponements, the conspirators decided on the conference of July 20, 1944, which von Stauffenberg would attend, as the occasion for their attempt. Von Stauffenberg flew to East Prussia, placed his briefcase with the bomb under the table around which Hitler and his military advisers gathered, left the meeting on a pretext, saw the explosion, which he assumed had killed Hitler, bluffed his way out of the headquarters, and flew back to Berlin. There and in Paris where conspirators held key posts the coup was attempted. In Berlin, the conspirators received the special signal and gathered at the Ministry of War; the code word of implementing Valkyrie went out to all military district headquarters, and orders to seize power went out over the teleprinter. In Paris, the military actually seized power and arrested top police officials. But Hitler had not been killed.

By an extraordinary mischance, the explosion that wounded and killed several left Hitler with only minor injuries. His headquarters in East Prussia immediately inaugurated countermeasures. The intended blocking of telephone and telegraph circuits could not be maintained, because Hitler had not been killed, and counterorders from East Prussia crossed those of Valkyrie from Berlin. The conspirators could not go back – and did not want to in any case. They tried to move on with their scheme, sending out their orders and proclamations, hoping to take over power in spite of Hitler's survival. In a few hours, the bulk of Germany's military leaders made their choice. As between a still living Hitler and his opponents, they sided with the dictator. In those few hours, the uprising was crushed, the most immediately implicated conspirators summarily shot, and the authority of the regime firmly reasserted. During the night Hitler spoke over the radio from East Prussia to reassure the people that he was still alive, obviously destined by fate to continue to lead them. And continue to lead them he did, to death and destruction for added millions.

The failure of the coup, in fact, left the National Socialist leadership in a stronger position than ever. The Gestapo had not fully understood the conspiracy; they knew something of it, but had been kept from picking up all of the conspirators by Himmler's own doubts about the outcome of the war. Now that most of the opposition had necessarily revealed themselves in the events of July 20, or by association with the conspirators or from seized records, a great haul of oppositionists was taken to jail and to the scaffold, while others previously arrested were now dealt with more harshly. As the war ground on along the shrinking fringes of Hitler's empire, hundreds were executed inside it for their real or suspected involvement in the conspiracy. Some were tried and then executed, some were simply murdered, still others committed suicide lest they endanger others under torture. Thus Hitler's control tightened, as the skeptical and the critical disappeared together and the atmosphere of terror intensified. He could now radically increase the power of the police at the expense of the army, and strengthen the Party at the expense of the army and the administration.

As Hitler's first triumph had been his assumption of power in 1933, so his last triumph was the maintenance of that power against internal enemies. A few of these were not discovered right away, and a few were never discovered at all, but no significant internal challenge to the Führer's power remained. He had not been overthrown either from below or from above; he could now be removed only by the armed might of the great anti-German coalition he himself had forged.

But, in spite of the continuing war, in spite of the increased Nazification of German life, in spite of failure, the events of that summer day remain significant for Germany and for world history. The Germans are the most numerous and potentially most powerful people in Europe after the Russians; whatever significantly affects them has important implications for the continent as a whole. The dramatic success of Germany's physical reconstruction after 1945 has obscured her far more difficult psychological reconstruction. If the German people are to find an integral place in Europe and their self-respect, they need a past to which they can relate positively. As the various European nationalities emerged from nonnational constructions in the nineteenth century, and as other nations have emerged out of the colonial empires in the twentieth, one distinguishing feature of that process has been the effort to relate the present to the past, to give independence a dimension in time, and to provide in difficult struggles the self-confidence and hope that comes from perceiving past struggles and accomplishments. The current developments in the former Russian colonial empire remind us of this need in the world at large even as the call for and discussion of African-American history and Chicano history do so within the United States. After 1945, with its total debacle and with revelations of greater horrors than the most determined foes of Hitler had ever imagined, Germany desperately needed the signposts, the examples, the heroes, and the traditions to which a new Germany might hark back and relate in the future. Here the conspiracy against Hitler is of central importance.

Not perfect men and women making perfect decisions, but fallible people facing hard choices and cruel alternatives, the members of the resistance provide a basis for a post-Nazi order and point to a future in which new issues can be measured by a standard of decency. In an age without heroes, in a country where the heroes have too often been those willing to sacrifice the spirit of humanity to the power of the state, a group that tried to assert the opposite – that the state must be subordinated to elemental rights – stands forth as a standard to which people can adhere and by which they can judge.

By no means all Germans have found this standard acceptable. In fact, the willingness or reluctance to do so may provide a touchstone by which most modern Germans can easily be assessed. Many have tried to avoid the Twentieth of July in uneasy distaste; many have condemned as traitors the very men and women who sacrificed their lives to save Germany from Hitler's frenzy of destruction. As the picture of the opposition, its hopes, plans, and aspirations has become clearer over the years, many have looked to it positively as representative of values that have meaning for all people, and as symbolizing a tradition which deserves a central place in a new beginning for their country, a country that desperately needs a new beginning.

This is important for Germany's relations with other countries as well. Hitler's tyranny had to be terminated by the exertions and sacrifices of others. But the others now know that inside Germany some brave men and women did try to end the tyranny themselves, at the risk of everything and at the price of their lives. Thus, the dead of the resistance, though sorely missed in postwar Germany, provided it with one of its most important assets.

There is, in addition, a point in all this for everyone. The judge who presided over the sham trials of some conspirators, Roland Freisler, was killed when a bomb fell on the People's Court. But sham trials did not end with Freisler's death, and tyranny did not end with Hitler's. Half a century later, the example of those who dared defy the tyrant is still worthy of remembrance.

When I became responsible for microfilming the captured German records held in the United States before their return to Germany, I was also responsible for assigning very personal papers among them to the privacy-protecting "privileged" category. One of the first films we wanted to make publicly available was that of the Gestapo reports to Hitler on the Twentieth of July, a group of records usually referred to as the Kaltenbrunner Reports because the head of the Reich Security Main Office signed them. The problem was that the last letters of some of the conspirators were attached to the reports. Certainly nothing could be more personal than the last letters to his wife, his mother, or his children of a man about to be executed; but it seemed to me that an exception to "privilege" could properly be made in this case so that the men of the resistance, not the Gestapo, would have the last word. The U. S. Army authorities then in charge of the documents were fortunately persuaded by this consideration – a judgment ironically confirmed when a neo-Nazi publication of the police reports carefully omitted every one of the letters.

One of the conspirators wrote to his mother before his execution on August 8, 1944:

> At the end of a life greatly blessed with love and friendship, I have only gratitude toward God and humility before His will. I greatly regret causing you this sorrow after all the sad things you have lived through. I ask you to forgive me for this. I have had more than two weeks to place my life and my actions before God, and I am convinced that I will find him a merciful judge. The extent of the internal conflict faced in recent years by men like myself is simply incomprehensible to those who are secure in their belief [in National Socialism] which I simply do not share. I can assure you that no ambitious seeking for power motivated my actions. My actions were motivated only by my patriotic feelings, the concern for Germany as it has developed over two millennia, and the worry over its internal and external development. Therefore I stand unashamed before my ancestors, my father, and my brothers. Perhaps a time will come when people will arrive at a different evaluation of our conduct, when we will be considered not bums but warners and patriots. I pray that the wonderful way in which we have been called will serve to honor God.[5]

---

5 Count Peter Yorck von Wartenburg to his mother, in Erich Zimmermann and Hans-Adolf Jacobsen (eds.), *20. Juli 1944* (Berlin: Berto-Verlag, 1960), p. 252. For additional details and an extensive bibliography, see Peter Hoffmann, *The History of the German Resistance, 1933–1945*, trans. Richard Barry (Cambridge, Mass.: MIT Press, 1977).

19

D-DAY AFTER FIFTY YEARS: ASSESSMENTS OF COSTS AND BENEFITS

When we look back on the events of D-Day and the campaign which followed, a number of images immediately appear before our eyes, even if no pictures are projected onto a screen. We see the vast fleets approaching the shore, men scrambling into the water from landing craft as the gates open or the ramps are lowered, parachutists jumping into the unknown, defensive fire – at first sporadic, then picking up – long siegelike warfare reminiscent of the trenches of World War I, Cherbourg surrendering and Caen obliterated, more and more French communities shattered by bombs and artillery, the carnage of the German forces trying to escape the Falaise pocket, the dash across France, the liberation of Paris, the failure of Market-Garden and the grinding campaign of the late fall, the German Ardennes offensive and death in the snow, the bridge at Remagen, the rush into Germany, the ruined towns of Germany with white – or more likely gray – sheets hanging out of the windows, ghastly scenes in the camps as Allied troops enter as liberators, the endless miles of German soldiers trudging to POW camps on one side of the road as Allied tanks and trucks roll forward on the other.

In these mental images, we glimpse some indications of the costs: death at Omaha Beach and parachutists hanging in the trees, destroyed towns and the gaunt looks of men too long under fire, crashed gliders and a storm-wrecked Mulberry harbor. And if we visit the battlefields today, we see much reconstruction from the physical damage of war, but not too far away the rows of crosses and stars of David in the cemeteries. A reasonably accurate compilation arrives at a total of over 850,000 Allied military casualties, a figure which does not include the sick or the tens of thousands of civilian casualties.[1] German casualties were substantially

Slightly revised from Theodore A. Wilson (ed.), *D-Day 1944* (Lawrence: University Press of Kansas, 1994), pp. 318–37, 389–90.

1 L. F. Ellis, *Victory in the West*, Vol. II: *The Defeat of Germany* (History of the Second World War, United Kingdom Military Series) (London: H.M. Stationery Office, 1968), p. 407.

higher, even if we exclude the enormous numbers of prisoners taken by the Allies in the last weeks of the fighting. A German estimate of 250,000 military casualties up to August 22, 1944, compared to 170,000 Allied casualties seems to provide a reasonable benchmark for the Normandy campaign as a whole.[2] If the human costs were high, the material ones were enormous. The 1944 joke, that the barrage balloons alone kept the British Isles from sinking under the weight of supplies stocked in preparation for the invasion, may serve as a reminder of the vast expenditure of money and material resources which went into the invasion and its follow-up operations.

If one raises the question, Was it worth it?, then one simply has to consider the alternatives first. After all, the Allies did not land in Normandy because they thought the scenery beautiful or the people charming, and the Germans did not try to hold on in Western Europe because they had always wanted to see Paris. The Allies were trying to defeat Germany in the quickest and least costly way possible, while the Germans were hoping to hold on until either victory in battle or a split in the hostile alliance they themselves had created provided them with the opportunity to continue that demographic revolution in the world on which they had set their hearts, to which they had harnessed their power, and which they were carrying forward with grim determination even as the fighting raged on. Alternatives to an invasion in northwest Europe for the Western Allies could be seen as of two basic types: geographical and chronological. They could have made their major push elsewhere or in the same place but at another time. These two types will be examined separately.

The geographic alternatives to northwest France were Italy or the Balkans, or a combination of these two. An assault on Norway, though repeatedly considered during the war, was quite correctly thought of as an operation for significant but *local* advantages even by its advocates and was never believed to be a substitute for a major invasion of Europe. The campaign in Italy was, of course, already in progress for almost a year by the time of D-Day. Why not reinforce it with massive strength, and perhaps supplement the operations there with a major landing in Greece or on the coast of Yugoslavia or both? At various times suggestions along these lines were made by some in the British leadership, though always with the claim that an invasion of northwest Europe at some time in the future would not thereby be precluded. In practice, however, that time in the future would most likely never have come before the Red Army

2 Dieter Ose, *Entscheidung im Westen: Der Oberbefehlshaber West und die Abwehr der Invasion* (Schriftenreihe des Militärgeschichtlichen Forschungsamtes) (Stuttgart: Deutsche Verlags-Anstalt, 1982), pp. 266–67.

overran all of Western as well as Central Europe or, alternatively, the first atomic bombs fell on Germany in August 1945.

The reason for this characteristic of the geographical alternative was twofold. In the first place, the logistical support needed for the sorts of operations and the size of forces which would have been engaged in the kinds of operations in Italy and southeastern Europe called for by such a strategy would have made any invasion of northwestern Europe impossible before the summer of 1945 or, more likely, the summer of 1946. It is worth noting that even the small-scale British operation in Greece in the winter of 1944–45 absorbed vast numbers of soldiers and great quantities of logistic support. In his diary, Field Marshal Brooke repeatedly lamented these diversions, but he at no time acknowledged how precisely this experience, limited though it was, proved the correctness of General Marshall's assertion that any added operation in the Mediterranean would act like a suction pump on the resources of the Allies and thereby preclude effective action elsewhere. And in Greece the British were not fighting any Germans; the Wehrmacht had already left!

The second reason why any larger operations in the central and eastern Mediterranean would have precluded an invasion in the West was the nature of the terrain Allied troops were certain to encounter. Just because Joseph Stalin was an accomplished liar, one ought not automatically to assume that all he ever said was false. His statement at the Moscow Conference on October 27, 1943, that a campaign in Italy would eventually run into the Alps can be confirmed by a look at any map.[3] In view of the trouble the Allied armies had pushing the Germans back in the mountainous terrain of Italy, there is no reason to assume that they would have found the even more difficult terrain of the Balkans any easier. As for the minimal openings, like the often mentioned Ljubljana Gap, they were about as promising avenues for the unfolding of Allied military power as the Moffat Tunnel through the front range of the Rocky Mountains of Colorado.

It has become something of an axiom among both historians and the public that the Italians cannot or will not fight. These assertions ought to be examined much more carefully than they usually are. James Sadkovich has done so for several engagements of World War II;[4] the point which needs to be made here relates to World War I, in which a great deal of

3 Keith Sainsbury, *The Turning Point: Roosevelt, Churchill, and Chiang Kai-shek, 1943; The Moscow, Cairo, and Teheran Conferences* (Oxford and New York: Oxford University Press, 1985), p. 96.

4 James J. Sadkovich, "Of Myths and Men: Rommel and the Italians in North Africa, 1940–1942," *International History Review* 13, no. 2 (May 1991): 284–313, and "Understanding Defeat: Reappraising Italy's Role in World War II," *Journal of Contemporary History* 24, no. 1 (January 1989): 27–61.

fighting took place in the very areas that Allied troops would have been obliged to traverse in moving from Italy into Central Europe. Anyone who has ever taken a good look at the Dolomite Alps, either from the air, on the ground, or by taking the train from Vienna to Venice, is likely to acquire a new view of Italian military effectiveness. Going up those steep slopes against an enemy entrenched in the higher elevations was an awesome task for any army; that the Italians advanced as far as they did in the Isonzo battles is a tribute to their bravery and persistence, even if they never reached their ultimate goal.

The terrain had in no way changed between the wars. On the contrary, a good case can be made for the assertion that the high rate of fire of modern weapons made a World War II army even more dependent on logistical support than a World War I force, so that the limitations of steep terrain and poor, narrow, roads would have imposed even greater obstacles on the Allied armies than on the Italian army of an earlier conflict. The reality of 1943–45 was that the "soft underbelly of Europe" might be slightly more difficult for the Germans to reinforce than any front in the West, as Brooke always argued; but as the beaches at Gela, Salerno, and Anzio, to say nothing of the mountains of Italy, showed all too dramatically, the Germans could always send in enough forces to combine with difficult terrain in holding the Allies to minute advances – when they could advance at all.

A further point which must be brought into the picture is the impossibility for the Allies of permanently concealing from the Germans that their main effort was in the South, not the Northwest, of Europe. Obviously German recognition of such an emphasis by the Western Allies would have encouraged them to redeploy units from the West to the Southeastern theater. Such a reallocation would, of course, have made fighting over the poor terrain even more difficult for the Allies – and in an area which could not have been reached by fighters and fighter-bombers from the highly developed system of air bases in the United Kingdom. A massive campaign in the South might have brought the Western Allies to the Alps and into Albania and Bulgaria as well as Greece, but hardly much farther. I shall return to this point later; suffice it to say here that there was simply no prospect ever of making a truly major contribution to the defeat of Germany in Italy and southeast Europe.

If there was no other place, what about another time? What about an invasion in the West earlier or later than June 1944? The possibility of an earlier invasion will be considered first. In 1980 Walter S. Dunn, Jr., published a book with the title *Second Front NOW – 1943*.[5] In great detail

---

5 Walter S. Dunn, Jr., *Second Front NOW – 1943* (University: University of Alabama Press, 1980).

it argued that an invasion in the West was not only possible in 1943 but would have been both militarily easier and politically more desirable. There are a number of difficulties with this line of argument. Moving the Allied victory over the submarines from the summer of 1943 forward to 1942 may provide a brilliant basis for arguing that there was no shipping problem and no submarine menace in 1943, but it in no way alters the sad reality that the Allies did not turn the tide in the war against the U-boats until May 1943 and that ship construction did not exceed total losses until the fall of 1943.[6] The shortage of ships constituted a stranglehold on the strategy of the Allies; here is a major factor in all World War II situations which is all too frequently disregarded.

Furthermore, there is something weird about the argument advanced by Dunn that the German units in the West were weak in 1943 because of the losses incurred in Tunisia, Sicily, and Italy, and would therefore have been overwhelmed easily by the Allies – under a set of assumptions which required that those prior battles should never and would never have been fought![7] Those who suggest alternative courses of action for specific operations or choices in the war all too often assume that everything else would have gone exactly the way it did, when the different course advocated necessarily implies changes in any number of other developments.

The fact is that the Allies originally did hope to land in the West still in 1943, and did not give up on this possibility until their loss of the race for Tunisia in late November 1942 showed them that a major campaign in North Africa was still ahead in 1943, and that this in turn would preclude the transfer of sufficient forces to England for a cross-Channel attack in 1943 before the weather turned too bad for such an operation. Although Sir Arthur Bryant excised the relevant portions of Brooke's diary, the fact is that the chief of the Imperial General Staff, like Churchill and the Americans, hoped until the events in North Africa determined otherwise that an invasion in Western Europe would be possible in 1943.[8]

When the Germans and Italians, as a result of the unwillingness of Vichy French forces in Tunisia to assist the Allies, won the race for Tunisia, the options for the Western Powers were really very limited. Given the complicated situation in French North Africa, there was never any possibility of simply leaving a force sufficient to contain the armies of

6 See the table in Jürgen Rohwer and Eberhard Jäckel (eds.), *Die Funkaufklärung und ihre Rolle im Zweiten Weltkrieg* (Stuttgart: Motorbuch, 1979), p. 165.
7 Dunn, *Second Front NOW – 1943*, pp. 100–102.
8 The specific references for this and most other statements in this piece are in Gerhard L. Weinberg, *A World at Arms: A Global History of World War II* (Cambridge: Cambridge University Press, 1994).

Erwin Rommel, Hans-Jürgen von Arnim, and Giovanni Messe in Tunisia while shifting resources and units to England for a summer 1943 invasion of France. The only option was to drive the German–Italian forces out of Africa entirely, and that was going to take some time. The real question was, what to do thereafter?

It is conceivable that not invading Sicily and the mainland of Italy in 1943 would have made it possible for the Allies to move D-Day in 1944 up a month or so, but at enormous political and military cost. The political cost would have been the great risk of a separate peace on the Eastern Front; had the Allies halted all serious fighting against the Germans for twelve months, what would the Soviet Union have thought? And why would the Germans, once they recognized that the Allies were through campaigning in the Mediterranean, not move additional units to meet an invasion of France, thus greatly increasing the risks of the invasion, risks which were much higher than generally thought. Whatever may or may not be said about the campaigns in Sicily and Italy in 1943–44, they certainly obliged the Germans to devote more forces to the Mediterranean theater than they wanted to, imposed substantial losses on those forces, increased the number of Allied units with substantial combat experience, and provided air bases of great significance for air attacks on portions of German-controlled Europe which were otherwise practically inaccessible at the time.

The other alternative in time for the Normandy invasion would have been to attack later than June, a possibility that Brooke preferred in order to push greater operations in Italy, and one that was in fact the alternative General Eisenhower was obliged to contemplate if the weather in early June was thought too bad for an invasion attempt. This issue has to be examined a bit more closely. Had the weather precluded an early June crossing, there would have been no choice but to wait, but the disadvantages were obvious, and Eisenhower knew what most of them were at the time. The issue of leaks would not have been there had the invasion *originally* been scheduled for a later date, so that this point, which surely weighed heavily with Eisenhower once the troops had been briefed for an early June landing, need not be considered here.

What does have to be looked at was a set of other factors. In the first place, the speculation that a later invasion would have been easier because of a greater weakening of German military strength by the fighting on the Eastern Front ignores the prior decision of the Allies to try to coordinate the timing of their respective attacks on Germany from east and west; had the invasion in the West *not* been scheduled for May or June, the Soviets would have had every reason to wait themselves. As for the offensive launched by the Allies in Italy on May 12, 1944, that was almost certainly not going to have any effect of further weakening German strength in France and hence not worth waiting on. Everything we knew then and everything we know now about German force allocations makes it clear that no additional German units were going to be transferred from the West to the Italian front in the summer of 1944 regardless of what happened on the latter front. Quite the contrary, the Germans in 1944 were strengthening, not weakening, their defenses in the West, and a postponed invasion would have run into heavier, not lighter, resistance. There is, in addition, another side to the issue of weather: the longer we waited, the shorter the good campaign weather in the West and the sooner storms in the Channel could be expected to interfere with the building up of any bridgehead.

This brings us back to the weather and one of the two factors which argued most strenuously for an invasion in early June. That date had two enormous advantages of which one was in part fortuitous and one was in part the result of careful Allied planning. The partially fortuitous event was a very short opening in the weather. The prior Allied success in sweeping the Germans out of both the waters of the North Atlantic and the skies over it enabled *them* to see its approach and to act on that knowledge – while the Germans had no idea of its coming. As a result, the success of the invasion was greatly favored by its attaining tactical as well as strategic surprise: the Germans simply assumed that in the terrible weather they *could* see, no invasion would be attempted. They therefore believed that they had a wonderful opportunity to arrange a conference of commanders who were obviously not needed at their own headquarters, while the rest, as well as their minimal sea and air reconnaissance forces, could take a few days off.

The other argument for an invasion at the earliest possible date is related to the success of the great deception operation.[9] The carefully designed Allied effort to deceive the Germans into thinking that the Normandy landing was a diversion and that the main invasion would come in the Pas de Calais area proved to be as important for the success of the invasion as the Allies had anticipated, a point to which I shall return; but no one could be certain beforehand how long it would work. We know today that the Germans were misled by this deception well into late July – an even longer time than the Allies had hoped for – and that the notional or imaginary divisions fabricated in the course of the deception were still showing up in German intelligence estimates in August.[10]

9 There is a vast literature on the subject; the most recent treatment is Michael Howard, *British Intelligence in the Second World War*, Vol. 5: *Strategic Deception* (New York: Cambridge University Press, 1990).

10 Ose, *Entscheidung im Westen*, p. 266. As of August 6, 1944 German intelligence had ten extra divisions in the Allied armies on the front in northern France.

The point which cannot be stressed too heavily is that Eisenhower simply could not count on the indefinite maintenance of the deception; every day that passed was another day when some slip or mischance could blow the whole scheme and with terrible implications for Allied efforts. Here was another factor that argued for the earliest possible date.

These two points, the great good fortune with the break in the weather, which the Germans had been prevented from learning about, and the extraordinary success of the deception operation bring up a major issue concerning the invasion which has not always been given the attention it deserves: the enormous risk in the whole enterprise. In retrospect the success of the landing is often seen as a foregone conclusion; the image created is one of great bravery but little doubt. German postwar scholars have at times referred to the extreme caution of the Western Allies and their reluctance to move at all unless assured of overwhelming odds in their favor. That is, frankly speaking, a lot of nonsense.

The element of risk in the invasion should be seen in two perspectives: German hopes and Allied fears. The Germans at the time not only hoped but seriously expected to defeat any invasion attempt in the West and believed themselves in an excellent position to accomplish this goal. They anticipated such a victory with considerable confidence and pleasure, among other reasons because they planned to follow it up with a massive transfer of forces to the Eastern Front for a resumption of their earlier string of victories there. They assumed, entirely correctly, that any second invasion attempt would take the Allies a long time to prepare, that the general time frame for such a renewed assault would be fairly easily predictable, and that they themselves would therefore have plenty of time to rebuild their forces in the West in anticipation of D-Day no. 2. In this way, the Germans hoped to take advantage of their interior lines, shifting units from front to front somewhat the way they had been able to do in World War I.

What gave the Germans this confidence? In the first place, it must be remembered that on three prior occasions the Germans had come close to throwing an Allied landing force back into the sea: at Gela in Sicily, at Salerno, and at Anzio. In the case of the last-named, they at one point actually thought they had done so. Having come so close three times, they anticipated doing better when the issue was closer to their main center of power, a center where their own forces in the initial stages were likely to be substantially larger than any invading army, and where their 1942 success at Dieppe looked like a marvelous precedent. There were indeed serious concerns on the German side, and there was much argument about the best way of conducting operations against an Allied landing, but there is simply not the slightest evidence that they believed the prospect hopeless; quite the contrary. In a portion of Europe which they had controlled for four years, they awaited an invasion with some awareness of the dangers ahead, but with very considerable confidence.

Reinforcing the hopes of the Germans of rebuffing any assault, there was at the very top the knowledge that two of the new V weapons, so often delayed by development problems and the impact of the Allied bomber offensive, were finally about to become operationally available. The expectations which the Germans attached to those weapons proved to be exaggerated, but that, of course, could not be known at the time. Furthermore, the Germans were also hoping, and by no means without considerable justification, that the new developments in U-boat warfare, which they had been feverishly working on for some time, would assist them in weakening any Allied invasion force by depriving it of reinforcements and supplies even if it did succeed in getting ashore.

The other side of this equation is the concern of the Western Allies that the invasion might fail. Their leaders, for obvious reasons, did not advertise these worries at the time, and they have tended to vanish in the afterglow of victory, but they were most certainly there beforehand. The Allies knew the size of force with which they intended to assault the Germans: even after the increase in the original concept on which General Montgomery had insisted and in which all others concurred, eight divisions would start an invasion against an area held by well over fifty-five, possibly as many as sixty, German divisions. It was obvious at the time, though often overlooked since, that in the initial weeks of operations the Germans would have a vast superiority in numbers of men, tanks, and guns in the West. The critical point was whether the Allies could get ashore and then build up their forces quickly while simultaneously restraining the Germans from concentrating their superior available strength against the beachhead. This objective was to be attained by a combination of deception – to keep a large proportion of German units tied up elsewhere in anticipation of a landing we did not intend to make – and by the disruption of the transportation system by bombing and on the ground sabotage – to slow down the rate of German reinforcement. These projects both ended up working; but there were no money back, or lives back, guarantees associated with them. The evidence is solid that the American air commanders were exceedingly doubtful about the success of the enterprise[11]; many of the British commanders had their doubts; Churchill himself came around to full support of the operation only in early May 1944.

The text of Eisenhower's draft announcement in case the invasion failed has long been known from his naval aide's publication of it in

---

11 See W. W. Rostow, *Pre-Invasion Bombing Strategy: General Eisenhower's Decision of March 25, 1944* (Austin: University of Texas Press, 1981), pp. 44–46.

1946.[12] It has also long been known that the famous picture of Eisenhower with the paratroopers the night before D-Day in part reflects his concern over having had to put aside the written objections to the American airborne operation because of anticipated excessive casualties. The possibility of a disaster was not discussed very much at the time, but it had to be in the back of all the leaders' minds. When President Roosevelt decided to appoint Eisenhower rather than Marshall to lead the invasion, the close calls in Sicily and Salerno were in the recent past. The Sicily landing was one of the few times when Roosevelt personally went to the Map Room during the war to get the first and most up-to-date reports on a military operation; in the early stages of the Salerno landing, Brooke thought it had failed.[13]

The appointment of Eisenhower to command the invasion should, in my judgment, be seen at least in part as a measure that would leave open the possibility of designating General Marshall to head up a second cross-Channel assault if the first one did not work out. And the gathering of the Combined Chiefs of Staff in England in June 1944 ought to be viewed as a part of the same conceivable scenario. Everyone wanted the invasion to be successful, would do what they could to make it so, and put on a serious but optimistic exterior. But there was, in the background, a recognition of the enormous risk, the possibility of failure, and the need to consider the option of a second try.

It was precisely because they thought it so unlikely that they could contribute in a major way to any second attempt that the British leaders, including Churchill, were so hesitant. Their army had been driven off the continent three times already: from Norway, from the West, and from Greece. If the cross-Channel invasion failed, there were only minimal contingents that would be available for a second try. The financial resources of the United Kingdom had been exhausted long since and the material resources were no longer adequate for the equipment of the nation's armed forces; only American aid and Commonwealth participation were keeping Britain in the war. But now the human resources were also running out: even before the liberation of Paris the first British division had to be broken up to provide replacements for others – the army was shrinking, not growing. And in the background, for those in charge, there were not only the terrible memories of Ypres, the Somme, and Passchendaele, but the more recent ones of mass surrenders at Singapore and Tobruk.

The Americans had gambled on creating fewer divisions than their

---

12 Harry C. Butcher, *My Three Years with Eisenhower* (New York: Simon and Schuster, 1946), p. 610.
13 The quotation from the diary of Field Marshal Brooke is in my book cited in n. 8; it was omitted in Sir Arthur Bryant's edition.

original program had once called for, but the possibilities of again reversing that decision or of shifting existing resources were open to them. It must be remembered that the very first time that a whole American army was engaged in the Pacific theater in one operation at one time – something which had occurred in Sicily in July 1943 – did not take place until the Leyte landing of October 1944. By that time, in turn, there were three whole Allied army groups already deployed in the ground fighting in the West whereas the first engagement of even one army group in the Pacific was never expected to take place until the spring of 1946, and then with an army from the European theater (First Army) included in it. From the American, unlike the British, perspective, therefore, a June 1944 landing looked much more like a great risk which was very much worth taking. If it should fail, there would just have to be another try; and the human and material resources to make it could and would be made available.

This weighing of risks necessarily raises the question of what precisely was at stake, both as seen at the time and as viewed in retrospect? A most important consideration then as well as from today's perspective is precisely the issue of costs. The record of wars in the preceding hundred years had shown all too clearly that the human and material costs go up, not down, as a conflict is prolonged. The second year is worse than the first; the third is worse than the second, and so on. In the very final days there may be a quick collapse of resistance and hence reduction in casualties, but up to that point, the record was and remains clear: casualties and destruction increase the longer a war lasts. Allowing the Germans more time to consolidate their hold on Europe, mobilize their own resources, exploit the occupied areas, develop their new weapons, and strengthen their defenses against amphibious assault, was sure to raise, not lower, the ultimate cost in lives and treasure regardless of the specific strategy adopted.

If the Americans pushed for the direct thrust as opposed to peripheral operations, that was in part due to a correct recognition of the way in which escalation in the needed sacrifices accompanies the passage of time. One has only to contemplate the possibility of the atomic bomb's being available a year earlier to end the war in Europe in August and September 1944 instead of May 1945 to get a sense of the millions of lives saved and cities preserved; or, alternatively, to think of yet a further period of struggle in Europe, ended by the explosions of August 1945 after additional deaths by the hundreds of thousands and further enormous destruction.

If the Americans and many British leaders favored an invasion of Western Europe, there was, in addition to the belief in the speediest possible attainment of victory, also a clear recognition of the importance of the Western Allies making a substantial contribution to the fighting. The Soviet Union was, as they well knew, carrying the overwhelming majority of the burden; was it really in their interest to have that situation continue to the end of hostilities in Europe? There was on the one hand the danger of exhaustion or defeat for the Soviet ally; there was on the other hand the possibility that the Soviet Union would practically win the war by itself. Neither looked like an inviting prospect. If Germany defeated the Red Army, then the burden that would have to be carried by American and British forces was certain to increase enormously; surely it made more sense to fight the Germans under circumstances in which the Soviet Union carried a substantial share. The horrendous price that the latter was paying for the stupidity of Stalin's earlier policy of helping the Germans drive the Allies off the continent in the North, West, and Southeast, only to find the Soviet Union having to fight them by itself in the East, showed dramatically just how much wiser it was to participate in a joint effort than to be by yourself.

But what if it all went the other way; if the Red Army defeated the Germans single-handed? Would it be in the interest of Britain and the United States to face a posthostilities Europe with the Red Army in control from the Pyrenees to the Black Sea? Could they expect the Russians to draw back to the lines which the British had proposed in the European Advisory Commission (EAC) in 1943 if they had, in effect, been left to fight the overwhelming bulk of the German army by themselves? And would it, in the meantime, have been helpful for Britain to have had to endure the whole onslaught of the V-1's and V-2's from nearby German launching sites all through 1944 and the first half of 1945? It must, in this connection, be remembered that the Western Allies had very considerable knowledge about those weapons *before* they began to fall on the United Kingdom so that this is not simply a matter of hindsight. They also knew a great deal about the German plans for a renewed offensive with new submarines; was it not in their interest to seize or neutralize the bases on the French Atlantic coast from which such an offensive would be mounted most effectively?

These considerations affected Great Britain as well as the United States. Would an already weakened Britain not have been even more exhausted had there been no cross-Channel invasion? However grim the road from Normandy to the Baltic, to use the title of Montgomery's memoirs, was it not preferable to being battered from the air and at sea until the Red Army displaced the Wehrmacht on the far shore – even if, in the interim, the Allied armies in Italy had, under British overall command, finally reached the Alps? To phrase the question is to answer it; and whatever the reservations and doubts entertained in London, there was always a belief in the need for invasion at some moment; and that belief, even though in a minimal form, had been held there even during the dark days when Britain stood alone.

As for the United States, the situation looked then and looks in retrospect as without any serious alternative. If the United States expected to play a major role in the postwar world, a role that might enable it not merely to assert its continued independence but also to adopt such policies as hopefully to preclude still a third world war, then it would have to do so after actually getting into Central Europe. One of the most important by-products of the German decision to call for an armistice in 1918 rather than to fight on had been that World War I had ended under circumstances very different from those which the Allies had anticipated. The expectation then had been that the war would run at least into 1919 and possibly into 1920, with the United States providing a very large proportion of the needed troops: the American buildup was geared to an eighty or one hundred division force on the Western Front on July 1, 1919. Had those expectations been fulfilled, the United States' role at the peace conference, as compared with that of Britain and France, would have been far greater than it became when the war ended so much sooner than expected and at a time when the American contribution was substantial but far smaller than had been anticipated. And the armies of the Allies, including the American one, had not reached Central Europe when the fighting ended.

In World War II there was no way to supply any American army in Italy with the Pogo sticks needed to hop the Alps; we would have to batter our way into Central Europe across France. The British had needed the army of Wellington at Waterloo, not only the navy of Nelson, to play their major role in the establishment of the settlement at the end of the Napoleonic wars. If the United States was to have a significant share in the organization of the post–World War II order, that could not be done from bases in Iceland, escort carriers in the North Atlantic, or a presence in the Mediterranean. It had to come from the establishment of a significant presence in the middle of the continent of Europe, and to this there was no other route than the one taken on D-Day. No one could predict just how great that American share would end up being, but it was clear to President Roosevelt, Secretary Stimson, and to our military leaders that a major invasion in the West, whatever the costs and whatever the details, was still the best road to a safer future for their own country and for the world as a whole.

Once the basic issue of costs has been faced, there remain some significant details. The questions which appear to me to have sufficiently broad implications to require at least brief discussion in the framework of a general review of D-Day and the subsequent campaign are the following: (1) matters of top-level personnel on both sides, (2) the role of Hitler in the direction of Germany's effort, (3) the argument over Anvil-Dragoon, (4) the issue of the broad versus the narrow front, (5) the various disputes over bombing policy, and (6) the question of Berlin and the related one of occupation zones.

As one looks back today on the leading figures on the Allied side, there seems to be only one appointment that is difficult to understand. In view of the difficulties that so many in the command structure, including that of the Royal Air Force, had with Air Chief Marshal Sir Trafford Leigh-Mallory, it is terribly hard to see why he was selected to head up the air component of the invasion force. His death in a crash en route to a new post in the Southeast Asia Command precluded his writing any memoirs, and the materials from his headquarters in the Public Record Office do not provide that much in the way of clues to his problems, so this may be an unfair assessment; but something of a puzzle remains.[14]

There was never any chance that Montgomery would retain an overall ground command, and it was a terrible mistake in judgment on the part of several of the British leaders to keep flogging this dead horse and encouraging Montgomery to believe that it could be resurrected. As Sir Michael Howard has pointed out in a thoughtful paper, "Monty" was well adapted to the special problems of Britain's World War II army,[15] but he was not the man to command a large Allied campaign. General Patton was repeatedly rescued from the effects of his own follies by Eisenhower, but that made the picturesque commander all the more eager to prove himself. It seems to me that he did so. The most striking demonstration is his breakthrough to Bastogne during the Battle of the Bulge; had Montgomery devoted more energy to a drive from the North to meet Patton than to making silly comments about the battle, the German spearheads might have been cut off instead of being pushed back.

On the German side, the personnel question which is most striking on even a cursory examination is the plethora of high-level commanders. Just as the German navy in World War II always seemed to have a vast excess of admirals and headquarters over available surface ships, so the German military bureaucracy in the occupied West had grown, and con-

---

14 Note Rostow, *Pre-Invasion Bombing Strategy*, pp. 46–47; Forrest C. Pogue, *The European Theater of Operations: The Supreme Command* (United States Army in World War II) (Washington, D.C.: GPO, 1954), p. 274.

15 See Sir Michael Howard's comments in Richard H. Kohn (ed.), "The Scholarship on World War II: Its Present Condition and Future Possibilities," *Journal of Military History*, 55, no. 3 (July 1991), 379–80. On the problems of the Canadian army, see John A. English, *The Canadian Army and the Normandy Campaign: A Study of Failure in High Command* (New York: Praeger, 1991).

tinued to grow, beyond all conceivable utility. It is, of course, very easy to understand the preference of field marshals, generals, and staff officers for cushy berths in France – especially in Paris – over assignments on the more dangerous and less comfortable Eastern Front. Precisely to cope with this type of problem the Germans in view of their great need for officer and enlisted replacements had established a special command, that of General Walter von Unruh, dubbed General *Heldenklau* or "hero kidnapper" by German soldiers. I have no explanation for the failure of von Unruh to carry out his assignment in the West. A 75 percent reduction in German headquarters in France would have immeasurably increased the effectiveness of the German, and the difficulties faced by the Allied, forces in the 1944 campaign.

Much has been made, especially in the memoirs of Hitler's former generals, of the Führer's defects as a military commander. This is a vastly more complicated subject than the postwar self-exculpations of those who shortly before were happily vying for medals, promotions, and bribes from him might lead one to expect. Whether a more mobile defense in Normandy would really have been better for the Germans, for example, is very difficult to assess, especially in view of the late but effective development of Allied close air support operations. While an argument can be made for the superior fire-power and armor of the German Mark V and VI tanks, two aspects of armor operations on a looser front need to be kept in mind: in the first place, the Sherman tank, whatever its deficiencies in other respects, had a far more reliable engine than any German tank, and second, the Germans were running short of fuel. Both of these considerations make it very doubtful that a more elastic German defensive posture would have been substantially more effective than the linear one adopted at Hitler's insistence.

The basic strategy of holding on to the ports just as long as possible and then wrecking them as completely as possible, very much a personal decision of Hitler's, certainly proved to be correct from the German perspective. The order to withdraw the two German armies threatened with being cut off in southwest France by the junction of Allied forces from the Normandy and Riviera landings was given reluctantly but in time for the bulk of the troops to avoid entrapment. Hitler still planned to win the war; there is not much evidence that his generals would have done better had they been kept on a longer leash. Certainly they were as much misled by the Allied deception operation and by their inability to read the weather correctly as he was.

The reference to the Riviera landings brings up the argument over Operation Anvil-Dragoon, certainly one of the bitterest differences between the British and the Americans during the campaign in the West.

Given the centrality of that campaign in the whole Allied effort, and the very serious logistical problems which it faced, it seems to me that one must now come down on Eisenhower's side. Barring his insistence, it is certainly conceivable that Roosevelt and Marshall might have deferred to Churchill's opposition. The prime minister, however, undermined his own argument by offering substitutes which could only look preposterous to the Americans. If one weighs the possibilities of a greater effort in Italy against the importance of the Mediterranean ports for the main front against Germany in the West, the balance clearly endorses Eisenhower's judgment.

Two further aspects of this question need to be drawn into the picture as well. Had there been no landing in southern France, the advance of the Allies from Normandy would have forced a withdrawal of the two German armies in southwest France anyway; these would then either have been moved into Italy to slow down Field Marshal Alexander's drive there, or they would have confronted a smaller Allied force in the West in the winter of 1944–45 on the old German–French border (or they could have been divided between the two fronts). None of these prospects looks so wonderful. A second point relates to the role of French forces in the war. As Arthur Funk has pointed out in several papers, Eisenhower was one of the few among the higher Allied leaders who managed to develop a reasonable working relationship with Charles de Gaulle – no mean accomplishment. It surely made sense to place the bulk of the reconstituted French army, and not just a token armored division, into the process of liberating France in the framework of Eisenhower's command instead of keeping them in the Italian campaign. Such a commitment of French forces, however, could be made most effectively in the south of France, directly across the Mediterranean from their major training and supply base in North Africa. There were, as is well known, some major incidents of friction about Strasbourg, Stuttgart, and a small piece of territory in the alpine border area between France and Italy, but there is no reason to assume that there would have been fewer of these under other deployment arrangements. The only thing the uproars occasioned by the incidents tell us is that they show how completely some historians have misread President Truman when they emphasize his rough treatment of Soviet Foreign Commissar Molotov during the latter's visit to Washington – a treatment which was positively sweet and gentle by comparison with his reaction to French conduct.

A fourth issue to be considered is the argument over the wide versus a narrow front for the advance to and across the Rhine into Germany. Here, again, one must endorse Eisenhower's judgment. Nothing in the record of Montgomery, by that time field marshal, justifies the belief that he could somehow have brought the war to a quick end by a drive across the Low Countries into Germany. Leaving aside entirely the possible responses of the Germans to such a narrow-front thrust, there is nothing in Montgomery's own record when he had both the upper hand at the front and an opportunity to move rapidly to suggest that such a procedure promised the results some have postulated. When he landed in southern Italy, he authorized his troops to sit tight while the Salerno bridgehead was in dire straits and newspaper correspondents were driving north freely. He forbade the American Ninth Army, the very army he always wanted kept under his control, to try to bounce the Rhine the way the American First and Third Armies did. In literally the last days of the war he was still thinking of staging a repeat on the Elbe River of the set-piece crossing of the Rhine; only the insistent prodding of both Churchill and Eisenhower could get him moving as rapidly as the situation at the front warranted. Numerous additional examples could be cited; whatever Montgomery's talents, mounting very rapid thrusts was not one of them.

Could a narrow front thrust by Patton have ended the war in 1944? The American Third Army was actually closer to the Rhine than Montgomery's armies, and on Patton's route the river was narrower and not divided into a series of separate waterways as is the case further north. The risks, however, were in this case, as compared with that of the invasion itself, much too high to run. With most of the ports in shambles or still in German hands, dependence on the beaches for logistic support of a massive thrust into Germany looked foolhardy then and looks equally – if not more – foolhardy now. The only avenue to an end of the war in 1944 that I can see is the one on the other side: a recognition by the Germans, as the Italians, Finns, Romanians, Bulgarians, and Hungarians had seen earlier and the Japanese would see later, that fighting until the bitter end only makes the end more bitter.

The issues of bombing policy appear in perspective to be considerably more difficult to comment on than the two just covered. Once the Allied victory over the German air force in the early months of 1944 had cleared the way for an invasion accompanied by control of the air over Western and much of Central Europe, the Allies probably had more alternatives available to them in this field than in most. The near sainthood status that Sir Arthur Harris had acquired in British eyes by this time probably made it practically impossible for the chief of the air staff to control him effectively. If the enormous resources of Bomber Command were to be fully harnessed to an integrated Allied war effort, Churchill would have had to intervene into matters of bombing policy even more directly than was already the case. Surely the man who had allowed Sir Hugh Dowding, the winner of the Battle of Britain, to be retired as his reward for gaining the most important British victory of the war could have found a way to handle this situation had he been so inclined. One must conclude that either he was not so inclined or his military advisors failed to impress upon him the significance of the issue. A larger and more continuous commitment of Bomber Command to either the bridge cutting, or the transportation, or the oil bombing plan would have contributed more to quick victory than the continuation of area bombing at a time when bombing technology and expertise, which had earlier dictated such an approach, had improved as much as they had by the summer of 1944.[16]

The last of the issues that need to be looked at is the interrelated questions of Berlin and the zonal division of Germany. In this field, the perspective of most people may have changed with the unification of Germany; but like so many other questions, this one must be examined at least some of the time in terms of what it looked like when decisions were originally made. President Roosevelt had repeatedly stated his preference for the Americans to reach Berlin first; but once the British had sold the Russians on their proposal for the zonal division of Germany, a division which left a four-power controlled Berlin deep inside the Soviet zone of occupation, that question was in effect one for the Germans rather than the Americans to answer. The German decision of the fall of 1944 to throw their last major reserves against the Americans in what they called the Ardennes Offensive and the Western Allies came to call the Battle of the Bulge meant that the winter fighting would bring the Red Army within fifty miles of Berlin at a time when the Western Allies had not yet reached the German portion of the Rhine. Under those circumstances, the resistance the Germans still put up meant that it simply made no sense for the Americans, who still expected a long and bloody campaign in the Pacific in which they wanted Soviet assistance, to pay a price for the capture of even more of the future Russian zone of occupation than they were already likely to take. From today's perspective, one may be tempted to ask the rhetorical question whether it really made any difference that the largest city in East Germany, Leipzig, had been cleared by U.S. troops and then turned over to the Red Army. That was the city in which the biggest demonstrations took place in 1989; is there anyone who thinks that the presence of American GIs there forty-four years earlier had anything to do with it?

As for the zonal conception that President Roosevelt originally drafted in 1943 while en route to the Cairo Conference with its huge American

---

16 On this whole subject, see Alfred C. Mierzejewski, *The Collapse of the German War Economy, 1944–1945: Allied Air Power and the German National Railway* (Chapel Hill: University of North Carolina Press, 1988); and the review article, "'Bomber' Harris in Perspective," *Journal of the United Service Institute for Defence Studies* 130, no. 2 (1985): 62–70.

zone reaching to Berlin,[17] that would certainly not have been acceptable to the Soviet Union in 1943 when the Western Allies had not yet landed in the West. Whether a postponement of drawing the lines in the EAC, as the president clearly would have preferred, could later have produced a division into zones with borders somewhere between the lines of the British proposal and the Roosevelt map is something we will never know. The possibility cannot be excluded, however; here as in so many other places, the picture Churchill painted of himself in his memoirs, a picture all too often reflected in discussions of the war, was the exact opposite of the contemporary reality. It was the British who, in the face of their diminishing power, wanted early agreements with the Soviet Union even at the cost of great concessions, while the United States opposed such concessions in the expectation of the slow but steady unfolding of American strength. Nothing in the record suggests that when Churchill changed his mind on this subject in the spring of 1945 Roosevelt would have followed a policy any different from that adopted by President Truman: the deal had been done, and the zonal borders stood.

In any case, if the Western Allies had not launched the invasion essentially when they did, one would hardly be examining such a question in the 1990s. The question instead, at the very least, would have been whether the Soviet leadership would have been willing to permit any role at all for the United States and Great Britain in the control of a Germany overrun by the Red Army. Without D-Day, the world would look very different indeed. What if the Western Allies had liberated Albania and occupied Bulgaria while the Soviet Union had come to control the human and material resources of all of Germany and most, if not all, of Western Europe?

As it is, the Western Powers, although doing far less of the fighting than the Russians, ended up with the most important and productive part of Europe. We will never know whether there could have been a Soviet school of revisionists who might have blamed Stalin for his foolishness in being bamboozled by Roosevelt into calling for an invasion in the West when any sensible Soviet leader would have invited the Western Allies to try their hands, or rather their feet, at mountain climbing in the Balkans while the tank armies of the Soviet Union roared through the richest part of the continent.

The passage of time, interestingly enough, makes the significance of

17 The map is reproduced photographically in Maurice Matloff, *The War Department: Strategic Planning for Coalition Warfare, 1943–1944* (United States Army in World War II) (Washington, D.C.: GPO, 1959), facing p. 341. See also Earl F. Ziemke, *The U.S. Army in the Occupation of Germany, 1944–1946* (Army Historical Series) (Washington, D.C.: GPO, 1975), pp. 116–22.

the invasion as the basis for major postwar developments of immense significance all the more, not the less, apparent. If one asks a similar question about some other major operations of World War II, one could come out with a different answer. If the Anzio landing had never taken place, if General MacArthur had not insisted on a massive campaign in the central and southern Philippines, if we had left the Japanese sitting and freezing on Attu and Kiska, would the world look substantially different today? The answer in these cases is almost certainly no. It is entirely true that in size, complexity, and costs none of these operations can compare with Overlord, but the point is still of interest. In the case of D-Day, we can see one example where in popular perceptions on both sides of the war at the time as well as in the public memory afterwards, image corresponds broadly with reality: here was an event in the greatest conflict in human history that was indeed of enormous importance and to which, in spite of the great cost, there was no realistic alternative.

20

GERMAN PLANS FOR VICTORY,
1944–1945

In most treatments of World War II, attention is centered on Germany and Japan for the early stages of the conflict, and then attention shifts to the Allies as they strove for victory in the second half of the war. From a perspective which looks backward rather than forward, the choices of the Germans and the Japanese in the latter portion of the war are seen as purely defensive. In fact, one might be tempted to think that the Germans and Japanese were fighting in the last two years of the war as if they had nothing better to do. There appears to be a general assumption that Germany, the focus of attention here, was continuing to fight because, unlike its European allies like Italy, Hungary, Romania, Bulgaria, and Finland, its leadership had no objective at all: the others all tried to get out of the war, only Germany seemed determined to go down in flames.

This perspective on the last stages of the war in Europe is excessively tainted with hindsight. On the one hand, it assumes that all was settled and sealed with the turning of the tide in 1943; on the other, it not only assumes that the Allied coalition was bound to hold together and that the Germans were bereft of all prospects of victory but also that the latter actually so saw themselves, having no concepts of their own but the simple – and terrible one – of fighting on to the bitter end.

I would like to propose a different way of looking at the last part of World War II and to suggest that all should recall the insistence of Clausewitz on the unpredictability of war, a subject recently reemphasized by Professor Alan Beyerchen.[1] It is important to look at the war at the end of 1943 from the perspective of the German leadership; to consider how the prospects looked to them, or at least to many of them.

Unless otherwise cited, the material in this piece is based on my book, *A World in Arms: A Global History of World War II* (Cambridge: Cambridge University Press, 1994), and the sources provided there. A slightly different version is published in *Central European History,* 27 (1994): 215–28.
1 Alan Beyerchen, "Clausewitz, Nonlinearity, and the Unpredictability of War," *International Security* 17, no. 3 (Winter 1992–93): 59–90.

Let us survey the war from such a perspective. The 1943 German summer offensive on the Eastern Front, on which so many hopes had been placed, had ended in disastrous failure and very substantial Red Army advances in the northern, central, and southern portions of the front. Furthermore, the Red Army's winter offensive had reclaimed for the Soviet Union much of the most important agricultural and industrial part of the Ukraine, in the process isolating the German and Romanian troops holding the Crimea.

In the face of these setbacks, how did the Eastern Front's future look to the German leaders? Three points should be noted. In the first place, the Red Army had been able to push forward, but it had at no time been able to rip open large segments of the German front and move rapidly. One could argue that something like that was indeed taking place in the Ukraine during the winter 1943–44, but that did not become obvious to the Germans right away (and was something they never quite grasped afterwards either). Furthermore, even there a seemingly solid front held the Red Army; certainly there was no comparison between the Soviet advances of 1943 and those of the Germans in 1941. In addition, there was a second factor, one which had once worked in favor of the Red Army and against the Germans and was now operating in reverse: the geography of Eastern Europe in which the front lengthened as one moved eastward. By definition that meant that it shortened as one moved westward so that defense would become easier for the Germans. It is hardly a coincidence that the army generals who rose in Hitler's esteem, and in rank to field marshal, in the latter years of the war were men who were not only fanatical National Socialists but also experienced defensive fighters: Ferdinand Schoerner and Walter Model. In the winter of 1943–44 Hitler fully expected to be able to retake the Ukraine, a view Heinrich Himmler shared; and the ability of the German army to hold on in the East was one element in this calculation. There were two others.

The two other factors, to which I shall return subsequently, were the possibility of the breakup of the alliance against Germany on the one hand, and the expectation of defeating the expected Allied landing in the West on the other. It should be noted that according to German calculations, the very advance of the Red Army exacerbated the strains in the Grand Alliance; Britain and the United States would be increasingly upset by Soviet advances, and the Germans were doing whatever they could by spreading rumors and disinformation to accentuate the rivalries and tensions which already strained the alliance they had by their own actions forged against themselves. An especially conspicuous symbol of these frictions was the Soviet break of relations with the Polish Government-in-Exile in 1943; more such problems for the Allies were gleefully anticipated in German headquarters.

In the general area of Southeast Europe, the Germans recognized at the end of 1943 that there were problems, but they had successfully taken over the territories previously occupied by Italy. Insufficient attention has been paid to the very considerable German success in the last months of 1943 in replacing Italian control of significant parts of Yugoslavia and Greece as well as all of Albania, the holding of the Aegean islands against British landing operations, and the detailed preparations under way in German military circles for the occupation of Hungary and Romania against the possibility of either of these countries trying to follow the example of Italy in getting out of the war. In the event, the Germans would occupy only Hungary while the Romanians managed to switch sides successfully, but that again is hindsight. The German rejection of all approaches from Marshal Tito's partisans in Yugoslavia for an accommodation with Germany in case the Western Allies landed in the Balkans should be seen not only as a reflection of German long-term aims for that portion of Southeast Europe, but also as a sign of confidence that German control of the region, even if challenged at some spots, was still basically solid.

In Italy, the Germans had been able to hold Allied advances to a quite literal snail's pace. Their defensive victory over the Americans at the Rapido River in January 1944, followed soon after by the containment of the landing at Anzio, show that German confidence in their defensive strategy here was still warranted. They were entirely willing to commit forces to a campaign in the Mediterranean which were vastly greater than they had ever been willing to deploy there in 1940 and 1941, when it was Italy's ambitions which were to be attained or in peril, *now* that they were defending Germany itself, preferably at a distance.

In the occupied areas of Western and Northern Europe all looked reasonably well. Norway's defenses had been built up against the possibility of an Allied invasion. The loss of the battleship *Scharnhorst* at the end of 1943 was a great blow to the German navy, whose leader, Admiral Dönitz, had offered up its crew as a sacrificial sign of his boundless devotion to Hitler; but the latter had by this time already lost faith in the practical utility of the big surface ships in the war. The new regime in Denmark appeared to be in firm control, in spite of its failure to get that country's Jews rounded up for killing, and the occupied West appeared reasonably quiet as well. To be sure, there were occasional acts of defiance and sabotage; but the situation there in the year since unoccupied France had been occupied by the Axis without a shot being fired was hardly especially menacing. As for an Allied invasion, a subject to be dealt with in detail subsequently, there had been all manner of preparations to meet that contingency. In order to infuse more energy into these preparations, Hitler had sent Erwin Rommel to inspect the defenses in November 1943 and soon after put him in charge of the most threatened portion of the coast along the Channel.[2]

The home front inside Germany also looked quite solid. The drops in morale which had been caused first by the defeat at Stalingrad and then by the defection of Italy had been largely contained in the fall of 1943.[3] Whatever their worries and concerns, the people inside Germany remained overwhelmingly and solidly behind their leaders and the war effort. The presence of millions of forced laborers – by 1943 about 10 percent of the people in prewar Germany – showed everyone what great advantages were to be gained by being a member of the master race, while the looting of a continent (and the government's worries about World War I memories) made sure that German rations were by far the highest in Europe. There were certainly individuals with divergent and even opposing viewpoints; 1943 was the year of the first real signs of opposition to the regime and of actions by conspirators against it. But the Nazi leadership had good reason to feel that it was fully in control.

This sense of confidence was assisted by what appeared to be a real prospect of defeating the Allied bomber offensive. The Hamburg disaster of July 1943 had been followed by a whole series of great raids, but the Royal Air Force's attacks on Berlin were clearly causing damage but no collapse of the capital or its population. Heavy losses inflicted on both the British and the American air forces suggested that before long the Americans would find daylight bombing as impossible as the Germans and English both claimed it was, even as the British lost too many crews and planes to replace out of their already strained resources. If it looked to the Germans as if they were on the point of reclaiming control of the air over central Europe, that was an entirely correct perception. Only a new and, for the Germans, unanticipated change in the Allied air offensive would reverse the tide which appeared to be swinging inexorably in Germany's favor. From the perspective of those in charge in Germany, the prospect of a victory over the Allied bomber offensive offered not only the hope of a great boost to morale at home but also a more rapid increase in the production of weapons of war along with the possibility of diverting a substantial proportion of the enormous resources devoted to home defense to other assignments.

The Germans realized that the war was unlikely to be won by defensive measures alone; major offensive successes would be needed. What

---

2 The best account remains Alan F. Wilt, *The Atlantic Wall: Hitler's Defenses in the West, 1941–1944* (Ames: Iowa State University Press, 1975).

3 This process can be traced in vols. 13–15 of Heinz Boberach (ed.), *Meldungen aus dem Reich: Die geheimen Lageberichte des Sicherheitsdienstes der SS 1938–1945* (Herrsching: Pawlak, 1984).

were the plans and prospects for these at the turn of 1943 to 1944? In the air, the Germans had long been planning a renewed bomber offensive against Britain. The details of that project cannot be reviewed here; suffice it to say that it had originally been scheduled for 1943, had been set back by production and other difficulties, but now looked to the Germans as ready to begin in the spring of 1944. This set of attacks, sometimes referred to in the literature as the "baby-blitz," would produce far less effect on England and far greater losses for the Germans than Berlin had anticipated, but that again is a retrospective assessment. The point that needs to be made is that a very substantial level of effort was made, that considerable effect was anticipated, and that whatever the ultimate failure, one element in the German calculations must be acknowledged as having considerable validity.

This element was the thought that after so may years of war and supreme effort, British morale might be vulnerable. War weariness in an increasingly exhausted country, it was believed, might have a major impact when reinforced by a revival of bombing after two years of almost total absence of the Luftwaffe from the skies over England. All the evidence we now have suggests that this calculation of the Germans was mistaken, but not by nearly as much as superficial analysis and postwar mythology might lead one to believe.

The evidence on the problem of British war weariness comes from the effects of another portion of the planned German air offensive against England. For years the Germans had been working hard to perfect a series of four long-range bombardment devices, all designed with the destruction of London as their aim, all developed with enormous allocations of scarce labor and raw materials, and all no doubt an indication of that special love for the British which some historians have ascribed to the Führer. It had originally been anticipated in Germany that all four of the new weapons would be ready by late 1943, early 1944, but development problems, Allied bombing, and other difficulties made for delays. Only two, named V-1 and V-2, were ready in time to be employed against Great Britain, beginning in the summer of 1944, while the other two, V-3 and V-4, ended up being employed only against continental targets.

Three aspects of this enterprise require our attention. The first has already been mentioned briefly. These were not inventors' dreams supported by small allocations of resources to see whether they would work. These were huge projects requiring the allocation of vast resources in a strained war economy. Several of them required not only great numbers of workers and all sorts of scarce raw materials for their development and manufacture, but in addition could be launched only from large installations which in turn could be built only when a very substantial workforce and great quantities of steel, cement, and so on were provided for them. The point is that the development, manufacture and launching systems of the "V" weapons were an enormous drain on the German war economy, and this drain was accepted because the weapons were seen as a truly significant element in a war-winning strategy.

The second point to be made is that there was at the time no way to stop three of the four new weapons once they had been launched. They might in individual cases prove defective in some way, and lots of them did just that; but once a V-2, 3, or 4 was on its way, no existing or foreseeable technology could prevent its completing its trajectory, whatever that might be. Only the V-1, the pilotless jet-bomber, could be shot down – as many of them were – but then it was the easiest to produce in large numbers. What all this means is that the Germans could reasonably expect that the new weapons would cause great damage and casualties and have a major impact on morale.

It is important to note that one of the main reasons that there were not more casualties and damage was that the Allied invasion succeeded and led to the overrunning of most of the best sites from which the new weapons could be launched against London. For reasons which will be reviewed, the Germans confidently expected that an Allied invasion would be repulsed – and it is well known that until quite literally the last moment the British were exceedingly reluctant to launch it at all. In retrospect, once these factors are recalled, the German expectations may not seem so unrealistic.

This consideration is underlined by what is now known about the reaction of the British people and government to the new weapons. The government's surveys of morale showed a dangerous drop: after five years of war, this was really rather much. The concern of the leadership over the impact of the V weapons on the public in England is demonstrated clearly in the reaction of Winston Churchill. It was his concern over the impact of the new bombardment on the home front that led him to propose that the Allies retaliate by using poison gas on the Germans. Such a desperate measure, which the British had once considered and actually approved as a means of coping with any successful German invasion lodgement in the summer of 1940, was now advocated by the prime minister as a retaliatory action against German use of the V-1 and V-2. The proposal was opposed by the British chiefs of staff and vetoed by the Americans, but its having been made and seriously considered provides insight into the extent to which the German speculation that by 1944 morale in Britain was becoming quite brittle was not preposterous.

Plans and preparations for offensive operations in the West were not limited to the air. At sea the Germans anticipated the employment of new types of submarines to turn the Battle of the Atlantic once more in their favor. The Allied victory against the U-Boats in May 1943 was to have been reversed in the fall of that year by new defensive devices for German submarines and by the introduction of a new torpedo, but the Germans recognized these measures as inadequate by November 1943. Only entirely new types of submarines, ones which could both stay under water without surfacing to recharge their batteries and move under water at speeds high enough to overtake convoys and escape the escorts, would be up to the task of breaking the Allied lifeline across the Atlantic, thereby restoring the stranglehold on Allied strategy which the steady net loss of shipping had created until the fall of 1943. The Germans had greatly overestimated the effectiveness of their submarine campaign and do not appear to have realized that by the late fall of 1943 the Allies were building more tonnage than they were losing, but all the evidence points to genuine concern in Britain and the United States over the new submarine types being developed and built by the Germans.

We now know that these new types did not in fact go into service during the war, and we also know that they would have been effectively blind in the absence of German naval air units to locate the convoys, but again much of this is hindsight. One of the most important factors responsible for the long delay in the deployment of the new types of submarines by the Germans was the reversal in the air war over Central Europe in early 1944. That event is reviewed below, but the point to be made here is that the Germans, who anticipated with good reason that they had a real chance to defeat the bomber offensive, had grounds to believe as they looked toward 1944 that their new submarines could provide them with a great opportunity in the campaign against Allied shipping. That campaign would debilitate Britain, make an invasion of Western Europe impossible or at least difficult, and would strand without reinforcements and supplies any Allied force that might be able to hold onto a lodgement on the coast of France.

Here too resource allocation may serve as a rough measure of the importance attached to a project. Literally hundreds of the new submarines were ordered and begun; each by the most accurate estimate required Germany to forgo about thirty of its new heavy tanks, the Mark V Panther and Mark VI Tiger. Furthermore, here was a development of such importance in the German perception of possible victory in the war that they shared many of the details of these new submarines with their Japanese ally in the hope of getting Tokyo to follow Germany's good example by concentrating on the tonnage war. A by-product of this measure was that the Western Allies, who could read the codes in which Japanese civilian and military representatives transmitted such information to Tokyo, learned a great deal both about the nature of the new submarines and their progress toward completion and employment; but of course neither the Germans nor the Japanese knew that at the time.

The portion of this whole enterprise which remains simply inexplicable unless one factors in the National Socialist enthusiasm of Dönitz and the reciprocal devotion to him of Hitler is the absence from German planning of two otherwise fairly obvious concerns. As already mentioned, the new submarines would have been practically blind; without aircraft to spot convoys, how were the new submarines to locate their targets? Second, after the sad experience the Germans had had with their new weapons in the fall of 1943 in the face of Allied countermeasures, why was not the slightest thought given to the possibility that the Allies, too, might be working on new devices to cope with the submarine menace? We know that they were, but no one in Germany appears to have given this possibility any thought. I wonder if German tourists looking at Howard Hughes's Spruce Goose on exhibit on the American West Coast have ever pondered this question, and, in particular, have ever puzzled about a form of combat in which submarines which never come to the surface engage flying boats which do not land on it until they arrive in port?

The German offensives at sea and in the air were to be supplemented by what could be called a diplomatic offensive designed to divide the alliance against Germany. There is at this time no study which looks at German propaganda and diplomacy during World War II from this perspective, but there are bits of evidence in the available record. Every effort was made, especially in such neutral countries as Turkey, to spread rumors about such subjects as the alleged faithlessness of the Western Powers to their alliance with the Soviet Union – and the other way around. Given the level of friction and suspicion between the members of the alliance against Germany, the speculations about the possibility of its breaking up are by no means as preposterous as they often appear in retrospect. It can, in fact, be suggested that it was precisely the unwillingness of the Germans themselves to come to terms with a Soviet Union that might well have been willing to make a separate peace which kept the alliance together. But that is another story, and it hinges on Germany's war aims in the East, aims that Hitler was not about to relinquish.

All attempts by Germany's allies, satellites, and enthusiastic adherents like Pierre Laval and Ferenc Szálasi to persuade her to make peace with the Soviet Union and concentrate on fighting the Western Allies were rejected by Berlin. It was in this regard that one can see German concepts of the future during 1944 most sharply delineated. All the available evidence points to a strongly held belief that a Germany which had by dictatorial measures made certain that there could be no stab-in-the-back this time, was certain of victory over any enemy coalition if it simply held out. And such a victory, it was confidently expected, would be very much furthered by the defeat of an Allied invasion in the West.

The success of the D-Day invasion of 1944 has blinded most both to the enormous risks run by the Allies and the at least partially justified confidence of the Germans beforehand. Nothing in war is riskier than a large amphibious operation against a defended shore. At Gela in Sicily, at Salerno, at Anzio, the Germans had come close to driving the Allies into the sea. The one substantial landing operation in the West, that at Dieppe in August 1942, had produced a resounding German victory. The Germans expected to have overwhelming superiority in the West in the early stages of any invasion in regard to men, guns, and tanks, and this expectation was well founded. Even after the Allied plan was expanded to an eight-division assault, the odds on land promised to be marvelous for the Germans and fearful for the Allies: eight divisions attacking an area held by fifty-eight German divisions!

In view of prior experience and the relative size and experience of the forces of the two sides, the Germans had good reason to believe that such weaknesses as existed in their own forces in the West would be more than compensated for. In 1940 the Germans had not risked a cross-Channel invasion against a far weaker foe; the Channel had not become narrower in the interim; its weather was not likely to be much better. If many of the Allied leaders were careful to conceal in public their own private doubts about the likely success of this risky operation, the German leaders were certainly not reluctant in giving voice to their confidence about repulsing an invasion. Hitler was quite certain on this point and repeatedly explained his plans for the aftermath of such a victory; even so realistic an opponent as Colonel Count von Stauffenberg believed that the German chances of driving the Allies into the sea were 50-50.[4]

The strategy Hitler expected to follow after the repulsing of an invasion was based on the correct belief that a second attempt could not be made for some time after the failure of the first, that it was quite likely that the next attempt could not be made before the spring of 1945, and that in any case, there would be a substantial period of time in advance of any second attempt during which the Germans could get ready for it. The interval could safely be utilized by Germany for a massive transfer of forces from the West to the Eastern Front for a massive new blow at the Soviet Union. Whatever else such a blow might do, it was assumed that it would do two things: it would lead to a reclaiming for Germany of the

---

4 Klemens von Klemperer, *German Resistance against Hitler: The Search for Allies Abroad, 1938–1945* (Oxford: Oxford University Press, 1992), 378.

rich agricultural and industrial areas of the Ukraine for exploitation for its own war effort, and it would greatly weaken an already severely debilitated Soviet Union. Such a set of circumstances, in turn, would facilitate Germany's dealing with any new Allied effort in the West. It is in this context that one must see the extent to which the Germans welcomed rather than feared the invasion in the West; here would be the opportunity to obtain – even if at considerable cost – a substantial breathing space on one major front so that German power could be applied in a more concentrated form on another.

Why were the Germans' hopes dashed and how did they react to this disappointment? The answer to the first question is to be found in three factors. In the first place, the victory of the Allied long-range fighters over the German air force in February–March 1944 completely reversed the situation in the air: the Allies could henceforth bomb Germany practically at will on the one hand, and they could provide effective air support for their invading troops on the other. In the second place, the success of the Allied deception operation in convincing the Germans until the end of July 1944 that the Normandy landing was a feint for the "real" invasion yet to come in the Pas de Calais area prevented the Germans from concentrating their superior forces on Normandy during the critical time. In the third place, the Allied forces fought far better than the Germans had expected. Other factors played some role, but these were the critical ones.

What was the German reaction to this failure in their hopes, a failure which was made all the more conspicuous for them by the disappointing results of the V weapons offensive in the West and the highly successful Soviet summer offensive in the East? That reaction should be seen in the following three parts. First, there was the need for internal consolidation after the July 20, 1944, attempt on Hitler's life. The success of the regime in putting down the coup is symbolized for most by the terrible vengeance wreaked on those who had been obliged to come into the open in order to topple the government. We should also note another facet of the events of July 20. On that day, there was a final free election of sorts in Germany, one in which only the military area commanders were able to vote: they had to choose between two sets of orders coming into their headquarters over the teleprinter. One set came from the conspirators in the War Ministry building in Berlin; a second set came from Hitler's headquarters in East Prussia. The generals voted overwhelmingly for Hitler. The SS could do its grisly work secure in the knowledge that the luminaries in the military hierarchy would readily turn over their comrades to the hangman.

The second part of the German reaction to the setbacks in West and

East can be seen in those other measures which continued behind the front. The war had provided first the opportunity for the mass killing of allegedly useless Germans in the so-called euthanasia program; thereafter it had done the same thing for the mass killing of Jews, the Sinti and Roma, and others considered unworthy of life. In the summer of 1944, in the very days of catastrophic German defeats at the front, the killing program was pushed forward, if anything with ever greater haste. It was in July 1944 that the German division commander on the island of Rhodes, a place with the one group of Jews in Asia whom the Germans had managed to reach, arranged for them to be sent to Auschwitz.[5] Whatever the growing doubts of the Hungarian government, for example, there was certainly none among Germany's leaders as to what the war was all about and how and why it had to continue.

That brings up the third and final aspect of German policy in the face of the summer defeats. As their forces were driven back by the Allies in the summer and early fall, whole German army groups came in danger of being cut off. This happened practically simultaneously in southwest France, the southern Balkans, and western Latvia. In southwest France, the German army group defending the French Atlantic and Mediterranean coasts was threatened by the imminent meeting between the Allied forces which had broken out of the Normandy beachhead and those which in early August landed on the French Riviera. Reluctantly, but in time, Hitler authorized the withdrawal of these forces to buttress the defense of the German border in Alsace. In the southern Balkans, the switch of Romania from the Axis to the Allied side in August followed by the Red Army's occupation of Romania and Bulgaria threatened to cut off the German army group in southern Yugoslavia, Albania, and Greece. Once again Hitler agreed to the withdrawal of German forces, and the German commander on the spot moved out less rapidly than Hitler had thought appropriate.

The third of these army group situations proved to be different. In October the Red Army struck to the Baltic Sea on both sides of Memel (Klaipeda) and thereby cut off a German army group in western Latvia. Here Hitler insisted on holding on; and these forces, which came to be referred to as Army Group Courland, remained in control of much of western Latvia until the surrender of May 1945. If one asks, why of all places was this one to be held while the surely far more scenic and attractive parts of France and all of Greece could be given up, one cannot

5 Raul Hilberg, *The Destruction of the European Jews*, rev. ed. (New York: Holmes & Meier, 1985), pp. 707–8. There were evidently some who doubted that this was the highest priority for the German armed forces in July 1944, and General Kleemann found it expedient to issue an order explicating the need for such actions.

repeat the silly explanation so often found in the mendacious memoirs of German military leaders that Hitler refused all requests for withdrawals: he had just approved two big ones. The answer must be sought in Hitler's plans for winning the war even in this last stage.

Western Latvia was being held primarily at the insistence of Admiral Dönitz because the German navy had to retain control of the central portion of the Baltic to test, run in, and train the crews for the new types of submarines needed for Germany's return to the Battle of the Atlantic. Since Hitler saw in the combination of that return with the dogged holding of as many ports in France by German garrisons as possible the great opportunity for Germany to weaken the Allied invasion forces in the West by starving them of supplies and reinforcements, he was willing to subordinate strategy on the Eastern Front to the demands of the U-boat war. And once the decision to hold Courland had been made, that decision in turn was to force the holding of a whole series of bridgeheads on the Baltic Sea as the Red Army pushed forward, because otherwise the German navy could not support and supply the army group isolated in western Latvia.

If the hopes of Hitler and many of his associates were still pinned on the U-boats in the last months of 1944, that was by no means the only element in the equation. Germany was in the process of mobilizing its last reserves, and these, it was evident, could be utilized for only one truly major offensive. It is not a coincidence that this offensive, known to the Germans as the Ardennes Offensive and to Americans as the Battle of the Bulge, should have been aimed at the Americans and headed for Antwerp, the Western Allies' most important port. It was aimed at the Americans on the racially inspired belief that the American home front was the weakest of the three major powers allied against Germany and therefore the one most likely to buckle under the impact of a major defeat at the front. The offensive was headed for Antwerp as a corollary of Hitler's strategy of holding on to the ports and reinvigorating the submarine campaign. Many postwar writers fault Hitler's ignorance of oceanic and logistic problems; in reality the Führer was far more familiar with these matters than is often realized. Once his preoccupation with the Western Allies and his deference to the judgment of Admiral Dönitz is recognized, his final choice of the admiral as his successor may be easier to understand.

If there were major elements of unreality in all the German plans and assessments that have been recounted, these were to be found, not in the alleged absence of any strategic concept in the German leadership of 1944–45, but in quite different fields. In the first place, there was the continued ridiculous underassessment of the United States and of the

Soviet Union, both having their origins in the racial fantasies with which so many Germans were afflicted. In a moment I shall point out how these were by no means limited to Hitler.

What this meant, among other things, was that there was no real appreciation of the extent to which the Americans were dedicated to the invasion of northwest Europe and would certainly have staged a more massive second attempt if the first one had actually failed. Furthermore, there was no recognition of the fact that after its enormous prior exertions, the Soviet Union was quite likely to begin recovering as it reclaimed its formerly German-occupied territory, so that in the East as well as in the West, greater, not lesser dangers loomed ahead.

Finally, if the strategic concepts of the Germans had succeeded in prolonging the war beyond the surrender of May 1945, that would, of course, have meant that the first atomic bombs would have fallen on Germany instead of on Japan. Even a Hitler government might have found it expedient to get out of the war under such circumstances.

The German atomic scientists who were held in England at the time of the atomic bomb drop at first were sure that this was a fake; since they had not been able to build one, it was self-evident that no one else could be smart enough. Like the German naval code experts, who repeatedly examined and rejected the possibility that their fabulous machine codes were being read by the Allies – when they themselves in spite of their obviously greater brilliance had been unable to break Allied machine codes – so these German scientists were afflicted by racial preconceptions. As so often, Shakespeare had an apt phrase for it: "The fault, dear Brutus, is not in our stars but in ourselves that we are underlings."

21

——— • ———

REFLECTIONS ON RUNNING A WAR: HITLER, CHURCHILL, STALIN, ROOSEVELT, TOJO

Anyone who visits the regional museum in Bonn, for long the capital of the Federal Republic of Germany, will certainly want to look at the most famous monument on display there. It is the funeral monument of the centurion Caelius of the Roman eighteenth legion who lost his life in 9 A.D. when the Roman general Varus was defeated in the famous battle which set the border of the Roman empire and of Latin civilization at the Rhine River.[1] Those who contemplate this, the only surviving contemporary piece of evidence on one of the decisive battles of world history, are not likely to wonder why Varus did not call down an air strike on the Germanic tribesmen crushing his legions. All know that the Romans, whatever their engineering talents, did not have an air force, and that such speculation would be foolish rather than enlightening. When we consider events of the distant past, we are likely to view them in the context of their time and of the events which preceded them. Our examination of recent developments, on the other hand, is frequently distorted by the fact that we tend to look at these through the intervening years.

Few episodes of this century have been subjected to more such distortions than World War II. Questions are framed and problems are discussed in terms of what followed rather than what preceded; commentators look at the war in terms of the Cold War or Vietnam; in relation to the postwar rather than the prewar era. We need to remind ourselves that the contemporaries of those harsh years had their hopes and their fears, made their guesses and their projections, but in the rush of events had only the barest glimmer of possible future developments. As I ask readers to share with me some reflections on those who led their nations during World War II, I would remind them that all saw the world and the choices

Originally given and printed as the sixth annual distinguished lecture in history (1986) at the State University of New York at Albany.
1 Bonn, Rheinisches Landesmuseum, *Führer durch die Sammlungen* (Cologne: Rheinland-Verlag, 1977), pp. 55–56.

facing them through the past and the present as they perceived the past and the present at that time, and most certainly not in terms of the developments of the decades which separate them from our own day.

Though they may be referred to in other connections, it is not my intention to discuss the leadership of Karl Dönitz, of Neville Chamberlain or Clement Attlee, of Harry Truman, of Koiso Kuniaki or Suzuki Kantaro, or to deal with Benito Mussolini and Chiang Kai-shek. As the title indicates, there is quite enough to cover as it is.

It may be appropriate to begin by noting those aspects of war leadership which the five men to be discussed had in common. The first and most striking characteristic evident to any student of the time will be the small size of their immediate staffs. Whether the view was arrived at intuitively or by experience – or was a matter of institutional inheritance – all evidently came to realize that the only way to inform themselves quickly and directly and in turn act swiftly and directly on their military and civilian hierarchies was to keep their personal staffs very small. If many leaders on the current world scene seem more remote and less effective, a quick look at the size of their staffs will provide a quick explanation for this phenomenon: American vice-presidents now have a larger staff to schedule their appearances at political dinners and state funerals than President Roosevelt had to run the United States and its war effort in World War II.

A second factor common to most if not all the leaders of World War II was the memory of World War I as an experience which framed their views of the second conflict. Time and again one finds references to the "lessons" drawn from what was clearly a great formative experience; over and over a perception of what had been done correctly or incorrectly during or right before or after the prior war became an important element in the development of approaches by Hitler, Churchill, and Roosevelt; Stalin and Tojo appear to have been less influenced by World War I, but there are similar even if slightly different patterns in their cases as well.

Let me turn now to some discussion of the leaders individually and, since he started the war, begin with Adolf Hitler. The war leadership of Hitler was long seen through the fog of German military memoirs. These works of occasional interest but almost invariable self-serving unreliability babbled endlessly of "Lost Victories"[2] and brilliant strategies aborted by an unthinking amateur. Like many German diplomats, innumerable generals and admirals discovered after defeat that they had

2 Erich von Manstein, *Verlorene Siege* (Bonn: Athenäum-Verlag, 1955).

never liked the leader they had followed and that they had always known better than he what ought to have been done in the face of the situation into which Germany had projected herself against their own sage advice.

Now that a beginning of serious research in the German records of World War II allows for some correcting light to penetrate the fog of memoirs, we can see the outlines of a rather different situation. We can now recognize the great degree of commonality in the perception of major problems of the war between Hitler and his military advisors. On what were perhaps the most critical issues of all, there was practically no dissent. There was something approaching unanimity on the decision to attack Poland in 1939 and thus to initiate the conflict.[3] There was very little disagreement with either the decision to attack the Soviet Union or the misassessment of Soviet strength and potential which accompanied that decision.[4] As a fine study has shown, there was practically no objection to waging the war against the Soviet Union in an entirely new fashion: as a war of extermination rather than a conflict of states.[5] And there was once again unanimity on the decision to go to war with the United States.[6] This list could be extended to other political, military, and naval aspects of the war.[7]

This is not to suggest that there were no disagreements or arguments; there were indeed many differences over both strategy and detail, but it is not as obvious as the memoir writers claim that the military leaders always had the better alternatives to offer. In any case, with a tiny number of honorable exceptions – exceptions all the more remarkable and praiseworthy for their isolation – the overwhelming majority of Hitler's military advisors were both entirely loyal to him and generally in agreement on major issues. And in case any had their doubts, Hitler operated a vast program of bribery to keep them in line.[8] The broad impact and significance of this program await scholarly investigation; it is under-

3 Gerhard L. Weinberg, *The Foreign Policy of Hitler's Germany: Starting World War II, 1937–1939* (Chicago: University of Chicago Press, 1980; Atlantic Highlands, N.J.: Humanities Press, 1994), p. 677.

4 An excellent analysis is in Andreas Hillgruber, "Das Russland-Bild der führenden deutschen Militärs vor Beginn des Angriffs auf die Sowjetunion," in *Russland-Deutschland-Amerika: Festschrift für Fritz T. Epstein* (Wiesbaden: Steiner, 1978), pp. 296–310.

5 Christian Streit, *Keine Kameraden: Die Wehrmacht und die sowjetischen Kriegsgefangenen, 1941–1945* (Stuttgart: Deutsche Verlags-Anstalt, 1978).

6 "Germany's Declaration of War on the United States: A New Look," in Gerhard L. Weinberg, *World in the Balance: Behind the Scenes of World War II* (Hanover, N.H.: University Press of New England, 1981), pp. 75–95.

7 For the naval sphere, this has been demonstrated to a considerable extent by the works of Jost Dülffer and Michael Salewski.

8 I have reviewed one of the more spectacular examples of this practice in my "Zur Dotation an Generalfeldmarschall Ritter von Leeb," *Militärgeschichtliche Mitteilungen* no. 2 (1979): 97–99.

standably a sensitive matter on which almost all of the memoir writers –
most of whom had been the recipients of enormous tax-free bribes –
found it expedient to maintain a discreet silence.

There were some arguments over the proper conduct of operations in
the latter part of the war. It is important to note that these differences
arose out of a basic difference in perspective. Hitler was still planning to
win the war, while some of the military leaders had shifted to trying to
find a less messy way of losing it. Two examples, one from the southern
and one from the northern end of the eastern front, may serve to illustrate this point. In the winter of 1942–43, the great Soviet victory at
Stalingrad threatened to lead to the cutting off of the German forces
halted by the Red Army in the Caucasus. The German commanders
wanted to pull them all out, while Hitler insisted on maintaining a
bridgehead across the Kerch Straits on the Taman peninsula, what the
Germans came to call the Kuban bridgehead.[9] What was this argument
all about?

Hitler looked forward to a victory over the Soviet Union, a victory
which would require the seizure of the Soviet oil fields in the Caucasus
by Germany's armed forces, and such an operation, in turn, would be
enormously assisted by a jumping off base across the Kerch Straits. The
German military leaders who argued against holding the bridgehead
were looking toward some stalemate on the Eastern Front and hoped to
utilize the German units that would be evacuated for strengthening the
German lines in the creation of such a stalemate. It is by no means clear
which of these perceptions was the more unrealistic. Hitler anticipated a
renewed German offensive in the East covering enormous distances in
1943 or 1944; the generals thought it likely that Germany could hold on
to the richest agricultural and industrial area of the Soviet Union in the
weeks when the last Axis position in North Africa was crumbling and
they were desperately trying to patch the holes created by the destruction
of five Axis armies on the Eastern front.

Let me turn to the other example, this one from the northern end of
the mainland front in the East. In the fall of 1944, the Red Army cut off a
German army group in western Latvia, what the Germans referred to as
the Courland bridgehead. Once again some of Hitler's military advisors
urged evacuation, hoping to utilize the evacuated German soldiers in a
last-ditch effort to defend other portions of the Eastern Front against the
next Soviet offensives. Hitler was still planning to win the war, hoping to
push the Western Allies off the continent so that he could concentrate all

---

9 The details are reviewed carefully in Friedrich Forstmeier, *Die Räumung des Kuban-
  Brückenkopfes im Herbst 1943* (Darmstadt: Wehr und Wissen Verlagsgesellschaft, 1964).

of Germany's might at least for a year on the East. Such a strategy required a reversal of the tide in the Battle of the Atlantic where the Germans had been winning until well into 1943. The Germans believed themselves to be just short of the availability of the weapons required for that reversal: new types of submarines that could remain under water for long periods of time and cruise at a speed to overtake the convoys. But there was only one place where the crews for these new submarines could be trained in their use: the central and eastern Baltic Sea; and if this critical training area was to be accessible for submarine training, western Latvia had to be held. The fact that Hitler was supported in this view by the person then in command of the German navy, Admiral Dönitz, is perhaps not unconnected with the appointment of the latter by Hitler as his own successor. But in this instance also, the observer of events would be hard put to decide which view of the war in the winter of 1944–45 was the more preposterous, that of Hitler or that of the army chief-of-staff, General Guderian, who was the most determined and outspoken of the advocates of evacuation.

When all is said and done, what we see is a war program of quite extraordinary ideological coherence and consistency. A short war in the East, made necessary by Poland's refusal to subordinate herself to Germany, would clear the way for the great war in the West in which France would be crushed and Britain driven off the continent and then conquered or subordinated. This in turn would clear the way for a quick seizure of vast areas of Eastern Europe from a rapidly defeated Soviet Union, a process that would help rather than hold up the longer-term preparations for a war across the Atlantic with the United States.

None of these premises or concepts was ever abandoned, however much modified by the necessities imposed by a war which refused to take the contours Hitler wanted and anticipated. Whatever the arguments at the top, whatever the confusions in the administration at home, all was subordinated to these broader perspectives. Recent research which has concentrated on the internal rivalries and complexities of the Third Reich has tended to confuse rather than enlighten. The vast paper trail left behind by those rivalries and complexities has diverted scholars from the fundamental and extraordinary fact that the whole structure held together with almost unbelievable solidity until the bitter end. Hitler had insisted almost twenty years before assuming power that his Reich would either be "Weltmacht oder überhaupt nicht," world power or nothing at all.[10] On this point at least he would turn out to be correct.

10 Adolf Hitler, *Mein Kampf*, Vol. 2 (Munich: Eher, 1927), p. 742.

Winston Churchill, unlike any of the others discussed here, did not head
the government of his country at either the beginning or the end of the
war. His relentless opposition to the steps contemplated by his own party
– as well as all other parties – looking toward a greater degree of self-
government in India had taken him into the political wilderness where
this view hardly made him "The Prophet of Truth" of Martin Gilbert's
multivolume biography.[11] Neville Chamberlain had taken England and
led France into war with Hitler, the only leader of a great power who took
such a step without his own country being attacked. Clement Attlee, who
had served as Churchill's deputy prime minister, would direct the British
government in the last stage of the war, a stage that was originally expected to last well over a year. But from May 1940 to July 1945 Churchill
was at the helm, and no one had any doubt that he was in charge. A point
of great importance for our understanding of his role is to be found in the
fact that he was not only conscious of history – we have extremely good
evidence on this point in regard to both Hitler and Franklin Roosevelt –
but that he planned to write it himself.

Churchill had penned a highly influential account of the First World
War, and there are excellent reasons for believing that he always intended
to do the same thing the second time around. Occasionally one finds
reference in the contemporary documents to the possibility that perhaps
Churchill had drafted a particular document with his future publication
in mind.[12] Perhaps more significant are two critical and interrelated
aspects of the great work Churchill published after the war. This was not
only an enormously skillful presentation of his own point of view as he
wanted it seen in the years that it appeared. Those years were ones in
which no one else had access to or could publish the records available to
Churchill and his assistants. Not until the late 1960s and early 1970s
were others able to consult the British papers of the war years, and many
remain closed even today. Moreover, the memoirs not only presented the
events of the war as Churchill wanted them to be seen, they were published at a time when their author was himself a highly active participant
in the partisan politics and international affairs of the time. When the
first volume appeared, Churchill was leading the vocal opposition to his
successor; and when the sixth and final volume was issued, he was once
again prime minister. Today we can read, to take only one example, how
the discussion of the Teheran Conference of 1943 in the memoirs was
seen as in need of tempering in 1951 by the possible impression that the

---

11 Martin Gilbert, *Winston S. Churchill*, Vol. 5, *1922–1938: The Prophet of Truth* (Boston:
    Houghton Mifflin, 1977).
12 David Dilks, "The Twilight War and the Fall of France: Chamberlain and Churchill in
    1940," *Transactions of the Royal Historical Society* Ser. 5, 28 (1978): 68–69.

discussion of the German question might make in the Federal Republic and the comments about Charles de Gaulle on the latter if he came to power again in France.[13] This should not be taken as a depreciation of the great value of Churchill's magisterial work on the war but as a caution that here, too, a foggy road awaits the driver.

The problems as well as advantages presented to the historian by Churchill's own massive account of the war are complicated even more by the fact, only now fully evident, that the justly famous and widely distributed diary of Lord Alanbrooke was altered in a large number of ways by Sir Arthur Bryant in the two volumes *The Turn of the Tide* and *Triumph in the West*.[14] Field Marshall Brooke was chief of the Imperial General Staff from November 1941 to the end of the war. His diary is one of our most important sources on the high-level direction of the war; and until we have a systematic and careful collation of Bryant's text with the actual text, there is additional ground for extreme care.

With these caveats, let me suggest some ways in which the role of Churchill may come to be seen. The emerging image of the great British leader appears to be more one of inspiration and determination than of leadership in detail. At the most critical moment of the war, when Germany was triumphant in Western Europe, when to the cheers of Moscow and the apprehensions of Washington the German army had triumphed over their World War I nemesis, the French army, Churchill held together the British people and government. With the exception of de Gaulle and a minute number of others, the French leaders and their people were through fighting the Germans. Thereafter they would fight the British, the Americans, and other Frenchmen; but under no circumstances would they fight the Germans or the Japanese. While the men of Vichy imagined a future for their country in the shadow of Hitler, Churchill and his associates did not and could not. And he would inspire them to vast efforts to maintain themselves in the war and bring hostilities to a Germany which imagined itself in sight of total victory. And whatever further blows Great Britain suffered, whether at the hands of the Germans or, even more grievously, at the hands of the Japanese, Churchill would persevere, rally his people, and devise new means to maintain the fight.

It will take a great deal more work to untangle the extent to which his numerous efforts at direct intervention into the course of military planning and operations helped or hindered the progress of the war. There

13 Lord Cherwell to Winston S. Churchill, January 11, 1951, London, Kings College, Liddell Hart Centre for Military History Archives, Ismay Papers 11/3/267.
14 The two volumes were published in 1957 and 1959, respectively. The original diary is now accessible to scholars at the Liddell Hart Centre Archives at Kings College of the University of London.

can, however, be no serious question about several facets of his role. He followed the course of operations with minute attention and almost invariably used his enormous personal and constitutional powers to push all others forward. He could devote a very high proportion of his time and energy to the military and diplomatic aspects of the war because he deliberately delegated to others, particularly Sir John Anderson (later Viscount Waverly), the bulk of the responsibility for civilian and home affairs and because under the British system it was possible to postpone the election which would otherwise have been due in 1940 at the latest. From his vantage point the prime minister and minister of defence of an all-party coalition ran the country and tried to run the war, doing the latter through a control system that slowly weeded out the misfits in the military hierarchy, struggled continually to keep open the sea lanes upon which Britain depended for survival, and worked with Britain's allies to bring the war to the German enemy.

Unlike Hitler, Churchill saw the world as a whole and was always conscious of global interrelationships. But while his geographic perception was broad and accurate, his chronological one was anachronistic. For him, the world always looked a bit the way it had in the years before World War I. If there were those in Germany who wanted to board the ship of colonial empire just before it sank, Churchill would not or could not conceive of its ever disappearing under the waves of independence. There is a curious dichotomy between his vast and alert interest in the latest technological devices from radar to the atomic bomb on the one hand, and his inability to appreciate the possibility that colonialism was nearing its end and that China would rise to great power status on the other; and it was these blind spots which occasionally brought him into disputes with the Americans, whom he otherwise cultivated and appreciated.

Churchill did, however, have a foreboding sense of the necessarily declining power and role of Great Britain in the world. The converse of his role in rallying his country to continue the fight was his slow recognition that Britain's fighting a war that was beyond her means meant that she would become dependent on others not only for victory in this war but for safety in the future. It was this recognition of the fact that Britain's power was ebbing and would continue to diminish that must, in my judgment, be adduced to explain his constant insistence on concessions to the Soviet Union, an issue on which he was frequently also at odds with the American government. It is some measure of the reluctance with which he insistently urged a policy of concessions to Moscow during the war, preferably sooner rather than later, that this was to be one area where his memoirs are least to be trusted and in which he attempted –

with considerable success – to project himself in a posture opposite to the one he actually occupied during the war. After Chamberlain's death in 1940, Churchill set him an outstanding memorial in a moving tribute in the House of Commons. Churchill's own memorial must be the victory of the alliance over Hitler's Germany.

Unlike all the other leaders to be discussed in these reflections, Stalin led his country not in one war but through four: a war with Poland, a war with Finland, a war with Germany and her allies, and a war with Japan. This multiplicity of wars contrasts with a paucity of sources. Access to the archives of the former Soviet Union is just beginning to open up; and if records pertaining to the decisions made at the top of the Soviet hierarchy survive, they are only becoming known very slowly and unsystematically. This does not mean that the subject of Stalin's role can or should be avoided, only that here we are still on even more speculative grounds than elsewhere. Certainly John Erickson's great work and the recent writing of General Volkogonov bring us as close to the details of Stalin's handling of affairs as we are likely to see for some time.[15] We must pay the most careful attention to the evidence of Stalin's actions as well as to the records and testimonies of others in our efforts to reconstruct the view from the perspective of the Soviet leader.

The Soviet attack on Poland in conjunction with Hitler's Germany was launched the moment the Soviet Union had secured its victory in the border fighting with Japan. Polish units were quickly overwhelmed in about two weeks of fighting which, to use Stalin's own elegant phraseology, "cemented with blood" the friendship of the Soviet Union with Germany.[16] Two other decisions of Stalin in regard to Poland in the first months of World War II deserve attention as possibly significant indicators of his long-term views of the future of Soviet–Polish relations. The first was his offer to the Germans to hand over to Germany the section of Poland between the Vistula and Bug rivers, assigned to the Soviet Union in the original partition scheme, in exchange for most of Lithuania, which had been scheduled for incorporation into Germany. This trade, reminiscent of the way Russia and Prussia in prior centuries had traded bits of Poland the way youngsters trade marbles, left to Germany the bulk of the Polish territories actually inhabited by people of Polish nationality and hence a problem that he could hope would continue to be fought over between Germany and the Western Allies. If the Germans won the war, they would surely know how to deal with their Polish subjects. But

15 John Erickson, *The Road to Berlin* (Boulder, Colo.: Westview Press, 1983).
16 Stalin to Ribbentrop, December 22, 1939, R. Umiastowski, *Russia and the Polish Republic, 1918–1941* (London: Aquafondate, 1945), p. 182.

just in case Germany were defeated or forced to accept some type of real compromise – either of which contingency would produce a revived independent Poland – Stalin took another step designed to make certain that such a state would be greatly weakened, even if hostile. In late March 1940, the three camps holding 15,000 Polish active and reserve officers captured by the Red Army were ordered dissolved and their inmates were murdered soon after. The orders for this operation, carried out practically contemporaneously at geographically separated points in the Soviet Union, came from Stalin himself and had been approved by the Politburo as we now know. The explanation for this action offered by some, namely that this was a step taken by Stalin to make the Germans happy, fails to convince in the face of Stalin's keeping it secret from the very German government he was supposedly trying to impress with this sign of a firm anti-Polish policy. It is far more likely that this was his way of dealing with any possibly revived Poland which would by such action be deprived – as it was indeed deprived – of a very substantial proportion of its military and technical elite.

The Soviet war with Finland in the winter of 1939–40 appears to have been the result of quite different calculations from those preceding the attack on Poland. There was no doubt in Soviet minds that Poland was an enemy to be crushed by military operations which had to be and were launched on a massive scale. In the case of Finland, however, the evidence suggests a colossal miscalculation in which Stalin had been misled by his own credulity and the errors of his assistants into believing that the Finnish state would collapse at the blast of Soviet trumpets so that its government could be replaced by one subservient to Moscow. By the time the nature of this mistake had become evident to all, tens of thousands of Soviet and Finnish citizens had lost their lives. Stalin was evidently determined to avoid any risk of wider hostilities of any kind and adopted a new set of policies geared to that view. A massive military offensive crushed Finnish resistance; but even as that offensive ground down the forces of the Finnish state, Stalin dropped the puppet government he had planned to install in Helsinki and moved toward peace with the very regime he had intended to displace. And in that peace, he made sure that there would remain a buffer separating his country from Norway and hence possible future complications. At the northern end of the Soviet–Finnish border, he kept a small piece of the Finnish territory occupied during the fighting by the Red Army but returned to Finland a strategic strip of land including the port of Petsamo.

In the following year, Stalin was willing to join Germany in the great conflict then raging, hoping to make even greater gains from the destruction of the European equilibrium which he believed was an aim he shared with Hitler. But in anticipating extended negotiations about the Soviet offer to join with Germany, Italy, and Japan in the Tripartite Pact, he had miscalculated again; the German leader did not behave the way orthodox Marxists expected him to. Far from being the tool of monopoly capitalists in the search for markets and profits, Hitler was a believing National Socialist who seriously expected to seize huge portions of the Soviet Union for settlement by German farmers. The Germans never bothered to answer Stalin's offer; they were intent on getting all the economic and political help they could get from Russia until the moment of their own attack upon that country, an attack on which they had decided long before.

Stalin thus found himself in the shockingly dangerous situation of being attacked by German forces after having himself done what he could to be left facing them in Europe all alone. The critical issue before him was whether or not his regime could keep hold of the country. Under the impact of war, first the Romanov dynasty and then the Provisional Government had lost their grip on the Russian state during World War I. While mobilizing all possible military strength, and in particular using the time gained by the desperate exertions of the Red Army to build up new military forces, Stalin's primary emphasis had to be on the maintenance of control over those portions of the country not occupied by the Germans. Although the German army in a few months seized more territory than it had taken in three years of World War I, Stalin was able to retain firm control of the rest of the country. Furthermore, the evidence is clear that he was prepared to maintain that control from carefully designated locations in case the capital of Moscow were seized by German troops.[17]

Once Stalin had succeeded in retaining control of the unoccupied parts of the USSR, a control dramatically demonstrated by the Soviet counteroffensive in the winter of 1941–42, he could contemplate new options. After survival came choice. What evidence we have on this matter suggests that he saw three options, and that he saw them in the order of preference of the sequence which follows. His first choice appears to have been a renewed peace and alignment with Hitler's Germany; once it had been made clear to the German government that they could not crush the Soviet Union, Hitler might again reverse himself as he had in 1939 when, after years of waving aside Stalin's offers, he had agreed to a deal. A second alternative, pursued in part simultaneously with the first, was to make peace with a Germany ruled by a new govern-

---

17 See John A. Armstrong, "The Relocation of Soviet Commissariats in World War II," in Karl-Heinz Manegold (ed.), *Wissenschaft, Wirtschaft und Technik* (Munich: Bruckmann, 1969), pp. 92–97.

ment led by German military men who had displaced the dictator. The Soviet Union had found it both possible and profitable to deal with such types before; perhaps that could be done once again. The origins of the "National Committee for a Free Germany" and the "League of German Officers" should, in my judgment, be seen in this context. Finally, if all else failed, if neither the existing nor a replacement German government would make peace, then there was the third alternative: the long and bloody road to Berlin and the establishment, at the end of that road, of an entirely new government in Germany under a German Stalin, Walter Ulbricht, operating under the eyes – and arms – of Moscow.

The refusal of Hitler to consider a compromise peace with the Soviet Union and the solidity of the German military leadership left Stalin no choice but to pursue the third alternative. In the process, the Red Army would and did liberate and occupy all of Eastern and much of Southeast Europe. At the end of this terribly lengthy, bitter, and bloody endeavor Stalin was determined to push westward both the borders and the sphere of control of the Soviet Union, regardless of what the other enemies of Germany – to say nothing of the affected peoples – might do or think or say. The new perspective is perhaps most neatly symbolized by Stalin's handling of the question of the border with Finland this time. Petsamo was annexed to the Soviet Union, and far above the Arctic Circle, Russia came to have a common border with Norway.

In any contemplation of war with Japan, Stalin could think back not only to the border incidents in which his own forces had beaten the Japanese in 1938 and 1939 but to the humiliation imposed on Russia by Japan in the war of 1904–05. When for the first time in 1943 Stalin promised the British and Americans that he would join them in war against Japan, he was confident that there was no danger of the Soviet Union being defeated in the West. Here was the opportunity to fight Japan in alliance with the Western Powers and Nationalist China, an opportunity not likely to recur. The actual conduct of that war in August 1945 has tended to be overlooked by Western scholars preoccupied with other aspects of the final stages of the Pacific War and diverted by the fairy tales of German military memoirs from any reasonable appreciation of the Red Army's conduct of operations in the second half of World War II. Work on these issues is only just beginning.[18]

Stalin's manner of directing the gargantuan efforts which the Soviet Union made during the war has been obscured by alternating periods of idolatry and derision in Soviet literature on the war. The more balanced

---

18 David M. Glantz, *August Storm: The Soviet 1945 Strategic Offensive in Manchuria* (Fort Leavenworth, Kansas: Combat Studies Institute, 1983).

view emerging now is one of a leader increasingly willing to listen to his military advisors but always pressing them and pushing them, sometimes with disastrous results, sometimes to substantial effect. On this subject, too, we are just beginning to obtain glimpses which can be credited instead of caricatures that obscure the central figure in Russia's huge part of the war.

Franklin Roosevelt did not want to lead the United States in war at all. In 1968 in his Shaw Lectures, Robert Divine put forward a picture of Roosevelt as a man who was at heart an isolationist and pacifist, primarily as a result of his experiences in World War I, and who hoped until literally the last moment that it might be possible to keep the United States out of the war.[19] The evidence which has come to light in the intervening years has dramatically reinforced this view of the president (see Chapter 14). In the face of contrary advice, he had gambled on his judgment that Britain would hold out against German attack in 1940 – and been proved correct by events. He had bet on his own judgment again in 1941 that the Soviet Union would hold out in the face of German invasion – and been proved correct once more. Several of his advisors were certain that the United States would have to enter the war herself. Roosevelt hoped that they were mistaken; this time he would turn out to be in error.

Once the initiative of the Axis Powers had precipitated the United States' entering the war, however, he was absolutely determined to lead the nation through it. And he would make the tough decisions himself. When, in the face of the German attacks on Allied shipping which threatened to strangle Allied strategy, there were hesitations about placing many thousands of American soldiers on the fast British ships *Queen Mary* and *Queen Elizabeth*, the president accepted the military and political risks.[20] Day in and day out he worked his way through an enormous array of issues, keeping his finger on everything from individual promotions in the higher ranks of the armed services to a blizzard of reports from the OSS. One of the most striking impressions which I carried away from looking through the materials of this period at Hyde Park is the almost unbelievable amount of work the president got through. And his staff did not hesitate to place documents in French or in German on their chief's desk. Roosevelt kept track of the "ultra" materials and was highly

19 Robert A. Divine, *Roosevelt and World War II* (Baltimore: Johns Hopkins University Press, 1969), pp. 8ff. There is a somewhat similar picture in the still very useful chapter by William R. Emerson, "F.D.R. (1941–1945)," in Ernest R. May (ed.), *The Ultimate Decision: The President as Commander in Chief* (New York: George Braziller, 1960), pp. 135–77, 249–53.
20 Chester Wardlow, *The Transportation Corps: Responsibilities, Organization, and Operations* (Washington, D.C.: GPO, 1951), p. 224.

conscious of security considerations. Just once the log of the Map Room, the command center through which the most secret current reports on the war flowed, records that the president's dog Fala came in; but it also notes that the president immediately told him to leave as he was not permitted there.[21] The country's most famous Scottie lacked the necessary clearance.

Time and again the Hyde Park record shows the president influenced by his perception of World War I experiences, both his own and the country's. Time and again he drew on his personal acquaintance with key figures from his years as second man in the Navy Department during the Wilson administration.[22] More clearly than most later observers, he recognized the limitations on American military power during the first years of U.S. involvement. He had been informed by his army chief-of-staff, General Marshall, at the time of Germany's invasion of Holland and Belgium in May 1940 that the United States could field five divisions at a time when Belgium had eighteen.[23] It would take years to mobilize American resources and bring them to bear in the conflict, and it would take more than time; there had to be a will to harness and employ the resources of the nation. It seems to me that this perception of Roosevelt's had a great deal to do with a number of his most important decisions and policies during the war. For example, his insistence that the United States become actively involved in land operations against Germany during 1942 ought to be seen in the context of his belief that the psychic energies of the country had to be engaged as conspicuously against Germany as the Japanese had on their own arranged for them to be engaged in the Pacific.

Roosevelt's sense of the steady growth of American military might – in the very years that British military power had reached and passed its zenith – surely also contributed to his unwillingness to make early commitments and decisions and promises about the future. Here the memory of so-called lessons of World War I combined with a sense of power unfolding slowly but with assurance. The secret treaties of World War I were widely believed to have contributed to the failure of the peace settlement of 1919 to hold, and Roosevelt did not wish to repeat what he considered an error of the World War I allies where he believed he could help it. Furthermore, the growing strength of the United States and its

21 Hyde Park, Roosevelt Library, Map Room Log 1a (entry for June 6, 1943), Box 195.
22 An example is Roosevelt's acquaintance with Admiral Halsey since 1913; see Elmer B. Potter, *Bull Halsey: A Biography* (Annapolis: Naval Institute Press, 1985), p. 101.
23 Robert Dallek, *Franklin D. Roosevelt and American Foreign Policy, 1932–1945* (New York: Oxford University Press, 1979). p. 221.

anticipated eventual success in projecting that power into the European and Asiatic theaters on the spot would greatly improve the bargaining position of Washington. If the ebbing strength of Britain induced Churchill to push for early and extensive concessions to the Soviet Union, both memory of the past and a sense of weakness in the process of being remedied led Roosevelt to prefer postponement.

Like Churchill, Roosevelt had a view of the world which was indeed geographically global, but his chronological perception was focused on a future far different from that vanishing era at the turn of the nineteenth to the twentieth century in which the great British leader still lived. If anything, Roosevelt looked too far ahead. Like Churchill, he thought it essential that the German threat be really crushed this time; Roosevelt never had any doubt that there could be no negotiations with the Hitler regime. But thereafter, peace, if it could be preserved, would have to be preserved by what he called the four policemen: The United States, Britain, the Soviet Union, and China. The incredulous smiles of the British and Russians about Roosevelt's concept of China's future role never led the president to doubt the accuracy of his own vision. Few would doubt its accuracy now. As for relations with Britain, that is a subject to which I shall return.

Let me comment briefly on Roosevelt's view of relations with the Soviet Union. He had tried unsuccessfully in 1939 to persuade Stalin to cast his lot with the West rather than with Hitler.[24] Now Hitler had obliged the Soviet leader to join with Germany's enemies. In the great conflict under way, the Soviet Union, as Roosevelt realized more clearly than most, was carrying the bulk of the burden. Hopefully there could be a continuing relationship of accommodation and cooperation. While the available evidence suggests that he always assumed that the United States would not wish to maintain large standing military forces after the war against Germany and Japan had ended, Roosevelt could feel some degree of confidence by 1944 in the future implications of one of his own major decisions. He had insisted on the development and construction of atomic weapons, and he simultaneously insisted that this process be kept secret from the Soviet Union to the maximum extent possible. These weapons were being constructed at the president's direction in what was at first believed to be a race with the Germans; but when it became clear to the U.S. government in the late fall of 1944 that the Germans had abandoned the race, no consideration was given to America's reducing its work on the project. In consultation with Great Britain, any atomic weap-

24 Weinberg, *Foreign Policy*, pp. 578, 608.

ons produced would be employed in the continuing war; at its end, the United States would have in place the enormous research and production facilities which Roosevelt had ordered established.

It was entirely appropriate that Tojo Hideki should be prime minister of Japan when that country attacked Great Britain, the Netherlands, and the United States. As one of the key leaders of that element in the Japanese government which had urged that Japan take this step, he was now in a position to direct its actions as the country expanded the war already under way against China since July 1937 into a segment of the world conflict started by Germany. If Tojo's role in the Japanese government was to be substantially less commanding than that of the others who have been discussed, a number of personal and institutional factors must be brought into view.

Tojo was a man of extremely limited background, experience, and interests. His knowledge and understanding of the world was extraordinarily minute.[25] Whatever his limitations, Hitler had a vastly greater fund of knowledge about the countries with which he was at war than Tojo ever attained. Furthermore, the institutional arrangements within which Tojo functioned were radically different from those of the other leaders we have examined. Hitler and Stalin were dictators who used their dictatorial authority wherever and whenever it suited them. Churchill and Roosevelt were both subject to constitutional restraints and were very much aware of such limitations. But in both Britain and the United States these limitations applied more to domestic and legislative affairs as well as to procedures and long-term policies; they did not inhibit actual direction of the war. Churchill operated the military machinery of Britain from his position as minister of defence in addition to that of prime minister, and he was always insistent on keeping both offices.[26] The U.S. constitution specifies that the president is the commander-in-chief of the armed forces, and although Roosevelt, like Churchill, sought the counsel of his military advisors, he never hesitated to use his authority – and no one ever questioned it. The situation in Japan was entirely different.

Although Tojo kept the position of minister of war which he had held in the preceding cabinet of Konoye Fumimaro as well as holding several other cabinet posts at times, and in spite of the fact that the navy minister generally deferred to him, the Japanese military system was structured in

25 Robert J. C. Butow, *Tojo and the Coming of the War* (Stanford, Calif.: Stanford University Press, 1961), pp. 183–84.
26 See Alexander L. Cochran, Jr., "Churchill as Minister of Defence and British-American Strategy," unpublished paper read at the American Historical Association meeting, December 1983.

such a fashion that a number of military and naval officers could move practically on their own. The theoretical supreme commander was the emperor; but in practice issues were, until August 1945, only brought to the emperor when all others had reached an agreement. In effect this meant that there was no central coordinating person in the Japanese war effort. The Japanese army and navy either moved without coordination or negotiated with each other at arm's length. I do not mean to suggest that there were no rivalries or differences between the services of the other belligerents; the records are filled to overflowing with examples. The point to be noted is that the extent of rivalry and suspicion between the Japanese services was such as to make for a difference in kind, not degree.

This problem was accentuated for Tojo by the peculiar role of Admiral Yamamoto Isoroku. The latter had badgered a resisting naval staff into acceptance of the Pearl Harbor plan in the late fall of 1941. Once that attack had apparently succeeded, Yamamoto's prestige was higher than ever. Tojo never learned, or if he did, much too late, that Yamamoto's Pearl Harbor victory was illusory. By the end of December 1941, three of the battleships which Yamamoto imagined he had sunk had left Hawaii for repairs on the American West Coast. In the absence of any comprehension in Japan of what had actually happened, it should not be surprising that Yamamoto could have his way on the next big project. The best Japanese and the most recent Western accounts of the Battle of Midway do not mention Tojo a single time.[27]

From the summer of 1942 on, Tojo presided over a series of checks followed by a series of defeats. He certainly played a significant role in the development and implementation of Japan's defensive strategy, but there are no indications that he ever assumed a strong leadership role in either of the two drawn out stalemates of sorts in which a guiding hand might have made a substantial difference. From August of 1942 to the end of that year, the struggle for Guadalcanal absorbed Japan's forces and energies. At no time, as far as I can see, did Tojo insist on one of the two possible alternative strategies for Japan: a truly massive commitment of forces to reconquer the island or, instead, a cutting of losses with the units being dribbled away by Japan and instead being used for a new offensive elsewhere. By the time the Japanese decided to evacuate their remaining troops from Guadalcanal in early 1943, they had lost the opportunity for any initiative in the Pacific.

27 See Fuchida Mitsuo and Okumiya Masatake, *Midway: The Battle that Doomed Japan* (Annapolis: Naval Institute Press, 1955), and H. P. Willmott, *The Barrier and the Javelin: Japanese and Allied Pacific Strategies, February to June 1942* (Annapolis, Md.: Naval Institute Press, 1983).

A similar situation, though of a political rather than a military nature, developed in China. There the Japanese dabbled endlessly in tentative contacts and negotiations with Chiang Kai-shek about a possible compromise on the mainland.[28] No one in Tokyo, least of all Tojo, ever accomplished anything in this except to waste time – which Japan did not have. Whether or not there were ever any real prospects for an agreement with Chiang, the Japanese waited until 1944 to launch major land offensives in China which crushed Chiang Kai-shek and deprived the United States of bases for air and land offensives against Japan. By that time, however, all this made no major difference to the outcome of the war for Japan. It also could not save Tojo himself from dismissal. There is a certain irony in the fact that the final victory of the Japanese army over its Chinese enemy could not save the army's prime minister from losing his position because of the American victory in the Marianas. Others would have to preside over Japan's final agony.

A detailed examination of Tojo's own role in the conduct of the Pacific War remains to be written. Robert Butow and Alvin Coox have made a start,[29] but here is a topic to challenge the brave. Given the peculiar structure of the Japanese governing system of the time, there will probably always remain an elusive quality about the role of specific individuals in Tokyo. The prime minister who led Japan into the Pacific War was certainly more than a figurehead or symbol; he was a vigorous and opinionated person with considerable force of personality. But his specific imprint on the details of Japan's conduct of the war awaits clarification.

In conclusion, it may be appropriate to comment briefly on the willingness of the leaders to cooperate with one another during the war. Hitler and Tojo never understood each other particularly well and made almost no effort to remedy this deficiency; in fact there is no evidence to show that they thought it an important deficiency. Although their own choices had made them each other's most important ally, they were never able to coordinate their efforts at that stage of the war when they had some realistic opportunity to do so (see Chapter 16). By the time they realized the possible importance of such coordination, their ability to act on that recognition had been largely removed. There is a lesson to be drawn from the fact that only the Italians were able to establish a brief link by air

28 Gerald S. Bunker, *The Peace Conspiracy: Wang Ching-wei and the China War, 1937–1941* (Cambridge, Mass.: Harvard University Press, 1972), and John Hunter Boyle, *China and Japan at War, 1937–1945: The Politics of Collaboration* (Stanford, Calif.: Stanford University Press, 1972), both touch on these questions, as do numerous articles; but a general survey of the multitudinous efforts at a separate Sino–Japanese peace remains to be written.
29 Alvin D. Coox, *Tojo* (New York: Random House, 1975).

between the European and East Asian theaters of war – but I am not sure what that lesson is.

Stalin was never particularly enthusiastic about cooperating with his Western partners. He had not wanted to work with Britain and the United States, and he was not about to go out of his way for them once he was thrust into their company by Hitler. He would certainly take all the help he could get in his long and bitter and bloody fight with Germany, but he was generally cool to his allies. He avoided meeting Churchill and Roosevelt as much and as long as he could, and he generally kept the level and extent of cooperation to a minimum. There were occasional exceptions, but these were exceptions and recognized as such. The tone of Soviet negotiators was generally set at the top. Nothing is more instructive than the contrast in the reporting of the German diplomatic representatives on their relations with Soviet officials with those of United States and British representatives: it is obvious that the Soviet leadership greatly preferred to work with the Germans.

Churchill and Roosevelt, on the other hand, really tried very hard to be as helpful as possible to each other. There were times when things did not work out. Churchill failed to move the Admiralty into assigning an aircraft carrier to the Pacific when Admiral Ernest J. King asked for one in the spring of 1942.[30] The Americans refused to assist the British with Churchill's pet scheme of seizing some Italian islands in the Aegean in the fall of 1943. Both events left a good deal of anguish behind. But the postwar emphasis on friction between the United States and Great Britain, based on nasty comments about each other sometimes found in memoirs and diaries and focused on certain difficult debates about strategy and priorities, has become exaggerated. The basic impression which the record has made on me is one of quite astonishingly vast goodwill and a consistently high level of effort at mutual comprehension. It was cooperation that was the rule, and it was friction which was exceptional.

The cooperation between the two Western Powers is symbolized by a monument that in its own way is as unique as the funeral monument for the centurion Caelius. From the beginning of the Anglo–American military partnership until his death on November 4, 1944, Field Marshal Sir John Dill headed the British military mission in Washington. From that post, Dill had worked hard and successfully to harmonize the efforts of the Western Allies in the global struggle against the Axis. His death was a terrible personal blow to the American chief-of-staff, General Marshall. He insisted in the face of the rules restricting Arlington National Cemetery to American soldiers that the former chief of the Imperial General

30 Merrill Bartlett and Robert W. Love, Jr., "Anglo–American Naval Diplomacy and the British Pacific Fleet, 1942–1945," *American Neptune*, 42 (1982): 206.

Staff be buried there. And in the face of the rules prohibiting such monuments, Marshall further insisted that the grave be marked by an equestrian statue. That monument, dedicated by President Truman, now stands beside the main road into the cemetery.[31] It may well serve as a symbol as well as a reminder of an extraordinarily close alliance in a time of great peril.

31 Forrest C. Pogue, *George C. Marshall: Organizer of Victory, 1943–1945* (New York: Viking Press, 1973), pp. 481–83.

22

SOME THOUGHTS ON WORLD WAR II

The fiftieth anniversary of World War II stimulated vast interest in its major events. From the fiftieth anniversary of its outbreak through the fiftieth anniversary of the Battle of Britain and of Pearl Harbor and a whole series of such anniversaries, the parade continues until 1995. Because of my work on a general history of the war over a period of fourteen years,[1] I would like to suggest some issues which appear in need of further discussion and examination. When examined with care, these issues may cause us to look at the events of that war somewhat differently. For convenience matters are put forward a country at a time.

Since the Germans began the war with their invasion of Poland in 1939, they will be put first. The single most difficult task all those working on World War II in Europe and North Africa face is the need to penetrate the fog of distortion and confusion generated by the vast German memoir literature, especially that of the generals like Heinz Guderian and Erich von Manstein. Long the basic staple on which secondary literature was based, closer examination of these works with reference to contemporary evidence has shown the memoirs to be almost invariably inaccurate, distorted, and in some instances simply faked.

The memoirs of von Manstein, to take a particularly striking example, fail to reveal that he was the one high-ranking leader who broke with all other German army and air force commanders in insisting that Stalingrad could and should be held, thus encouraging Hitler in his decision to opt for an air supply and relief effort which all others (except Hermann Göring) rejected. The field marshal also pretends in his memoirs that on December 19, 1942, he had provided General Paulus, the commander of

Originally given as a luncheon talk to the Society for Military History, this was first published in *The Journal of Military History* 56, no. 4 (October 1992): 659–68.
1 *A World at Arms: A Global History of World War II* (Cambridge: Cambridge University Press, 1994).

the German forces in Stalingrad, with orders to break out; as the major study of the Stalingrad battle by Manfred Kehrig proves, this order is a postwar invention.[2]

The West German government's Military History Research Office in Freiburg has made a laudable effort to write its impressive series of volumes currently appearing on the history of Germany and World War II on the basis of the real evidence; the uproar this has at times caused in some circles in the Federal Republic is greatly to their credit.[3] Those vocal objections illustrate the extent to which the authors in Freiburg have honestly portrayed a past which others had found it expedient to alter. The truth often hurts, especially liars.

A continuing issue in the writing of the history of World War II, therefore, will be a new liberation. This time the Allies do not have to liberate the occupied peoples from Axis control; instead, scholars in all countries need to liberate their own minds and their own writings from a preoccupation with an enormous collection of dubious works and from the influence of an even larger mass of secondary works largely based on those memoirs. It is not only that the memoirs are filled with errors and distortions, they also omit important information, very well known to their authors, which is essential for an understanding of the events of that era and the roles played in them by many who loom large in the story. The most obvious example of this sort, which has already been examined by some, is that of the involvement of key German military men in the Holocaust. There is another example which is not so frequently mentioned, and to which attention ought to be paid. This is the systematic bribery of German military figures by Hitler, bribery on a colossal scale.

Practically all field marshals and four-star generals received enormous sums secretly from Hitler, partly in huge sums and partly in regular monthly secret supplements to their already very high pay.[4] It is understandable that most have displayed a discreet silence on this score. There is, for example, almost no record in Guderian's memoirs of the year between his being sacked as commander of Second Panzer Army in the crisis before Moscow in the winter of 1941–42 and his appointment as inspector general of armored troops in February of 1943, when he spent much of his time traveling around occupied Poland to select an estate to be stolen for him by the German government. He was given a huge estate worth 1.25 million Marks – and there is a thick file of his correspon-

---

2 Manfred Kehrig, *Stalingrad: Analyse und Dokumentation einer Schlacht* (Stuttgart: Deutsche Verlags-Anstalt, 1974), esp. pp. 224, 390f., 395, 396.
3 The series is entitled *Das Deutsche Reich und der Zweite Weltkrieg* (Stuttgart: Deutsche Verlags-Anstalt, 1979). An English language edition is being published by Oxford University Press.
4 A summary in Peter Meroth, "Vorschuss auf den Endsieg," *Stern*, June 12, 1980, pp. 86–92.

dence complaining that this princely gift was not large and elegant enough![5]

Bribery always requires two parties: one who wishes to bribe and one who is willing to be bribed. There is a world of difference between a publicly announced gift in gratitude to a victorious commander after a war, of the sort Prussia had repeatedly awarded her military leaders and Britain had given the Duke of Marlborough and the Duke of Wellington on the one hand, and sums secretly slipped into the accounts of field marshals and admirals during hostilities with equally secret assurances that these gifts from the Führer were exempt from taxes. The whole subject awaits scholarly investigation, but those who wonder about the curious willingness of German military leaders to honor their oath to Hitler, while disregarding earlier oaths to uphold the Weimar Constitution and laws – which included the Treaty of Versailles – or their postwar oaths to tell the truth in court proceedings, may wish to look at the authors of the memoir literature rather more closely.

One wonders what German soldiers, struggling against overwhelming odds in the latter part of the war, would have thought had they known that for each month the war continued, every field marshal could secretly pocket an extra 4,000 Reichsmark, every four-star general an additional 2,000 Reichsmark? (The regular monthly pay for both was 2,000.) Those who are interested in the cohesion of the German army into the last weeks of World War II will want to reexamine the impact of large-scale bribery. They will also want to consider the effect of the terror exercised by the so-called "military justice" system of the German armed forces which, by latest estimates, had well over 25,000 German soldiers, sailors, and airmen shot![6] Huge bribes for many at the top and bullets for thousands at the bottom; not the picture of the German army projected by much of the literature.

For those who might like to see a specific sample of the type of distortion in the postwar books by participants in the events of those years, there is a publication which is in many ways unique. Although it comes from the diplomatic rather than the military sphere, it provides extremely useful insight into the problems created by the whole genre of writings on which so many have relied. A middle-level German diplomat by the name of Curt Prüfer kept a diary during part of World War II. After the war, he decided to publish this diary, but he revised it exten-

---

5 The file on Guderian's search for an estate he considered appropriately large enough to be stolen for him is in the German Federal Archives in Koblenz in the records of the Reichskommissar für die Festigung deutschen Volkstums, R 49, RDV 40.
6 Manfred Messerschmidt and Fritz Wüllner in *Die Wehrmachtjustiz im Dritten Reich: Zerstörung einer Legende* (Baden-Baden: Nomos, 1987), argue that over 30,000 death sentences were issued and that most of these were carried out.

sively. Prüfer never did publish that diary, but his son made it possible for a distinguished American scholar, Donald McKale of Clemson University, to print both versions together in a single volume. As the editor explains in his introduction to *Rewriting History: The Original and Revised World War II Diaries of Curt Prüfer, Nazi Diplomat:* "The handwritten original diaries, kept between the time Prüfer returned to Germany in the fall of 1942 . . . and September 1943 . . ., showed him supporting overwhelmingly the nationalism, dictatorship, and anti-Semitism of the Nazi government and despising the Anglo–American and Russian enemies. The revised diaries, on the other hand, which Prüfer claimed to have written during 1942–43 but which he wrote after Germany's defeat and occupation by the Allies, portrayed the reverse: Prüfer and the Germans appeared therein as anti-Hitler and anti-Nazi, sympathetic to the Jews, and much less hostile toward the Reich's conquerors."[7] There are numerous examples in the text: the story of the impact of the "unconditional surrender" demand at the Casablanca Conference of February 1943 is a postwar insertion; Prüfer's vehement anti-Semitism and knowledge of mass extermination are carefully shrouded in the revised version which he intended to publish, pretending that it was "in no way changed." The editor wisely warns readers not to trust other Third Reich diaries which cannot be verified by comparison with the originals. To pursue this matter further in the archives, the best place to start is the German Military Archive in Freiburg where in the papers of some of the military figures one can follow the deliberate attempts to "cook" the record.

Let me now turn to Great Britain. The way in which the memoir history of Winston Churchill has dominated the writing of World War II history by others has been the subject of considerable discussion in recent years. We can now see more easily than earlier what the documents from which he quoted actually said in full, the answers to his notes which he generally omitted, and the effect of contemporary issues in Britain's domestic politics and foreign policy which influenced the writing of particular portions during the postwar years when Churchill was in opposition or again leading the government. The papers of General Ismay, who played a key role in the preparation of Churchill's six-volume set, are particularly useful in illuminating how contemporary political and foreign policy perspectives influenced the way specific events and personalities were portrayed. These papers are now accessible at the Liddell Hart Centre at King's College of the University of London.

7 (Kent, Ohio: Kent State University Press, 1988).

Furthermore, it has not yet become sufficiently widely known that the diary of the chief of the Imperial General Staff for most of the war, Field Marshal Lord Alanbrooke, was issued by Sir Arthur Bryant in a manner that will not stand up to scrutiny. Some of the changes in the printed from the original text, which is now also accessible to scholars at the Liddell Hart Centre, can be understood in terms of needed protection for security interests and personal susceptibilities; but other changes have the effect of either distorting the original or at least omitting important clues to Brooke's thinking at the time. Brooke's certainty that the September 1943 Allied landing at Salerno would fail and that the British faced disaster in the Japanese invasion of India in early 1944 was quietly eliminated by the editor. A psychohistorian will find it of interest that, as the original text shows, Brooke never was able to spell correctly the name of General William Simpson, whose American Ninth Army he always wanted kept in Field Marshal Sir Bernard Montgomery's Twenty-first Army Group.

Next it is France's turn. Here an entirely different kind of topic requires scrutiny. It is a puzzle to which someone ought to provide a satisfactory answer; as yet, no one as far as I know has even formulated the question. The puzzle is the following: why was the army of Vichy France willing and able to fight everyone on the face of the earth except for the Germans, the Italians, and the Japanese? In 1940, at the same time as the army at Dakar was fighting off the British and the Free French, the army in northern Indo-China was not called on to defend that French colony against Japan. In the summer of 1941, the French army in Syria fought desperately against the British, the Australians, and the Free French; at the same time, there was no resistance to the Japanese occupation of southern Indo-China. In early 1942, the Vichy government urged the Germans to agree to joint efforts to try to get the Japanese to land on Madagascar. When, with strong U.S. endorsement, British forces landed at the northern end of Madagascar, the French army fought; in fact, it fought on that island for months later in the same year. When American soldiers landed in Northwest Africa in November 1942, hundreds of them were killed by French bullets; but not one German or Italian soldier was as much as scratched when they landed in Tunisia or occupied the unoccupied portion of France. The literature on Vichy deals with each of these incidents in isolation without ever putting them together, without considering the general pattern which is so extraordinary.

The French forces in all these events were commanded by leaders who had made their way up the promotion ladder in prewar years. They had carefully weeded out all Jewish officers and noncommissioned officers in a delayed reaction to the Dreyfus Affair of the turn of the century. This was then what its leaders saw as the true army of France. And it would fight only the friends but never the enemies of the country! It is my hope that someone will address this problem. Now that the French archives for those years are beginning to open, we may learn more about these issues.

It is essential that attention next focus on the former Soviet Union. A great deal could be said about the matter of access to Soviet archives, surely one of the most important matters affecting work on that theater in which a majority of the fighting of the whole war took place. One can only hope that recent changes in the former Soviet Union as in the other countries of Eastern Europe will bring a major change in the hitherto restrictive policy on access to archives. That is essential not only so that scholars can write some solidly based accounts of the war, but also if the record itself is not to vanish from sight before anyone has had an opportunity to use it. The wartime paper used is of such poor physical quality that unless opened to access now and preserved on microfilm in the immediate future, it will have decomposed beyond retrieval. Denial of access into the next century, when the paper itself will have vanished, will result in these countries cutting themselves off from a major portion of their own history.

The first returns are suggestive but not reassuring. The archives appear to be both in very poor condition and in many instances poorly organized, but access to them is handled in a manner that is best described as a mixture of confusion with bribery. In the process, the contexts of many files are likely to be lost, some records may vanish forever, and systematic work is likely to be delayed for years into the future. This is not to denigrate in any way those serious studies which are beginning to appear but rather to call attention to the fact that the collapse of the old regime has by no means led to an archival millennium.

On the substantive side of research in newly opened archives, this is where we are likely to see the most extensive changes in our understanding of the war in coming decades. Earl Ziemke, John Erickson, and David Glantz have carried us about as far as possible in following the war on the Eastern Front prior to the opening of the Soviet archives. The debates about Stalin's role will continue, but perhaps they will now be informed by contemporary evidence instead of being a continuation of political debate by other means. The official Soviet revisions of views about the secret protocol to the Nazi–Soviet Pact of 1939 and the murder of Polish POW's at Katyn, both announced while the Soviet state still existed, suggest that there is lots still to come. Some of these revelations will shed light on old controversies – like the Red Army halt before Warsaw in the

summer of 1944 – but others may very well open up entirely new perspectives on major issues which we have simply not been able to examine
effectively before at all.

Let me point to only two examples: how did the Red Army come to
underestimate the size of the Axis force trapped inside the Stalingrad
encirclement by such a large factor; how did the Soviet high command
see the German bridgehead in western Latvia, what the Germans called
the Courland bridgehead, in the winter of 1944–45? The first of these
puzzles is related to the Soviet shift in approach which concentrated on
the Stalingrad pocket instead of a drive to the Black Sea at Rostov which
would have cut off the German army group in the Caucasus; the second
might shed light on the interaction between Soviet and German strategy
on the Eastern Front in the six months' period October 1944–March
1945.

China and Japan had been at war for years before Japan decided to
expand that war into a part of the war which began in Europe in 1939.
Much of the discussion of China in the war has focused on the defeats
and weaknesses of the Chinese and their government. There is without
doubt much good sense in that approach, but there might be another
question worth investigating. Why did not the Chinese collapse earlier
than 1944 when their resistance fell apart before the Japanese offensive
of that year? A comparison with the prior Sino–Japanese War of 1894–95
and the earlier wars of the Chinese Empire against Western invaders in
the nineteenth century suggests that the consolidation of China under
the Nationalist regime during the 1920s and 1930s may have gone further than scholars have often been willing to admit. The Nationalist
regime with all its faults held on from 1937 to 1944; would a different
government have been able to defy the Japanese even longer – or might it
have collapsed much earlier as the Japanese evidently expected? Surely
here is a set of issues deserving of further thought.

The other side of all this is the extraordinary and repeated inability of
Japan to make anything substantial or lasting out of a long series of
victories. One is sometimes reminded of Germany's performance in
World War I when that country won its way through repeated victories to
total defeat. Even more intriguing is what appears to have been the truly
astonishing incompetence of the leaders of the Japanese navy. How is one
to explain the development of plans so complicated as practically to invite
defeat, repeated failure of nerve at critical moments, and what appears to
have been an extraordinary lack of imagination? With some of the best
warships in the world, with dedicated and well-trained crews, the admirals of the Imperial Navy managed to accomplish astonishingly little.

They neither grasped the significance of the Indian Ocean when it was open to them in 1942 nor harvested the fruit of their own plans in the great naval battle off Leyte in October 1944. The performance of Japanese naval leadership in Alaskan waters can only be described as feebleminded. How come? Again, as in the French case, what intrigues the retrospective observer is the pattern, not just the individual case. What could have happened in earlier personnel policies, training systems, or other aspects of Japanese recruitment and preparation of naval officers to produce this astonishing pattern?

The Pacific War, its origins and its course, have become something of a taboo subject in Japan (unlike Germany). There is a great reluctance to deal with dark passages in the country's past such as the atrocious conduct toward prisoners of war – after Japanese forces had acquired a reputation for exemplary treatment of prisoners in the Russo-Japanese War and World War I. This neglect can only come back to hurt Japan; a renewed effort to come to grips with the war could provide both a needed catharsis and new light on major questions.

A subject related to the role of Japan is that of the extreme nationalists who sided with Japan in the Pacific War somewhat the way certain other extreme nationalists sided with the Germans in Europe and the Middle East. These individuals, one thinks first of the Indian Subhas Chandra Bose, had in front of them the model of Japanese colonialism in Korea, undoubtedly the worst record of any colonial power. What on earth made them believe that a Japan and Germany which had defeated Britain, the Soviet Union, and the United States would treat the inhabitants of the colonial empires of the Western Powers any more kindly than they already treated their own? How did they imagine themselves working for independence against a triumphant Axis? Here is a question that surely deserves a new look now that the immediate passions of war and of decolonization are, or at least ought to be, past.

There are things which could be said about a large number of other participants, but let us now turn to the United States. It can be argued that the relationship of the United States to its allies has not always been discussed in a proper light. This is, I believe, because some things were so obvious that no one referred to them at the time, either because they were too obvious to deserve mention or because alluding to them would have been impolite and inexpedient. Their not being mentioned meant their not appearing in the record and hence, all too frequently, their being overlooked by subsequent analysts. In regard to the United States' relations with the Soviet Union, the fact that the latter was carrying most of the burden of the war was so obvious from daily news reports, however inaccurate in detail, that no one needed to point it out. Day after day the newspapers and intelligence reports, the newsreels, and the intercepts of messages showed in public and in secret that the bulk of the German army was engaged in the bloodiest fighting on the Eastern Front. If Americans at home and in Washington, in the White House and in the military, sought to provide help, that must always be seen against the background of contemporary reality.

The recent events in Eastern Europe and the former Soviet Union ought also to make us take another look at the origins of the Cold War in the latter stages of World War II. Perhaps there is more merit to the traditional view that the Western Powers were reacting to the Soviet imposition of an unwanted system on unwilling peoples than was fashionable in some circles. It should be noted that the word "totalitarian," which was for so long decried as an inappropriate term for talking about Nazi Germany and Stalin's Russia, and whose use was seen for some time almost as a form of Red-baiting, has reappeared in the political discourse: it is now regularly used by individuals in Eastern Europe and the former Soviet Union to describe the system under which they lived.

In regard to occasional difficulties of American leaders with the British during the war, there is an entirely different matter, in this case one which – at least to judge by the record – Americans were too polite to mention: the extraordinary string of British defeats, disasters, and surrenders. The contrast between American forces holding out in the Philippines for months and the defenders of Singapore marching off to POW camps in huge numbers practically as soon as the Japanese obtained a foothold on Singapore island is a case in point. After almost three years of war, the garrison of Tobruk surrendered in the summer of 1942. British military leaders made a practice of deprecating the military ability of their American ally, a matter now much easier to follow in the record; but what about their own forces? Two years after the Kasserine Pass defeat in Tunisia, American troops were chasing the remnants of the Wehrmacht in the Rhineland. Had they not learned rather more quickly than their British cousins? What the American military did on Guadalcanal in 1942 took the British until 1944 to accomplish in Burma. These comments are not designed to minimize the significance of the British effort in the war or to deprecate the bravery of its soldiers, sailors, or airmen; it is merely to suggest that the supercilious tone often found in British records and subsequent writings might well bear reassessing.

A last aspect of the American effort to which reference must be made is the discussion of the dropping of the atomic bombs. This is all too frequently done without reference to a question often asked in other contexts during the conflict: "Don't you know that there is a war on?" It is very intriguing that much of the literature on the subject deals with it as if one fine day the Americans had thought they had nothing else to do that weekend so they dropped A-bombs on Japan. Neither Martin J. Sherwin's well-known book, *A World Destroyed: The Atomic Bomb and the Great Alliance,*[8] nor a recent bibliographic article in *Diplomatic History,*[9] reviewing the whole literature and controversy on the subject, contains a discussion of the fighting on Okinawa. The American reading of Japanese diplomatic telegrams, which showed that the Japanese government had discussed but rejected the alternative of surrender, is similarly absent from the literature in spite of the records on this being available in the National Archives for years.

Let me turn finally to a point which becomes both more important to an understanding of the war but more difficult to work out as the time passes. The personal element at the highest levels seems to me to have been often far more significant than considerations of nationality or service rivalry which are often put forward to explain particular controversies. It is clear, for example, that Field Marshal Montgomery could not get along with many Canadians and with most British generals, as well as Americans. Were those British generals and admirals who did not have this trouble any less British than he? General MacArthur could not abide Admiral Hart or General Brett but worked very effectively with Admiral Halsey and General Kinney. Were the latter any less navy or air force than the former? To pose the question is to answer it, and that ought to turn our attention to the personality problems actually involved as distinct from the national and service rivalries which are so frequently trotted out as obvious explanations. There certainly were plenty of instances of interservice and national friction; but we should be cautious in many instances where quite different factors were at work.

It may be useful to close this brief discussion of the personality question with an example having significant implications for postwar developments. Perhaps the bitterest Anglo–American difference over an appointment in World War II was the American refusal to accept Air Marshal Sir Sholto Douglas as South East Asia Commander when he was proposed by the British in 1943. The evidence on this lengthy controversy that I have seen suggests both that this was due to the belief of American military leaders that Douglas could not or would not work well with Americans and that this belief, though honestly held, was probably mistaken. The result of this fracas was that the British eventually

8 (New York: Knopf, 1975).
9 J. Samuel Walker, "The Decision to Use the Bomb: A Historiographical Update," *Diplomatic History* 14 (1990): 97–114.

proposed Admiral Lord Louis Mountbatten, who was immediately accepted by the Americans. This was, of course, a major step toward Mountbatten's later appointment as the last viceroy of India. What is sometimes forgotten is that Sir Sholto Douglas became Montgomery's successor as British commander in Germany. Who knows; if the Americans had not objected to Douglas's appointment, the roles of the two men might well have been reversed. Mountbatten would presumably have worked as well as anyone in the complicated situation in postwar Germany, but how would Douglas have coped with the upheaval in India?

There cannot be any certain answer to a speculative question like the one just raised, but there are surely many other issues of World War II which remain to be illuminated. That vast conflict is not only certain to attract the attention of scholars long after the fiftieth anniversaries have been concluded, but it deserves it.

23

A NEW GERMANY IN A NEW WORLD

When American soldiers entered German towns at the end of World War II, they painted on the remainders of walls sticking up out of the rubble the words of a famous assertion of Hitler: "Gebt mir vier Jahre Zeit, und Ihr werdet Deutschland nicht wiedererkennen" (Give me four years' time and you will not recognize Germany). His years were over, and it was indeed difficult to recognize Germany. Most German cities had been very badly battered by bombing and in the fighting of the last half year of war. Unlike World War I, which had been fought out practically entirely over the towns and lands of others, this time the physical damage caused by war was visible not only elsewhere but in Germany itself.

There could be, furthermore, no doubt whatever this time in the mind of anyone inside the country that Germany had lost the war, that it had in fact been utterly crushed and defeated on all fronts. The presence of Allied troops in almost all of prewar Germany by the time hostilities ended with the surrender of May 1945, quickly followed by the occupation of the small portions not yet seized by the forces of Germany's enemies, drove home to all the reality of defeat, a reality which this time, as contrasted with 1918, had been making itself felt in the preceding months as the fronts moved ever closer to and into Germany itself. Defeat this time was neither unexpected nor deniable. It had been stalled by desperate exertions since the fall of 1944; but once the Western Allies had successfully established a new front in the West and the Red Army had torn open the Eastern Front, both in the summer of 1944, there could be no doubt that the nation was headed for defeat.

It was true that during most of the war the Germans had lived better at home than in World War I; in fact, their looting of much of the continent had enabled them to have the highest rations in Europe, but there had been first the disruption of bombing and evacuations, then the flight of millions westward in the winter of 1944–45, and finally the disruption of the whole transportation system in the last months of fighting. Privation at home thus came later to the mass of Germans than in the prior war, but it came all the harder this time because the disruption Germany had brought to the economy of Europe and the world meant that in the years after 1945 – and especially the first three winters – hunger stalked the land. This time it was not only the others who faced the problem of recovering from the ravages of fighting in years of scarcity and deprivation.

The difficulties faced by the Germans were greatly increased by three aspects of the postwar situation which, ironically, they had brought down on themselves. The peace settlement of 1919 had attempted to adjust the boundaries of the European states to the way populations were distributed; it had not always done so entirely fairly and accurately, but the effort had been a comprehensive one and had, on the whole, worked to Germany's advantage as discussed in the first essay in this collection. The Germans, however, had rejected this concept and the effort to implement it and had insisted on its replacement by the opposite procedure: the establishment of boundaries to be followed by the shoving of people to whichever side they were now supposed to be on. This new notion was now applied on a massive scale to the Germans.[1] Over 3 million people of German background were driven out of Czechoslovakia; some 9 million had fled or were driven out of the pre-1937 German territories east of the new border with Poland; hundreds of thousands had also fled or were now expelled from Southeast Europe. And all these millions – minus those many thousands who were killed or died along the way – now had to crowd into the territory left to the Germans, a territory in which more than half the housing units had been destroyed or damaged in the war.

This substantially reduced Germany was not, however, a single unit. During World War II, unlike World War I, the members of the coalition Germany had forced together against herself had come to the conclusion that a unified Germany was incompatible with the safety and survival of other countries and hence had decided that Germany would have to be split up into separate entities once again. The term used at the time was "dismemberment," and all the major Allies had come to accept this concept. In the course of looking more closely at the implementation of any scheme to divide Germany into several separate countries, the Allies had one by one abandoned the "dismemberment" concept in theory, but they instead came to implement something very much like it in practice

---

1 There is an excellent illustration of the transition from shifting boundaries to fit people toward shifting people to fit boundaries in Detlef Brandes, " 'Eine verspätete tschechische Alternative zum Münchener Diktat': Edvard Benes und die sudetendeutsche Frage, 1938– 1945," *Vierteljahrshefte für Zeitgeschichte* 42 (1994): 221–41.

by establishing occupation zones which would be commanded by their respective field commanders.

The zonal division of Germany, which came to include a Soviet zone, a British zone, an American zone with two enclaves in the British zone, a French zone essentially consisting of two separate parts, and a Berlin zone divided into four sectors, created a patchwork of entities which were to a considerable extent cut off from each other, in which different policies were frequently adopted, and over which there was no effective central government or administration. The government of Admiral Dönitz was arrested in May 1945 by unanimous agreement of the occupying powers, and the French government blocked the creation of any administrative apparatus for occupied Germany as a whole. The defeat of 1945 thus ended, at least for the time being, the unity which had been established in 1871. Furthermore, the temporary incorporation of Austria into Germany in 1938 had convinced the majority of Austrians that they were not Germans after all; even if the victorious Allies had not insisted on a restored independent Austria, the aspiration for a greater Germany, which had been much discussed in the preceding hundred years, had evaporated for good.

A third factor which would impede any restoration of German self-confidence, self-esteem, and consolidation for decades was also the result of German policies and actions in the years of the Third Reich: this was the legacy of endless brutalities, mass murders, and crimes committed on so vast a scale that it would take years to grasp their extent. Many Germans were required by the victors to view for themselves the scenes of torture and death in the liberated camps; others could see them in films and pictures; many tried to avert their eyes or pretend to themselves and others that they had known nothing of what had happened – with many pretending so long that they came to believe their own pretense.

But as there had been those who had mustered the courage to defy the Nazi regime when it was still in power, there were now some who faced the truth about their country; and over the subsequent years, increasing numbers came to confront the reality of what had happened. Ironically the elite segments of German society – the doctors, the lawyers, the civil servants, the academicians – would take longest to begin to engage their own often shameful past, but some began early, and others slowly joined. Similarly, the churches, which had generally remained mute in the face of the most awful crimes, appeared at first to be concerned primarily with protesting the trials and sentences of those who had committed murder on a scale which defied the imagination[2]; but over time some recognition of past reality and of further obligations began to make itself felt here too.

---

2 See Thomas Alan Schwartz, "Die Begnadigung deutscher Kriegsverbrecher: John J. McCloy und die Häftlinge von Landsberg," *Vierteljahrshefte für Zeitgeschichte* 38 (1990): 375–414.

If the defeat of Germany was complete this time, the reintegration of Germany as a single state into a new European system was to be complete as well, even if it took almost half a century to bring it about. In many ways the two processes were integrally related. The complete occupation of the country by the victorious Allies implied that they would take the steps they considered wise, and if the Germans did not like any of them, they could blame either their own prior government or the Allies – but not a successor government of their own, since at first none existed. If the Republic of Weimar instead of the prior regime had constantly been blamed for the terrible mess it had inherited and struggled to straighten out, no one in Germany could so easily put the blame for the disaster into which they had allowed the Nazi regime to lead them on anyone but themselves. And the new government which began to be organized in the Western zones of occupation was very obviously not responsible for developments which preceded its establishment.

It was this new system which would provide a focus for Germany's internal reconstruction and external reintegration into a civilized society. There was a tendency in some circles in Germany in the 1970s and 1980s to assert that the Americans had prevented a complete break with the past after 1945 and had acted to restore rather than renew and change German society, but the reality was the exact opposite. The United States, like the other occupying powers, had banned the Nazi Party and successor organizations, thereby freeing postwar Germany of the threat of extremist parties from the political right, parties of the sort which had wrecked the Weimar Republic and could very well have done so again.[3] Instead, as the leading occupying power in the West, the United States had assisted the Germans in rebuilding government from the local level on up, and had kept extremist political parties from being formed.

Ironically the process was hastened by Soviet moves which threatened the freedom of the inhabitants of the western sectors of Berlin and appeared to threaten all Germans with the imposition of a system modeled on that of the Soviet Union. It was in the shadow of the Berlin airlift of 1948–49 that the Federal Republic was founded by leaders from the Western zones who saw themselves and were seen as aligned with the Western Powers in the construction of a democratic, federal, and Europeanized Germany. As this state organized itself as a functioning parliamentary democracy, it received more and more of the attributes of sovereignty, its economy revived – with crucial assistance from the

3 Daniel Rogers, "The Western Allies and the Restoration of German Political Parties, 1945–1949," unpublished Ph.D. dissertation, University of North Carolina, 1990, and "Transforming the German Party System: The United States and the Origins of Political Moderation, 1945–1949," *Journal of Modern History* 65 (1993): 512–41.

United States – and its successes in physical reconstruction and economic development attracted ever more support from a citizenry slowly becoming accustomed to the workings of a democratic state.

If the leaders of the Allies had drawn from their World War I experience the lesson that this time Germany must be required to surrender, so the leader, or at least a few of the leaders, of the new Germany learned some significant lessons as well. After World War I, Germany had tried to assert itself by throwing off the burdens of repair costs onto the shoulders of others. First by wrecking its currency in the great inflation of 1920–23 and then by wrecking its own economy again in the great deflation of 1930–32, the Germans had demonstrated their alleged inability to pay reparations – but at a cost to themselves as well as to others which proved disastrous to all. This time a far smaller and more damaged Germany under leaders, especially Konrad Adenauer, who saw things very differently, decided that the opposite course made more sense: Germany would prosper if it paid reparations rather than wreck its own economy to avoid having to do so. And contrary to the fears of some, this worked very well. Germany emerged from a far worse ordeal than World War I greatly strengthened in its economic life and its social cohesion as a result of a deliberate effort to accommodate rather than cheat its creditors as well as at least some of its victims.

As other powers observed the changes inside Germany, they too changed their policies toward the Germans. Though undoubtedly hastened in this process by the pressures of the Cold War, increasingly the occupying powers in the West came to see the Germans as changing and as changed. The willingness of the understandably most anxious of the former enemies of Germany – France – to allow the return of the Saar area to Germany in the mid-1950s demonstrates perhaps more clearly than any other single event of the first postwar decades how much reciprocal changes within the Western alliance moved into new directions.

If the airlift of 1948–49 made this obvious in regard to the United States and Great Britain, the rapprochement between Germany and France symbolized a new order in Western Europe. Nothing marks this dramatic alteration in Europe more clearly than the two men who played key roles in it. Charles de Gaulle had upheld the independence and honor of France in its darkest hour; whatever anyone might say about or against him, no one could accuse him of being in some subversive way pro-German. On the contrary, it was he who had led and symbolized the insistence of at first a few and eventually far more Frenchmen that France had to regain its full independence from an intolerable German occupation. Konrad Adenauer had defied the most obvious political considerations in Weimar Germany by arguing for good relations with France at a time when the alleged political wisdom of Germany argued for bitter hatred of all things French or associated in the remotest way with France. No one could claim that his post–World War II advocacy of close German–French relations was a move of expediency and opportunism; here was the man who had argued for the same policy when it had been most inexpedient to do so.

Germany's crushing defeat in the war had involved not only enormous casualties and massive destruction, but it had brought the reality of war to all at home, including especially the young, who not only missed fathers off to war but were themselves frequently sent to the outskirts of town to handle the searchlights and fire the antiaircraft guns. As they grew up in the years after the war, they lived in a country slowly recovering from the war, and at first recovering very slowly indeed. At the beginning of the century, the youthful German emperor William II had promised to lead his people to great times; the postwar generation of Germans had encountered all the "great times" they ever needed. Their most recent leader had promised to settle them on farms carved out of the possessions of others; one may well doubt that many of them would have left their homes voluntarily to live in villages in the Ukraine or northern Caucasus; nothing suggests that they became more enthusiastic about this prospect after defeat had terminated its possibility. Their last emperor had called for Germany to have a bigger "place in the sun," by which Germans at the beginning of the century meant a larger colonial empire and sphere of influence outside Europe and an even more dominant position inside it; if the new generation of Germans used the term "place in the sun" at all, it was to refer to a winter vacation on the south coast of Spain or on some pleasant and sunny island.

The heritage of the past does remain with the Germans as it does with those who fought against them in World War II. Monuments and memories survive the changes of generations; some apprehensions remain outside Germany; and there is always a small number who yearn for what they consider the "good old days" when they could slaughter others to their hearts' content.[4] To these are added some disoriented and miseducated young people who have emerged from forty years of Stalinist dictatorship in the former German Democratic Republic, having been deliberately kept from any real confrontation with the Nazi past by an ideology which pretended that National Socialism was a tool of capitalism and not an independent ideological system with its own imperatives – of which racism was the central one.

After two world upheavals brought about by German might, it is not

---

4 Ernst Klee, Willi Dressen, and Volker Riess (eds.), *"The Good Old Days": The Holocaust as Seen by Its Perpetrators and Bystanders* (New York: Free Press, 1992). The title is taken from the photo album of the Treblinka killing center commander Kurt Franz (who was recently released from jail by a German court).

surprising that the antics of unreconstructed old or rowdy new fanatics in Germany should cause apprehension elsewhere. But unlike the prior German experiment at democratic self-government, this one has brought forth countervailing forces: individuals and groups who recognize the dangers posed by extremists for a civilized society. The attractiveness of freedom and prosperity in the West which helped bring about the collapse of the East German state as soon as the Soviet leadership decided to allow it to fall is likely to sustain the reunified Germany through the difficult transition that is taking place currently. The Israeli statesman Abba Eban once asserted that history teaches us that men and nations adopt wise policies once they have exhausted all other possibilities. Surely this aphorism applies to modern Germany; they indeed exhausted all other possibilities, including several that no one else would have thought conceivable.

For other Europeans and for those in the world outside Europe, the changes in Germany have led and will continue to lead to changes in attitude toward Germany and Germans. The legacy of the past cannot and will not and should not disappear; the appropriate prescription after half a century is amnesty, not amnesia. But if Robert Hutchins was correct in referring to the advent of nuclear weapons in 1945 as the "good news of damnation," the ultimate incentive to avoid another world war, then the terrible experience of World War II provides Germans and non-Germans alike every incentive to avoid a repetition, regardless of the form or weapons involved. And if that is possible, as all evidence of the recent past suggests that it is, then there may be hope for other issues and conflicts on the globe as well.

APPENDIX

———— • ————

THE END OF RANKE'S HISTORY?
REFLECTIONS ON THE FATE
OF HISTORY IN THE TWENTIETH
CENTURY

The basic way in which historians identify Ranke's approach to history with their own – to the extent that they do so at all – is related to his use of archives. The location, analysis, and interpretation of records created during or close to the time of the events to be described are seen as essential to the historian's craft. If may well be helpful to locate and to consult later accounts and interpretations, but the first concern of the historian must be the effort to find contemporary records.

This approach to the research for and the writing of history has influenced the training of historians in the United States and throughout the world in the nineteenth and twentieth centuries and also placed a premium on making records available. Locating, preserving, and utilizing archival materials have come to be central to the training of students as well as to the professional practice of historians. Governments and other institutions responded, at least to some extent, to the pressures created by this trend in scholarship. The modern system of archives, the development of finding aids for their use, the regularization of access procedures, and the concern for the collection of manuscripts in private hands for transfer into generally accessible institutions all received a major impetus from this perception of the historical discipline.

The practice of history as it has evolved in the century since Leopold von Ranke's death in 1886 would be inconceivable without the emphasis on archival research associated with his work. In spite of this integral connection between archival research and the kind of history Ranke wrote, few who read his works today are likely to concern themselves with the preconditions required for the writing itself. The famous Venetian diplomatic relations, accounts of local developments sent home by the

This was originally presented at the conference in Syracuse on the hundredth anniversary of Ranke's death. A version was published in *Syracuse Scholar* 9, no. 1 (1988): 51–59, but it was excised from the published proceedings of the conference at the insistence of the Syracuse University Press.

diplomatic service of the Republic of Venice, to which Ranke turned in his search for evidence, had survived into his lifetime and were accessible to him. Accessibility and survival of records are prerequisites for the historian, and both are presently endangered to such an extent that the discipline itself as modern society has come to know it is threatened.

The United States at one time took a proud lead in making its records openly and promptly accessible to the public. It was assumed that in a democracy the government's records were the public's. They should be open for use, and there should be no copyright in government records. The great wars of this century temporarily interfered with this concept as secrecy came to be considered essential. Security classification closed many records, but the basic belief in the principle of open records reasserted itself in the post–World War II era. A series of executive orders first brought coherence into the classification system and then at least began to reinstate some reasonable procedures for opening the files. Whatever one might say about the specific details of each of these orders, they all went in the same general direction under Republican and Democratic administrations alike. This is not the place to recount the terms of the various orders; suffice it to say that until 1980 there was a steady development toward the application of the principle that within a reasonable period of time, the people should have access to the records of their government, and that, in addition, practical administrative and budgetary procedures had to be instituted to make that principle effective in reality.

This process has been dramatically and emphatically reversed. President Reagan's executive order on security classification, E.O. 12356, took effect on August 1, 1982; it reversed the post–World War II trend. Designed to get the people off the government's back by keeping records closed to public access, this order did more than put a drastic halt to the process which had been under way in the preceding thirty-five years. It invited the reclassification of previously opened records. It shifted all the presumptions from favoring opening to favoring the closing of records. It called for favoring longer over shorter closing periods. In its original White House draft, it called for no time limits at all;[1] that is, it showed the administration's preference for the perpetual closing of records, a cherished goal up to now only reached by the perpetual exemption of the operational records of the Central Intelligence Agency from the application of the Freedom of Information Act.[2]

1 Counsellor to the President Edwin Meese III, "Memorandum: Executive Order on Classification," December 23, 1981. A copy of this draft revision of the Executive Order was made available to the American Historical Association.
2 98th Congress, 1st Session, Senate Report No. 98-305, *Intelligence Information Act of 1983*, November 9, 1983; 98th Congress, 2d Session, *Legislation to Modify the Application of the Freedom of Information Act to the Central Intelligence Agency: Hearing before the Subcommittee on*

Simultaneously with the reversal in the purpose of the rules there came an equally dramatic reversal in the budgetary implementation of the declassification process. The vast majority of the positions of declassifiers were abolished, so that the more difficult rules might be applied ever more slowly by fewer personnel. It is not surprising that the result, as intended, was a great and continuing reduction in declassification actions and an equally enormous upswing in the annual net increase in classified documents. It was appropriately in the Orwellian year of 1984 that the Information Security Oversight Office, the agency charged with supervising this process, in its annual report hailed the reduction in the opening of archives with "special delight" and asserted that it "looks forward to even greater progress" in the same retrograde direction[3] – a prediction fully borne out by subsequent experience. A later report shows that the declassification process during the 1980s normally left a net increase of almost 7 million pages of classified material in the stacks: to keep up with the current production of classified records, the National Archives would have had to act on 10 million pages per year, but in the fiscal year 1985 they were able to act on a little over 3 million.[4] For Orwell's fans in the Information Security Oversight Office, the signs of "progress" are dramatic; for the other 250 million Americans, they are disheartening indeed.

What this means in practice is that serious research in American history will be halted chronologically at some point in the early 1950s into the indefinite future. It also means that historians in other countries, who in the past have often used the American example as an argument for earlier opening of their own government's records, will no longer be able to do so. Quite the reverse. Instead of British historians arguing with their own government, eventually successfully, that their government should shift from a fifty- to a thirty-year rule so that they would not have to cross the Atlantic to study their own nation's history, there may well be influences moving the other way. The determination of the U.S. government to keep its own records closed is almost certain to influence American allies in the same deplorable direction.[5] And this problem is accentu-

Legislation of the Permanent Select Committee on Intelligence, House of Representatives, February 8, 1984.

3 Information Security Oversight Office, *Annual Report to the President FY 1983,* March 16, 1984, p. 27.

4 Information Security Oversight Office, *Annual Report to the President FY 1985,* March 24, 1986, p. 17. It is worth noting that the Clinton administration appointed the head of this same agency to chair the review of the declassification issue.

5 The British author Chapman Pincher provides numerous examples in his book *Too Secret Too Long* (New York: St. Martin's, 1984), of American records that had been closed to him because of requests to close them from the British to the American government. Presumably there is reciprocity.

ated for all by the very mass of modern records with the attendant enormous costs of declassification once the mountains of closed papers have been allowed to grow to Himalayan proportions.

A further aspect of this problem which may in time cause the government of the United States to rethink its policy on secrecy is the relationship of trying to keep everything secret to the problem of keeping anything really important secret at all. It is hardly a coincidence that the very years – the 1980s – which saw the secrecy screen cast widest was also the time when the most serious penetrations of U.S. security took place. If one tries to stretch the security screen over too much, then by definition that screen becomes thinner where it really counts. The point is obvious, but was perhaps for that very reason systematically ignored. The finite security resources of a society had best be concentrated on those items and files which really do need to be protected, and this surely does not include files from World War II and even earlier periods.

It might be added that what is true of the United States is true for the United Kingdom as well. The files and the individual documents pertaining to the Duke of Windsor's flirtations with the Germans during the war could surely be made available by now. Concealing such materials for additional decades only makes him and his wife look even more foolish and even traitorous than disclosure of the records would reveal. And the British intelligence records of the prewar and wartime years are long overdue for declassification.

The general governmental mania for secrecy has further hidden, but in some ways even more dangerous, implications for the discipline of history. In the 1970s, when I was involved in representations to the National Security Agency (NSA) in behalf of the Conference Group for Central European History of the American Historical Association for the declassification of German World War II cryptologic records, I warned the officials of the NSA that they absolutely had to microfilm that large portion of the records they were still refusing to declassify because otherwise, by the time they did declassify them later in this or during the next century, the records themselves would have disintegrated. One of these decades we will find out whether or not the NSA did what they should have done; but the issue alluded to is, of course, applicable to most records of this century. It is the physical deterioration of the acidic paper used for most records and books in the twentieth century, paper which is practically guaranteed to disintegrate chemically after thirty to sixty years, depending on original quality and the conditions under which it is kept.

What this means in practice is that the records of this century, unlike those of the eighteenth and earlier centuries, simply will not survive. A couple of centuries hence, people may well conclude from the survival of a minuscule number of books and scanty archives from the 1980s, that the overwhelming majority of people in our age were illiterate and that, as in most ancient times, only a minute minority could read and write, using acid-free stationery and printing books on acid-free paper. The point which is ignored far too frequently is the relationship between keeping records closed for long periods of time on the one hand, and their physical deterioration on the other. At one point in the 1980s there were references to a concern of the Reagan administration about its place in history. There was little need to worry; had they had their way, it would certainly have been blank. If the records are kept closed for as long a period of time as the Reagan administration preferred, all or almost all of them will have yellowed and crumbled into dust by the time historians are finally allowed access to them.

Far from being a peculiarity of this country, the problem is worldwide. Until the Chernobyl disaster, the leaders of the Soviet Union assured their people that only in profit-seeking capitalist societies could there be serious safety problems with nuclear reactors. It has become evident that graphite can burn even under the watchful eyes of Lenin's picture. Now that scholars are finally beginning to be allowed access to Soviet archives, they discover that modern paper deteriorates in Eastern as in Western Europe depending on its acidity and conditions of storage rather than on the political and social system which produced it. Those European countries which are currently carefully excluding their own and foreign scholars from their recent archives are in fact, whether they realize it or not, destroying the basis for their own historical record in this process.

The same thing is true for what is often called the Third World; in fact, it is almost certainly even more the case for these countries. A disproportionate number of Third World countries is in areas of higher temperature and often of higher humidity than the more developed countries, with the result that their records deteriorate even more rapidly, since temperature and humidity are major determinants in the self-destruction of paper. The lack of resources for the proper care of records hastens the process as do major hydroelectric projects which raise the humidity in nations like Egypt. If these countries keep their recent records closed, they face the ironic situation where eventually the only records of their past available to historians are likely to be those papers of their former colonial masters which were generated before the introduction of wood acetate paper in the late nineteenth century. Independence no more guarantees survival of records than the imaginary advantages of a different social or political system.

There is even more bad news. The turn to computerization in the last forty years hastens the danger of societies being left with little or no material for the study of their own past. There is, quite obviously, the disappearance of preliminary drafts and stages in the preparation of important documents. This aspect of the computer eliminates one type of evidence historians have often found helpful, especially in tracing the process of policy formulation. But this is not all; it is the smallest portion of the problem. It is not just the drafts which vanish quite literally with the push of a button; it is the final clean copy which will disappear as well. Several aspects of the computer revolution combine to create this situation.

First there is the problem of changing hardware. Machine-readable records presuppose machines which are literate in those records. Given even the present rate of change in this field, it is safe to predict that by the end of this century almost no machine-readable cards, disks, tapes, wires, and so on, generated up to now will in fact be readable. There will be no machines capable of reading them, and if any machines survive, there will be no spare parts for them, and if there are spare parts, no one will know how to make them work. This situation already exists. One can work with American census schedules of the nineteenth century, but it is impossible to use those of the 1960 census. Of the two machines left in the world which can handle those tapes, one is in Japan and the other has been retired to the Smithsonian Institution.[6] Some years ago there was a scheme to convert these tapes to another format which the machines of the early 1970s could read, but the money was never appropriated. It is just as well that this was *not* done, partly because the machines now in use would be as illiterate toward these tapes as toward the original ones, partly for still another aspect of this catastrophic situation.

The various types of tapes, wires, and disks not only change at such a rate that the new generations of hardware cannot handle them after a few years, but they themselves deteriorate. We do not as yet have full experience with this only slightly slower variant of the self-destructing tape that used to open each episode of the television series "Mission Impossible." The proud promises on the cartons of floppy disks, however, promising that these disks are guaranteed to last five or as many as ten years provide a clue. No doubt some of the disks and tapes will last longer, but it is unlikely that many of them will be in physical condition for use in fifty years. Currently known methods of transferring existing machine-readable information onto new tapes, disks, or other media do not provide a realistic solution to the problem; the fact is that for the most part this is simply not done. There is here an exact analogy to the fact that society knows very well how to make acid-free paper but rarely uses it.

6 Committee on the Records of Government, *Report* (Washington, D.C., March 1985), p. 9.

People are in this case repeating with open eyes the disastrous story of the early movies unthinkingly made with nitrate base film, a kind of film that deteriorates rapidly even when it does not destroy itself and anything stored nearby by spontaneous combustion. In the movie field as with microfilm, there has been a shift to silver halide film, a subject which will be reviewed below; but a similar emphasis on long-term survivability has barely begun to enter the world of machine-readable records. The text from which this talk was originally read in 1986 at the Ranke Conference was printed from a floppy disk prepared on an IBM Personal Computer. Even if the historian two centuries hence who is researching the disappearance of most twentieth-century records could locate a machine that can read a 1980s floppy disk, the disk itself will long since have vanished into dust; and these dire predictions can be tested against experience only if they have in the meantime been printed on acid-free paper.

There is still another aspect of the machine-readable records disaster for historians. The information maintained in one or another form of automated storage is frequently accessible through indexing or other entry devices which are in the form of software programs or special scan-sensitive markings on the tape or other material. If these software and indexing scan systems are themselves lost or cannot be manipulated by a later generation of machines, the originals are to all intents and purposes lost, even if they survive physically, because no one can access them. Examples of calamities of this type are already upon us; two involving important records from the Vietnam War are described in the very suggestive report of the Committee on the Records of Government.[7] It is safe to assume that there will be more incidents of this kind.

What professional historians face is a need to rethink the requirements for the discipline of history as Ranke developed it. Whatever else they need, historians must have access to a surviving record. The reader is invited to imagine Ranke going from his library to Washington to negotiate for access to Venetian diplomatic reports on acidic paper or seventeenth-century magnetic tapes. Some of these reports will pertain to Venetian intelligence operations at the Court of Naples and hence under current U.S. law, proposed by the administration and enacted in 1984, permanently closed to research. In the case of such materials, neither mandatory review nor the Freedom of Information Act would help; as the executive director of the American Historical Association attempted to explain at the congressional hearing, perpetuity is a very long time.[8] But for those records *not* covered by continuing se-

---

7 Ibid., p. 31.
8 The statement and testimony of Dr. Samuel R. Gammon may be found in 98th Congress, 2d Session, *Legislation* . . . (see n. 2), pp. 72–82.

curity restrictions, there would still be nothing to work on either. Any paper reports would have vanished by the self-destruction of that paper, and even the Smithsonian has no machinery for reading surviving seventeenth-century magnetic tapes. This is the situation any historian working on the current era will face a mere seventy-five years hence.

There are two possible ways of engaging the prospect unfolding before us. Historians can continue to ignore it – as they largely have. If no basic changes are made, it will be necessary for future historians to be trained and to work on the twentieth century essentially the way ancient history is done now. Combining careful analysis of a few fragmentary surviving texts with archaeological and numismatic evidence, historians will have to attempt to recover a society which, ironically, is characterized by the generation of enormous volumes of records. They will be working with survivals that will be proportionately very much *smaller* than those surviving from Athens or Rome and *minuscule* when contrasted with the comparatively voluminous papyri and cuneiform tablets of ancient Egypt and Mesopotamia. Only the occasional university press book on acid-free paper will remain of the millions of tomes in the libraries, and only letters on rag bond paper will survive out of the vast paper production of the world's Pentagons.

If this prospect seems especially sad to me, it is because my own current research field, the Second World War, will be affected dramatically. The paper of all the belligerents was particularly bad in those years of wartime shortages. This is as true for the United States as it is for others. Only one agency comes to mind as having been equipped with an exemplary stock of paper: a special German official appointed by Heinrich Himmler and having the title "Bevollmächtigter des Reichsführers-SS für das gesamte Diensthunde und -Taubenwesen," the Plenipotentiary of the National Leader of the SS for All Military Dog and Pigeon Affairs. It will be interesting to read histories of World War II based on the surviving records of that agency, appropriately bound in leather and chained to a reading desk in the Laurentian Library in Florence alongside the surviving codices of ancient texts preserved there.

There is a second possibility. Historians can work together with archivists and librarians in a major effort to publicize the problem as a whole and possible solutions for it. There exist today feasible solutions for each of the three aspects of the basic issue that have been described: long-term closing of records, disintegration of records, and the effective disappearance of machine-readable records. The answers to each of these that will now be described briefly are not necessarily the only possible ones; it is just that no other currently feasible ones have as yet been proposed.

First, long-term closure of records. The only realistic answer to the practical problem of declassifying the enormous volumes of records generated in ever increasing quantities by the modern state is the imposition by legislation of a requirement for self-declassification, a requirement that in this country would mean amending the Federal Records Act. Every document that is classified must have included in the initial classification a declassification schedule with dates in it. No other form of classification would be valid and no penalty would be imposed on the publication of documents not carrying such a declassification schedule. A document would therefore carry a notation, for example, that it was top secret, would go down to secret on January 1, 1999, and would be declassified as of January 1, 2009. No further review of the document would be needed unless the declassification were either to be speeded up or postponed. The overwhelming majority of the millions of pages of classified documents created each year would never need to be reviewed again at all, and the burden of examining the endless pages of classified paper would be placed on those who wish to hasten or slow the previously established pace. Since any extension of classification would also have to have termination dates to be valid, the volume of truly long-term document closures would shrink steadily. The backlog of records classified before the imposition of the self-declassification requirement would at least be a finite quantity, however huge, and could be addressed over a period of perhaps ten years, with the National Archives given broad authority to act itself on documents thirty years old.

It should be clear that all modern societies which expect to make their records accessible will eventually be forced by the practical problems posed by the classification mess to turn to some variant of the self-declassification system. And they will also find it essential to include the costs of declassification in the budgets of the agencies which create the classified documents just as they now include the cost of safes in their budgets. Again, all modern societies will find that their archival institutions will either not have the resources for the massive declassification reviews needed or would otherwise have to divert an inordinate and increasing proportion of their resources to it. The management and servicing of the mountains of paper which the modern state creates is quite enough for archives; the costs of declassification will have to be considered a part of the cost of classifying. The sooner self-declassification becomes the legally required norm in any country, the sooner that country can look forward to a day when the pile of closed records will start to shrink instead of continuing to grow; the longer it waits, the bigger the pile will become in the interim.

Let us consider next the problem of deteriorating paper. There have been some encouraging experiments with the deacidification of paper as a means of saving books and records from complete destruction by halting the process of deterioration. Certainly such techniques need to be applied, especially to library holdings.[9] It is, however, highly unlikely that such methods will ever be applied on an adequate basis to archives; and since in any case they can only halt, not reverse, the deterioration, the available effective technology must take precedence over the possibly some day appearing new procedure. That available effective technology is microfilming. Even if all future Ph.D.'s must be provided with a seeing eye dog along with their doctoral hood, this is the one practical way to cope with the problem. Silver halide film lasts, and copies can be made for readers and for eventual replacement.

When I first visited the German Federal Archives in Koblenz, I warned the archivist then in charge that any major record groups which had not been processed by the microfilm projects in England or the United States would have to be filmed by the German authorities for preservation purposes. He refused to believe me. He was certain that once the German records had been saved from Allied clutches and were in the beautiful surroundings of Koblenz, they would – like carefully kept medieval parchment – last forever. And he was not about to follow me into the stacks when I offered to show him examples of paper continuing to deteriorate in spite of its return to German custody. The current leadership of the Bundesarchiv fortunately has a more realistic view of the issue. Their great microfilming program, together with the accompanying series of Findbücher or Guides, could serve as a model of what ought to be done everywhere.[10] The National Archives in Washington at one time operated similarly but has more recently turned to private microfilm projects which leave the reader uninformed about the identity of the editors as well as the principles of selection and omission, a disastrous departure from the very fine microcopy program the Archives once operated. Microfilming done properly and according to archival preservation standards is something done best under the control of archivists, not salesmen; and – with the costs again charged to the records-creating agency – must be seen as a function of the permanent custodians of the film.

9 Committee on the Records of Government, pp. 104–5. See also the summary of this issue by the Director, Office of Preservation, National Endowment for the Humanities, Harold C. Cannon, "Necessary Choices," in the *ACLS Newsletter* 37 (Winter-Spring 1986): 24–28. It should be noted that the Library of Congress has experienced two fire incidents at its book deacidification pilot plant in December 1985 and February 1986. Any books lost in such fires can presumably be replaced, but what about records?

10 The series "Findbücher zu Beständen des Bundesarchivs" is published by the German Federal Archives in Koblenz.

In the future, it may well be possible to reduce concern over this issue by enactment into law of the suggestion of the Committee on the Records of Government that "archivists and record managers could be given the authority to require archival-quality paper for the production of all government records deemed important enough to justify retention in their original form,"[11] a proposal partially enacted into law during the Bush administration. Even if such a procedure were ever completely adopted by the United States or any other government, however, there will always be masses of records unlikely to satisfy that standard. Microreproduction in some form is likely to remain a major part of any preservation program. Whatever changes in technology may be ahead, magnification will always be possible. It is absolutely essential that this crucial point remain in the forefront of archival preservation projects: as long as the original letters are maintained in the original form, they can be brought back by magnification.

This reference to technology brings up the third issue, that of machine-readable records, to automated storage and retrieval. There are those who hold out the hope that at some point in time standardization will assure the long-term maintenance of accessibility from the technological point of view as well as physical survival of the material on which the machine-readable information has been placed. This happy event is most likely to take place some decades after the Greek Calends; but even if it ever does come, there will be all the vanishing material created in the meantime. The video disk with laser-imprinted information under an acrylic shield is supposed to be a possible remedy for all these problems and is currently being utilized by the Library of Congress for purposes of long-term preservation of books as well as other materials. One cannot help wondering about the machines of future centuries scanning these disks with a technology we cannot now imagine – and most likely illiterate vis-à-vis what will then look primitive and hopelessly outmoded. What would we do with a stack of seventeenth-century disks today?

There appears to be no alternative to the recourse once again to the currently available technology which does not change the format of the text. What that means is the requirement that agencies which create records of machine-readable disks, tapes, or wires be obligated by the national archives of the country where these are to be kept, to produce and turn over with those that deserve permanent retention a hard paper copy together with funds for the archivists to prepare a microfilm. Alternatively, Computer Output Microfilm (COM) can be prepared directly from machine-readable records; but this procedure will produce usable

11 Committee on the Records of Government, *Report*, p. 109.

film only if it is carried out under strict archives control and according to very high standards.

Film we *know* we can preserve and make accessible. By the time any other currently anticipated solution to the problem has been developed technically and applied in practice, the overwhelming majority of the existing machine-readable records and those created between now and that ever-receding horizon will be inaccessible by available hardware or deteriorated beyond recall or more likely both. It should be noted that a major study commissioned by the National Archives has come to essentially the same conclusion.[12] Here is a challenge to daunt the brave; but as we enter an era in which technology is greeted not only with enthusiasm but also with a little skepticism, it ought not to be impossible to engage a problem far easier than that of disposing of high-level radioactive waste. In this field we at least have a known and workable procedure.

The problems spelled out here are both difficult and massive. They threaten to put an end to the discipline of history as we have come to know it, at least as it is applied to the last decades of the nineteenth century and to the twentieth century as a whole. Unless historians take these matters seriously, and begin to work on them energetically and successfully, the future of the discipline is dim indeed. The line of those wanting a seat in the Laurentian Library to inspect the few remaining records of this century could be a very long one.

12 National Research Council, *Preservation of Historical Records* (Washington, D.C.: National Academy Press, 1986). The National Research Council is the operating agency of the National Academy of Sciences and the National Academy of Engineering.

INDEX

Poland (*cont.*)
  German attack on, 4, 89, 90–91,
    118, 129–50, 144–45, 170, 177,
    289
  German refugees from, 319
  and German war plans, 42–43, 76,
    130–31, 154, 174, 175
  military preparedness of, 77–78
  and Nazi–Soviet Pact, 169, 170–71
  and Soviet Union, 174, 177–78,
    275, 295–96, 312
  Warsaw Ghetto uprising in, 226–28
  Zegota, 226
Potemkin, Vladimir P., 168
Prague, Treaty of, 12
Prüfer, Curt, 309–10
Prussia, 31, 59, 66, 131, 295, 309
  annexations of 1866, 12
  and Polish corridor, 15–16, 77, 149

Queen Elizabeth, 299
Queen Mary, 299
Quisling, Vidkun, 105, 231

race doctrine, 32–34, 41, 49, 52, 58,
    60, 61, 69, 71, 241
Raeder, Erich, 85, 86, 114, 198
Ranke, Leopold von, 325–26
Rauschning, Hermann, 23, 36
Reagan, Ronald, 326
Reichenau, Walther von, 133, 134, 139
Remarque, Erich Maria, 51
Renzetti, Giuseppe, 45
Rhineland, 77, 90, 98, 99
Ribbentrop, Joachim von, 39, 85, 89,
    91, 102, 117, 149, 195, 234, 238
  in Britain, 87–88
  and Danzig question, 122–23, 125,
    127
  and Nazi–Soviet Pact, 168, 169–70
Rintelen, Anton, 97, 98
Röhm, Ernst, 132
Romania, 16, 21, 156, 162, 169, 187,
    221
  German occupation of, 244, 276
  Jews in, 239–40, 244
  Soviet occupation of, 178, 284
Romans, 287
Rome, 235, 245
Rommel, Erwin, 207, 259, 277
Roosevelt, Franklin D., 166–67, 189,
    223, 263, 269

and Winston Churchill, 305
on Nazi–Soviet pact, 167, 172, 185,
    301
and U.S. neutrality, 185–87
war leadership of, 299–302
and zonal division of Germany, 271–
    72
Rosenberg, Alfred, 38–39, 40, 45
Ruhr area, 25, 43
Rundstedt, Gerd von, 194
Russia, 1, 13, 16, 21, 41, 42, 295, 297
  see also Soviet Union

SA (Sturm-Abteilung), 26, 132
Saarland, 106
St. Germain, Treaty of, 46
St. James, Declaration of 1942, 242
Salonika (Greece), Jews of, 235–36
San Sabba death camp, 235
Savo Island, Battle of, 208
Schacht, Hjalmar, 79, 166, 184
Scharnhorst, 81, 276
Scheubner-Richter, Max Erwin von,
    48
Schleicher, Kurt von, 97, 132
Schmidt, Paul, 91
Schoerner, Ferdinand, 275
Schönerer, Georg von, 48
Schulenburg, Friedrich Werner von
    der, 89
Schuschnigg, Kurt von, 105–6
Seeckt, Hans von, 138–39
Serbia, 13, 48, 237
Seyss-Inquart, Arthur, 105, 106
Sicily, invasion of, 219, 222, 263
Silesia, 11, 31
Singapore, 200, 315
Slavs, in racial doctrine, 41–42, 70,
    166, 241
Smigly-Rydz, Edward, 123n
Sobibor death camp, 229, 230, 233
Social Darwinism, 32, 68
Sofia, 239
Solomon Islands, 208–9, 303, 315
Somaliland, 207
Soviet–Japanese Neutrality Pact of
    1941, 206
Soviet Union, 67, 78, 89, 144, 242
  army purges of, 115, 156
  Berlin Treaty of 1926, 72, 155
  and Britain, 159–60, 163, 171, 189,
    272, 294